I0013773

François Gobert

Towards Putting Abstract Interpretation of Prolog into Practice

François Gobert

Towards Putting Abstract Interpretation of Prolog into Practice

Design, Implementation, and Evaluation of a
Tool to Verify and Optimise Prolog Programs

VDM Verlag Dr. Müller

Imprint

Bibliographic information by the German National Library: The German National Library lists this publication at the German National Bibliography; detailed bibliographic information is available on the Internet at http://dnb.d-nb.de.

Any brand names and product names mentioned in this book are subject to trademark, brand or patent protection and are trademarks or registered trademarks of their respective holders. The use of brand names, product names, common names, trade names, product descriptions etc. even without a particular marking in this works is in no way to be construed to mean that such names may be regarded as unrestricted in respect of trademark and brand protection legislation and could thus be used by anyone.

Cover image: www.purestockx.com

Publisher:
VDM Verlag Dr. Müller Aktiengesellschaft & Co. KG , Dudweiler Landstr. 125 a, 66123 Saarbrücken, Germany,
Phone +49 681 9100-698, Fax +49 681 9100-988,
Email: info@vdm-verlag.de

Zugl.: Louvain-la-Neuve, Université catholique de Louvain, UCL, Diss., 2007

Copyright © 2008 VDM Verlag Dr. Müller Aktiengesellschaft & Co. KG and licensors
All rights reserved. Saarbrücken 2008

Produced in USA and UK by:
Lightning Source Inc., La Vergne, Tennessee, USA
Lightning Source UK Ltd., Milton Keynes, UK
BookSurge LLC, 5341 Dorchester Road, Suite 16, North Charleston, SC 29418, USA

ISBN: 978-3-8364-8858-7

Abstract

Logic programming is an attractive paradigm that allows the programmer to concentrate on the meaning (the logic) of the problem to be solved - the *declarative layer*. An execution model is then used as the problem solver - the *operational layer*. In practice, for efficiency reasons, the semantics of the two layers do not always match. For instance, in Prolog, the computation of solutions is based on an incomplete depth-first search rule, unifications and negations may be unsound, some builtin language primitives are not multidirectional, and there exist extralogical features like the cut or dynamic predicates. A large number of work has been realised to reconcile the declarative and operational features of Prolog. Methodologies have been proposed to construct operationally correct and efficient Prolog code. Researchers have designed methods to automate the verification of specific operational properties on which optimisation of logic programs can be based. A few tools have been implemented but there is a lack of a unified framework.

The goal and topic of this thesis is the design, implementation, and evaluation of a static analyser of Prolog programs to integrate 'state-of-the-art' techniques into a unified abstract interpretation framework. Abstract interpretation is an adequate methodology to design, justify, and combine complex analyses. The analyser that we present in this thesis is based on a non-implemented original proposal. The original framework defines the notion of *abstract sequence*, which allows one to verify many desirable operational properties of a logic procedure. The properties include verifying type, mode, and sharing of terms, proving termination, sure success or failure, and determinacy of logic procedures, as well as linear relations between the size of input/output terms and the number of solutions to a call. An abstract sequence maintains information about the input and output terms, as well as the non-failure conditions on input terms, and the number of solutions for such inputs. The domains of abstract sequences cooperate together and improve each other. The abstract execution is performed during a single global analysis, and abstract sequences are derived at each program point (the information of the various domains are computed simultaneously). The intended operational properties of a procedure are written in formal specifications.

The original framework is an interesting starting point for combining several analyses inside a unified framework. However, it is limited and inaccurate in many ways: it is not implemented, and therefore, it has not been validated by experiments, it accepts only a subset of Prolog (without negation, cut, conditional and

i

disjunctive constructs), and some of the proposed domains are not precise enough. The basic framework is only oriented towards the verification of Prolog programs, but it cannot always prove the desirable properties. In this thesis, we implement and evaluate the basic framework, and, more importantly, we overcome its limitations to make it accurate and usable in practice: the improved framework accepts any Prolog program with modules, new abstract domains and operations are added, and the language of specifications is more expressive. We also design and implement an optimiser that generates specialised code. Optimisation is essential in Prolog, but it is not easy to perform by hand and it is error prone. The optimiser uses the information to safely apply source-to-source transformations. Code transformations include clause and literal reordering, introduction of cuts, and removal of redundant literals. The optimiser follows a precise strategy to choose the most rewarding transformations in best order.

This thesis shows the feasibility of a unified framework that integrates many complex analyses in a single global analysis. Practically and theoretically, a single global analysis is more attractive than a combination of a lot of separate analyses and frameworks. Many extensions have been performed to obtain an accurate and usable tool devoted to verification and optimisation of Prolog programs.

Keywords. Abstract debugging, abstract interpretation, automated optimisation, automated verification, cut insertion, logic programs, program construction, Prolog, source-to-source transformation, static analysis.

Acknowledgements

Making a doctoral thesis is a unique experience, professionally and humanely speaking. The thesis comprised many challenges, and also, it brought to me much joy. My first gratitude goes to God and Mary, to whom I owe everything.

The realisation of this intellectual work would not come to its end without the support of many people. I apologise in advance the persons who aren't listed here.

I cordially thank my thesis adviser Baudouin Le Charlier. Five years ago, he supervised my Ms. degree dissertation in the Faculés Universitaires Notre-Dame de la Paix in Namur, and during the four last years, my doctoral research in Louvain-la-Neuve. I want to thank him for his human qualities. He dedicated significant time to me and was really patient with me. I have appreciated his invaluable advice that guided me throughout these years. I have benefited from his great research experience to achieve this thesis. He encouraged me providing several comments, advice, and suggestions for the writing of drafts, reports and articles, and for the publication of this thesis.

I want to show my gratitude and appreciation to the members of my jury: Yves Deville, Germán Puebla, Wim Vanhoof and Kim Mens. Yves Deville, at the very beginning of my research, agreed to form part of my training committee, and he advised me for this work structure. I also thank him for his research on logic programming [45] on which my work is partially based. The development team of CiaoPP of Universidad Politécnica in Madrid, Spain, welcomed me at the beginning of January 2007. There, I met a very dynamic and active team in the field of logic programming. I keep particularly in mind the profitable discussions with Germán Puebla, Manuel Hermenegildo, Pedro López and Jesús Correas. I am grateful for the time they granted to me and for their relevant remarks. Wim Vanhoof, from University of Namur, also encouraged me, and provided constructive feedback to improve my articles, and finally, my thesis. I thank also Kim Mens, for the interest he showed in this work, and for his useful comments.

I am also grateful to Agostino Cortesi and Sabina Rossi, who received me in Venice, Italy, during five months in 2003, when I was working on my Ms. degree dissertation. I have also appreciated the interesting discussions with Christophe Leclère, who was the co-adviser of that dissertation.

I thank all professors who taught me computer science, in Namur, Mons, Liège and Louvain-la-Neuve. I want also to thank all my students, and especially two grade students, Cindy and Sooky, who contributed in extending the framework of the analyser that I present in this thesis.

I do not forget to acknowledge all my colleagues of the INGI department in Louvain-la-Neuve. I want to quote particularly the colleagues who shared my office, Xavier Martin and José Vander Meulen, as well as the colleagues who were my next door office neighbours, Isabelle Dony, Nicolas Vanderano and Gustavo Ospina. With all of them, I had enthusiastic and enriching discussions. I wish José success for the end of his thesis. Gustavo, co-author of [112], helped me a lot in the implementation of the analyser; I thank him for his knowledge on language interoperability. Isabelle was always present and encouraged me in the most difficult moments. I also want to acknowledge the administrative and technical staff of the department, who rendered good services to me.

During my stay in Louvain-la-Neuve, I accommodated in *la Maison du Chemin* and in *la Maison Saint-Pierre*. I would like to thank all the persons who were my so-called 'cokoteurs': Christophe, Anne-Catherine, Béata, Céline, Michel, Aude, Isabelle, Tanguy, Florence, David and Martha, Claire, Galia-Irena, David, Bogdan, and Albert. I also thank particularly my good friends Charles (Carlitos) and Olivier (le 'sacré renard') for their encouragement, as well as the nice people that I have known from the students parish of Louvain-la-Neuve.

I want to thank my family that have continually supported me: my grandparents, my parents, my four sisters and brother. The work of this thesis would not exist without the love and education provided by my parents. I am grateful that they have allowed me to study and to make research.

Finally, I dedicate this thesis to a very important person for me, 'mi alma gemela' Alicia, for her love and tireless support. Thank you for having endured the omnipresence of my work, and especially for always having been present at my sides. I thank you with all my heart.

François Gobert
December 11, 2007

This doctoral research was supported by the Belgian National Fund for Scientific Research (F.N.R.S.).

Contents

List of Figures

xi

List of Tables

Chapter 1

Introduction

1.1 Context of this thesis

The fundamental idea behind *logic programming* is that *logic could be used as a programming language* [28, 74]. Logic is used to declare the problem to solve, and a theorem prover or execution model is used as the problem solver (e.g., the Warren Abstract Machine [131]). Therefore, the problem solving task is split between the programmer, who is responsible only for ensuring the correctness of programs expressed in logical form, and the model generator, which is responsible for solving problems efficiently. This idea is very appealing: at the programmer side, solving a problem amounts only to specifying the problem in logic. Another interest of programming in logic is the ability to write so-called *multidirectional* procedures, in the sense that the same code of a procedure can be used in more than one way (the arguments being either input data or output results).

However, in practice, logic programming languages like Prolog do not follow, strictly speaking, this ideal view, mainly for efficiency reasons (in terms of space utilisation and of execution time). In order to be competitive with conventional imperative languages, Prolog allows the user to add control (extralogical) information. So, Prolog is not purely declarative, and is accompanied by two semantics: the declarative semantics and the operational semantics. The declarative semantics is based on first-order logic, and deals with the logical consequences of a logic program. The operational semantics is based on execution mechanisms (SLD resolution, computation rule, search rule), and deals with the computation of answer substitutions. The programmer needs to consider both semantics to write a correct and efficient Prolog program. Unfortunately, the two semantics do not always match, due to the incompleteness of the depth-first search rule for computing solutions, the unsoundness of unifications (without occur-check) and of negations (as failure), the use of extralogical features like the cut and dynamic predicates, as well as the use of arithmetic built-ins that are not multidirectional.

Despite its drawbacks, logic programming attracted many people over the years. Prolog is widely used in the fields of artificial intelligence, expert systems, natu-

1

ral language processing, and database applications. Due to its high-level nature, Prolog is useful to quickly build prototypes for logical problems. Furthermore, Prolog has been enhanced by many extensions such as parallelism and constraints facilities. Many other programming languages are based on (some of) the ideas of Prolog, e.g., Ciao [61], Mercury [123], Oz [128].

Many works have been achieved to reconcile (at least partially) the declarative and the operational natures of Prolog, to compute or to verify some operational properties of programs, and to optimise automatically programs. Methodologies were proposed to construct systematically correct and efficient programs, e.g., [3, 45]. For instance, the methodology of Y. Deville [45] consists of three main steps for the construction of a program: (1) specify the problem; (2) provide a logic description of the problem from the specification; and (3) derive correct and efficient code from the logic description and the specification. The Deville development process is systematic but is not automated. Automatic or semi-automatic tools aim to check or to compute some operational properties of programs, or to optimise programs [52]. Many of such frameworks are based on abstract interpretation [34], which is a static analysis technique that aims at deriving general information about the execution of a program at compile-time, without actually running it. Abstract interpretation of Prolog was initiated by Mellish [95] and further developed by many researchers [14, 35, 41, 70, 76, 91]. For instance, there exist frameworks for proving or inferring termination [15, 27, 51, 75, 96], occur-check freeness of unifications [6], and cardinality information [12, 19, 43, 79, 89, 90]. Other frameworks are devoted to optimise programs at the code generation stage. For instance, mode [41, 44, 121], type [9, 31, 48, 69, 72, 106, 133, 119], and aliasing [24] analyses collect information about the state of variables during the execution and are useful to speed up term unification and make memory allocation more efficient [64]. Sharing analysis [104] is similar to aliasing except that it refers to the sharing of memory structures to which program variables are instantiated; it is useful to perform compile-time garbage collection [100] and automatic parallelisation [17]. Reference chain analysis [129] attempts to determine an upper bound to the length of the pointer chain for a program variable. Trailing analysis [126] aims at detecting variables that do not need to be trailed. Liveness analysis [99] determines when memory structures can be reused and is useful to perform update-in-place. Detecting mutual exclusion of the clauses in a procedure may allow the compiler to generate code to select the right clause deterministically. Automatic complexity analysis [42] can be applied to select the most efficient version of a Prolog procedure. Some optimisations can be expressed by source-to-source transformations such as introduction of cuts, replacement of negated literals by cuts, and partial evaluation [2, 39, 45, 47, 71, 85, 88, 114]. The CiaoPP preprocessor performs a lot of analyses which are devoted to verification and optimisation [18, 40, 42, 43, 66, 89, 116, 118].

It is desirable to have a global system that can serve to verify and to optimise Prolog code, or more generally, to support a methodology for constructing reliable and efficient programs. Unfortunately, there is a huge disparity between the above-mentioned Prolog analysis frameworks. Some works concentrate on a specific problem of verification or optimisation, and some of them only present theoretic solutions without providing any implementation. Therefore, it is not easy to combine them into a global system. As stressed by B. Le Charlier and P. Flener [77], it is difficult to use abstract interpretation for designing a complex analysis that is provably correct, practically implementable, and scalable. The design of such an ambitious analysis requires the use of complex abstract domains made of several communicating components. Practical methods of combining abstract domains have been proposed (e.g., [25, 33]). There exist good experiences of abstract interpretation for building a complex analysis, like the PLAI abstract interpreter used in CiaoPP [104, 105], or the GAIA system [80] and its extensions (see, [33, 78, 79]). PLAI integrates and combines many domains (e.g., sharing/freeness/types), but CiaoPP is still composed of several separated analyses, which are performed in sequence (for instance, the non-failure and determinacy analyses are performed after a size analysis, which is performed after the sharing/freeness/type analysis of PLAI).

The goal and topic of this thesis is to develop an analyser that integrates some of the 'state-of-the-art' techniques into a unified abstract interpretation framework. The different analyses are realised simultaneously into a single global analysis. The developed tool can be used for different purposes. We can distinguish two main uses for it depending on whether we consider the operational semantics only, or both the declarative and the operational semantics of a program. In its first use, the analyser collects and verifies operational properties at each program point (e.g., modes, types, sharing, linearity, sizes, number of solutions). The declarative meaning of the program is not considered during the analysis. The abstract information is used to verify some intended operational properties as well as to automatically apply some optimisation techniques. In its second use, the abstract information that is collected during the static analysis helps to remove or reduce the gap between the declarative and operational semantics. Sufficient conditions on programs are checked to ensure that the operational meaning complies with its declarative meaning. For instance, the analyser proves that the procedure terminates, that a program is occur-check free, that a negation is sound, that a cut is green.

1.2 Contributions of this thesis

In this thesis, we concentrate on the development of a static analyser of Prolog programs that integrates and combines several analyses devoted to verification and optimisation. The developed system is based on the work presented in [78], which is an evolution of GAIA [80]. In the rest of this thesis, the abstract interpretation framework of [78] is called the *basic framework*. The basic framework introduces the notion of *abstract sequence*, which makes it possible to collect a lot of desirable information, including relations between the input and output sizes of terms, multiplicity, and termination. Abstract sequences enable the integration of many individual analyses previously proposed in the literature as well as new ones. The desirable operational properties of a procedure are described by so-called *formal specifications* and are provided by the user. Our work validates the basic framework, which was not implemented before: we implement and complete the basic framework to obtain a practicable and accurate analyser (that we call also the *checker* or the *verifier*) able to verify useful operational properties.[1] We also design and implement an *optimiser*, which performs abstract specialisation of procedures with respect to their formal specifications.[2] Several formal specifications may be attached to one procedure, and thus, multiple specialised versions can be generated. The optimiser uses the checker to safely apply source-to-source transformations, like clause reordering, literal reordering, green cut insertion, dead and redundant code removal. Even if the tool concerns the Prolog language, the ideas behind the framework and techniques explained in this thesis can be applied to other logic programming languages similar to Prolog.

Major remark.   As explained in [69], there are two different approaches towards obtaining abstract information. *Declaration-based (prescriptive)* systems require the user to provide declarations which characterise the predicates (e.g., mode declarations) and with which the program can be checked to be consistent. Providing the declarations requires a considerable discipline of the programmer, but they are useful for program development tools and for code generation. In *inference-based (descriptive)* systems, all the information is inferred from the program text itself and describes the properties of the program at several points in a successful execution. Code generation or specialisation can be based on the derived information, whereas programming errors are indicated by the derivation of unexpected results. Usually, the word *verifier* is used for declaration-based systems (typically, the abstract execution needs not to perform a fixpoint), and the word *analyser* is used for inference-based systems (typically, the abstract execution is performed by applying a fixpoint). Our approach is essentially declaration-based. In the rest of this thesis, we use the words *analyser*, *checker* and *verifier* interchangeably: each of these words must be understood with the meaning of *verifier*.

The objective of making the checker and optimiser accurate and usable in practice has required many non-trivial development efforts. The theoretical contributions of this thesis are summarised below.

1.2.1   Complete and extend the basic framework

The basic framework is limited: it is incomplete, not sufficiently accurate, and it is not implemented. Therefore, we needed to complete and extend the basic frame-

---

[1]The checker has been presented at AFADL'2007 [56, 57].
[2]The optimiser has been presented at WLPE'2007 [58].

work in the following ways. We extend the basic framework to accept more Prolog programs, to augment the expressiveness of the formal specifications, and to improve the accuracy of the analysis.

Handling full Prolog

The basic framework only considers *pure* normalised Prolog programs, with explicit unifications. A practical analyser must consider the full Prolog syntax, with its main characteristic features. Such features include the cut, negation as failure, disjunctive and conditional constructions, dynamic predicates, and the meta-call facility. Those features are extra-logic but occur in many real Prolog programs. We integrate new abstract domains into abstract sequences in order to model accurately the execution of such built-ins. The integration of the new abstract domains involves the refinement of the abstract operations, as well as new cooperation between abstract domains.

Extend the expressiveness of formal specifications

Formal specifications are written by the user and describe the expected operational behaviours of a procedure. The language of formal specifications allows the user to represent abstract sequences in a syntax that is more convenient than the mathematical formalism of abstract substitutions and sequences. In addition, we make the formal specifications (and thus abstract sequences and abstract substitutions) more expressive in order to describe more accurately the way a procedure is used.

An abstract domain for linearity is added in abstract substitutions. It allows us to describe more kinds of calls to a procedure, and to prove the occur-check freeness of programs. This domain is combined with the other components of an abstract substitution (e.g., mode, type, sharing).

The basic framework considers a simple type system: it is only able to describe lists (the type `list`), terms instantiable to a list (the type `anylist`) and unrestricted terms (the type `any`). A unique size-measure is also considered in the basic framework: the list-length norm. We define a new type system to describe and to analyse more accurately the behaviours of programs using structures other than lists. The user is now able to declare its own parametric types, as well as new norms attached to them. The possibility to combine several norms (user-defined and primitive norms) into the interargument size relations is useful for proving termination. Terms and subterms described in abstract sequences are assigned to so-called *type expressions*. A type expression is a primitive type (e.g., `int`, `any`) or an instantiation of a parametric type (by replacing the type parameters by primitive types or by other type expressions). A type expression denotes a set of (possibly non-ground) terms. The way we combine type and mode information is similar to the type graphs of G. Janssens and M. Bruynooghe [69]. Parametric type declarations have similarities with the types and modes declarations of Mercury [123].

Improving the accuracy of the analysis

We perform several improvements to the basic framework to make the global analysis more accurate. The abstract operations are refined to take into account the new abstract domains added to the basic framework (e.g., linearity, type expressions).

A new abstract domain for untouched terms is integrated into abstract sequences, and models the input terms that are left uninstantiated during the execution. It allows us to describe accurately the execution of built-ins and predicates that do not instantiate their arguments. It is useful for proving the sure success as well as the termination of procedures using such predicates.

In the basic framework, the induction parameter is required to be a single linear expression in function of the size (list-length) of the input terms. We extend the expressiveness of such induction parameters. Several (user-defined and primitive) norms can now be combined in such an expression. Furthermore, induction parameters are now defined as *sequences of linear expressions*. The system proves the termination of a procedure by checking that the sequence of linear expressions decreases through (mutually) recursive calls, according to the lexicographic order.

Special attention is made to obtain precise cardinality information about the execution of a procedure (including the sure success and the determinacy). Several abstract operations are discussed in this thesis. The detection of the exclusivity between two goals (or two clauses) is improved by using *non-failure* components. We also improve the design of the concatenation of abstract sequences, which computes the abstract sequence modelling the behaviour of a procedure composed of several clauses (possibly with cuts).

The basic framework performs a single pass in the program, by annotating procedures with abstract sequences, at each program point. The non-failure conditions of abstract sequences can be used to (partially) reexecute the procedure in order to obtain more accurate information. We propose such a strategy of reexecution.

Implementation and experimental evaluation of the checker

We implement the framework with its improvements. The distribution is publicly available [55]. The analyser is written in Java and C. It is interfaced with the Parma Polyhedral Library [8] written in C++, which maintains the linear relations between the sizes of input/output terms. The checker is validated experimentally on a large set of programs. The framework gets accurate results, especially about cardinality information.

1.2.2   Using the checker to optimise programs

A solution for optimising a Prolog procedure is to generate specialised code for each particular use of the procedure. Given a procedure and a formal specification of this procedure, one can try to find a more efficient ordering of clauses and literals, such that the program still remains operationally correct in the context of that specification. In Prolog, we can also try to insert cuts to prune the search tree without removing solutions. This can greatly reduce the size of the search tree, and improve the efficiency. Applying correct code transformations is not obvious and is tricky to be done manually, because it is very error-prone. This thesis describes an *optimiser* based on the integrated abstract interpretation framework (the *checker*), which performs this task automatically.

Applying source-to-source transformations

Our approach is inspired by Deville's methodology [45], where it is proposed to apply some code transformations, in order to produce more efficient programs. Our optimiser also applies other code transformations not described in [45]. Such code transformations include clause reordering, literal reordering, green cut insertion, and removal of useless literals. It is not obvious to ensure by hand the correct application of those transformations. The analysis results of the checker are used to safely apply the source-to-source transformations. For instance, the insertion of a green cut at a valid position in the procedure requires information about the cardinality and exclusivity with subsequent clauses. Such information is available in abstract sequences.

Strategy to generate specialised code

There exist several ways to order and combine the source-to-source transformations. Furthermore, some transformations may be conflictual, like clause reordering and cut insertion. We define a strategy for choosing a suitable order to safely apply the transformations. The strategy is inspired from [45] and from the knowledge of Warren's Abstract Machine (e.g., see [1, 131]).

Implementation and experimental evaluation of the optimiser

The optimiser is implemented and is publicly available [55]. We test the optimiser on a large set of programs to validate the strategy of the optimiser. Experiments show the speedup and the gain of the local stack utilisation between the original code and the code generated by the optimiser.

1.2.3 Modular verification and optimisation

In many Prolog systems, a program can be divided into different modules. A module is a part of the program that can be imported by several other modules. Module systems are an essential feature of programming languages as they facilitate the reuse of existing code and the development of general purpose libraries and of larger programs. We enhance the analyser to verify and optimise programs decomposed in modules. Type and norm declarations, as well as formal specifications may be private inside a module or public to other modules. The system verifies and/or optimises a module without having to reanalyse its imported modules (except if they are modified).

1.3   Structure of this thesis

Chapter 2 recalls the main operational issues of Prolog and presents some related work that tries to overcome those issues: Deville's methodology [45], which proposes a systematic way to construct reliable and efficient programs, the Termin-Web tool [27], which proves or infers termination, the CiaoPP environment [66], which performs a lot of analyses similar to ours, and the declarative language Mercury [123].

The core of the thesis is divided in two parts.

Part I presents the *checker*. The basic abstract interpretation framework [78] is described in Chapter 3. The various improvements to the basic framework are provided in the next chapters. In Chapter 4, extensions are realised to handle the full Prolog syntax (negation, cuts, disjunctive and 'if then else' constructs, dynamic and higher-order predicates). In Chapter 5, the expressiveness of the specifications is augmented (linearity domain, type and norm declarations). In Chapter 6, the abstract analysis is made more accurate. A discussion about the implementation is provided in Chapter 7, and we present the experimental evaluation of the checker in Chapter 8.

Part II presents the *optimiser*. Chapter 9 describes the different optimisation techniques and the sufficient conditions to apply them (those conditions are verified by the *checker*). It presents the strategy of the optimiser for choosing which transformations to apply on a procedure (in the context of some formal specification) and in which order to combine them, in order to generate efficient code. We provide finally the experimental evaluation of the optimiser.

Several appendices are provided. Appendix A and B list the procedures and the formal specifications used in this thesis, respectively. Appendix C presents the abstract syntax of the Prolog language dialect accepted by the system. Appendix D describes the abstract syntax of formal specifications. Appendix E presents the implementation of *constrained mappings*, which manipulate indices in the size components of abstract sequences. Appendix F provides the implementation of the abstract sequence concatenation. Appendix G provides the implementation of the source-to-source transformations performed by the optimiser. Appendix H provides detailed tables on the experimental results of the optimiser. Appendix I describes how to use the system.

Chapter 2

Background and related work

The Prolog language is accompanied with a *declarative* (or *logic*) semantics and an *operational* (or *procedural*) semantics. The declarative semantics is based on first-order logic, and it deals with the logical consequences of a logic program. The operational semantics is based on execution mechanisms (SLD resolution, computation rule, search rule), and deals with the computation of answer substitutions. Declarative semantics are easier to think about and to program in terms of, and operational semantics are needed for implementations. Unfortunately, for efficiency reasons, there is a gap between the two semantics of Prolog: they do not always coincide. The operational semantics is incomplete (depth-first search rule), unsound (negation by failure, unification without occur-check), and uses extralogical features (cuts, dynamic predicates). Consequently, to write a correct and efficient program, the programmer cannot reason about the declarative meaning of a program only, but he must also consider its operational semantics.

The difference between the two semantics of Prolog complicates the programmer's life, and many approaches are proposed to assist the user for writing reliable and efficient Prolog programs. Some methodologies try to reconcile (at least partially) the declarative and operational behaviours of logic programs (e.g., [3, 45]), by proposing a systematic development of programs based on logic specifications of the problem. Other approaches propose to construct programs by relying on the operational features of Prolog only, and are not directly concerned with the declarative semantics of Prolog. The resulting code has not always a clear declarative meaning (e.g., a lot of books about Prolog [13, 124]). Pragmatic approaches try to automate the verification or the inference of some interesting and intended operational properties of programs. Such analyses may also serve to optimise programs. Another solution to support the construction of logic programs is to improve the logic programming language. For instance, the declarative programming language Mercury [123] removes the conflict existing between the declarative and the operational semantics, by restricting the class of accepted logic programs and by compelling the user to write declarations besides its program. The Mercury compiler performs optimisations thanks to the specified properties.

The tool that we present in this thesis is related to all the above-mentioned approaches. This chapter describes and compares some of them with our system. Our tool can be used to support a methodology for constructing operationally correct logic programs. Some sufficient conditions are checked to ensure that the operational behaviour of a procedure conforms with its declarative meaning (for instance, verifying termination, occur-check freeness, soundness of negations). Also, by considering only the operational semantics of a program, our system can be used to check operational properties at each program point (for instance, modes, types, sharing, linearity of terms, relations between input/output terms, cardinality information). Thanks to all those properties, the tool can generate optimised versions of a given Prolog procedure with respect to user-given formal specifications.

The rest of this chapter is organised as follows. Section 2.1 recalls the main operational issues in Prolog. Section 2.2 presents the Deville's methodology, which proposes a systematic development of reliable and efficient programs. Section 2.3 presents the tool TerminWeb, which is designed to infer or to check the termination of logic programs. Section 2.4 describes the CiaoPP preprocessor, which performs a lot of analyses and optimisations on Prolog programs. Section 2.5 presents Mercury, a purely declarative language.

2.1   Programming with Prolog: some operational issues

In this section, we follow the discussion of [45] in order to present the main operational issues encountered when programming in Prolog. Such operational issues break the declarative nature of Prolog. We assume a preliminary knowledge of logic programming; see, for instance, [3, 87, 124].

2.1.1   Incompleteness

Given a program and an input query, answer substitutions are computed according to a depth-first search strategy with backtracking, where clauses are selected from top-to-bottom, and literals are executed from left-to-right inside a clause. Some input-output patterns can thus loop. For instance, consider the following program.

```
append([], L2, L2).
append([X|L1], L2, [X|L3]) :- append(L1, L2, L3).

append3(A, B, C, D) :- append(A, B, AB),
                       append(AB, C, D).
```
Procedure 2.1   append3(A,B,C,D)

This example shows procedures implementing the append(L1,L2,L3) and append3(A,B,C,D) relations (the latter holds if D is the concatenation of lists A, B and C). The query append3([a],[],[],D) produces the solution D=[a] and the program terminates. If we try the query append3(A,B,C,[a]), then we obtain the three expected solutions, but after that, the program loops. Indeed, with this query, the first call to append is executed when A, B and AB are distinct variables. Such a call has an infinite number of solutions, and thus, Prolog infinitely backtracks to that point.

Consider now another version of append3 where the two subcalls to append have been switched.

```
append3bis(A, B, C, D)  :- append(AB, C, D),
                           append(A, B, AB).
```

Procedure 2.2 append3bis(A,B,C,D)

The query append3bis(A,B,C,[a]) still produces the three expected solutions, and the program now terminates. However, the first query considered does not behave as expected: the execution of append3bis([a],[],[],D) produces the solution D=[a], but after that, the program loops. The two programs append3 and append3bis have the same declarative semantics but different operational semantics. The programmer must pay attention to the order of literals inside a clause. This problem can be solved using delay declarations [5, 20, 68, 109]. The idea is to replace the Prolog selection rule by a more flexible selection mechanism according to which atoms are delayed until they become 'sufficiently' instantiated. At each stage of the execution of a logic program only atoms satisfying the delay declarations can be selected. However, Prolog with delay declarations is still incomplete: it is well-known that it has the risk of floundering if the conditions of a delay declaration never hold. Prolog with delay declarations has a more complicated and less efficient implementation than standard Prolog.

The order of clauses in a procedure must also be considered, as it is shown in the following program.

```
connected(X,Y)  :- connected(X,Z), connected(Z,Y).
connected(1,2).
connected(2,3).
connected(3,4).
connected(4,5).
```

Procedure 2.3 connected(X,Y)

The procedure connected describes the relation between two points X and Y such that there exists a path between them. Declaratively, it is easy to see that the points 1 and 5 are connected. However, the query connected(1,5) produces no answer but loops. This is because the first clause is always selected. If the first clause was placed at the end of the procedure, after the basic cases, then the query would succeed.

2.1.2 Unfairness

By reconsidering Procedure 2.1, a call to append3(A,B,[2],D) will produce the following answers:

A	B	D
[]	[]	[2]
[]	[H1]	[H1,2]
[]	[H1,H2]	[H1,H2,2]
...	...	...

This shows the unfairness of the execution: A is always an empty list, although other instantiations also exist. Note that unfairness can lead to incompleteness. For instance, the goal append3 (A, B, [2], D), A=[1] will never succeeds, whereas append3 ([1], B, [2], D) is a logical consequence of this program.

2.1.3   Unsoundness

Prolog uses a general algorithm for unification, with no restriction on the terms being unified. However, most Prolog compilers do not perform the occur-check test during the unification for efficiency reasons. For instance, consider the following code.

```
append([], L2, L2).
append([X|L1], L2, [X|L3]) :- append(L1, L2, L3).
```
Procedure 2.4   append(L1,L2,L3)

We know that the list [1|L] is not the concatenation of [] and the list L. However, for some Prolog implementation, the query append([],L,[1|L]) succeeds, and it tries to print an infinite list whose elements are all 1. This Prolog result is unsound.

2.1.4   Green and red cuts

Cuts can be used to make programs more efficient, by allowing us to prune redundant parts of the search tree. The effect of the cut is to suppress the choice points, so that the next clauses are not selected when the cut is executed. Such control feature can force a procedure to be deterministic, and it can allow us to remove useless literal tests in successive clauses. We distinguish two kinds of cuts. A *green* cut is one which does not change the semantics of the program. A *red* cut is one which changes the semantics of the program, pruning away solutions that would have been found if the cut had not been there.

Using cuts is tricky and error-prone, because it can lead to undesirable run-time errors. For instance, consider the minimum1 code below.

```
minimum1(X,Y,X) :- X =< Y, !.
minimum1(X,Y,Y) :- X > Y.
```
Procedure 2.5   minimum1(X,Y,Z)

This procedure can be used when input X and Y are integers, and when input Z is a variable or an integer. The cut at the end of the first clause is *green* because its execution does not suppress a solution. Consider now the same program where the arithmetic test in the second clause has been removed:

```
minimum2(X,Y,X) :- X =< Y, !.
minimum2(X,Y,Y).
```
Procedure 2.6 `minimum2(X,Y,Z)`

The above cut is *red*. The procedure `minimum2` behaves as expected when input X and Y are integers, and when input Z is a variable. However, it does not work properly when Z is an integer. For instance, the query `minimum2(2,5,5)` succeeds using the second clause, but this is clearly false. The correct code for this use should be:

```
minimum3(X,Y,Z) :- X =< Y, !, Z=X.
minimum3(X,Y,Y).
```
Procedure 2.7 `minimum3(X,Y,Z)`

The above example shows that it is quite intricate to use cuts correctly. Several authors claim that the programmer should not use the cut, and that cuts should be automatically inserted (e.g., [39, 45], and see Section 9.4).

2.1.5 Negation

Negation is generally handled as failure [23]: a call to `not(p(X1,...,Xn))` succeeds if the execution of `p(X1,...,Xn)` fails. The variables occurring in the negation are not instantiated after the execution of the negation. So, negation in Prolog is different from the negation used in logic. For instance, consider the two procedures p and q:

```
p(a).    q(a).
p(b).
```

Consider the two queries `p(X),not(q(X))` and `not(q(X)),p(X)`. Declaratively, the two queries have the same semantics. However, operationally, they produce different results: the first query succeeds by instantiating X to b, although the second one fails (because the call to `q(X)` succeeds). Only the first goal is operationally correct and corresponds to the declarative meaning of negation. The second result is unsound. A sufficient condition to have a sound negation by failure is that it applies to a ground literal. Other approaches to negation exist [10, 21, 22, 107], but they are rather complicated (see Section 4.1.1).

2.1.6 Extralogical features

Prolog also proposes features that have little or no declarative semantics: test-predicates (e.g., `var/1`, `nonvar/1`), input/output primitives (e.g., `write/1`, `read/1`), dynamic predicates (e.g., `assert/1`, `retract/1`), higher-order predicates (e.g., `findall/3`). Such features cannot be described in first-order logic. Thus, they increase the gap between the declarative and operational semantics.

2.1.7   Multidirectionality

An attractive feature of Prolog is that procedures can be used in more than one way
(the arguments being either input or output). However, for efficiency reasons, some
built-ins are not multidirectional (e.g., arithmetic and comparison predicates).

2.2   Deville's methodology

The author of [45] proposes a methodology to systematically construct correct and
efficient Prolog programs. The development of a program is decomposed into several steps: (1) elaboration of a specification of the problem, (2) construction of
a logic description in pure logic (independent from any operational semantics),
and (3) derivation of a correct and efficient Prolog program from the logic description. The method involves a number of transformation and verification steps.
The methodology is inspired from Kowalski's equation 'Algorithm = Logic + Control' [73]: the final executable algorithm results from the addition of control to the
logic description.

The following sections summarise the different steps of the methodology.

2.2.1   Specification schema

Deville's methodology proposes a standard schema for specifying a procedure. It
contains, among other things, the name and the formal parameters of the procedure, an informal definition of the relation between the arguments, and pre-post
conditions on its execution. For instance, the procedure `efface/3` can be specified in this way:

---
procedure `efface(X,L,LEff)`
Type: X: Term
               L, LEff: Lists
Relation: X is an element of L and LEff is the list L without the first
                     occurrence of X in L.
Application conditions:
          in(ground,ground,any):**out**(ground,ground,ground) $\langle 0, 1 \rangle$
          in(any,ground,any):**out**(ground,ground,ground) $\langle 0, * \rangle$
          in(ground,any,ground):**out**(ground,ground,ground) $\langle 0, * \rangle$

The *application conditions* (or *directionalities*) describe the possible uses of the
procedure: each directionality specifies the allowed instantiations of the parameters
before the execution (the **in** part), and the corresponding instantiations after the
call (the **out** part). Type information (a type is here defined as a set of ground
terms) acts as pre-post conditions too. The cardinality information $\langle Min, Max \rangle$
specify the minimum and maximum lengths of the sequence of computed answer

substitutions returned by a procedure call respecting the **in** part of the directionality. The symbol ∗ (resp. ∞) expresses that there is a finite (resp. infinite) number of solutions. In this example, the first directionality expresses the following. Before the execution, the first and second parameters must be ground lists, and the third argument may be any term. After a successful execution, all parameters are ground. In that case, the procedure is deterministic (at most one solution).

In our system, the user can write so-called *formal specifications*, which partially correspond to Deville's specifications (see Section 3.1.1 for details). They express input and output conditions on terms, as well as operational properties such as the number of solutions. For instance, the first directionality of efface can be expressed as follows in our framework:

```
efface/3
   in(X:ground, L:ground list, LEff:any)
   out(_, _, ground list)
   sol(sol =< 1)
```

Our specification language expresses various behavioural properties that are verified by the analyser. Such properties include many of the operational aspects proposed by Deville. They are sometimes even more precise and expressive. For instance, the number of solutions can be explicitly related to the size of input terms, and the information on sure success and failure can be expressed with respect to a refinement of the information on the input terms. Other operational properties not present in Deville's specification can be expressed in our formal specifications and checked by our analyser (e.g., the input terms that are left uninstantiated during the execution (see Section 6.1), the induction parameter that decreases through recursive calls (see Section 6.2), etc.). However, our system cannot currently express (and prove) that the procedure has an infinite number of solutions (the symbol ∞ in Deville's specification).

2.2.2 Logic description

A logic description is a formula in typeless first-order logic. It is an *if and only if* definition of the predicate. It uses the declarative semantics of pure logic, and negation is real negation (and not negation as failure). The logic description is constructed from the formal specification [45].

The logic description for $efface(X, L, TEff)$ is:

$$efface(X, L, LEff) \Leftrightarrow$$
$$L = [] \land false$$
$$\lor\ L = [H|T] \land (\ H = X \land LEff = T$$
$$\lor H \neq X \land efface(X, T, TEff) \land LEff = [H|TEff])$$

2.2.3 Derivation of a correct and efficient Prolog program

The last step of the methodology is the derivation of a logic program (in Prolog) from the logic description. It starts with the translation of the logic description into program clauses. To obtain a correct Prolog program, an abstract interpretation (using the type and directionality information of the specification) is performed to determine a permutation of the literals such that incompleteness, unfairness, unsoundness, and negation problem do not occur. This step has to solve all the problems that make the declarative and operational semantics different.

For instance, a Prolog code that is operationally correct for each directionality expressed in the specification is the following:

```
efface(X,L,LEff) :- L=[H|T], H=X, LEff=T.
efface(X,L,LEff) :- L=[H|T], LEff=[H|TEff],
                    efface(X,T,TEff), not(H=X).
```

The Prolog code is finally transformed by the introduction of control information and optimisations. For instance, if we consider the first directionality of the specification of `efface`, the procedure can be transformed into a more efficient procedure:

```
efface(X,[X|T],LEff) :- !, LEff=T.
efface(X,[H|T],[H|TEff]) :- efface(X,T,TEff).
```

The Deville's construction process is not automated. The transformations leading to an operationally correct and optimised Prolog code are systematic but tedious to perform by hand. Our tool can be used to automatically check that, in the context of the considered formal specifications, the above code is occur-check free (see Section 5.1), the negation is sound (see Section 4.1), and the program terminates (see Section 6.2). This allows us to reduce the gap between the two semantics of Prolog. Our tool can also be used to verify that a procedure meets its formal specification (see Section 3.5), and it can be used to automatically apply code transformations making the code more efficient (see Chapter 9). Note that Deville's methodology is not always applicable. Some programs have non-logical aspects (e.g., input/output procedures).

2.3 TerminWeb: termination analysis and inference

A main operational issue encountered when programming in Prolog is the possible non-termination of a Prolog program, due to the depth-first search rule for computing solutions. Termination analysis of logic programs has received a lot of attention. The objective of such analysis is either to prove that the execution of a Prolog program terminates for some class of input queries, or more generally, to infer the input conditions for which the execution terminates. A detailed survey can be found in [38, 84].

In this section, we briefly present the TerminWeb [15, 26, 27, 50] tool, which performs termination checking and termination inference as well. The termination analysis in TerminWeb is based on the *binary unfolding* semantics. A given program P is unfolded into a possibly infinite set of binary clauses that represent the dependencies between calls in a computation of some given goal (query). A binary clause is a clause whose body consists of exactly one atom. Intuitively, a binary clause a:-b specifies that a call to a in a computation implies an eventual subsequent call to b. A clause of the form a:-true is a fact, i.e., it indicates a success pattern. It is shown that the termination behaviour of a program is equivalent to that of its binary unfolding. So, there is a direct connection between termination and the *calls-to* relation expressed by the unfolding program. Termination of a program P and a query G is determined in the absence of an infinite chain in the binary unfolding of P starting with G.

The first step of TerminWeb is to compute a *finite* description of the binary unfolding description, by applying abstract interpretation and widening to the binary unfolding semantics. The abstract interpreter derives a finite set of *abstract binary unfoldings* which approximates the possibly infinite set of binary unfoldings. The resulting abstract program expresses relations on the sizes of the program's argument positions. Several norms (or size measures) can be automatically inferred and combined (e.g., term-size, list-length).

The second step of TerminWeb is a backwards analysis to infer modes for an initial goal for which a logic program is guaranteed to terminate. This analysis extracts boolean conditions on the instantiation of variables to guarantee that the loops (identified in the abstract binary unfolding program) can be executed only a finite number of times. TerminWeb uses the abstract domain of Pos [32, 127, 94] to compute instantiation dependencies.

The analyser presented in this thesis makes use of similar notions as Termin-Web (see Section 5.3 and Section 6.2): term norm (i.e., a function that maps terms to natural numbers), and interargument relation (i.e., a relation between the norm values of terms). Our system is able to relate the size of input terms to the size of other terms arising in any subsequent computation step. Several norms can also be combined. We do not impose that the norm of a term remains invariant under instantiation. For instance, our system is able to prove the termination of the following 'impure' Prolog procedure, for any possible input, using the list-length norm:

```
close(X)  :- var(X), X=[].
close(X)  :- nonvar(X), X=[H|Xs], close(Xs).
```

Our system requires more information from the user than other automatic methods since the user has to specify norms and interargument relations in the behaviours of the procedures. But this drawback is counterbalanced by the advantage that the user can often invent a size expression or an interargument relation which could not be easily found automatically. We perform all analyses (modes, types, sharing, term sizes) at the same time, which allows the analyses to interact and thus to improve each other (see Section 3.5).

Furthermore, our abstract interpretation framework is built on the $\text{Pat}(\Re)$ construction [33, 80], which automatically enhances an abstract domain $\Re$ with structural information (abstract values are computed not only for procedure arguments, but also for subterms of them). TerminWeb uses an alternative approach to the $\text{Pat}(\Re)$ construction. Rather than enhancing the abstract domain $\Re$ with pattern information, the program itself is enhanced. First, a pattern analysis is applied to the program. Then, a transformation that portrays the derived information is applied. This involves two steps: specialisation and untupling [26]. Finally, the program is analysed over the original domain $\Re$. The effect is an improvement in the precision of the $\Re$ analysis similar to that obtained in the $\text{Pat}(\Re)$ analysis.

2.4   CiaoPP: multiple analyses for Prolog

CiaoPP [66] is a preprocessor of the Ciao [16] multi-paradigm programming system, allowing programming in logic, constraint, and functional styles, as well as in a particular form of object-oriented programming. The heart of Ciao is a logic programming-based kernel language. The design philosophy of Ciao (and of CiaoPP) is discussed in [63]. Ciao subsumes ISO-Prolog and is extensible via libraries. The preprocessor CiaoPP uses modular, incremental, abstract interpretation to infer properties of program predicates and literals, including types, variable instantiation properties (sharing and freeness), non-failure, determinacy, bounds on computational costs, bounds on sizes of terms in the program. Such properties are expressed using assertions [116]. This information is used to validate programs, to detect bugs with respect to user-given assertions, to generate and simplify run-time tests, and to perform high-level program transformations for optimisation. Program transformations include abstract specialisation (removing redundant literals), multiple abstract specialisation (different specialised versions are generated depending on the use of the predicate), partial evaluation, dead code removal, goal reordering, parallelisation, resource usage control, reduction of concurrency, low-level optimisation [62]. The input to CiaoPP consists of a logic program, possibly decomposed in modules and optionally annotated with assertions. The output consists of error/warning messages, the results of the static analysis (expressed using assertions), and the transformed logic program (specialised code with additional run-time tests).

In the next sections, we present CiaoPP and we compare it to our tool with respect to the language of assertions (Section 2.4.1), the abstract interpretation framework (Section 2.4.2), the sharing and freeness analysis (Section 2.4.3), the type analysis (Section 2.4.4), the non-failure and determinacy analysis (Section 2.4.5), the size, cost and termination analysis (Section 2.4.6), and the optimising program transformation (Section 2.4.7).

2.4.1 Assertions

Assertions in Ciao serve many purposes [116]. They are used to express analysis results, to provide input to the analyser (verifier or optimiser), and to provide program specifications for debugging and validation. Assertions can also be processed to generate documentation [65].

To illustrate the assertion language in CiaoPP, consider for instance the predicate select(X,L,Ls), which holds iff X is an element of the list L and Ls is the list L without an occurrence of X:

```
select(X, [X|L], L).
select(X, [H|L], [H|Ls]) :- select(X, L, Ls).
```

A possible operational behaviour of the above procedure can be described by the following assertion in CiaoPP:

```
:- check pred select(X,L,Ls)
   : ( var(X), list(L,gnd), var(Ls), indep(X,Ls) )
  => ( gnd(X), list(Ls,gnd),
       size(L,length(L)), size(Ls,length(L)-1) )
   + ( terminates,possibly_fails,steps_ub(length(L)+1)).
```

Conditions on input arguments are placed between the ':' and '=>' tags, and conditions on output arguments are placed after the '=>' tag. Operational properties such as termination and non-failure can be described after the '+' tag. The above assertion expresses the following. If input X and Ls are two independent (distinct) variables and input L is a ground list, then after success of the execution, X becomes a ground term and Ls becomes a ground list whose size (list-length) is equal to the size of L minus one. The procedure terminates, it may fail, and the upper bound of resolution steps is the list-length of L plus one. Note also that in CiaoPP, information about the determinacy can be described using, for instance, the tags is_det (at most one solution, or not terminate), or non_det (at least one solution), or possibly_non_det (nothing can be ensured about determinacy nor termination).

In our system, the formal specification corresponding to the above assertion can be written as follows (see Section 3.1.1 for more details):

```
select/3
   in(X:var, L:ground list, Ls:var; noshare(<X,Ls>))
   out(ground, _, ground list)
   srel(Ls_out = L_in-1)
   sol(sol = L_in)
   sexpr(< L >)
```

The in part of the specification describes the class of input calls where X and Ls are two distinct variables (presence of the noshare tag) and where L is a ground list. The out part of the specification describes the form of the arguments at the end of the execution, when the execution succeeds. In a formal specification, information that can be implicitly deduced needs not to be explicitly written (the symbol '_' is used). In this case, X becomes a ground term, and Ls becomes a ground list. The srel part describes linear relations between the size of input and output terms: the list-length of output Ls is equal to the list-length of input L minus one. The sol part expresses that the number of solutions is exactly the list-length of L. In particular, the procedure select(X,L,Ls) succeeds only if input L is a non-empty ground list. Thus, if L is an empty list, the execution surely fails. Unlike our specification language, assertions in CiaoPP cannot express the number of solutions in function of the size of input terms. CiaoPP is not able to specify conditions of sure success and sure failure inside a single assertion (consequently, CiaoPP only proves that the procedure may fail for input calls satisfying the in conditions). However, it is possible to provide the following two assertions for the select predicate in CiaoPP, splitting the cases of sure success and sure failure explicitly:

```
:- check comp select(X,L,Ls)
   : ( var(X), list1(L,gnd), var(Ls), indep(X,Ls) )
   + not_fails.
:- check comp select(X,L,Ls): nil(L) + fails.
```

where the property list1/2 holds for a non-empty list, and where the property nil/1 holds for an empty list (they are defined as regular types, see Section 2.4.4).

The sexpr part in formal specifications describes the induction parameter, which decreases through recursive calls (this is used for proving termination). In this case, it is the list-length of the second argument L. In CiaoPP, one cannot specify an induction parameter. Other properties can be written in assertions (and checked by CiaoPP) but not in our formal specifications (e.g., lower and/or upper bounds of cost functions [110]).

If a procedure is not specified in our system, then the procedure is simply not analysed. In CiaoPP, assertions are optional. Note that every part of a formal specification does not need to be specified in our system (it depends on the kind of properties we want to check). The minimum information that must be provided by the user are the conditions on input arguments. In general, the accuracy of the analysis depends on the information that is described in the formal specifications or in the assertions.

CiaoPP and our system have the same approach to deal with the system built-ins (e.g., arithmetic comparisons, test-predicates) and with predicates whose code is unavailable. Their behaviour is described by assertions or formal specifications. Both systems allow the user to express that an assertion has to be statically checked or can be trusted (i.e., assumed, but not checked).

In CiaoPP, there exist entry annotations, that are a class of predicate level annotations. They state that calls to a predicate with a given abstract call may exist at execution time. For instance, the following annotation states that there can be a call to predicate `p/2` in which its two arguments are ground:

```
:- entry(p(X,Y), (ground(X),ground(Y))).
```

Such entry annotations specify a restricted class of calls to the module entry points as acceptable. No call patterns other than those specified by the entry annotations in the program may occur from outside the program text. The list of entry annotations includes all calls that may occur to a program, apart from those which arise from the literals explicitly present in the program text. Such assertions are optional. If entry annotations are not present, CiaoPP takes the module declaration as starting point and analyses exported predicates for their 'top' abstract substitution. The user may provide several entry declarations for the same predicate. Entry declarations can be provided for predicates that are not explicitly exported but which can be called by meta-calls such as `call/1` and `findall/3`.

2.4.2 Abstract interpretation framework

The fundamental functionality behind CiaoPP is a static global program analysis, based on abstract interpretation. The CiaoPP abstract interpreter, called PLAI [103, 104, 105], is based on the framework of Bruynooghe [14], and includes many extensions, e.g., incrementality [67], modularity [18, 30, 113], analysis of constraints [49], and analysis of concurrency [92].

The PLAI abstract interpreter computes (and infers), at each program point, abstract substitutions modelling the variable states until that point. Abstract substitutions combine several domains. Some abstract domains are used for gathering term-type information (regular types [48, 130]). Other domains are used to keep track of variable dependence (e.g., sharing+freeness [104]). PLAI follows a top-down goal-dependent strategy to compute the information that pertains to the particular set of queries (entries) to be considered. The abstract interpretation produces an abstract AND-OR tree (which approximates the concrete AND-OR tree). An AND-node contains a clause head whose children are all the literals in the body of the clause. An OR-node contains a literal in a body of a clause whose children are the different clause heads that unifies with the literal. PLAI computes abstract substitutions at all points in the program.

The analysis results of PLAI are then used by CiaoPP for several other *computational* analyses, for instance, size analysis, cost analysis, determinacy analysis, non-failure analysis, termination analysis, as well as bounds on resource consumption (e.g., time or space cost). Those analyses are instrumental to verify an assertion (by checking that the assertion is entailed by the results of the analysis), to generate run-time tests, or to safely apply optimisation techniques.

In the presence of recursive predicates, the analyses require a fixpoint computation. A general fixpoint algorithm is proposed for PLAI [103, 104, 105], which localises fixpoint computations to only the strongly connected components of (mutually) recursive predicates. Memo tables are used to contain information about the particular goal called and its location within the program. Additionally, an initial approximation to the fixpoint is computed from the non-recursive clauses of the recursive predicate. The construction of the abstract AND-OR graph is updated each time the success abstract substitution of a procedure is becoming more accurate. The process stops when a fixpoint is reached. The fixpoint algorithm is independent of the abstract domain used in the abstract interpreter, as it is the case in GAIA [80]. Ad-hoc fixpoint algorithms are designed for the additional analyses, performed after the execution of PLAI (e.g., [43] for the non-failure analysis).

Our abstract interpretation framework is based on [78]. Unlike CiaoPP, our analyser does not compute any fixpoint. Indeed, our analyser abstractly executes[1] a literal in a clause by relying directly on the information present in the related specifications, which are provided by the user (see Section 3.5). Our framework is thus entirely compositional.

The PLAI framework is based on abstract substitutions (modelling set of program substitutions), but our framework is based on abstract sequences (modelling sequences of answer substitutions, see Section 3.4). Abstract sequences are richer and more expressive than abstract substitutions. In particular, the whole analysis is done in a single pass, where abstract sequences are collected at each program point (components are verified simultaneously and thus improve each other). It is not the case in CiaoPP, where several analyses are performed in sequence. For instance, PLAI first infers modes, types, sharing and freeness information. Further analyses are then performed to compute the information about the cardinality, the sizes relations, determinacy, and termination. In our framework, the abstract operation responsible to compute the global behaviour (abstract sequence) of a procedure is more complex (see Section 6.4): it abstractly concatenates the abstract sequences modelling the execution of each clause, instead of performing a simple least upper bound of abstract substitutions as it is done in PLAI.

To simplify the design of the abstract operations dealing with abstract sequences, our framework executes *normalised* programs (see Section 3.2.1), which are similar to the superhomogeneous form of Mercury programs [123]. In CiaoPP, the input program is abstractly executed, without having to normalise it.

2.4.3 Sharing and freeness analysis

The user can parametrise CiaoPP by choosing the abstract domains to combine in abstract substitutions. Usually, at least sharing and freeness domains are used in abstract substitutions [104]. The *set-sharing* component provides information

---

[1]The meaning of 'abstractly execute' in our work and in CiaoPP are different. In our framework, the abstract execution of a literal denotes the computation of the abstract sequence modelling the literal execution. In CiaoPP, this is a program transformation operation whereby a literal is eliminated from a program [118]. It mostly involves calls to external predicates (builtins, libraries) for which CiaoPP knows sufficient conditions for 'executing them at compile-time'. Note that our optimiser is also able to remove redundant literals, by relying on the abstract information derived by the checker.

about potential aliasing and variable sharing among the program variables (as well as groundness). Its structure is defined in [103]. The set-sharing component of the abstract substitutions for a clause is defined as a set of sets of program variables in that clause. Informally, a set of program variables appears in the sharing component if the terms to which these variables are bound share a variable. For instance, the value of a sharing component may be $\{\{X\}, \{X, Y\}\}$. It corresponds to a set of substitutions in which X and Y are bound to terms t_X and t_Y such that (1) at least one variable occurs in both t_X and t_Y (represented by the element $\{X, Y\}$), and (2) at least one variable occurs only in t_X (represented by the element $\{X\}$). Thus, a program variable is ground if it does not appear in any set, and two program variables are independent if they do not appear together in any set. Instead of using set-sharing, CiaoPP can use *pair-sharing*, which is defined by a set of pairs of the form (X, Y). A pair (X, Y) in this set denotes that the terms bound to X and Y possibly share a variable. The freeness component of an abstract substitution for a clause gives the mapping from its program variables to the set $\{G, F, NF\}$ of freeness values, where G stands for *ground*, F stands for *free*, and NF stands for potentially not free (it can be bound to terms which have functors).

In our framework also, abstract substitutions are made of several abstract components (among them, the *mode*, the *linearity*, and the *possible sharing* domains), which can increase the accuracy of each other (see Section 3.3). Our mode, sharing, and linearity domains are defined over indices (an index represents a term or a subterm in a substitution, and the structure of a term is represented thanks to the `Pattern` component [33, 80, 102]). In CiaoPP, the sharing and freeness components are defined only for program variables occurring in the clauses and not for subterms of them. Like the freeness domain in CiaoPP, the mode component can describe groundness (`ground`), freeness (`var`), and possible non freeness (`any`), but it can also describe more accurate modes (e.g., `gv` for terms that are variable or ground, `ngv` for terms that are neither ground nor variable). Our analyser uses a *pair-sharing* component (and not a set-sharing component like in CiaoPP). Set-sharing is more expressive than pair-sharing. For instance, in a pair-sharing domain, we cannot describe the fact that *all* variables occurring in Y share with X, which can be expressed by the set $\{\{X\}, \{X, Y\}\}$. In such a case, X becoming ground implies that Y is ground too.

2.4.4 Type analysis

CiaoPP automatically infers (parametric) regular types, based on the framework described in [48, 119, 130]. A regular type [37] is a type representing a class of terms that can be described by a regular term grammar. A regular term grammar describes a set of finite terms constructed from a set of functors, and from productions (rewriting rules) of the form $T \rightarrow rhs$, where T is an non-terminal and the right hand side *rhs* is either a non-terminal or a term $f(T_1, ..., T_n)$, constructed from an n-ary functor and n non-terminals. In CiaoPP, specific *base* types are predefined, e.g., `term` denotes the set of any terms, `gnd` denotes the set of any ground terms, `int` denotes the set of integers. They are considered as non-terminals in the regular grammar. A non-terminal in such a grammar is a *type*. The concretisation of a non-terminal is the set of terms derivable from its productions.

The regular types considered in CiaoPP are constructed on *deterministic* regular grammars: none of the right hand sides are non-terminals, and for each non-terminal T the function symbols are all distinct in the right hand sides of the productions for T. Deterministic grammars are less expressive than non-deterministic grammars. Deterministic regular grammars can only express sets of terms that are *tuple-distributive*, i.e., if the concretisation of a type contains two terms with the same principal functor (for instance, $f(a, b)$ and $f(c, d)$), then necessarily, it contains terms with the same principal functor obtained by exchanging subterms of the two terms in the same argument positions (in this case, it contains also the terms $f(c, b)$ and $f(a, d)$).

CiaoPP allows the user to provide regular type declarations, written in Prolog style. Such declared types can then be used in assertions to specify the input and output types of procedure arguments. For instance, a regular type for a list can be declared as follows in CiaoPP:

```
:- regtype list/1.
list([]).
list([_|Xs]) :- list(Xs).
```

It corresponds to the regular grammar rules *list* $\rightarrow$ $[]$ and *list* $\rightarrow$ $[term|list]$. Similarly, the regular type `nil/1`, used in Section 2.4.1, holds for an empty list and is defined as follows:

```
:- regtype nil/1.
nil([]).
```

The declared types can also be *parametric*, where non-terminals are parametrised by *type variables*. For instance, a regular type defining parametric lists can be defined as follows in CiaoPP, where `T` is the type parameter denoting the type of the elements of the list:

```
:- regtype list/2.
list([], T).
list([X|Xs], T) :- T(X), list(Xs, T).
```

Similarly, the regular types `list1/2`, used in Section 2.4.1, holds for an non-empty list and is defined as follows:

```
:- regtype list1/2.
list1([X|Xs], T) :- T(X), list(Xs, T).
```

In our system also, the user can declare parametric regular types (see Section 5.2), by using the following syntax (`T` is the type parameter):

```
list(T) ::= [] | [T|list(T)]
```

The constructors of the declared types must be different, making our types also *tuple-distributive*.

Assertions in CiaoPP and formal specifications in our system are not polymorphic. The actual types in formal specifications are called *type expressions* (see Section 5.2.4). A type expression denotes a set of (possibly non-ground) terms. It is a primitive type (e.g., any, ground, int) or a declared type where each of its type variables has been instantiated by a type expression. For instance, the type expression list(list(int)) denotes the set of lists of lists of integers, the type expression list(list(any)) denotes the set of lists whose elements are lists of any terms. Only type declarations are parametric in both systems. They are introduced to represent families of non-parametric types.

The algorithm used in CiaoPP for inferring regular types is described in [48, 119, 130]. It consists of approximating a logic program P by transforming it into *regular unary logic programs* (RUL programs, defined in [133]). A RUL program is composed of regular unary clauses of the form $t_0(f(X_1, ..., X_n))$:-$t_1(X_1),...,t_n(X_n)$ ($n \geq 0$), where $X_1, ..., X_n$ are distinct variables, and where $t_1, ..., t_n$ are unary procedure names defined in the RUL program. In a RUL program, no two different clause heads have a common instance.

In our framework, non-parametric type expressions are computed for all indices described in the abstract sequences, during the abstract execution of the procedure. Type expressions are built upon the declared parametric types provided by the user and the primitive types, only. If a concrete (sub)term cannot be described by some declared type, a general primitive type is used (e.g., ground, any) (see Figure 5.3). Unlike our system, CiaoPP may infer regular types besides the user-declared types. The way we combine type and mode information is also similar to the integrated types of [31, 69], but to avoid combinatorial explosion problems arising in these proposals, the user is restricted to declare disjoint types (two different types must have different principal functors).

2.4.5 Non-failure and determinacy analysis

CiaoPP includes a non-failure analysis, based on [19, 43], which detects procedures and goals that are guaranteed not to fail (they produce at least one solution or they do not terminate). The technique is based on a covering decision procedure. The non-failure analysis takes as input the results of the type, sharing and freeness analyses performed in PLAI. CiaoPP then attempts to detect predicates that cover their types. A predicate covers its types if there is at least one clause whose 'tests' (head unification and body built-ins) succeeds, for any well typed input. A predicate p is non-failing if there is no path in the call graph of the program from p to any predicate q that does not cover its types.

In our framework, the non-failure input conditions, as well as the information about the number of solutions are approximated into the abstract sequences (see

Section 3.4.4). The covering algorithm in our system consists of checking that the least upper bound of the non-failure input conditions (`ref` component) of all clauses of a procedure is an exact union and is equal to the `ref` component of the considered specification (see Section 6.4).

CiaoPP also includes a determinacy analysis based on [89], which detects predicates that produce at most one solution, and predicates whose clauses are mutually exclusive, even if they are not deterministic. In our system, determinacy can be verified by detecting the exclusivity of abstract sequences (based on the non-failure conditions, see Section 6.3), and by looking at the cardinality information maintained in abstract sequences (see Section 6.4).

2.4.6   Size, cost, and termination analysis

CiaoPP can infer lower and upper bounds on the size of terms and the computational cost of predicates [40, 42, 110]. The size and cost analyses are performed by using the results of the PLAI analysis (sharing/freeness/types). The cost bounds are expressed as functions on the size of the input arguments. Various measures are used for the size of an input, such as list-length, term-size, term-depth, integer-value. Termination is proved by checking that the number of computational steps (which is a cost function) has a finite upper bound. Lower-bound on size and cost functions are derived on the basis of the non-failure analysis.

Our analyser performs all analyses (modes + types + sharing + term sizes + cardinality) at the same time, which allows the analyses to interact and thus to improve each other (see Section 3.4 and Section 3.5). Our analyser does not perform cost analyses, but it can check linear relations between the number of solutions and the sizes of input terms (several norms can be combined). Our system uses norms similar to CiaoPP, and allows the user to declare its own norms (see Section 5.3). Termination is proved by checking that a given induction parameter (which can be a sequence of linear expressions on the sizes of input terms) decreases through (mutually) recursive calls, according to the lexicographic order (see Section 6.2). Our system uses the Parma Polyhedra Library [8] to compute and compare the sizes components of abstract sequences (systems of linear (in)equations).

2.4.7   Source program optimisation

Several kinds of program optimisations are available in CiaoPP. They include (multiple) abstract specialisation [118], partial evaluation [114], parallelisation [17]. All optimisations perform source-to-source transformations, based on the abstract analysis results.

Similarly, our system performs source-to-source transformations. The code transformations that we apply are inspired by the Deville's methodology [45]. Given a procedure and a formal specification for it, the optimiser generates a specialised version of the procedure. During this step, clauses are reordered, control information (cuts) is automatically inserted, redundant literals are removed, explicit unifications are removed and clause heads are instantiated. Our source-to-source transformations are thus related to [39], the authors of which propose to avoid the use of cuts in programs, and to let the system automatically insert them. Cut insertion as well as replacement of negations by cuts are not performed by CiaoPP.

2.5 Mercury: a purely declarative logic language

Mercury [123] is a purely declarative programming language. This language re-solves the conflict existing between the declarative and the operational semantics of Prolog, by restricting the class of accepted logic programs and by asking the user to enhance his program with type, mode and determinacy information. Mercury provides declarative counterparts for Prolog's non-logical features. It uses a syntax very similar to Prolog with additional declarations. The Mercury system performs semantic checks at compile-time to certify these declarations. The compiler tries to help the user by locating as much as possible errors in the program. Declarations are also useful to document the code. The execution model of Mercury takes ad-vantage of the type, mode and determinacy information to generate efficient code. The execution model is split into three execution algorithms, depending on the de-terminacy information: deterministic, nondeterministic, and semideterministic.

The approach of our system bears many similarities with Mercury. In our sys-tem also, the user has to annotate its program with formal specifications, which de-scribe operational properties of the procedures (including modes, types, and cardi-nality information). However, our system accepts any Prolog program. Less logic programs are accepted by Mercury, because only limited forms of unification are allowed. Our system statically checks the operational properties described in the annotations, as well as general properties that are needed to ensure the equivalence between the declarative and the operational meanings of the program (termination, occur-check freeness, sound negations, green cuts). The information verified by the system is also used to generate specialised code.

In the next sections, we compare Mercury and our tool with respect to the types (Section 2.5.1), the modes (Section 2.5.2), the determinism (Section 2.5.3), and the termination analysis (Section 2.5.4).

2.5.1 Types

Mercury types are polymorphic, modelled after ML [97], and equivalent to the Mycroft-O'Keefe type system [106] and to the type system of Gödel [68]. For instance, the polymorphic type for lists can be defined as follows:

```
:- type list(T) ---> [] ; [T | list(T)].
```

There are also some primitive (built-in) types, like `int` for integers and `float` for real numbers. A feature in Mercury allows the user to provide different names for the same type (this is not available in our analyser). In Mercury, it is an error to mix values of different types inside a list, because there is no way to give a type to values such as `[1, "2", 3.4, X]`. In our Prolog analyser however, we can approximate such a list by the type expression `list(any)`, denoting the set of lists whose elements are any (possibly non-ground) terms.

The type of every argument of a predicate must be declared. The Mercury compiler then automatically infers the types of all variables at each program point. A program is *type correct* if there is a unique most general assignment of parametric polymorphic types to the variables and function symbols occurring in the program such that the type of every argument of every atom in the program is identical to the declared type of the corresponding formal argument.

In our framework, we do not use our parametric type declarations (see Section 5.2) to perform the same kind of type checking. Our type declarations are used to build non-parametric type expressions. Type expressions are used in formal specifications and are also related to the so-called *instantiatedness trees* in Mercury (see next section).

2.5.2 Modes

In Mercury, a *mode* of a predicate is a mapping from the initial state of instantiation of the arguments to their final state of instantiation. States of instantiation are described by the types annotated with mode information. Types can be viewed as regular trees, with two kinds of nodes: *or-nodes* representing types, and *and-nodes* representing function symbols. The children of an or-node are the function symbols that can be used to construct terms of that type; the children of an and-node are the types of the arguments of the function symbol. An or-node is attached with mode information, i.e., *free* or *bound*. If the node is *free*, then the corresponding node in the term is a free variable that does not share with other variable in the tree. If the node is *bound*, then the corresponding node in the term is a function symbol. In Mercury's terminology, the type tree with mode information on its or-nodes is called a *instantiatedness tree*. The mode system provides `free` and `ground` as names for instantiatedness trees, all of whose nodes are free or bound respectively. A partially instantiated value is one whose instantiatedness tree is of the form `bound(...)`, where the `...` part contains `free` sub-instantiatedness, either directly or indirectly. For instance, the following instantiatedness tree, called `listskel`, describes the lists containing distinct free variables:

```
:- inst listskel == bound([] ; [free | listskel]).
```

Actually, partial instantiation in Mercury is currently not fully supported for several reasons, including the difficulty of analysing such code, the difficulty of maintaining such code, and the difficulty of compiling such code efficiently [122]. Thus, only the `free` and `ground` instantiatedness trees are well-supported in Mercury.

Instantiatedness tree are similar to the type expressions used in our formal specifications (see Section 5.2). Like an instantiatedness tree, a type expression is built on the parametric user-declared type, and combines mode (e.g., `ground`, `any`) and type information. Our mode and primitive types are partially redundant. More general type expressions can be described in our system, for instance, `list(any)` denotes the set of lists whose elements are any (possibly non-ground) term. However, not every instantiatedness tree corresponds to a type expression. For instance, the `listkel` of Mercury cannot be expressed in our system, but it can be approximated by the type expression `list(any)`.

In Mercury, a *mode* m is a mapping from an initial instantiatedness tree (say `inst1`) to a final instantiatedness tree (say `inst2`), which can be declared as follows:

```
:- mode m == (inst1 >> inst2).
```

In our system, the initial and final type expressions of the predicate arguments are described in the `in` and `out` parts of the formal specifications, respectively (see Section 3.1.1). Mercury provides the two usual modes `in` (input) and `out` (output) as follows:

```
:- mode in == (ground >> ground).
:- mode out == (free >> ground).
```

A *predicate mode declaration* assigns a mode mapping to each argument of a predicate. For instance, the predicate `select/3` can be annotated with the following type and mode declarations:

```
:- pred select(T,list(T),list(T)).
:- mode select(out,in,out).
:- mode select(in,out,in).
```

The compiler rejects programs that violate the mode or type declaration constraints. Mercury uses a *well-modedness* notion that is easy for the compiler to check. A predicate p is *well-moded with respect to a given mode declaration* if given that the predicates called by p all satisfy their mode declaration constraints, there exists an ordering of the literals in each clause of p such that p satisfies its mode declaration constraints, and p satisfies the mode constraints of all the predicates it calls.

The mode analysis algorithm works with clauses in *superhomogeneous form*, where each atom has one of the forms `p(X1,...,Xn),Y=X,Y=f(X1,...,Xn)`. The *superhomegeneous* form in Mercury corresponds to the *normalised* form that is abstractly executed by our analyser (see Section 3.2.1). The Mercury mode analysis algorithm abstractly interprets each clause of the predicate, keeping track of the instantiadeness tree of each variable, and selecting a mode for each call and unification in the clause body. To ensure that the mode constraints of called predicates are satisfied, it may reorder the literals in the clauses; it reports an error if no satisfactory order exists. In Prolog, literals are executed from left to right. However, our analyser can also serve to perform literal reordering inside a clause, to generate a Prolog code that correctly calls subprocedures (i.e., respects the `in` parts of their specifications).

To the contrary of Prolog, only few modes for unifications are accepted: instances of `Y=X`, where `X` is input and `Y` is output (denoted by `Y:=X` and called *assignment*); instances of `Y=X`, where both `X` and `Y` are input (denoted by `X--Y`, and called *equality test*), instances of `Y=f(X1,...,Xn)`, where `Y` is an output and the `Xi`'s are either input or void (i.e., this is their only appearance in the clause) (denoted by `Y:=f(X1,...,Xn)` and called *construction*); instances of `Y=f(X1,...,Xn)`, where `Y` is input, and `Xi`'s are either output or void (denoted by `Y==f(X1,...,Xn)` and called *deconstruction*). As a result, to the contrary of Prolog, all unification in Mercury are occur-check free, all terms are linear, and two program variables cannot be bound to terms that share a variable.

2.5.3   Determinism

For each mode and type of a predicate, information about the number of solutions that can be returned to a call must be described. Mercury provides several *determinism categories*: either `det` (exactly one solution), or `semidet` (zero or one solution), or `multi` (at least one solution), or `nondet` (zero or more solutions), or `failure` (zero solution). For instance, the possible types, modes and determinism declarations of `select/3` are as follows.

```
:- pred select(T,list(T),list(T)).
:- mode select(out,in,out) is nondet.
:- mode select(in,out,in) is multi.
```

The Mercury compiler checks that the determinism declarations are correct [59]. The compiler issues an error if a procedure can fail or have multiple solutions when its declared determinism category says otherwise. The determinism analysis phase of the Mercury compiler runs after the type and the mode analyses. The determinism analysis is a bottom-up process; it combines the determinism of primitive goals to find the determinism of compound goals. In our analyser, the verification of the cardinality is performed during the global analysis. The cardinality information that can be checked by our analyser is more expressive, because it can be expressed in function of the size of the input sizes (several norms can be combined). Furthermore, additional information about the sure success and the sure failure to a call allows us to describe more accurately the number of solutions.

Note that in Mercury, the determinism of a goal with no output arguments is either `det`, `semidet` or `failure`. This is not always the case in Prolog. For instance, in Prolog, a call to `select(a,[a,a,a],[a,a])` provides three solutions (each solution is the empty substitution), although it is considered semi-deterministic in Mercury.

2.5.4 Termination

Mercury is endowed with a termination analyser [46]. Mercury approximates interargument size relationships with convex constraints. These relationships are derived during an analysis based upon abstract interpretation (through a fixpoint algorithm). The analysis takes as input the results of the type and mode analyses. In our framework, we maintain also linear relations between the input and output sizes, but this is performed during the global abstract execution. Our framework uses the information provided by the user, and can thus be more accurate.

Part I

Automated verification of
operational properties

Chapter 3

Design of the checker: original abstract interpretation framework

This chapter describes the checker, based on the basic abstract interpretation framework presented in [78], that we called the *basic framework* in the rest of this thesis. The main aspects of the basic framework can be summarised as follows.

- The notion of abstract sequence models sets of pairs of the form $\langle \theta, S \rangle$, where θ and S denote an (input) substitution and the sequence of answer substitutions resulting from executing a clause, a goal, or a procedure with this input. Abstract sequences make it possible to relate the number of solutions and the size of input terms in full generality. For instance, we can relate the input and output sizes of the same term (i.e., bound to the same program variable) without requiring invariance under instantiation.

- The framework integrates several analyses into a single one. The abstract domains cooperate together to improve on each other.

- The framework does not perform a fixpoint computation but instead it verifies the correctness of the program with respect to a set of abstract descriptions provided by the user. Such descriptions are called *behaviours* and consist of abstract sequences and size expressions that must strictly decrease through recursive calls (the analyser only accepts terminating procedures). Such behaviours allow us to express the desirable operational properties to be checked.

- The domain of abstract sequences is generic and its elements have the form $\langle \beta_{in}, \beta_{ref}, \beta_{out}, \beta_{ref\_out}, E_{sol} \rangle$, where β_{in} describes a set of input substitutions, β_{ref} is a refinement of β_{in} modelling the input substitutions leading to a successful execution, β_{out} describes the set of output substitutions, E_{ref_out} is a set of constraints between the size of terms in β_{ref} and the size

35

of terms in β_{out}, E_{sol} is a set of constraints between the size of terms in β_{ref} and the number of solutions. The β_{ref} component improves the accuracy of E_{ref_out} and E_{sol}, as constraints have only to deal with successful executions.

- The generic domain of abstract sequences has been instantiated by fixing a particular domain of abstract substitutions (for the β's) and a particular domain of constraints (for the E's). The domain of abstract substitutions is an instantiation of the domain $\text{Pat}(\Re)$ [33, 80, 102]. The domain of constraints consists of sets of integer linear equalities and inequalities.

Section 3.1 provides an overview of the functionalities of the checker on some examples. The formal specification language and the domain of abstract sequences is introduced. We show an example where the analysis is capable of proving the given specification, and another one where the analysis fails. Section 3.2 describes the concrete domains, the syntax of normalised programs, and the way we express the concrete execution of programs. Section 3.3 defines the domain of abstract substitutions and Section 3.4 defines the domain of abstract sequences. Section 3.5 shows how a program is executed at the abstract level for proving the operational properties described in formal specifications.

3.1   Overview of the checker

The checker takes as input a Prolog program (without negations nor cuts) that is annotated with formal specifications. Section 3.1.1 presents the language of formal specifications that allows the user to describe the expected operational properties of a procedure. There may exist several specifications for a procedure, typically one specification for each kind of use of the procedure. Formal specifications provide a convenient syntax allowing the user to represent abstract sequences. Section 3.1.2 gives an example of abstract sequence that models the behaviour of a procedure, a clause, or a goal. Section 3.1.3 illustrates a successful analysis of the checker and Section 3.1.4 shows an unsuccessful analysis.

3.1.1   Specification of operational properties of a procedure

This section illustrates what the checker can prove, and introduces the language of formal specifications. The purpose of the analyser is to verify a set of operational properties. Such properties include verifying mode, type, and sharing of terms. The system can prove termination, sure success or failure of the execution, and determinacy of logic procedures. It also checks linear relations between the size of input/output terms and the number of solutions to a call. It can detect that the program is occur-check free. The following examples are small for clarity, and cover the usual operational mechanisms and features of Prolog. The formal specification language used by the analyser is introduced progressively, by refining step by step the operational properties the system is able to prove.

Example 1: specifying `select`

Consider the predicate `select(X,L,Ls)` that holds iff X is an element of the list L and Ls is the list L without an occurrence of X:

```
select(X, [X|L], L).
select(X, [H|L], [H|Ls]) :- select(X, L, Ls).
```
Procedure 3.1 `select(X,L,Ls)`

The programmer can query the system for proving termination, checking the number of solutions, verifying the conditions of sure success or sure failure, the type correctness of procedure calls, and the occur-check freeness of the program.

Checking input/output modes.   The analyser is able to check that the two following specifications hold:

```
select/3
  in(X:var, L:ground, Ls:var)
  out(ground, _, ground)

select/3
  in(X:ground, L:var, Ls:ground)
  out(_, ground, _)
```

The `in` part specifies conditions on the input arguments. The symbol `var` (resp. `ground`) denotes that the argument is bound to a free variable (resp. a ground term). The `out` part describes the form of the arguments at the end of the execution, when the execution succeeds. The symbol '_' is used when we do not provide refined information about an argument. Other mode information can be specified (e.g., `any` denotes all terms, `gv` denotes the set of ground terms or variables, `ngv` denotes the set of non-ground terms that are not a variable). For instance, the two specifications can be combined, using the `gv` mode:

```
select/3
  in(X:gv, L:gv, Ls:gv)
```

Checking correct-typing.   Specifications can also be express the input/output types of the arguments as follows:

```
select/3
  in(X:any, L:list, Ls:any)
  out(_, _, list)

select/3
  in(X:any, L:any, Ls:list)
  out(_, list, _)
```

The type `any` denotes the set of all terms, and the type `list` denotes the set of (non-necessarily ground) lists. Modes and types can be combined together as follows:

```
select/3
  in(X:var, L:ground list, Ls:var)
  out(ground, _, ground list)

select/3
  in(X:ground, L:var, Ls:ground list)
  out(_, ground list, _)
```

Checking no sharing and occur-check freeness.   No sharing between terms is sometimes needed to prove occur-check freeness of the procedure.

```
select/3
  in(X:var, L:list, Ls:var; noshare(<X,L,Ls>))
  out(_, _, list)
```

The `noshare` tag in the `in` part of the above specification expresses that the three input arguments do not share any variable. The analyser is then able to prove that the procedure is not subject to the occur-check.

Checking cardinality information and proving termination.   The system can check information about the number of solutions in function of the size of the input terms, and it can prove the termination of the execution.

```
select/3
  in(X:var, L:ground list, Ls:var)
  out(ground, _, ground list)
  srel(L_in = Ls_out+1)
  sol(0 =< sol =< L_in)
  sexpr(< L >)

select/3
  in(X:ground, L:var, Ls:ground list)
  out(_, ground list, _)
  srel(L_out = Ls_in+1)
  sol(sol = Ls_in+1)
  sexpr(< Ls >)
```

The `srel` part describes linear relations between the size of input and output terms. The basic framework only considers the list-length size measure. The size of an input (resp. output) term T is denoted by `T_in` (resp. `T_out`). The `sol` part describes the number of solutions to the call. The symbol `sol` denotes the number of solutions, which depends on the value of the input terms. In the first case, the number of solutions is checked to be between zero and the length of the input list `L`. The sure success of the execution is indeed not guaranteed, because the input arguments `X` and `L` may possibly share a variable (the `noshare` tag is not present), and because `L` may be an empty list. Sure success is proved for the second specification. The termination of the execution is proved for the two specifications. The `sexpr` part specifies the induction parameter decreasing through recursive calls.

Proving sure success/failure, and refining cardinality information. Refined conditions for sure success and sure failure of the execution can be specified, and the analyser is then able to prove more accurate cardinality information. Constraints of the `srel` and `sol` parts of a specification only have to deal with successful executions.

```
select/3
    in(X:var, L:ground list, Ls:var; noshare(<X,Ls>))
    ref(_, [_|_], _)
    out(ground, _, ground list)
    srel(Ls_out = L_in-1)
    sol(sol = L_in)
    sexpr(< L >)
```
Specification 3.1   `select(X,L,Ls)`

```
select/3
    in(X:ground, L:var, Ls:ground list)
    out(_, [ground|ground list], _)
    srel(Ls_in+1 = L_out)
    sol(sol = Ls_in+1)
    sexpr(< Ls >)
```
Specification 3.2   `select(X,L,Ls)`

Specification 3.1 considers input calls where `X` and `Ls` are two distinct variables (presence of the `noshare` tag). The `ref` part specifies necessary conditions on the input arguments to obtain a success of the execution (at least one solution). The procedure `select(X,L,Ls)` succeeds only if input `L` is a non-empty ground list. (If `L` is an empty list, then the execution surely fails.)[1] Information that can be implicitly deduced needs not be explicitly written (the symbol '_' is used). Specification 3.2 describes the output pattern of `L`, which is a non-empty ground list.

---

[1] Actually, the `ref` part of Specification 3.1 needs not to be explicitly written. The analyser is able to derive this information from the `sol` component: if the predicate surely succeeds, then `L_in` must be greater or equal to one, i.e., `L` must be a non-empty list.

Example 2: specifying `append`

Consider the well-known `append(L1,L2,L3)` procedure, that concatenates two lists `L1` and `L2` into the list `L3`.

```
append([], L2, L2).
append([X|L1], L2, [X|L3]) :- append(L1, L2, L3).
```
Procedure 3.2   `append(L1,L2,L3)`

Assume that the following conditions hold on the input arguments: `L1` and `L2` are two ground lists and `L3` is a variable. The analyser is then able to verify that the procedure meets the following formal specification:

```
append/3
  in(L1:ground list, L2:ground list, L3:var)
  out(_, _, ground list)
  srel(L1_in+L2_in = L3_out)
  sol(sol = 1)
  sexpr(< L1 >)
```
Specification 3.3   `append(L1,L2,L3)`

Specification 3.3 describes the following operational properties. Input arguments `L1` and `L2` are ground lists and `L3` is a variable. All output arguments are ground lists. The system checks that, at the end of the execution, the list-length of output `L3` is equal to the list-length sum of inputs `L1` and `L2`. There is exactly one solution: the procedure is fully-deterministic. The induction parameter is the list-length of the first argument. The analyser verifies that the procedure is occur-check free when it is executed with input arguments satisfying the `in` part.

A more general call to `append(L1,L2,L3)` can be described when input `L1` and `L2` are non-necessarily ground lists, when `L3` is a variable, and when `L1`, `L2` and `L3` do not share a variable (presence of the `noshare` tag in the `in` part of the specification).

```
append/3
  in(L1:list, L2:list, L3:var;
    noshare(<L1,L2,L3>))
  out(_, _, list)
  srel(L1_in+L2_in = L3_out)
  sol(sol = 1)
  sexpr(< L1 >)
```
Specification 3.4   `append(L1,L2,L3)`

Other interesting classes of calls to `append(L1,L2,L3)` can be verified. Consider for instance the situation where input `L1` and `L2` are distinct variables and where input `L3` is a ground list.

```
append/3
  in(L1:var, L2:var, L3:ground list;
     noshare(<L1,L2>))
  out(ground list, ground list, _)
  srel(L1_out+L2_out = L3_in)
  sol(sol = L3_in+1)
  sexpr(< L3 >)
```
Specification 3.5 append(L1,L2,L3)

The analyser can prove that the procedure surely succeeds. At the end of the execution, both L1 and L2 are ground lists. The number of solutions is exactly the list-length of input L3 plus one. The program terminates, given the induction parameter (list-length of L3), and it is occur-check free.

Example 3: specifying append3

Consider the procedures 2.1 and 2.2. They can be specified and checked as follows according to the way they are used:
```
append3/4
  in(A:ground list, B:ground list,
     C:ground list, D:var)
  out(_, _, _, ground list)
  srel(A_in+B_in+C_in = D_out)
  sol(sol = 1)
```
Specification 3.6 append3(A,B,C,D)

```
append3bis/4
  in(A:var, B:var, C:var, D:ground list;
     noshare(<A,B,C>))
  out(ground list, ground list, ground list, _)
  srel(A_out+B_out+C_out = D_in)
  sol(sol >= 1)
```
Specification 3.7 append3bis(A,B,C,D)

Example 4: specifying reverse

The analyser can deal with programs that use accumulating parameters. For instance, consider the program reverse(L,Lrev) that reverses the list L into the list Lrev.
```
reverse(L,Lrev) :- reverse_acc(L,Lrev,[]).

reverse_acc([],A,A).
reverse_acc([H|T],A,B) :- reverse_acc(T,A,[H|B]).
```
Procedure 3.3 reverse(L,Lrev)

Usually, the procedure is called when input L is any (possibly non-ground) list and when input Lrev is a variable that does not occur in L:

```
reverse/2
  in(L:list, Lrev:var; noshare(<L,Lrev>))
  out(_, list)
  srel(L_in = Lrev_out)
  sol(sol = 1)
  sexpr(< L >)
```

Specification 3.8   reverse(L,Lrev)

The subprocedure reverse_acc can be checked with respect to the following specification:

```
reverse_acc/3
  in(L:list, A:var, B:list; noshare(<L,A>, <A,B>))
  out(_, list, _)
  srel(L_in = A_out-B_in)
  sol(sol = 1)
  sexpr(< L >)
```

Specification 3.9   reverse_acc(L,A,B)

The noshare tag expresses that L and A do not share a variable, and that A and B do not share a variable. However, L and B may possibly share a variable.

Remark.   In this section, we have provided detailed specifications. However, the user needs not to specify everything. The way a user specifies a procedure depends on the purpose of the verification. One can be interested in proving only termination, or occur-check freeness, or determinacy of the procedure, for some input context. There exist several ways to specify a procedure, and a specification can be more or less accurate. In Section 8.3, we discuss what is the minimal information to be specified in order to prove a specific operational property for a given 'use' of the procedure.

3.1.2   Abstract sequences for modelling the execution

Technically, a formal specification defines a so-called *abstract sequence*. The semantics of abstract sequences is defined in Section 3.4. Abstract sequences contain the same information as the corresponding specifications, but the information is expressed in a form better suited for defining and implementing abstract operations. For instance, the abstract sequence corresponding to Specification 3.1 of the procedure select(X,L,Ls) is depicted in Figure 3.1.

In this abstract domain, the information is expressed on *indices*, not directly on the procedure variables. Indices represent terms bound to the program variables or subterms of those terms. For instance, the β_{ref} component characterises a set of substitutions θ as follows: the *same-value* component sv binds the program

$$\beta_{in} \quad : sv \quad = \{X \mapsto 1, L \mapsto 2, Ls \mapsto 3\}$$
$$frm = \{\}$$
$$mo \quad = \{1 \mapsto var, 2 \mapsto ground, 3 \mapsto var\}$$
$$ty \quad = \{1 \mapsto anylist, 2 \mapsto list, 3 \mapsto anylist\}$$
$$ps \quad = \{(1,1), (3,3)\}$$
$$\beta_{ref} \quad : sv \quad = \{X \mapsto 1, L \mapsto 2, Ls \mapsto 3\}$$
$$frm = \{2 \mapsto [4|5]\}$$
$$mo \quad = \{1 \mapsto var, 2 \mapsto ground, 3 \mapsto var, 4 \mapsto ground,$$
$$5 \mapsto ground\}$$
$$ty \quad = \{1 \mapsto anylist, 2 \mapsto list, 3 \mapsto anylist, 4 \mapsto any,$$
$$5 \mapsto list\}$$
$$ps \quad = \{(1,1), (3,3)\}$$
$$\beta_{out} \quad : sv \quad = \{X \mapsto 1, L \mapsto 2, Ls \mapsto 3\}$$
$$frm = \{2 \mapsto [4|5]\}$$
$$mo \quad = \{1 \mapsto ground, 2 \mapsto ground, 3 \mapsto ground, 4 \mapsto ground,$$
$$5 \mapsto ground\}$$
$$ty \quad = \{1 \mapsto any, 2 \mapsto list, 3 \mapsto list, 4 \mapsto any, 5 \mapsto list\}$$
$$ps \quad = \{\}$$
$$in_{ref} \quad : \{1 \mapsto 1, 2 \mapsto 2, 3 \mapsto 3, 4 \mapsto 4, 5 \mapsto 5\}$$
$$in_{out} \quad : \{1 \mapsto 6, 2 \mapsto 7, 3 \mapsto 8, 4 \mapsto 9, 5 \mapsto 10\}$$
$$E_{ref\_out} : \{sz(8) = sz(5)\}$$
$$E_{sol} \quad : \{sol = sz(2)\}$$

Figure 3.1: Abstract sequence corresponding to Specification 3.1 of the procedure `select(X, L, Ls)`.

variables X, L and Ls to the indices 1, 2 and 3, which represent the terms t_1, t_2 and t_3 respectively bound to X, L and Ls in θ. The *frame* component frm states that the term t_2 is of the form $[t_4|t_5]$. The *mode* component mo provides information about the modes of terms. It states that t_1 and t_3 are variables and that t_2, t_4 and t_5 are ground terms. The *type* component ty provides information about the types of terms. The basic framework only considers three types, namely list (lists), anylist (all terms that can be instantiated to a list), and any (all terms). The terms t_1 and t_3 have type anylist because they are variables. The *possible sharing* component ps consists of the pairs of indices of terms that may share a variable. Since the pair $(1,3)$ does not belong to ps, t_1 and t_3 are distinct variables. The E_{ref_out} component relates the sizes of terms in an input substitution to the sizes of terms in the corresponding output substitutions. Terms are represented by indices, but as the same indices can be used in β_{ref} and β_{out}, we express the relation on the *disjoint union* of the two sets. The functions in_{ref} and in_{out} maps the original indices to their image in the disjoint union. In this case, the constraint $sz(8) = sz(5)$ means that the output size (list-length) of Ls is equal to the input size of the tail of L. Finally, the component E_{sol} defines the constraints on the number of solutions.

3.1.3   Illustration of a successful analysis

In the rest of this document, we use the syntax of formal specification instead of the less readable format of abstract sequences (with indices). This section illustrates the verification analysis of the procedure `select(X,L,Ls)` according to Specification 3.1. The checker does not analyse Procedure 3.1, but it analyses a normalised version of the procedure (where unifications are explicit and variables occurring in the head of the clauses and in the literals are distinct):

```
select(X1,X2,X3):-1 X2=[X4|X5]2,  X4=X13,  X5=X34 .5
select(X1,X2,X3):-6 X2=[X4|X5]7,  X3=[X4,X6]8,
                     select(X1,X5,X6)9 .10
```

We have annotated the procedure with natural numbers identifying its program points. The analyser attaches an abstract sequence Bi to every program point i. Every abstract sequence Bi describes the set of pairs $\langle\theta, S\rangle$ such that θ is described by the `in` part of the specification and S is the sequence of computed answer substitutions produced by the literals before the program point i. Note that the abstract sequences B4 and B5 both model the execution of the first clause, but they are distinct: the output part of B4 maintains information for each program variable occurring in the clause (as it is the case for B1, B2, and B3), although the output part of B5 is restricted to the program variables occurring in the clause head only. The same difference applies to B9 and B10, modelling the execution of the second clause.

The trace of the execution is as follows. In what follows, the `in` part of each abstract sequence Bi is not shown, since it is always identical to the `in` part of Specification 3.1.

The checker starts to analyse the first clause. The abstract sequence B1 is:

```
B1:
  ref(X1:var, X2:ground list, X3:var;
      noshare(<X1,X3>))
  out(X1:var, X2:ground list, X3:var,
      X4:var, X5:var; noshare(<X1,X3,X4,X5>))
  sol(sol = 1)
```

The `ref` part is identical to the `in` part of Specification 3.1 because the head of the clause is unifiable with any call since it contains distinct variables. The `out` part is obtained by extending the `in` part with information about the local variables X4 and X5. They are distinct new variables, which is expressed by the mode and the sharing components of B1. The component `sol` expresses that the unification of the head of the clause succeeds exactly once.

The three next literals are unifications. They result in the following abstract
sequences:

```
B2:
  ref(X1:var, X2:[ground|ground list], X3:var;
      noshare(<X1,X3>))
  out(X1:var, X2:[X4:ground|X5:ground list],
      X3:var, X4:ground, X5:ground list;
      noshare(<X1,X3>))
  sol(sol = 1)


B3:
  ref(X1:var, X2:[ground|ground list], X3:var;
      noshare(<X1,X3>))
  out(X1:ground, X2:[X1:ground|X5:ground list],
      X3:var, X4=X1:ground, X5:ground list)
  sol(sol = 1)


B4:
  ref(X1:var, X2:[ground|ground list], X3:var;
      noshare(<X1,X3>))
  out(X1:ground, X2:[X1:ground|X3:ground list],
      X3:ground list, X4=X1:ground,
      X5=X3:ground list)
  sol(sol = 1)
```

The first unification succeeds if and only if X2 is a non-empty list of the
form $[t|t']$ because X4 and X5 are distinct variables as specified by the mode and
sharing components in the out part of B1. Thus, in B2, the analyser updates
the frame component of the ref and out parts with the structural information
about X2. The sol component is not modified because unification surely succeeds
for all terms X2 of the form $[t|t']$. The next two unifications X4=X1 and X5=X3
both surely succeed because X1 and X3 are distinct variables as indicated by the
mode and sharing components of B2. The result of the unification is recorded by
mapping corresponding variables to the same index, in the same-value component.
In the user syntax of specification, this is expressed by the equality X4=X1 and
X5=X3 in the out part of B3 and B4. The final abstract sequence for the first
clause is obtained by removing the local variables from the same-value component. The abstract sequence B5 is thus:

```
B5:
    ref(X1:var, X2:[ground|ground list], X3:var;
        noshare(<X1,X3>))
    out(X1:ground, X2:[X1:ground|X3:ground list],
        X3:ground list)
    sol(sol = 1)
```

The second clause is treated similarly but contains a recursive call, which deserves a special treatment. The abstract sequence B8 corresponding to the program point just before the recursive call is:

```
B8:
    ref(X1:var, X2:[ground|ground list], X3:var;
        noshare(<X1,X3>))
    out(X1:var, X2:[X4:ground|X5:ground list],
        X3:[X4:ground|X6:var], X4:ground,
        X5:ground list, X6:var; noshare(<X1,X6>))
    sol(sol = 1)
```

The analyser first checks that the size expression (provided by the sexpr part of Specification 3.1) is smaller for the recursive call than for the initial call, i.e., that the size of X5 is smaller than the initial size of X2. This can be deduced by reasoning on the modes and the structural information of the ref and out parts of B8. Next, the analyser checks that the information given by the out part about the actual parameters X1, X5 and X6 is compatible with the in part of the specification, which is the case, since X1 and X6 are distinct variables and X5 is a ground list. Thus, the analyser may use the information from Specification 3.1 to update B8. The abstract sequence B9 is obtained:

```
B9:
    ref(X1:var,
        X2:[ground|X5:[ground|ground list]],
        X3:var;
        noshare(<X1,X3>))
    out(X1:ground,
        X2:[X4:ground|X5:[ground|ground list]],
        X3:[X4:ground|X6:ground list], X4:ground,
        X5:[ground|ground list], X6:ground list)
    srel(X6_out = X5_ref-1)
    sol(sol = X5_ref)
```

All information of B9 is deduced by mapping the indices of the components of B8 to those of Specification 3.1, and reexpressing the information of Specification 3.1 on the indices of B8. In particular, note that the frame component of the `ref` part of B8 has been updated to take into account the sure success condition of the execution: X2 is a list of at least two elements.

The final abstract sequence for the second clause is obtained by removing the local variables from the same-value component of the `out` part in B9:

```
B10:
  ref(X1:var,
      X2:[ground|X5:[ground|ground list]],
      X3:var;
      noshare(<X1,X3>))
  out(X1:ground,
      X2:[X4:ground|X5:[ground|ground list]],
      X3:[X4:ground|X6:ground list])
  srel(X3_out = X2_ref-1)
  sol(sol = X2_ref-1)
```

The abstract sequence B10 states that the second clause succeeds only for a list X2 of at least two elements (and actually succeeds for all of them) and that the output size of list X3 is equal to the size of X2 minus one; moreover, the number of solution is also equal to size of input X2 minus one.

The final step of the analyser is to combine the abstract sequence B5 and B10 to compute an abstract sequence Bfinal describing the global behaviour of the procedure. In this case, Bfinal is identical to Specification 3.1. Its components `ref` and `out` are computed from those of B5 and B10 by a least upper bound operation. A careful analysis is once again necessary to get the most accurate result about the number of solutions: when X2 is a list of at least two elements, the first clause succeeds once and the second one succeeds X2_ref-1 times, so the procedure succeeds X2_ref times. However, when the length of X2 is equal to one, the second clause fails and the first one succeeds once; so the procedure also succeeds X2_ref times. Hence, putting the abstract sequences B5 and B10 together, the analyser is able to reconstruct exactly the information provided by the user, such that the procedure respects its specification.

This verification analysis is realised automatically by the checker and is formally described in Section 3.5.

3.1.4   Description of an unsuccessful analysis

Consider the following specification for the procedure `select(X,L,Ls)`:

```
select/3
    in(X:var, L:ground list, Ls:var)
    ref(_, [_|_], _)
    out(ground, _, ground list)
    srel(Ls_out = L_in-1)
    sol(sol = L_in)
    sexpr(< L >)
```
Specification 3.10   `select(X,L,Ls)`

The above specification is the same as Specification 3.1 where we have removed the `noshare` conditions between input `X` and `Ls`. In this situation, the abstract sequence placed just after the unification `X4=X1` of the first clause is as follows:

```
B3:
    ref(X1:var, X2:[ground|ground list], X3:var)
    out(X1:ground, X2:[X1:ground|X5:ground list],
        X3:gv, X4=X1:ground, X5:ground list)
    sol(sol =< 1)
```

The unification still surely succeeds but since `X1` and `X3` may be bound to the same variable, it gives the mode `gv` (ground or variable) to `X3`. Now, since `X3` is possibly ground, the analyser cannot prove that the next unification `X5=X3` surely succeeds. The component `sol` of `B4` is thus `sol =< 1` instead of the expected `sol = 1`. As a consequence, the analyser is globally unable to prove that the number of solutions is equal to the size of `X2`.

3.2   Concrete domains and execution

This section presents the concrete domains and the way we express the concrete execution of a terminating procedure, clause, or prefix of a goal. The analysis is defined for normalised programs that make explicit all unifications.

3.2.1   Syntax of normalised programs

The basic framework accepts only pure Prolog programs with no cut and no negation. The abstract interpretation framework is defined for *normalised* programs. The abstract syntax of a normalised Prolog program is depicted in Figure 3.2.

The variables occurring in a literal or in the head of a clause must be distinct. All clauses of a procedure of name p and of arity n have exactly the same head

$$
\begin{array}{ll}
P & \in \ Programs \\
pr & \in \ Procedures \\
c & \in \ Clauses \\
h & \in \ Heads \\
g & \in \ Goals \\
l & \in \ Literals \\
b & \in \ Builtins \\
p & \in \ ProcedureNames \\
X & \in \ ProgramVariables \\
f & \in \ FunctorNames
\end{array}
\qquad
\begin{array}{lll}
P & ::= & pr \mid pr \ P \\
pr & ::= & c \mid c \ pr \\
c & ::= & h \ \text{:-}\ g. \\
h & ::= & p(X, \dots, X) \\
g & ::= & <>\mid g, l \\
l & ::= & p(X, \dots, X) \mid b \\
b & ::= & X = X \mid X = f(X, \dots, X)
\end{array}
$$

Figure 3.2: Abstract syntax of normalised Prolog programs.

$p(X_1, \dots, X_n)$. If a clause uses m different program variables, these variables are $X_1, \dots, X_m$ $(n \leq m)$.

As an example, the normalised version of Procedure 2.4 is as follows.

```
append(X1, X2, X3)  :- X1=[], X3=X2.
append(X1, X2, X3)  :- X1=[X4|X5], X3=[X4|X6],
                       append(X5, X2, X6).
```

The translation from a pure Prolog procedure to its normalised version is realised automatically by the checker.

3.2.2 Basic semantic domains: substitutions and sequences

The following notions are introduced to allow us to express in a suitable way the execution of a procedure, a clause, a prefix of a goal, or a literal in the context of some given program. We use the notations of [78].

Variables and terms

Program variables are variables occurring in the program source. Standard variables are variables that are created during the execution of a procedure, a clause, a goal or a literal; they are used for performing unification and variable renaming. The sets of program variables and of standard variables are disjoint. Program (resp. standard) terms are built using program (resp. standard) variables only. A Prolog construct o is either a literal, a prefix of a goal in a clause, or a clause. The set of program variables occurring in a Prolog construct o is denoted by $pvars(o)$. The set of all standard terms is denoted by $\mathcal{T}$. The set of standard variables occurring in a standard term t is denoted by $vars(t)$. Let $I = \{i_1, \dots, i_n\}$ be a set of indices (we assume that I is a subset of N). The set of all term tuples $\langle t_i \rangle_{i \in I}$ is denoted by $\mathcal{T}^I$, and $\mathcal{T}_I^*$ denotes the set of all "frames" of the form $f(i_1, \dots, i_n)$ where f is a functor of arity n.

Program substitutions

A program substitution θ is a set of the form $\{X_1/t_1, ..., X_n/t_n\}$ where $X_1, ..., X_n$ are program variables, and where $t_1, ..., t_n$ are standard terms. The set of program substitutions is denoted by PS. The domain of θ is $\{X_1, ..., X_n\}$ and is denoted by $dom(\theta)$. We denote by PS_D the set of program substitutions whose domain is D. The codomain of θ, denoted by $codom(\theta)$, is the set of standard variables occurring in $t_1, ..., t_n$. The restriction of θ over the set of program variables D is denoted by $\theta_{/D}$. Composition of program substitutions cannot be performed. A program substitution θ can be applied to a Prolog construct o, provided that $pvars(o) \subseteq dom(\theta)$, and is denoted by $o\theta$.

Standard substitutions

A standard substitution σ is a mapping from standard variables to standard terms. Standard substitutions are substitutions in the usual sense, such that the composition of standard substitutions can be performed. The set of program substitutions is denoted by SS. The domain and codomain of σ are denoted by $dom(\sigma)$ and $codom(\sigma)$, respectively. Renamings, i.e., standard substitutions that define a permutation of SS, are denoted by the letter ρ. A standard substitution σ can be applied to a standard term t, and is denoted by $t\sigma$. The composition of a program substitution $\theta = \{X_1/t_1, ..., X_n/t_n\}$ with a standard substitution σ is the program substitution $\{X_1/t_1\sigma, ..., X_n/t_n\sigma\}$ and is denoted by $\theta\sigma$. A program substitution θ is *more general* (or *less instantiated*) than θ' if there exists a standard substitution σ such that $\theta' = \theta\sigma$, and is denoted by $\theta' \leq \theta$. We denote the set of standard substitutions that are a most general unifier of t_1 and t_2 by $mgu(t_1, t_2)$.

Substitution sequences

A program substitution sequence S is either a *finite* sequence of the form $< \theta_1, ..., \theta_n > (n \geq 0)$, an *infinite* sequence of the form $< \theta_1, ..., \theta_i, ... > (i \in N)$, or an *incomplete* sequence of the form $< \theta_1, ..., \theta_n, \perp > (n \geq 0)$, where the θ_i are program substitutions with the same domain. We use the notation $< \theta_1, ..., \theta_i, \_ >$ to represent a program substitution sequence when it is not known whether it is finite, infinite or incomplete. The set of all program substitution sequences is denoted by PSS. We denote by $Subst(S)$ the set of program substitutions that are elements of S. The domain of S is defined when $S \neq <>$ and $S \neq < \perp >$. In this case, $dom(S)$ is the domain of program substitutions belonging to $Subst(S)$. Let D be a finite set of program variables. PSS_D denotes the set of program substitution sequences over the domain D augmented with $<>$. The restriction of S over the set of program variables D, denoted by $S_{/D}$, is the program substitution sequence $< \theta_{1/D}, ..., \theta_{n/D}, \_ >$. The number of elements of S, including the special element $\perp$, is denoted by $Ne(S)$. The number of elements of S that are substitutions is denoted by $Ns(S)$. Sequence concatenation is denoted by :: and it is used only when its first argument is a finite sequence.

3.2.3 Expressing concrete terminating executions

This section presents the notations used to express the result of the execution of some query (either a procedure call, a prefix of a clause[2], a literal after the execution of a goal, or a clause). The basic framework only considers queries that terminate. Thus, we only consider *finite* substitution sequences. In the remainder of this document, the underlying normalised program is denoted by P.

Execution of a procedure call

Let p be the name of a procedure pr of arity n, and let θ be a program substitution whose domain is $\{X_1, ..., X_n\}$. The execution of the query $p(X_1, ..., X_n)\theta$ under the Prolog operational semantics, yields a standard substitution sequence $< \sigma_1, ..., \sigma_k > (k \geq 0)$. This behaviour is expressed as follows:

$$\langle \theta, p \rangle \mapsto_P S$$

or, alternatively, by:

$$\langle \theta, pr \rangle \mapsto_P S$$

where S is the program substitution sequence $< \theta\sigma_1, ..., \theta\sigma_k >$, whose domain is $\{X_1, ..., X_n\}$. In what follows, we alternatively use both notations (with p or with pr). The second notation (with pr) is notably used to characterise the denotational semantics of Prolog (see [78, 79]), and to define the concatenation operation (see Section 4.2.1).

Execution of a prefix of a clause

Let c be a clause, $D = \{X_1, ..., X_n\}$ be the set of all variables occurring in the head of c, and $D' = \{X_1, ..., X_m\}$ $(n \leq m)$ be the set of all variables occurring in c, and g be a prefix of the clause c. Let θ' be the extension of θ on the set of variables in D to the set of variables in D' such that $X_i\theta' = X_i\theta$ $(1 \leq i \leq n)$ and $X_{n+1}\theta', ..., X_m\theta'$ are distinct standard variables not belonging to $codom(\theta)$. The execution of the query $g\theta'$ yields a standard substitution sequence $< \sigma_1, ..., \sigma_k >$. This behaviour is denoted as follows:

$$\langle \theta, g, c \rangle \mapsto_P S$$

where S is the program substitution sequence $< \theta'\sigma_1, ..., \theta'\sigma_k >$, whose domain is D'. When the prefix of the clause is empty, we have $\langle \theta, <>, c \rangle \mapsto_P < \theta' >$.

Execution of a literal in a clause

Let l be a literal following a prefix g of a clause c, and assume that l is of the form $q(X_{i_1}, ..., X_{i_r})$. Let θ be a program substitution whose domain is the set of program variables occurring in the head of the clause c. Assume that the execution of

---

[2]A *prefix of a clause* is a prefix of the body of that clause.

the prefix g of the clause c is $\langle \theta, g, c \rangle \mapsto_P S'$. Let θ' in $Subst(S')$. The execution of the query $q(X_{i_1}, ..., X_{i_r})\theta'$ yields a standard substitution sequence $< \sigma_1, ..., \sigma_k >$. This behaviour is described by:

$$\langle \theta'', q \rangle \mapsto_P S''$$

where θ'' is the program substitution $\{X_1/X_{i_1}\theta', ..., X_r/X_{i_r}\theta'\}$, and where S'' is the program substitution sequence $< \theta''\sigma_1, ..., \theta''\sigma_k >$. We use the same notations when the literal l is a unification.

Execution of a clause

Let c be a clause whose body is g, let D be the set of program variables occurring in the head, and let θ be a program substitution whose domain is D. The result of the execution of c with input θ is denoted by:

$$\langle \theta, c \rangle \mapsto_P S$$

where $\langle \theta, g, c \rangle \mapsto_P S'$, and where $S = S'_{/D}$.

3.3   Abstract substitutions

The domain of abstract substitutions is an instantiation to modes, types, and possible sharing of the generic abstract domain $\text{Pat}(\Re)$ described in [33, 80]. More specifically, an abstract substitution β over program variables $X_1, \dots, X_n$ is a triplet of the form $\langle sv, frm, \alpha \rangle$ and represents a set of program substitutions of the form $\{X_1/t_1, \dots, X_n/t_n\}$. It provides information not only about terms $t_1, \dots, t_n$ but also about subterms of them. If t_i is a term of the form $f(t_{i_1}, \dots, t_{i_m})$, then β is expected to represent information about $t_{i_1}, \dots, t_{i_m}$. Each term described in β is denoted by an index. The same-value component sv maps each program variable of the substitution to its index. The frame component frm gives information about the structure of the terms. The abstract tuple α provides information about modes, types and possible sharing of the terms and subterms.

This section formally describes the various components of abstract substitutions. In the rest of this section, D denotes the set of program variables $\{X_1, ..., X_n\}$, and I denotes the set of indices occurring in β.

3.3.1   The same-value component

Definition 3.1

The *same-value* component sv assigns a term to each variable in the substitution. We denote by $\text{SV}_{D,I}$ the set of total functions (non necessarily surjective) from D to I. The semantics of an element $sv \in \text{SV}_{D,I}$ is given by the following concretisation function $Cc : \text{SV}_{D,I} \to 2^{PS_D}$, that makes sure that two variables assigned to the same index have the same value (i.e., they are bound to the same term):

$$Cc(sv) = \{\theta \in PS_D \mid \forall X_i, X_j \in D : sv(X_i) = sv(X_j) \Rightarrow X_i\theta = X_j\theta\}$$

3.3.2 The frame component

Definition 3.2

The *frame* component frm associates with some of the indices in I an expression of the form $f(i_1, \ldots, i_q)$, where f is a functor symbol of arity q and where $i_1, \ldots, i_q$ are indices in I. We denote by FRM_I the set of partial functions from I to $\mathcal{T}_I^*$ that provides information about the structure of terms. The fact that no frame is associated with an index i is denoted by $frm(i) = undef$. The meaning of an element $frm \in \mathrm{FRM}_I$ is given by the following concretisation function $Cc : \mathrm{FRM}_I \rightarrow 2^{\mathcal{T}^I}$, that specifies that the terms corresponding to the indices satisfy simultaneously all pattern constraints:

$$Cc(frm) = \left\{ \langle t_i \rangle_{i \in I} \in \mathcal{T}^I \;\middle|\; \begin{array}{l} \forall i, i_1, \ldots, i_q \in I : \\ frm(i) = f(i_1, \ldots, i_q) \Rightarrow t_i = f(t_{i_1}, \ldots, t_{i_q}) \end{array} \right\}$$

3.3.3 The mode component

Definition 3.3

The following set of modes, denoted by Mode, is considered:

$$M \in \text{Mode} = \{\bot, \text{ground}, \text{var}, \text{ngv}, \text{novar}, \text{gv}, \text{noground}, \text{any}\}$$

The concretisation function $Cc : \text{Mode} \rightarrow 2^{\mathcal{T}}$ is defined as follows:

$$
\begin{array}{lll}
Cc(\bot) & = & \emptyset \\
Cc(\text{ground}) & = & \{t \in \mathcal{T} \mid t \text{ is a ground term}\} \\
Cc(\text{var}) & = & \{t \in \mathcal{T} \mid t \text{ is a variable}\} \\
Cc(\text{gv}) & = & \{t \in \mathcal{T} \mid t \text{ is either a ground term or a variable}\} \\
Cc(\text{noground}) & = & \{t \in \mathcal{T} \mid t \text{ is not a ground term}\} \\
Cc(\text{novar}) & = & \{t \in \mathcal{T} \mid t \text{ is not a variable}\} \\
Cc(\text{ngv}) & = & \{t \in \mathcal{T} \mid t \text{ is neither a ground term nor a variable}\} \\
Cc(\text{any}) & = & \mathcal{T}
\end{array}
$$

The partial ordering relationship $\leq$ over modes is such that, for all M_1, M_2 in Mode, $M_1 \leq M_2$ implies $Cc(M_1) \subseteq Cc(M_2)$. This is deduced by the diagram depicted in Figure 3.3, where an arc between M_1 and M_2 with M_1 above M_2 means that $M_1 > M_2$.

Definition 3.4

The *mode* component mo binds to each index in I a value from Mode. We denote by Modes_I the set of total functions from I to Mode augmented with $\bot$. The

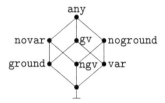

Figure 3.3: The partial ordering relationship over modes.

semantics of an element $mo \in \text{Modes}_I$ is given by the following concretisation function $Cc : \text{Modes}_I \rightarrow 2^{T^I}$. If $mo = \perp$, then $Cc(mo) = \emptyset$. Otherwise, $Cc(mo) = \{ \langle t_i \rangle_{i \in I} \in T^I \mid \forall i \in I : t_i \in Cc(mo(i)) \}$.

3.3.4   The type component

Definition 3.5

The basic framework considers the following set of types, denoted by Type:

$$T \in \text{Type} = \{\perp, \texttt{list}, \texttt{anylist}, \texttt{any}\}$$

The concretisation function $Cc : \text{Type} \rightarrow 2^T$ is defined as follows:

$$
\begin{array}{rcl}
Cc(\perp) & = & \emptyset \\
Cc(\texttt{list}) & = & \{t \in T \mid t \text{ is a list}\} \\
Cc(\texttt{anylist}) & = & \{t \in T \mid \exists \sigma \in SS \text{ such that } t\sigma \text{ is a list}\} \\
Cc(\texttt{any}) & = & T
\end{array}
$$

The type `anylist` denotes the set of terms that can be instantiated to a list. A term t is an `anylist` if it is a standard variable, or if it is the empty list [ ], or if it is of the form $[t_1|t_2]$, where t_1 is any term and t_2 is an `anylist`. Note that every `list` is an `anylist`.

The total ordering relationship over types is such that, for all T_1, T_2 in Type, $T_1 \leq T_2$ implies $Cc(T_1) \subseteq Cc(T_2)$. We have $\perp \leq \texttt{list} \leq \texttt{anylist} \leq \texttt{any}$.

Definition 3.6

The *type* component ty defines a total function binding each index in I with its type. We denote by Types_I the set of total functions from I to Type augmented with $\perp$. The semantics of an element $ty \in \text{Types}_I$ is given by the following concretisation function $Cc : \text{Types}_I \rightarrow 2^{T^I}$. If $ty = \perp$ then $Cc(ty) = \emptyset$. Otherwise, $Cc(ty) = \{ \langle t_i \rangle_{i \in I} \in T^I \mid \forall i \in I : t_i \in Cc(ty(i)) \}$.

3.3.5   The possible sharing component

Definition 3.7

The *possible sharing* component ps specifies possible variable sharing between terms. We denote by PSharing_I the set of all binary and symmetrical relations

$ps \subseteq I \times I$ augmented with $\perp$. The semantics of an element $ps \in \texttt{PSharing}_I$ is given by the following concretisation function $Cc : \texttt{PSharing}_I \rightarrow 2^{T^I}$. If $ps = \perp$ then $Cc(ps) = \emptyset$. Otherwise,

$$Cc(ps) = \{ \langle t_i \rangle_{i \in I} \in T^I \mid \forall i, j \in I : vars(t_i) \cap vars(t_j) \neq \emptyset \Rightarrow (i, j) \in ps \}$$

In the rest of this document, $ps(i, j)$ denotes that the pair (i, j) belongs to ps and $\neg ps(i, j)$ denotes that the pair (i, j) does not belong to ps.

3.3.6 The abstract tuple component

Definition 3.8

The *abstract tuple* component α of an abstract substitution provides information about the modes, types, and possible sharing of the terms described in the abstract substitution. In the $\texttt{Pat}(\Re)$ terminology [33, 80], it is an instantiation of the so-called $\Re$-component. The set of abstract tuples over indices I is denoted by $\texttt{Alpha}_I$. Formally, an abstract tuple $\alpha \in \texttt{Alpha}_I$ over a set of indices I is either $\perp$ or a tuple of the form $\langle mo, ty, ps \rangle$ where $mo \in \texttt{Modes}_I$, $ty \in \texttt{Types}_I$, and $ps \in \texttt{PSharing}_I$, with $mo, ty, ps \neq \perp$ and for all $i \in I$, $mo(i), ty(i) \neq \perp$. The semantics of an abstract tuple α over I is given by the following concretisation function $Cc : \texttt{Alpha}_I \rightarrow 2^{T^I}$. If $\alpha = \perp$ then $Cc(\alpha) = \emptyset$. Otherwise, $Cc(\langle mo, ty, ps \rangle) = Cc(mo) \cap Cc(ty) \cap Cc(ps)$.

We are now able to provide the semantics of an abstract substitution.

3.3.7 Abstract substitutions: definition and concretisation

An abstract substitution denotes a set of program substitutions. It is an instantiation to modes, types, and possible sharing of the abstract domain $\texttt{Pat}(\Re)$ described in [33, 80].

Definition 3.9

The set of abstract substitutions with domain D, and defined over the set of indices I, is denoted by $\texttt{AS}_{D,I}$. It is defined as follows:

$$\beta = \langle sv, frm, \alpha \rangle \in \texttt{AS}_{D,I} = (\texttt{SV}_{D,I} \times \texttt{FRM}_I \times \texttt{Alpha}_I) + \{\perp\}$$

In the rest of this document, we will often represent an abstract substitution β where the α tuple is explicit:

$$\beta = \langle sv, frm, \langle mo, ty, ps \rangle \rangle$$

Note that the set of indices assigned to the variables by the *same-value* component sv does not cover all the indices used by the other components of the domains (e.g., if a term has a pattern then the *frame* component frm will keep some information about its subterms). The domain of β is D and is denoted by $dom(\beta)$.

The semantics of an abstract substitution β is given by the following concretisation function $Cc : \mathrm{AS}_{D,I} \to 2^{PS_D}$. If $\beta = \bot$ then $Cc(\beta) = \emptyset$. Otherwise,

$$Cc(\langle sv, frm, \alpha \rangle) = \left\{ \theta \in PS_D \mid \exists \langle t_i \rangle_{i \in I} \in T^I : \begin{array}{l} \forall X \in D, \ X\theta = t_{sv(X)} \\ \langle t_i \rangle_{i \in I} \in Cc(frm) \cap Cc(\alpha) \end{array} \right\}$$

In the rest of this thesis, unless it is specified otherwise, β denotes $\langle sv, frm, \alpha \rangle$, β_k denotes $\langle sv_k, frm_k, \alpha_k \rangle$, and β' denotes $\langle sv', frm', \alpha' \rangle$.

Let β_1 in AS_{D,I_1} and β_2 in AS_{D,I_2}. The *greatest lower bound* of β_1 and β_2 is denoted by $\beta_1 \sqcap \beta_2$, and is such that $Cc(\beta_1 \sqcap \beta_2) = Cc(\beta_1) \cap Cc(\beta_2)$. The *least upper bound* of β_1 and β_2 is denoted by $\beta_1 \sqcup \beta_2$, and is such that $Cc(\beta_1 \sqcup \beta_2) \supseteq Cc(\beta_1) \cup Cc(\beta_2)$. The greatest lower bound and least upper bound over abstract substitutions are defined in [80].

3.3.8   Decomposition of substitutions

Given one particular program substitution θ with domain $\{X_1, \ldots, X_n\}$ and represented by an abstract substitution β over I, the correspondence between indices in I and (sub)terms in $X_1\theta, \ldots, X_n\theta$ is made explicit by the function DECOMP. This operation computes a term tuple that is a *decomposition of θ with respect to the abstract substitution β.*

Let θ be a substitution and $\beta = \langle sv : \{X_1, \ldots, X_n\} \to I, frm, \alpha \rangle$ be an abstract substitution over I such that $\theta \in Cc(\beta)$. DECOMP(θ, β) returns the term tuple $\langle t_i \rangle_{i \in I} \in T^I$ such that the following properties hold:

- $\theta = \{X_1/t_{sv(X_1)}, \ldots, X_n/t_{sv(X_n)}\}$;
- $\forall i \in I, \ frm(i) = f(i_1, \ldots, i_m) \Rightarrow t_i = f(t_{i_1}, \ldots, t_{i_m})$;
- $\langle t_i \rangle_{i \in I} \in Cc(\alpha)$.

Note that if $\theta \notin Cc(\beta)$ then DECOMP(θ, β) is undefined.

For instance, consider the abstract substitution β_{ref} of Figure 3.1. Let θ be the program substitution $\{X/x, L/[a, b, c], Ls/y\}$, where x and y are two distinct standard variables, and where a, b and c are constants. We have that $\theta \in Cc(\beta_{ref})$. Then, the operation DECOMP(θ, β_{ref}) gives the term tuple $\langle t_1, t_2, t_3, t_4, t_5 \rangle$, where:

$$
\begin{array}{rcl}
t_1 & = & x \\
t_2 & = & [a, b, c] \\
t_3 & = & y \\
t_4 & = & a \\
t_5 & = & [b, c]
\end{array}
$$

3.3.9 Structural mapping between abstract substitutions

A structural mapping between two abstract substitutions is a mapping on their corresponding indices preserving same-value and frame. Finding structural mapping between abstract substitutions is instrumental to detect that an abstract substitution is less or equal than (i.e., satisfies the conditions imposed by) another abstract substitution (see Section 3.3.10). Furthermore, structural mappings, through 'constrained mapping' operations (see Section 3.4.2), are used to manipulate indices in the size components of abstract sequences. Typical structural mappings are the ones between abstract substitutions and their greatest lower bound, and the ones between the least upper bound of abstract substitutions and the abstract substitutions (see Appendix F.1).

Let β in $\mathrm{AS}_{D,I}$ and β' in $\mathrm{AS}_{D',I'}$ be two abstract substitutions, such that the domain D is a subset of the domain D'. A *structural mapping* between β and β' (if it exists) is a total function tr from I to I' that satisfies the following two conditions:

- $\forall X \in D : tr(sv(X)) = sv'(X)$;
- $\forall i, i_1, \ldots, i_q \in I$:
  $$frm(i) = f(i_1, \ldots, i_q) \Rightarrow frm'(tr(i)) = f(tr(i_1), \ldots, tr(i_q)).$$

The structural mapping between β and β' is denoted by $tr : \beta \to \beta'$.

For instance, consider the two following abstract substitutions β_a and β_b:

$$
\begin{aligned}
\beta_a: sv &= \{\mathtt{X1} \mapsto 1, \mathtt{X2} \mapsto 2, \mathtt{X3} \mapsto 3\} \\
frm &= \{2 \mapsto [4|5]\} \\
mo &= \{1 \mapsto \mathtt{novar}, 2 \mapsto \mathtt{ground}, 3 \mapsto \mathtt{var}, 4 \mapsto \mathtt{ground}, \\
& \qquad 5 \mapsto \mathtt{ground}\} \\
ty &= \{1 \mapsto \mathtt{any}, 2 \mapsto \mathtt{list}, 3 \mapsto \mathtt{anylist}, 4 \mapsto \mathtt{any}, \\
& \qquad 5 \mapsto \mathtt{list}\} \\
ps &= \{(1,1), (1,3), (3,3)\}
\end{aligned}
$$

$$
\begin{aligned}
\beta_b: sv &= \{\mathtt{X1} \mapsto 1, \mathtt{X2} \mapsto 2, \mathtt{X3} \mapsto 3\} \\
frm &= \{1 \mapsto [4|5], 2 \mapsto [6|7]\} \\
mo &= \{1 \mapsto \mathtt{novar}, 2 \mapsto \mathtt{ground}, 3 \mapsto \mathtt{var}, 4 \mapsto \mathtt{any}, \\
& \qquad 5 \mapsto \mathtt{any}, 6 \mapsto \mathtt{ground}, 7 \mapsto \mathtt{ground}\} \\
ty &= \{1 \mapsto \mathtt{any}, 2 \mapsto \mathtt{list}, 3 \mapsto \mathtt{anylist}, 4 \mapsto \mathtt{any}, \\
& \qquad 5 \mapsto \mathtt{any}, 6 \mapsto \mathtt{any}, 7 \mapsto \mathtt{list}\} \\
ps &= \{(1,1), (3,3)\}
\end{aligned}
$$

The structural mapping $tr : \beta_a \to \beta_b$ exists and is:

$$tr = \{1 \mapsto 1, 2 \mapsto 2, 3 \mapsto 3, 4 \mapsto 6, 5 \mapsto 7\}$$

3.3.10   Pre-ordering on abstract substitutions

The checker abstractly executes a procedure call $q(X_{i_1}, ..., X_{i_m})$ by relying on a suitable specification of q/m. A specification B_q of the procedure q/m can be applied if β_{inter}, which is the output abstract substitution of the abstract sequence situated at the program point just before the call, restricted to the program variables $X_{i_1}, ..., X_{i_m}$, satisfies the input abstract substitution β_{in}^q of B_q. This is performed by checking that β_{inter} is less or equal ($\leq$) than β_{in}^q. The $\leq$ relation over abstract substitutions is also used to check that an abstract sequence B implies a specification B_p. In particular, the checker verifies that the refined substitution of B implies the conditions imposed by the refined substitution of B_p (i.e., $\beta_{ref} \leq \beta_{ref}^p$) and that the output substitution of B implies the conditions of the output substitution of B_p (i.e., $\beta_{out} \leq \beta_{out}^p$) (see Section 3.4.5).

We define a pre-ordering $\leq$ over abstract substitutions as follows. Let β_1 in AS_{D,I_1} and β_2 in AS_{D,I_2} be two abstract substitutions over the same domain D. Semantically, if $\beta_1 \leq \beta_2$ holds then β_1 imposes the same as or more constraints on all components than β_2 does, that is, $Cc(\beta_1) \subseteq Cc(\beta_2)$.

We have $\beta_1 \leq \beta_2$ if $\beta_1 = \perp$ or if there exists a structural mapping $tr : \beta_2 \rightarrow \beta_1$ satisfying:

- $\forall i \in I_2 : mo_1(tr(i)) \leq mo_2(i)$;
- $\forall i \in I_2 : ty_1(tr(i)) \leq ty_2(i)$;
- $\forall i, j \in I_2 : frm_2(i) = frm_2(j) = undef : ps_1(tr(i), tr(j)) \Rightarrow ps_2(i, j)$.

Note that the constraints over the same-value and the frame components of β_1 and β_2 are also considered, by the definition of the structural mapping tr (see Section 3.3.9). The relation $\leq$ is a *pre-order*, i.e., it is reflexive and transitive, but not necessarily antisymmetric. Indeed, two distinct abstract substitutions can represent the same set of substitutions simply by permuting some indices. It is not difficult to obtain a partial ordering relation by considering equivalence classes of abstract substitutions. The equality test '=' between abstract substitutions is such that $\beta_1 = \beta_2$ implies $Cc(\beta_1) = Cc(\beta_2)$.

For instance, considering the two abstract substitutions β_a and β_b defined in Section 3.3.9, we have that $\beta_b \leq \beta_a$.

3.4   Abstract sequences

This section formalises the notion of abstract sequence introduced in Section 3.1. We first introduce the domain used to represent size relations. We then define the notions of constrained mappings and of disjoint unions, which are useful to express the semantics of abstract sequences, as well as to implement abstract operations of abstract sequences.

3.4.1 Size relations

A size measure, or norm, is a function from terms to naturals $\mathcal{T} \to \mathbb{N}$. The norm of a term t is denoted by $\|t\|$. In the basic framework, the unique norm that is considered is the list-length measure. Abstract sequences maintain relations between the size of input and output terms (the `srel` part in a specification), and the number of solutions in function of the size of input terms (the `sol` part in a specification). Furthermore, the `sexpr` part of a specification expresses a linear relation between the size of input terms, which must decrease through recursive calls. We first define the domain of linear expressions, and then, we define the size domain.

Definition 3.10

Let V be a set of variables. We denote by Exp_V the set of all linear expressions with integer coefficients on the set of variables V. Let $X_1, ..., X_m$ be variables. An element $le \in Exp_{\{X_1,...,X_m\}}$ can also be seen as a function from $\mathbb{N}^m$ to $\mathbb{N}$, as size expressions are positive. The value of $le(\langle n_1, \ldots, n_m \rangle)$ is obtained by evaluating the expression le where each X_i is replaced by n_i.

For instance, let $2 * X_1 + X_2$ be a linear expression of $Exp_{\{X_1,X_2\}}$. Assume that the size of X_1 is 3, and the size of X_2 is 5. Then, the expression $(2 * X_1 + X_2)(\langle 3, 5 \rangle)$ is equal to 11.

Definition 3.11

We denote by $Sizes_I$ the set of all systems of linear equations and inequations over Exp_I, extended with the special symbol $\bot$. In order to distinguish indices of I, considered as variables, from integer coefficient and constants when writing elements of Exp_I, we wrap up each element i of I into the symbol $sz(i)$. The domain $Sizes_I$ is endowed with a concretisation function $Cc : Sizes_I \to 2^{\mathbb{N}^I}$. For all $E \in Sizes_I$, if $E = \bot$ then $Cc(E) = \emptyset$. Otherwise,

$$Cc(E) = \{\langle n_i \rangle_{i \in I} \in \mathbb{N}^I | \ \langle n_i \rangle_{i \in I} \text{ is a solution of } E\}$$

Let $E_1, E_2 \in Sizes_I$. Then, $E_1 \leq E_2$ implies $Cc(E_1) \subseteq Cc(E_2)$. The least upper bound is denoted by $E_1 \sqcup E_2$, and is such that $Cc(E_1 \sqcup E_2) \supseteq Cc(E_1) \cup Cc(E_2)$ (the least upper bound operator $\sqcup$ between (in)equation systems is implemented as convex hull, see [7, 120]). The greatest lower bound is denoted by $E_1 \sqcap E_2$ and is such that $Cc(E_1 \sqcap E_2) = Cc(E_1) \cap Cc(E_2)$.

For instance, consider the following two size components E_1 and E_2 over the same set of indices $\{i, j\}$:

$$
\begin{aligned}
E_1 &= \{1 \leq sz(i) \leq 3, 1 \leq sz(j) \leq 3\} \\
E_2 &= \{2 \leq sz(i) \leq 4, sz(j) \leq sz(i)\}
\end{aligned}
$$

The intersection $E_1 \sqcap E_2$ is the system $\{2 \leq sz(i) \leq 3, 1 \leq sz(j) \leq sz(i)\}$. The convex hull $E_1 \sqcup E_2$ is $\{1 \leq sz(i) \leq 4, sz(i) + sz(j) \geq 2, 3 * sz(j) - sz(i) \leq 8\}$.

3.4.2   Constrained mappings

Constrained mappings have been introduced in [82, 83] as a formalism to manipulate indices, to duplicate, eliminate, equalise, introduce and rename place-
holders occurring inside abstract descriptions. Constrained mappings are motivated
by one of the fundamental difficulties encountered when designing the operations
of $\text{Pat}(\Re)$: the fact that abstract substitutions may have different structures in the
pattern component and that equality constraints are enforced implicitly by repeated
use of the same index. As a consequence, it is non-trivial to establish a correspondence between the elements of the respective components of two abstract substitutions or sequences. The need for such a correspondence appears, in one form
or another, in many abstract operations such as the abstract concatenation operation (see Section 6.4), and the ordering relation over abstract substitutions (see
Section 3.3.10) and over abstract sequences (see Section 3.4.5). The constrained
mapping provides a uniform solution to this problem and simplifies dramatically
the implementation of many abstract operations.

The constrained mapping operation takes as input an abstract object (in this
case, a size component E_1, over the set of indices I_1) and a mapping $tr : I_1 \to I_2$.
The mapping tr contains two implicit pieces of information: first, a set of equality
constraints for terms whose indices are mapped onto the same value by tr; second,
it ignores terms whose indices are not the image of some index in I_2. So, such a
mapping indicates how to transform the size component E_1 in I_2, by removing su-
perfluous terms and duplicating some others, yielding the new size component E_2.
There are two dual constrained mapping operations, depending on whether the operation computes E_2 from E_1 and tr (this is called a *direct constrained mapping*),
or whether the operation computes E_1 from E_2 and tr (this is called an *inverse
constrained mapping*).

Definition 3.12
   Let $E_1 \in \text{Sizes}_{I_1}$ and $tr : I_1 \to I_2$ be a (possibly partial) function. The *direct
constrained mapping* of E_1 w.r.t. tr, denoted by $tr^>(E_1)$, is $E_2 \in \text{Sizes}_{I_2}$, such
that:
$$\left. \begin{array}{l} \langle n_i^1 \rangle_{i \in I_1} \in Cc(E_1) \\ n_i^1 = n_{tr(i)}^2 \; (\forall i \in dom(tr)) \end{array} \right\} \Rightarrow \langle n_i^2 \rangle_{i \in I_2} \in Cc(E_2)$$

   Let $E_2 \in \text{Sizes}_{I_2}$ and $tr : I_1 \to I_2$ be a (possibly partial) function. The
inverse constrained mapping of E_2 w.r.t. tr, denoted by $tr^<(E_2)$, is $E_1 \in \text{Sizes}_{I_1}$,
such that:
$$\left. \begin{array}{l} \langle n_i^2 \rangle_{i \in I_2} \in Cc(E_2) \\ n_{tr(i)}^2 = n_i^1 \; (\forall i \in dom(tr)) \end{array} \right\} \Rightarrow \langle n_i^1 \rangle_{i \in I_1} \in Cc(E_1)$$

In what follows, (in)equations will be written between double brackets $[\![\cdots]\!]$,
meaning that they are syntactic objects, not semantic relations. If tr is a function
from one set of indices to another one, such that $tr(i) = i'$ and $tr(j) = j'$, the
expression $[\![sz(tr(i)) = sz(tr(j)) + 1]\!]$ has to be read as the syntactical equation

$sz(i') = sz(j') + 1$.

For instance, consider the system of constraints E_1 over the set of indices $I_1 = \{1, 2, 3, 4\}$ (each index represents an input or output term in an abstract substitution or sequence):

$$E_1 = \{[\![sz(1) = sz(2) + sz(3)]\!], [\![sz(2) = sz(4) + 1]\!]\}.$$

Assume now that the term bound to index 3 becomes the same as the term bound to index 2, and that the indices 3 and 4 have not to be considered any more in the constraints system. Such conditions can be expressed through the structural mapping tr, which is defined from the set I_1 to the set $I_2 = \{1, 2\}$ as follows:

$$tr = \{1 \mapsto 1, 2 \mapsto 2, 3 \mapsto 2\}.$$

The direct constrained mapping of E_1 w.r.t. tr is $E_2 = tr^>(E_1)$:

$$E_2 = \{[\![sz(1) = 2 * sz(2)]\!], [\![sz(2) \geq 1]\!]\}.$$

In the first constraint, $sz(3)$ has been replaced by $sz(tr(3))$, i.e., by $sz(2)$. In the second constraint, $sz(4)$ has been removed, but the fact that the size of the term bound to index 2 is greater than one has been maintained in E_2, by projection.

The interested reader can find the implementation of the constrained mapping operations for the size domain in Appendix E.

3.4.3 Disjoint unions

In abstract sequences, terms are represented by indices, and the same indices can be used in β_{ref} and in β_{out}. As indices from different abstract substitutions can occur in the (in)equations of the size components (e.g., we use indices from β_{ref} and β_{out} to compare the size of the terms before and after the execution of a procedure), we first need to rename the refined and output indices, since they refer to different terms. For this reason, we introduce the notion of 'disjoint union' that allows us to "merge" two sets of indices into one set of indices. Thanks to this operation, elements from both sets remain distinct (the indices that are present in both abstract substitutions should remain distinct, as they refer to different terms).

For instance, consider the β_{ref} and β_{out} components of the abstract sequence corresponding to Specification 3.1 of the procedure select(X, L, Ls), depicted in Figure 3.1, page 43. The set of indices in β_{ref} is $I_{ref} = \{1, 2, 3, 4, 5\}$ and the set of indices in β_{out} is $I_{out} = \{1, 2, 3, 4, 5\}$. Although the same indices are used in β_{ref} and β_{out}, the input and output indices refer to different terms. In order to relate the size of input and output indices, we first map each refined and output index to a new index in the disjoint union set. The disjoint union set, denoted by $I_{ref} + I_{out}$, is the set $\{1, 2, 3, 4, 5, 6, 7, 8, 9, 10\}$. The refined and the output indices are mapped into $I_{ref} + I_{out}$ (through the injection functions in_{ref} and in_{out} respectively, also depicted in Figure 3.1). The size component E_{ref_out} of the abstract sequence is defined on the disjoint union. In particular, the system of constraints relates the size of index 8 (which corresponds to the output index 3, and which is different from the refined index 3) to the size of refined index 5.

Definition 3.13
    Let A and B be two (possibly non disjoint) sets. The *disjoint union* of A and B is an arbitrarily chosen set, denoted by $A + B$, equipped with two injections functions in_A and in_B satisfying the following property: for any set C and for any pair of functions $f_A : A \rightarrow C$ and $f_B : B \rightarrow C$, there exists a unique function $f : A + B \rightarrow C$ such that $f_A = f \circ in_A$ and $f_B = f \circ in_B$ (where the symbol $\circ$ is the usual function composition). Since the function f is uniquely defined, we can express it in terms of f_A and f_B. In the following, it is denoted by $f_A + f_B$. The functions in_A, in_B, f_A, f_B, and $f_A + f_B$ satisfy the commutative diagram depicted in Figure 3.4.

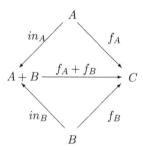

Figure 3.4: Disjoint union of functions.

3.4.4   Abstract sequences: definition and concretisation

The domain of abstract sequences is the main abstract domain of the abstract interpretation framework. It is made of several abstract components that cooperate together. An abstract sequence describes a set of pairs $\langle \theta, S \rangle$, where θ is an input substitution, and S is a sequence of answer substitutions resulting from executing a piece of code (a procedure, a clause, a goal in a clause, a literal). It maintains information about the input substitution θ, output substitutions (elements of S), linear relations between the size of input and output terms, as well as the number of solutions to a call ($|S|$) in function of the size of input terms (including determinacy and sure success or failure of the execution).

Definition 3.14

An abstract sequence B with input domain $D = \{X_1, ..., X_n\}$ and output domain $D' = \{X_1, ..., X_m\}$ $(n \leq m)$ is a tuple $\langle \beta_{in}, \beta_{ref}, \beta_{out}, E_{ref\_out}, E_{sol} \rangle$ where:

- The *input* component β_{in} is an abstract substitution over I_{in} whose domain is D, i.e., $\beta_{in} \in \mathrm{AS}_{D,I_{in}}$

- The *refined* component β_{ref} is an abstract substitution over I_{ref} whose domain is D, i.e., $\beta_{ref} \in \mathrm{AS}_{D,I_{ref}}$

- The *output* component β_{out} is an abstract substitution over I_{out}, and whose domain is D', i.e., $\beta_{out} \in \mathrm{AS}_{D',I_{out}}$

- The *size relations* component E_{ref_out} is a system of linear equations and inequations, whose variables are the disjoint union between the indices of β_{ref} and of β_{out}, i.e., $E_{ref\_out} \in \mathrm{Sizes}_{I_{ref}+I_{out}}$

- The *solutions* component E_{sol} is a system of linear relations whose variables are *sol* and indices of β_{ref}, i.e., $E \in \mathrm{Sizes}_{\{sol\}+I_{ref}}$

The set of abstract sequences is denoted by ASeq; $input(B)$ denotes β_{in} and $output(B)$ denotes β_{out}. Moreover, $dom_{in}(B)$ denotes $dom(\beta_{in})$, which is equal to $dom(\beta_{ref})$. Similarly, $dom_{out}(B)$ denotes $dom(\beta_{out})$. The set of abstract sequences where $dom_{in} = dom_{out} = D$ is denoted by ASeq_D.

An abstract sequence B describes a set of pairs $\langle \theta, S \rangle \in PS_D \times PSS_D$ such that:

- θ is a program substitution with $dom(\theta) = D$, and such that $\theta \in Cc(\beta_{in})$.

- S is a *finite* program substitution sequence with $dom(S) = D'$, and such that, for all θ' in $Subst(S)$, we have $\theta'_{/D} \leq \theta$ and $\theta' \in Cc(\beta_{out})$.

- The substitution θ that is not described by β_{ref} leads to unsuccessful calls, i.e., $S \neq <> \Rightarrow \theta \in Cc(\beta_{ref})$.

- The E_{ref_out} component describes the system of relations that must hold between the size of input and output terms. Let $\langle t_i \rangle_{i \in I_{ref}}$ be the terms of θ corresponding to the indices in β_{ref}, i.e., $\langle t_i \rangle_{i \in I_{ref}} = \mathrm{DECOMP}(\theta, \beta_{ref})$. For all $\theta' \in Subst(S)$, let $\langle s_i \rangle_{i \in I_{out}}$ be the terms of θ' corresponding to the indices in β_{out}, i.e., $\langle s_i \rangle_{i \in I_{out}} = \mathrm{DECOMP}(\theta', \beta_{out})$. Then, $\langle \|t_i\| \rangle_{i \in I_{ref}} + \langle \|s_i\| \rangle_{i \in I_{out}} \in Cc(E_{ref\_out})$.

- The E_{sol} component describes the system of relations that must hold between the length of S (number of substitutions) and the size of the input terms. Let $\langle t_i \rangle_{i \in I_{ref}}$ be the terms of θ corresponding to the indices in β_{ref}, i.e., $\langle t_i \rangle_{i \in I_{ref}} = \mathrm{DECOMP}(\theta, \beta_{ref})$. Then, $\{sol \mapsto Ns(S)\} + \langle \|t_i\| \rangle_{i \in I_{ref}} \in Cc(E_{sol})$.

The set of $\langle \theta, S \rangle$'s represented by B is denoted by $Cc(B)$. In the rest of this document, unless it is specified otherwise, B denotes $\langle \beta_{in}, \beta_{ref}, \beta_{out}, E_{ref\_out},$

$E_{sol}\rangle$, B_k denotes $\langle \beta_{in}^k, \beta_{ref}^k, \beta_{out}^k, E_{ref\_out}^k, E_{sol}^k \rangle$, and B' denotes $\langle \beta_{in}', \beta_{ref}', \beta_{out}', E_{ref\_out}', E_{sol}' \rangle$.

Each abstract sequence is associated with two structural mappings (see Section 3.3.9): $tr_{in\_ref} : \beta_{in} \to \beta_{ref}$ and $tr_{ref\_out} : \beta_{ref} \to \beta_{out}$.

An example of abstract sequence is depicted in Figure 3.1 and corresponds to Specification 3.1 of the procedure `select/3`.

3.4.5   Pre-ordering on abstract sequences

The $\leq$ relation over abstract sequences is used to check that an abstract sequence B_1 'implies' (i.e., imposes the same as or more constraints on all components than) another abstract sequence B_2. This is used to check that the abstract sequence modelling the execution of the whole procedure (which is computed through the abstract concatenation operation, see Section 6.4) satisfies a given specification.

We define a pre-ordering $\leq$ over abstract sequences as follows. Let B_1 and B_2 be two abstract sequences over the same domain D (i.e., $B_1, B_2 \in \mathtt{ASeq}_D$). Semantically, if $B_1 \leq B_2$ holds then B_1 imposes the same as or more constraints on all components than B_2 does, that is, $Cc(B_1) \subseteq Cc(B_2)$.

If $B_1 = \perp$ then $B_1 \leq B_2$. If $B_1 = \langle \beta_{in}, \perp, \perp, \perp, \{[\![sol = 0]\!]\} \rangle$ and if $\{[\![sol = 0]\!]\} \leq E_{sol}^2$ then $B_1 \leq B_2$. Otherwise, we have $B_1 \leq B_2$ if there exist two structural mappings $tr_{ref} : \beta_{ref}^2 \to \beta_{ref}^1$ and $tr_{out} : \beta_{out}^2 \to \beta_{out}^1$ satisfying the following conditions:

$$
\begin{aligned}
&(1)\quad \beta_{in}^1 = \beta_{in}^2 \\
&(2)\quad \beta_{ref}^1 \leq \beta_{ref}^2 \\
&(3)\quad \beta_{out}^1 \leq \beta_{out}^2 \\
&(4)\quad E_{ref\_out}^1 \leq (tr_{ref} + tr_{out})^{>}(E_{ref\_out}^2) \\
&(5)\quad E_{sol}^1 \leq (tr_{ref} + \{sol \mapsto sol\})^{>}(E_{sol}^2) \\
&(6)\quad (E_{sol}^2 \leq \{[\![sol \geq 1]\!]\}) \Rightarrow \beta_{ref}^1 = \beta_{ref}^2 .
\end{aligned}
$$

Condition (1) imposes that the input substitutions of B_1 and B_2 are equivalent (up to a renaming of indices). Conditions (2) and (3) describe that the refined and output components of B_1 impose the same as or more constraints than the refined and output components of B_2, respectively (see Section 3.3.10). Condition (4) expresses that the size constraints of B_1 must imply the size constraints of B_2. The constraints system $E_{ref\_out}^2$ is projected onto the set of indices of B_1, i.e. onto the disjoint union $I_{ref}^1 + I_{out}^1$ (see Section 3.4.3), through a direct constrained mapping (see Section 3.4.2). Condition (5) expresses that the number of solutions of B_1 must imply the number of solutions of B_2. The constraints system E_{sol}^2 is projected onto the set of indices $I_{ref}^1 + \{sol\}$ through a direct constrained mapping. The last condition expresses that, if the number of solutions of B_2 is greater than one (i.e., if there is a sure success), then the two refined components β_{ref}^1 and β_{ref}^2

must be identical, since they are exact descriptions of the input conditions to have a sure success of the execution.

3.4.6 Abstract behaviours and formal specifications

A behaviour for a procedure is a formalisation of the specification of behavioural properties provided by the user. Formal specifications have been introduced in Section 3.1, and their abstract syntax can be found in Appendix D.

Definition 3.15

A *behaviour* Beh_p for a procedure name p of arity n is a finite set of pairs $\{\langle B_1, se_1 \rangle, \ldots, \langle B_m, se_m \rangle\}$ where $B_1, \ldots, B_m$ are abstract sequences such that $dom_{in}(B_k) = dom_{out}(B_k) = \{X_1, \ldots, X_n\}$ $(1 \leq k \leq m)$; and $se_1, \ldots, se_m$ are positive linear expressions from $Exp_{\{X_1, \ldots, X_n\}}$.

Each pair of the form $\langle B, se \rangle$ is called a behavioural pair (or, if no confusion is possible, a behaviour). The positive linear expression se is required to strictly decrease through recursive calls of the described procedure to ensure termination. In the following, $SBeh$ is a family of behaviours containing exactly one behaviour Beh_p for each procedure name p occurring in the program.

3.5 Abstract execution

This section presents how the checker executes a procedure at the abstract level. The verification is realised on normalised procedures (see Section 3.2.1). The analyser follows the standard top-down verification technique: for a given program, it analyses each procedure; for a given procedure, it analyses each clause; for a given clause, it analyses each atom. If an atom in the body of a clause is a procedure call, then the analyser looks at the given behaviours to infer information about its execution. The analyser succeeds if, for each procedure and each behaviour describing this procedure, the analysis of the procedure yields abstract sequences that are covered by the considered behaviour.

Section 3.5.1 presents the abstract execution of a clause. Section 3.5.2 presents the abstract execution of a procedure. Section 3.5.3 presents the abstract execution of a program. Finally, Section 3.5.4 formally defines the annotated clauses and procedures, that are the results of the verification process.

3.5.1 Abstract execution of a clause

Let $c ::= p(X_1, \ldots, X_n) : -l_1, \ldots, l_s.$ be a clause of the procedure p, let $\langle B, se \rangle$ be a behaviour of the procedure p to be checked, and let $SBeh$ be the set of abstract behaviours (i.e., specifications) corresponding to each procedure in the program. Then, the abstract execution of clause c is depicted in Figure 3.5.

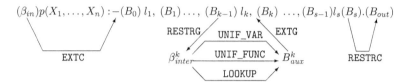

$$(\beta_{in})p(X_1,\ldots,X_n):-(B_0)\,l_1,\,(B_1)\ldots,\,(B_{k-1})\,l_k,\,(B_k)\,\ldots,(B_{s-1})l_s(B_s).(B_{out})$$

Figure 3.5: Abstract execution of a clause.

The analysis of the above clause consists in the following steps:

1. extending the input substitution β_{in} of B to an abstract sequence B_0 on all the variables in the clause through the operation EXTC;

2. computing B_k from B_{k-1} and l_k $(1 \le k \le s)$;

3. restricting B_s to the variables in the head of c through the operation RESTRC.

Each B_k is computed from B_{k-1} and l_k by:

1. restricting the domain of the output abstract substitution β_{out} of B_{k-1} to the variables $X_{i_1},\ldots,X_{i_z}$ of l_k and renaming them into $X_1,\ldots,X_z$, by computing $\beta_{inter}^k = \text{RESTRG}(l_k,B_{k-1})$;

2. executing the literal l_k with β_{inter}^k which returns an abstract sequence B_{aux}^k;

3. propagating this result on B_{k-1} by computing $B_k = \text{EXTG}(l_k,B_{k-1},B_{aux}^k)$.

The execution of l_k with β_{inter}^k depends on the form of l_k:

1. if l_k is a built-in of the form $X_{i_1} = X_{i_2}$ then $B_{aux}^k = \text{UNIF\_VAR}(\beta_{inter}^k)$;

2. if l_k is of the form $X_{i_1} = f(X_{i_2},\ldots,X_{i_n})$ then B_{aux}^k is the result of $\text{UNIF\_FUNC}(\beta_{inter}^k, f)$;

3. if l_k is a non-recursive call $q(X_{i_1},\ldots,X_{i_z})$ (i.e., $q \ne p$) then the analyser looks at $SBeh$, the set of behaviours, to find an abstract sequence general enough to give information about this call (this is performed through the operation $\text{LOOKUP}(\beta_{inter}^k, q, SBeh)$ that succeeds if such a behaviour exists);

4. if l_k is a recursive call $p(X_{i_1},\ldots,X_{i_n})$ then the analyser checks whether the size the arguments decreases (w.r.t. the size expression se) through the operation $\text{CHECK\_TERM}(l_k, B_{k-1}, se)$. The system also checks if the actual parameters of the subcall satisfy the input substitution of the specification, i.e., if $\beta_{inter}^k \le \beta_{in}$.

The algorithm execution of the clause is depicted in Figure 3.6.

PROCEDURE analyse_clause$(c, B, se, SBeh) =$
   $\beta_{in} \leftarrow input(B)$
   $B_0 \leftarrow$ EXTC(c, β_{in})
   for $k \leftarrow 1$ **to** s **do**
      $\beta^k_{inter} \leftarrow$ RESTRG(l_k, B_{k-1})
      switch (l_k) **do**
         case $X_{i_1} = X_{i_2}$:
            $B^k_{aux} \leftarrow$ UNIF_VAR(β^k_{inter})
         case $X_{i_1} = f(X_{i_2}, \dots, X_{i_m})$:
            $B^k_{aux} \leftarrow$ UNIF_FUNC(β^k_{inter}, f)
         case $q(X_{i_1}, \dots, X_{i_m})$ **and** $q \neq p$:
            $\langle success_k, B^k_{aux} \rangle \leftarrow$ LOOKUP$(\beta^k_{inter}, q, SBeh)$
         case $p(X_{i_1}, \dots, X_{i_n})$:
            $B^k_{aux} \leftarrow B$
      $success_k \leftarrow$ CHECK_TERM$(l_k, B_{k-1}, se) \wedge \beta^k_{inter} \leq \beta_{in}$
      $B_k \leftarrow$ EXTG$(l_k, B_{k-1}, B^k_{aux})$
   if there exists k **in** $\{1, \dots, s\}$ **such that**
      either $l_k ::= q(X_{i_1}, \dots, X_{i_m}) \wedge \neg success_k$
      or $l_k ::= p(X_{i_1}, \dots, X_{i_n}) \wedge \neg success_k$
      then $success \leftarrow false$
      else $success \leftarrow true$ **and** $B_{out} =$ RESTRC(c, B_s)
   return $\langle success, B_{out} \rangle$

Figure 3.6: Algorithm for the abstract execution of a clause.

3.5.2 Abstract execution of a procedure

After each clause of a procedure has been abstractly executed, then the analyser concatenates the output abstract sequences through the CONC operation, as it is depicted in Figure 3.7. The number of solutions of a procedure is the sum of the numbers of solutions of its clauses, not an "upper bound" of them. The analysis of the procedure succeeds if the computed abstract sequence B_{out} implies the specification B, i.e., if $B_{out} \leq B$. The algorithm for verifying a procedure is depicted in Figure 3.8.

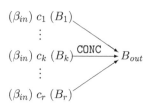

Figure 3.7: Abstract execution of a procedure.

PROCEDURE analyse_procedure($p, B, se, SBeh$) =
    for $k \leftarrow 1$ **to** r **do**
        $\langle success_k, B_k \rangle \leftarrow$ analyse_clause($c_k, B, se, SBeh$)
    if there exists $k \in \{1, \ldots, r\}$ **such that** $\neg success_k$
        then $success \leftarrow false$
        else $B_{out} \leftarrow$ CONC($B_1, \ldots, B_r$)
            $success \leftarrow (B_{out} \leq B)$
    return $success$

Figure 3.8: Algorithm for the abstract execution of a procedure.

3.5.3 Abstract execution of a program

Let P be the normalised program and $SBeh$ be the set of abstract behaviours corresponding to each procedure in P. The analyser succeeds to verify the program P according to $SBeh$ if, for each procedure and each behaviour describing this procedure, the analysis of the procedure yields abstract sequences that are covered by the considered behaviour. This verification process is depicted in Figure 3.9.

PROCEDURE analyse_program($P, SBeh$) =
    $success \leftarrow true$
    for all p in the program P, **for all** $\langle B, se \rangle \in Beh_p$ **from** $SBeh$
        $success \leftarrow success \wedge$ analyse_procedure($p, B, se, SBeh$)
    return $success$

Figure 3.9: Algorithm for the abstract execution of a program.

3.5.4 Annotated clauses and procedures: result of the checker

During the abstract execution of a procedure, the checker derives and computes abstract sequences at each program point (see Figure 3.5 and Figure 3.7). After the checker analysis, that abstract information is used by the optimiser to safely apply source-to-source transformations to specialise the procedure (see Part II, and especially, Section 9.4). For this reason, the checker needs to record in specific data structures the abstract information at each program point. In this section, we define an *annotated clause* that contains, at each program point of the clause, an abstract sequence modelling the execution of the clause until that point, and an abstract sequence modelling the execution of the literal situated at that position. Similarly, an *annotated procedure* contains its annotated clauses and the result of the abstract concatenation.

Annotated clauses

Let c be a clause of the form $h : -l_1, ..., l_s.$, let D be the set of all variables occurring in the head of c, let D' be the set of all variables occurring in c, and let β_{in}^c be an abstract substitution whose domain is D. An *annotated clause* of the clause c with input β_{in}^c, denoted by $\tilde{c}$, is a construct of the form:

$$(\beta_{in}^c)h : -(B_0)\tilde{l}_1, (B_1)..., (B_{s-1})\tilde{l}_s(B_s). \ (B_c)$$

where:

- B_i is an abstract sequence with $dom_{in}(B_i) = D$ and $dom_{out}(B_i) = D'$, for all i in $\{0, ..., s\}$. Note that the input domain of B_i is only composed of the program variables occurring in the clause head, whereas the output domain of B_i is composed of the program variables occurring in the clause (including the local variables).

- $\tilde{l}_i$ is a tuple of the form $\langle l_i, \beta_{l_i}^{inter}, B_{l_i} \rangle$, for all i in $\{1, ..., s\}$, where:
  l_i is a literal whose parameters are $X_{i_1}, ..., X_{i_r}$;
  $\beta_{l_i}^{inter}$ is an abstract substitution whose domain is $\{X_1, ..., X_r\}$;
  B_{l_i} is an abstract sequence whose input and output domain are $\{X_1, ..., X_r\}$.

- B_c is an abstract sequence $\langle \beta_{in}^c, ... \rangle$ with $dom_{in}(B_c) = dom_{out}(B_c) = D$. Note that only the program variables occurring in the clause head are maintained in the input and output substitutions of B_c.

Safe approximation of clauses

An annotated clause $\tilde{c}$ is a *safe approximation* of the clause c if the following conditions hold. Let $\theta \in Cc(\beta_{in}^c)$. Consider the execution of the clause $\langle \theta, c \rangle \mapsto_P S$, the execution of the prefixes of the clause $\langle \theta, (l_1, ..., l_i), c \rangle \mapsto_P S_i$ $(0 \leq i \leq s)$, and the execution of each literal after the execution of the goal preceding it, i.e., $\langle \theta_{\tau,i}, l_i \rangle \mapsto_P S_{\tau,i}$ $(1 \leq i \leq s)$, where τ is in $Subst(S_{i-1})$, $X_{i_1}, ..., X_{i_r}$ are the parameters of l_i, and $\theta_{\tau,i} = \{X_1/X_{i_1}\tau, ..., X_r/X_{i_r}\tau\}$. Then, the following conditions on θ, S, S_i's, $\theta_{\tau,i}$'s and $S_{\tau,i}$'s must be satisfied:

- the abstract sequence B_c models the execution of the whole clause, i.e., $\langle \theta, S \rangle \in Cc(B_c)$;

- at each program point i $(0 \leq i \leq s)$, the abstract sequence B_i models the execution of the sequence of literals until that point, i.e., $\langle \theta, S_i \rangle \in Cc(B_i)$;

- at each program point i ($1 \leq i \leq s$), the abstract substitution $\beta_{l_i}^{inter}$ approximates the call to the literal l_i, i.e., $\theta_{\tau,i} \in Cc(\beta_{l_i}^{inter})$, for all $\tau \in Subst(S_{i-1})$;

- at each program point i ($1 \leq i \leq s$), the abstract sequence B_{l_i} models the execution of the literal l_i, i.e., $\langle \theta_{\tau,i}, S_{\tau,i} \rangle \in Cc(B_{l_i})$, for all $\tau \in Subst(S_{i-1})$.

The procedure `analyse_clause`$(c, B, se, SBeh)$ depicted in Figure 3.5 produces a safe approximation of the clause c.

Annotated procedures

Let pr be a procedure whose name is p, whose arity is n, and that is composed of the clauses $c_1...c_r$. Let $B_{pr} = \langle \beta_{in}^{pr}, ... \rangle$ be an abstract sequence whose input and output domain is $\{X_1, ..., X_n\}$. An annotated procedure of pr (in the context of B_{pr}), denoted by $\tilde{pr}$, is a pair $\langle B_{pr}, < \tilde{c}_1, ..., \tilde{c}_r > \rangle$, where $\tilde{c}_k$ is an annotated clause of c_k with input β_{in}^{pr} ($1 \leq k \leq r$).

Safe approximation of procedures

An annotated procedure $\tilde{pr} = \langle B_{pr}, < \tilde{c}_1, ..., \tilde{c}_r > \rangle$ is a *safe approximation* of pr if the following conditions hold. For all $\theta \in Cc(\beta_{in}^{pr})$, consider the execution of the procedure $\langle \theta, p \rangle \mapsto_P S$. Then, we have $\langle \theta, S \rangle \in Cc(B_{pr})$, and each annotated clause $\tilde{c}_k$ is a safe approximation of the clause c_k ($1 \leq k \leq r$).

The procedure `analyse_procedure`$(p, B, se, SBeh)$ depicted in Figure 3.7 produces a safe approximation of the procedure p.

Chapter 4

Towards handling full Prolog

The kind of programs that are given to our analyser depends on the use of the tool.

The system can be used as a support of a methodology to construct reliable and efficient programs. For instance, in the context of Deville's methodology [45], the analyser takes as input formal specifications and a Prolog program that is a (direct) translation of the logic description of the problem (see Section 2.2.2 and 2.2.3). The input program resembles a normalised code (see Section 3.2.1) on which the abstract execution applies. A logic description may possibly use negations, but it does not contain extralogical features like control information or dynamic predicates. The control information is generated during the last step of the methodology, where source-to-source transformations are automatically and safely applied.

The system can be used for other particular purposes. One can be interested only in checking some operational properties of a procedure (expressed by the formal specifications), without any concern about the logic meaning of the procedure. Similarly, one can use the system with the objective to specialise a given procedure with respect to a formal specification. In such cases, the input of the analyser can be any Prolog program, possibly with negations, cuts, 'if then else' constructs, dynamic predicates, higher-order predicates, etc.

The basic framework (presented in the previous chapter) only accepts as input a pure Prolog program (no negation, no cut, no dynamic and higher-order predicates, etc.). This chapter presents the various extensions that we have performed on the basic framework, to accept more Prolog programs as input. The abstract syntax of the full Prolog which is now accepted by the extended framework is depicted in Appendix C. The analyser deals with negations as failure (Section 4.1), it handles green and red cuts (Section 4.2), it analyses disjunctive and conditional constructs (Section 4.3), dynamic procedures (Section 4.4), as well as higher-order procedures (Section 4.5). Finally, Section 4.6 briefly presents Prolog enhanced with dynamic scheduling, in which some calls are dynamically 'delayed' until their arguments are sufficiently instantiated to allow the call to run correctly.

The treatment of such new features imply several extensions. In addition of extending the accepted Prolog syntax, abstract operations are designed to model the execution of these features. New domains are integrated into abstract sequences to get a precise analysis, allowing the system to prove the operational properties provided in formal specifications. The language of formal specifications is also extended to reflect the additional information maintained in the new abstract domains.

4.1   Negation

The SLD-resolution of Kowalski [74] allows us to derive only positive consequences from a logic program. However, in many circumstances, it is useful to derive *negative* consequences. For instance, negation is particularly useful in knowledge representation, where many of its uses cannot be simulated by positive programs. This section describes the improvements to the basic framework to handle the behaviour of *negation as failure* [23] accurately, which is implemented in most Prolog compilers.

Section 4.1.1 presents the various approaches to incorporate negation in logic programs: negation as failure (*naf*) [23], use of delays to apply *naf* in a secure way [107], intensional negation [10, 11], and constructive negation [21, 22]. Section 4.1.2 illustrates inaccuracies in the basic framework for proving determinacy as well as the sure success of the execution of procedures using negation as failure. To remedy the limitations of the basic framework, Section 4.1.3 defines a new component of abstract sequences, namely the *failure* component, that describes the conditions on input substitutions for which the execution surely fails. Section 4.1.4 refines the pre-ordering relation between abstract sequences by considering the new failure component. Section 4.1.5 describes the main modifications to be realised on the abstract execution algorithm for verifying a procedure containing negations. Finally, Section 4.1.6 defines another extension (not implemented) that could be done to the basic framework to make the failure component more precise.

4.1.1   Negation in logic programming

The inclusion of negation among the logical facilities of logic programming has been a very active area of research. A lot of efforts have been done to propose different ways to understand and to incorporate negation into logic programming languages. Several proposals differ in expressiveness and in semantics. This section presents some well-known negation techniques (we follow the discussion of [101]).

Negation as failure

The negation as failure rule of Clark [23] is a builtin or a library in most Prolog compilers (e.g., SWI-Prolog, Quintus, SICStus, Ciao, Bin Prolog). The negation as failure not (Q) is a consequence of a program P if a finitely failed SLD-tree for the query Q w.r.t. P exists (i.e., if the execution of Q finitely fails). The operational behaviour of negation as failure can be described by the following Prolog program:

```
not(Q)  :- Q, !, fail.
not(Q).
```

The procedural negation as failure is known to have two important drawbacks: it can only be used safely on ground subgoals and on some particular types of non-ground goals, and it cannot generate any new bindings for query variables (if the execution of not (Q) succeeds, the variables occurring in Q are not instantiated). The behaviour of negation as failure is unsound and it corrupts the declarative character of logic programs as it is illustrated in Section 2.1.5. A sufficient condition to have a sound negation as failure is that the negation applies to a ground literal. This soundness condition can be checked by the abstract interpretation framework, by considering the output substitution of the abstract sequence corresponding to the program point situated just before the call to the negation.

Also, the termination of the negation as failure not (Q) depends on the termination of the query Q. If Q terminates, so does not (Q). If Q does not terminate, then not (Q) may or may not terminate depending on whether a solution is found during the execution of Q.

Negation as failure with delays

The technique of negation as failure can be adapted to a sound version by using delay directives (e.g., when), to ensure that the call to negation as failure is made only when the variables of the negated goal are ground [107]. A call to not (q(X)) is replaced by the goal when (ground(X), not (q(X))). So, for instance, in the context of the program P of previous section, the execution of when (ground(X), not (q(X))), p(X) delays the execution of not (q(X)) so that the negation is executed after the call to p(X). Negation with delay is sound but incomplete: it is well-known that it has the risk of floundering if the arguments of the negation never become ground. It is present in Nu-Prolog [108], Gödel [68], and Prolog systems which implement delays.

In order to eliminate delays, techniques can be used which, given a program with delays, try to identify those that are not needed, perhaps after some safe reordering of literals, as described in [117]. Such techniques are based on groundness analysis (e.g., [105]). Even if our abstract interpretation framework does not describe the behaviour of delay declarations, it provides enough information to detect whether delay conditions are satisfied or not, so that the optimiser could safely eliminate or shift such delay declarations (see Section 4.6 and Chapter 9).

Intensional negation

Intensional negation uses a different approach to handle negation [10, 11]. It consists of obtaining a program that is a transformation of the original program P which introduces the 'only if' part of the predicate definitions (i.e., interpreting implications as equivalences). For instance, the transformation of the following program (from [10]):

```
even(o).
even(s(s(X)))  :- even(X).
```

yields a new predicate not__even that is the *complement* of even (i.e., that succeeds when even fails):

```
not__even(s(o)).
not__even(s(s(X)))  :- not__even(X).
```

The difficulty with such a negation technique is that the new program needs to handle some kinds of universal quantification construct, when there are logical variables in the body of a clause. For instance, consider the program (from [98]):

```
has_even(L)  :- member(X, L), even(X).
```

The transformed code representing not(has_even(L)) will be:

```
not__has_even(L)  :-
    forall([X], (not__member(X, L) ; not__even(X))).
```

where the forall/2 predicate implements the universal quantification, and ; is the disjunction.

Constructive negation

The constructive negation scheme, proposed by Chan [21, 22] and formalised in the context of CLP by Stuckey [125], removes the main drawbacks of negation as failure because constructive negation can handle non-ground negative subgoals and generates new bindings for query variables.

When the negated goal Q has a finite number of answers, then the constructive negation can be performed as follows. Firstly, the solutions of Q are obtained, getting a disjunction $S_1 \vee ... \vee S_n$. Each component S_i can be understood as a conjunction of equalities $S_i^1 \wedge ... \wedge S_i^{m_i}$. Then, the formula is negated and a normal form constraint is obtained:

$$
\begin{aligned}
\neg Q \quad &\equiv \quad \neg(S_1 \vee ... \vee S_n) \\
&\equiv \quad \neg S_1 \wedge ... \wedge \neg S_n \\
&\equiv \quad \neg(S_1^1 \wedge ... \wedge S_1^{m_1}) \wedge ... \wedge \neg(S_n^1 \wedge ... \wedge S_n^{m_n}) \\
&\equiv \quad (\neg S_1^1 \vee ... \vee \neg S_1^{m_1}) \wedge ... \wedge (\neg S_n^1 \vee ... \vee \neg S_n^{m_n})
\end{aligned}
$$

For instance, consider the program:

```
less(o,s(Y)).
less(s(X),s(Y))  :- less(X,Y).
```

Then, the constructive negation not(less(X,s(s(o)))) will give the solutions $\neg$ X=o $\wedge$ $\neg$ X=s(o).

If Q has infinitely many answers, then a full constructive negation is needed. In order to compute not(Q), an SLD computation for the goal Q is started. A frontier of Q is a finite set of nodes (which are goals) of the SLD resolution tree such that every resolution branch of Q is either a failure or passes through exactly one node in the set. A frontier can be expressed as $\{(\theta_1, Q_1), ..., (\theta_m, Q_m)\}$, where each θ_i is a substitution and Q_i is a subgoal. Any frontier can be interpreted as the logic formula $(\theta_1 \wedge Q_1) \vee ... \vee (\theta_m \wedge Q_m)$ (viewing substitutions as equalities) that is equivalent to the original goal Q. The constructive negation of Q is obtained by negating the frontier formula.

Combination of negation techniques using abstract interpretation

The authors of [98, 101] propose a strategy to combine all the above techniques to get a system to handle general negation. They use the preprocessor CiaoPP [66] to choose which techniques to apply. In particular, a groundness analysis is used to check soundness of negation as failure [105]. A technique is used to eliminate delays when they are not necessary, by possibly reordering literals [117]. To determine finiteness in the number of solutions, the upper bounds complexity and execution cost analysis can be used, to decide whether either the finite or the full constructive negation can be applied [40].

4.1.2 Inaccuracies in the basic framework

Our abstract interpretation framework is based on the standard semantics of Prolog with no delay declarations. In what follows, we consider negation as failure only, which is the most common negation technique used in Prolog. The basic framework can be used to check that a negation is sound, by checking that its arguments are sufficiently instantiated. However, the behaviour of a negation as failure cannot be described accurately. In particular, the basic framework is usually unable to prove the determinacy or the sure success of the execution of a procedure containing a negation as failure.

Consider the predicate delete(Xs,X,Ys) that holds iff Ys is the list Xs where all occurrences of X have been removed from Xs.

```
delete([], X, []).
delete([X|Xs], X, Ys) :- delete(Xs, X, Ys).
delete([X|Xs], Z, [X|Ys]) :- not(X=Z),
                             delete(Xs, Z, Ys).
```
Procedure 4.1 delete(Xs,X,Ys)

Consider that the procedure is called when input Xs is a ground list, X is a ground term, and Ys is a variable. The expected behaviour in such conditions can be described by the following formal specification:

```
delete/3
  in(Xs:ground list, X:ground, Zs:var)
  out(_, _, Zs:ground list)
  sol(sol = 1)
  sexpr(< Xs >)
```
Specification 4.1   `delete(Xs,X,Ys)`

The output Zs becomes a ground list and the procedure is fully-deterministic. In order to check the specification, the checker abstractly executes a normalised version of the procedure:

```
delete(X1,X2,X3):-₁ X1=[]₂, X3=[]₃ .₄
delete(X1,X2,X3):-₅ X1=[X2|X4]₆,
                    delete(X4,X2,X3)₇ .₈
delete(X1,X2,X3):-₉ X1=[X4|X5]₁₀, X3=[X4|X6]₁₁,
                    not(X2=X4)₁₂,
                    delete(X5,X2,X6)₁₃ .₁₄
```

Checking soundness of negation

The computed abstract sequence $B11$, corresponding to the program point 11 situated just before the negation `not(X2=X4)`, contains the following information:

```
B11:
  ref(X1:[ground|ground list],X2:ground,X3:var)
  out(X1:[X4:ground|X5:ground list],
      X2:ground,
      X3:[X4:ground|X6:var],
      X4:ground, X5:ground list, X6:var)
  sol(sol = 1)
```

At that program point, by considering the `out` part of $B11$, the analyser is able to check that $X2$ and $X4$ are ground terms, so that the negation `not(X2=X4)` is sound.

Checking sure success

The abstract sequence $B12$ after the execution of the negation is:

```
B12:
  ref(X1:[ground|ground list],X2:ground,X3:var)
  out(X1:[X4:ground|X5:ground list],
      X2:ground,
      X3:[X4:ground|X6:var],
      X4:ground, X5:ground list, X6:var)
  sol(0 =< sol =< 1)
```

The `ref` and `out` parts of B12 are the same as the ones of B11. However, because the negation may fail for such input conditions, the number of solutions is now zero or one (0 =< sol =< 1). The abstract sequence B14 modelling the execution of the third clause is thus:

```
B14:
   ref(X1:[ground|ground list],X2:ground,X3:var)
   out(X1:[X4:ground|ground list],
       X2:ground,
       X3:[X4:ground|ground list])
   sol(0 =< sol =< 1)
```

It results that the sure success of the whole procedure cannot be proved in the basic framework.

Checking determinacy

To verify the whole procedure, the analyser concatenates the abstract sequences modelling the execution of the three clauses (and in particular, it starts by concatenating the last two clauses). The abstract execution of the second clause yields the abstract sequence B8:

```
B8:
   ref(X1:[X2:ground|ground list],X2:ground,X3:var)
   out(X1:[X2:ground|ground list],
       X2:ground,
       X3:ground list)
   sol(sol = 1)
```

The second clause is fully-deterministic if and only if the input list X1 is a nonempty list whose first element is the input X2. This is expressed by the `ref` part of B8. The concatenation between the two abstract sequences B8 and B14 models the behaviour of the two first clauses:

```
CONC(B8,B14):
   ref(X1:[ground|ground list],X2:ground,X3:var)
   out(X1:[ground|ground list],
       X2:ground,
       X3:ground list)
   sol(0 =< sol =< 2)
```

The exclusivity between the two clauses cannot be checked, because the intersection between the concretisation of the `ref` parts of B8 and B14 is not empty:

the `ref` part of B8 is included in the `ref` part of B14. Therefore, the checker sums the number of solutions of each clause, and the upper bound is 2. Thus, the basic framework is unable to prove that the procedure is deterministic.

4.1.3   Modelling sure failure conditions in abstract sequences

As it is illustrated in the previous section, the basic framework is usually unable to prove the sure success and determinacy of a procedure using negation. To overcome such inaccuracies, abstract sequences are enhanced with a new *failure* component that imposes additional conditions on input arguments for which the execution surely fails. The language of formal specifications (that represents abstract sequences in a syntax more convenient for the user) has been enriched with a new optional tag `fail` corresponding to the failure component. This new component allows us to model accurately the execution of negation as failure. For instance, the execution of the negation `not(X1=X2)` when input X1 and X2 are ground terms can be described by the following abstract sequence `Bnot`:

```
Bnot:
    in(X1:ground, X2:ground)
    fail(X1:ground, X2=X1:ground)
    sol(sol = 1)
```

The above abstract sequence captures the exact behaviour of the negation: it is fully deterministic (`sol = 1`) if and only if X1 and X2 do not respect the conditions imposed by the failure component `fail`, i.e., if and only if X1 and X2 are not the same term.

Definition 4.1

   Formally, an abstract sequence B is now defined as a tuple of the form $\langle \beta_{in}, \beta_{ref}, \beta_{fails}, \beta_{out}, E_{ref\_out}, E_{sol} \rangle$, where β_{fails} is a set of abstract substitutions whose domains are $dom_{in}(B)$. The failure component β_{fails} imposes additional conditions over the pairs $\langle \theta, S \rangle$ of $Cc(B)$ as follows. For all $\theta \in Cc(\beta_{in})$, if there exists an abstract substitution $\beta_f \in Cc(\beta_{fails})$ such that $\theta \in Cc(\beta_f)$, then $S = <>$. Importantly, the size components E_{ref_out} and E_{sol} apply only on every input substitution θ satisfying $Cc(\beta_{ref})$, and such that θ does not belong to the concretisation of any β_f in β_{fails}. Constraints only deal with successful executions. In the rest of this document, the concretisation of the set β_{fails}, denoted by $Cc(\beta_{fails})$, is defined by $\bigcup_{\beta_f \in \beta_{fails}} Cc(\beta_f)$.

   Thanks to this new *failure* abstract component, the checker is now able to verify Specification 4.1 of the procedure `delete(Xs,X,Ys)`. In particular, the analyser checks the sure success of the execution, and it verifies that the procedure is deterministic.

Checking sure success thanks to the failure component

The abstract sequence B12 after the execution of the negation not(X2=X4) is
now:

```
B12:
   ref(X1:[ground|ground list], X2:ground,X3:var)
   fail(X1:[X2:ground|ground list],X2:ground,X3:var)
   out(X1:[X4:ground|X5:ground list],
       X2:ground,
       X3:[X4:ground|X6:var],
       X4:ground, X5:ground list, X6:var)
   sol(sol = 1)
```

There is exactly one solution for any input X1 that is a non-empty list (this is expressed by the ref component), and such that the first element of X1 is not the
input X2 (this is expressed by the fail component). It follows that the third
clause surely succeeds for those input conditions, which is expressed by the abstract sequence B14:

```
B14:
   ref(X1:[ground|ground list],X2:ground,X3:var)
   fail(X1:[X2:ground|ground list],X2:ground,X3:var)
   out(X1:[X4:ground|ground list],
       X2:ground,
       X3:[X4:ground|ground list])
   sol(sol = 1)
```

The sol part only concerns inputs satisfying the ref component but not satisfying the fail component. If the input does not satisfy the ref part or satisfies
the fail part, then the number of solutions is zero.

Checking determinacy thanks to the failure component

The analyser is now able to prove that the two abstract sequences B8 (modelling
the execution of the second clause) and B14 (modelling the execution of the third
clause) are exclusive: they cannot both succeed for the same input substitution.
Indeed, because the ref part of B8 is the same as the fail part of B14, then
the two clauses are exclusive. The checker finally concludes that the procedure is
deterministic.

4.1.4 Pre-ordering on abstract sequences with the failure component

The pre-ordering relation $\leq$ between two abstract sequences has to be refined to
consider the new failure component. Let $B_1, B_2 \in \texttt{ASeq}_D$. We have $B_1 \leq B_2$ if

the conditions defined so far are satisfied (see Section 3.4.5), and if the following
two additional conditions hold:

$$(*) \quad \forall \beta_f^2 \in \beta_{fails}^2 : \beta_f^2 \sqcap \beta_{ref}^1 = \bot \vee \exists \beta_f^1 \in \beta_{fails}^1 : \beta_f^2 \leq \beta_f^1$$
$$(*) \quad E_{sol}^2 \leq \{[\![sol \geq 1]\!]\} \Rightarrow \beta_{ref}^1 = \beta_{ref}^2 \wedge \beta_{fails}^1 = \beta_{fails}^2$$

The first condition expresses that each failure component of B_2 must be described
by B_1. The second condition applies when the refined and failure components
of B_2 are an exact description of the sure success. In that case, the refined and
failed components of B_1 and B_2 must coincide.

For instance, consider the following two abstract sequences B_1 and B_2:

```
B1:                                    B2:
    in(ground,any)                         in(ground,any)
    ref(a, _)                              fail(c, _)
    fail(_, ground)                        fail(_, d)
    sol(sol =< 1)                          sol(sol >= 0)
```

We have that $B_1 < B_2$, because the first condition on the failure components
is satisfied: `fail(c,_)` is incompatible with `ref(a,_)`, and `fail(_,d)` is
included in `fail(_,ground)`.

4.1.5   Abstract execution with negations

The abstract execution of a clause `analyse_clause`, explained in Section 3.5,
is modified to take into account negated literals (the new algorithm is depicted
in Figure 4.1, page 89). In case the next literal to be executed l_k is a negation
of the form `not(l)`, where l is a literal, then the abstract sequence B_{aux}^k, which
models the execution of the literal l_k, is computed through the new abstract operation NOT_AI$(\beta_{inter}^k, l_k, SBeh) = \langle success_k, B_{aux}^k, sound\_neg \rangle$, where $SBeh$ is
the family of behaviours attached to the procedures in the program. This operation
is responsible for checking that the negation is sound (boolean $sound\_neg$), i.e.,
by ensuring that the program variables occurring in the inner literal l are bound to
ground terms. This operation computes the *failure* component of B_{aux}^k attached
to the negation as follows. The checker first executes the inner literal l with in-
put β_{inter}^k, resulting in the abstract sequence $B_l = \langle \beta_{inter}^k, \beta_{ref}^l, ..., E_{sol}^l \rangle$. The
failure component β_{fails} of B_{aux}^k is the β_{ref}^l component of B_l, provided that this
refined component of B_l is an exact description of the sure execution of l, i.e.,
$E_{sol}^l \leq \{[\![sol \geq 1]\!]\}$. In that case, the negation is fully deterministic if and only if
the inputs in β_{inter}^k do not satisfy the conditions imposed by β_{ref}^l.

The abstract operation EXTG that extends the result of the execution of the literal l_k (described by B_{aux}^k) into the abstract sequence B_{k-1} (corresponding to the
program point before the literal l_k) also has to be refined. In particular, the failure component of B_{aux}^k must be propagated inside B_{k-1}, yielding the abstract sequence B_k.

The abstract concatenation CONC is also modified to deal with the new failure components. In particular, the β_{fails} components must be considered for detecting the exclusivity between abstract sequences (see Section 6.3), and for proving the sure success of the execution (see Section 6.4).

4.1.6 Further extensions

Consider the predicate remove_red(Xs,Rs) that holds iff Rs is the list Xs where every redundant element of Xs has been removed.

```
member(X, [X|Ys]).
member(X, [Y|Ys]) :- not(X=Y), member(X,Ys).

remove_red([X|Xs], Rs)  :- member(X, Xs),
                               remove_red(Xs, Rs).
remove_red([X|Xs], [X|Rs]) :- not(member(X, Xs)),
                               remove_red(Xs, Rs).
remove_red([],[]).
```
Procedure 4.2 remove_red(Xs,Rs)

The desirable behaviour can be specified as follows when input Xs is a ground list, and when input Rs is a variable.

```
remove_red/2
  in(Xs:ground list, Rs:var)
  out(_, ground list)
  sol(sol = 1)
  sexpr(< Xs >)
```
Specification 4.2 remove_red(Xs,Rs)

The formal specification for the subprocedure member(X,Xs) is

```
member/2
  in(X:ground, Xs:ground list)
  out(_, ground list)
  sol(sol =< 1)
  sexpr(< Xs >)
```
Specification 4.3 member(X,Xs)

The analyser cannot prove that the first two clauses of remove_red are exclusive (and therefore, that the procedure is deterministic). Indeed, the abstract sequence corresponding to the first clause is B1.

```
B1:
  ref(X1:[ground|ground list],X2:var)
  out(X1:[ground|ground list],X2:ground list)
  sol(sol =< 1)
```

Abstract sequences are not expressive enough to describe the sure execution of the negation not(member(X,Xs)) with the *failure* component. The abstract sequence corresponding to the second clause is thus identical to B2.

A solution to remedy this problem is to refine the ref and fail components by maintaining the set of relations that must hold between the terms in order to have a sure success (or a sure failure) of the execution. With such information, one can compute the following two abstract sequences corresponding to the execution of the first two clauses of remove_red:

```
B1:
    ref(X1:[X3:ground|X4:ground list],X2:var;
        relation(member(X3,X4)) )
    out(X1:[ground|ground list],X2:ground list)
    sol(sol = 1)

B2:
    ref(X1:[ground|ground list],X2:var)
    fail(X1:[X3:ground|X4:ground list],X2:var;
        relation(member(X3,X4)) )
    out(X1:[ground|ground list],X2:ground list)
    sol(sol = 1)
```

The new tag relation specifies the set of relations that must hold between the terms described in the abstract substitutions (in the in and in the fail parts). Because the ref part of B1 and the fail part of B2 are identical, then the two clauses are exclusive, and the system is able to prove the determinacy. Furthermore, the number of solutions has been refined to take into account the relation property, and the sure success of the clauses can be proved.

Definition 4.2
    The following definition depends on the program P that is currently analysed. Formally, the abstract tuple α of a substitution β over the set of indices I is now defined as a tuple of the form $\langle mo, ty, ps, rels \rangle$. The new *relations* component *rels* is a set of constructs of the form $q(i_1, ..., i_n)$, where q is a predicate symbol of arity n that belongs to the program P, and where $i_1, ..., i_n$ are indices of I. The *relations* component imposes additional conditions between the terms of substitutions described by the abstract substitution. Let $\theta \in Cc(\beta)$, and let $\langle t_i \rangle_{i \in I} = \text{DECOMP}(\theta, \beta)$. Then, for each $q(i_1, ..., i_n) \in rels$, the execution of the query $q(t_{i_1}, ..., t_{i_n})$ surely succeeds in the program P.

The *rels* component of abstract tuples should only be maintained for a procedure that contains negation of the form $\text{not}(q(X_{i_1}, ..., X_{i_n}))$. This extension is not easy to implement, because the property of sure success of a query is not decidable in general, and because we need to justify that abstract operations with such a new component still remain correct (i.e., that they are sound w.r.t. the standard semantics of Prolog).

4.2 Cuts

This section presents the extensions of the basic framework to handle cuts. First, Section 4.2.1 refines the way we express the concrete execution for procedures, clauses, and prefixes of clauses that contain cuts. Then, Section 4.2.2 illustrates how the analyser detects whether a cut is *green*. Finally, Section 4.2.3 describes the domain that maintains the conditions on input substitutions such that a cut is surely executed for such substitutions.

4.2.1   Concrete execution of clauses with cut flag

When a procedure, a clause, or a prefix of a clause contains some cuts, we have to consider whether the cut has been executed or not. So, the way to express the concrete execution (see Section 3.2.3) has to take into account the information about the execution of a cut. We use the notations of [79].

Definition 4.3
    A *substitution sequence with cut information* is a pair $\langle S, cf \rangle$ where S is a program substitution sequence (in PSS) and the *cut flag* cf is either *cut* or *nocut*.

Execution of a prefix of a clause with cut

Let c be a clause of arity n such that the program variables occurring in c are $X_1, ..., X_m$ ($n \leq m$). Let g be a prefix goal of the clause c. Let θ be a program substitution whose domain is $\{X_1, ..., X_m\}$. The execution of the goal g with input θ is described by:

$$\langle \theta, g, c \rangle \mapsto_P \langle S, cf \rangle$$

where S is the answer substitution sequence (as it is defined in Section 3.2.3) and cf is the cut flag describing whether a cut has been surely executed or not during the execution of g. Assume that the literal to be executed after the goal g in c is a cut, then only the first substitution of S is conserved. If $S = < \theta_1, ..., \theta_k >$ ($k \geq 1$), then we have:

$$\langle \theta, (g, !), c \rangle \mapsto_P \langle < \theta_1 >, cut \rangle$$

Otherwise, if $S = <>$ then we have:

$$\langle \theta, (g, !), c \rangle \mapsto_P \langle <>, cf \rangle$$

Execution of a clause with cut

Let c be a clause of arity n that contains some cut. Let θ be an input program substitution over domain $\{X_1, ..., X_n\}$. The concrete execution of c with input θ is denoted by:

$$\langle \theta, c \rangle \mapsto_P \langle S, cf \rangle$$

where S is the answer substitution sequence (as it is defined in Section 3.2.3), and where the value of the cut flag cf is cut (resp., $nocut$) implies that some cut of the clause c has been surely executed (resp., surely not executed). Note that, if there are several cuts in a clause, the cut flag cf attached to the execution of the clause only depends on the execution of the leftmost cut in the clause.

Execution of a procedure with cut

Let pr be a procedure that contains some cut. Let θ be an input program substitution for this procedure. The execution of the procedure can be described as follows. If the procedure pr is composed of a unique clause c, then:

$$\langle \theta, pr \rangle \mapsto_P S$$

where $\langle \theta, c \rangle \mapsto_P \langle S, cf \rangle$. Otherwise, if the procedure pr is of the form $c\ pr'$ (c is the first clause of pr and pr' is the sequence of clauses that follows c in pr), then:

$$\langle \theta, pr \rangle \mapsto_P \langle S, cf \rangle \Box S'$$

where $\langle \theta, c \rangle \mapsto_P \langle S, cf \rangle$, where $\langle \theta, pr' \rangle \mapsto_P S'$, and where operation $\Box$ denotes the concatenation between a substitution sequence with cut information and a substitution sequence without cut information. Formally, the operation $\Box$ is defined as follows:

$$\langle S, cf \rangle \Box S' \quad = \quad \begin{array}{ll} S & \textbf{if } cf = cut \\ S :: S' & \textbf{otherwise} \end{array}$$

4.2.2   Checking green cuts: exclusivity and determinacy

Green cut characterisation

A cut is *green* if it does not remove any solution in the procedure execution. In other words, the execution of the procedure with the green cut and the execution of the procedure without the green cut produce the same answer substitution sequence (for the same input substitution).

Let pr be a procedure (with arity n) of the form $c_1 \ldots c_k \ldots c_r$. Assume that the clause c_k is of the form $h\ :-\ g_1, !, g_2.$, where h is the head of the clause and where g_1 and g_2 are the goals before and after the cut, respectively. Let θ be an input program substitution over domain $\{X_1, ..., X_n\}$. Assume that the execution of the prefix goal g_1 with input θ is as follows:

$$\langle \theta, g_1, c \rangle \mapsto_P \langle S_{g_1}, cf_{g_1} \rangle$$

Assume that the execution of the clause c_i with input θ is as follows ($1 \leq i \leq r$):

$$\langle \theta, c_i \rangle \mapsto_P \langle S_i, cf_i \rangle$$

The cut of the clause c_k in the procedure pr is a green cut for input θ if the following two conditions hold:

(1) the execution of the goal g_1 is deterministic for θ, i.e., $0 \leq Ns(S_{g_1}) \leq 1$;

(2) for all $i \in \{k+1, ..., r\}$, the goal g_1 is exclusive with the clause c_i for input θ, i.e., the execution of g_1 and of c_i with input θ cannot both succeed. In other words, we have either $S_k = <>$, or $S_i = <>$, or both $S_k = <>$ and $S_i = <>$.

The above conditions are sufficient (but not necessary) to characterise that a cut is green. When encountering a cut, those two conditions are checked by the analyser, as it is illustrated on the following example.

Checking green cuts: illustrating example

Consider the procedure `efface(X,T,TEff)`, seen in Section 2.2, describing a relation that holds iff X is an element of the list T and if TEff is the list T without the first occurrence of X.

```
efface(X,[X|T],T)   :- !.
efface(X,[H|T],[H|TEff])   :- not(X=H),
                             efface(X,T,TEff).
```
Procedure 4.3   `efface(X,T,TEff)`

Assume that input X is a ground term, T is a ground list, and TEff is a variable. The behaviour corresponding to such inputs can be specified as follows:

```
efface/3
   in(X:ground, T:ground list, TEff:var)
   out(_, _, ground list)
   sol(sol =< 1)
   sexpr(< T >)
```
Specification 4.4   `efface(X,T,TEff)`

The analyser is able to detect that the cut executed in the first clause is a *green* cut because the abstract sequence at the program point before the cut is deterministic (1) and it is exclusive with the abstract sequence of the second clause (2).

The abstract sequence B_before_cut corresponding to the program point just before the cut looks like:

```
B_before_cut:
   ref(X1:ground,X2:[X1:ground|ground list],X3:var)
   out(X1:ground,X2:[X1:ground|ground list],
       X3:ground list)
   sol(sol = 1)
```

Condition (1) holds at the view of the `sol` part of this abstract sequence. The cut is surely executed if the input terms satisfy the conditions described by the `ref` part of `B_before_cut`. The abstract execution of the second clause yields the abstract sequence `B_clause2`:

```
B_clause2:
  ref(X1:ground,X2:[ground|ground list],X3:var)
  fail(X1:ground,X2:[X1:ground|ground list],
       X3:var))
  out(X1:ground,X2:[ground|ground list],
       X3:ground list)
  sol(sol =< 1)
```

The `ref` part of `B_before_cut` and the `fail` part of `B_clause2` are identical, such that the two abstract sequences are exclusive. Thus, Condition (2) holds and the system proves that the cut is *green*.

4.2.3   Dealing with red cuts: sure execution of cuts

A cut is called *red* if it is not *green*.

Red cuts: illustrating example

If one of the two conditions characterising a *green* cut is not satisfied, then the system has possibly detected a *red* cut. For instance, consider the following version of `efface(X,T,TEff)` where the negation has been removed.

```
efface(X,[X|T],T) :- !.
efface(X,[H|T],[H|TEff]) :- efface(X,T,TEff).
```
Procedure 4.4   `efface(X,T,TEff)`

Specification 4.4 still holds for this code. The analyser checks that the cut is *red* because Condition (2) is not satisfied. The abstract sequence corresponding to the program point before the cut is not exclusive with the abstract sequence modelling the second clause.

Maintaining information about the sure execution of cuts

The abstract sequence modelling the execution of a clause is enhanced with additional information about the execution of a cut. The additional information describes the input conditions for which a cut has been surely executed or not inside the clause. The notion of *abstract sequence with cut information* is defined as follows.

Definition 4.4

Let D be a set of program variables. Formally, an *abstract sequence with cut information* C over domain D is a tuple of the form $\langle B, acf, \beta_{cut}, \beta_{nocuts} \rangle$. B is an abstract sequence from ASeq_D; acf is *the abstract cut flag* whose value belongs to $\{nocut, cut, weakcut\}$; β_{cut} is an abstract substitution from AS_D and β_{nocuts} is a set of abstract substitutions from AS_D. The components β_{cut} and β_{nocuts} are defined only if the value of the flag acf is either *cut* or *weakcut*. Otherwise, those components have the special value *undef*. In what follows, if the component β_{nocuts} is defined, then the notation $Cc(\beta_{nocuts})$ is used to represent its concretisation, which is defined by $\bigcup_{\beta \in \beta_{nocuts}} Cc(\beta)$. The set of abstract sequences with cut information is denoted by ASeqC, and the set of abstract sequences with cut information over the domain D is denoted by ASeqC_D. The concretisation of an abstract sequence with cut information $C = \langle B, acf, \beta_{cut}, \beta_{nocuts} \rangle$, denoted by $Cc(C)$, represents a set of tuples $\langle \theta, S, cf \rangle$ such that:

- the input substitution θ and its related output substitution sequence S satisfy the constraints of the abstract sequence B, i.e., $\langle \theta, S \rangle \in Cc(B)$;

- if $acf = nocut$ then no cut is executed for any input θ, i.e., $cf = nocut$;

- if $acf = cut$ then a cut is surely executed if and only if the input substitution θ satisfies the conditions of β_{cut} and does not satisfy the conditions imposed by the abstract substitutions β_{nocuts}, i.e.,

$$\left. \begin{array}{l} \theta \in Cc(\beta_{cut}) \\ \theta \notin Cc(\beta_{nocuts}) \end{array} \right\} \Leftrightarrow cf = cut;$$

- if $acf = weakcut$ then the β_{cut} and β_{nocuts} components impose necessary (but not sufficient) conditions for the sure execution of a cut, i.e.,

$$cf = cut \Rightarrow \left\{ \begin{array}{l} \theta \in Cc(\beta_{cut}) \\ \theta \notin Cc(\beta_{nocuts}) \end{array} \right.$$

The extended analyser now annotates each clause c of a procedure with such an abstract sequence with cut information. The notion of *annotated clause* that safely approximates the execution of a clause (see Section 3.5.4) is refined as follows.

Definition 4.5

Let pr be a procedure in the program P, and let c be a clause of the procedure pr that possibly contains a cut, and let β_{in} be an input abstract substitution for the clause c. An *annotated clause* of the clause c with input β_{in}, denoted by $\tilde{c}$, is enhanced with an abstract sequence with cut information C as follows:

$$(\beta_{in})h \text{:} -(B_0)\tilde{l}_1, (B_1)..., (B_{s-1})\tilde{l}_s(B_s). \ (C)$$

Such an annotated clause is a safe approximation of the clause c with input β_{in} as it is defined in Section 3.5.4; and the abstract sequence with cut information C

models the execution of the clause and the sure execution of the cut as follows. Let $\theta \in Cc(\beta_{in})$ and consider the execution of the clause $\langle \theta, c \rangle \mapsto_P \langle S, cf \rangle$. Then, the tuple $\langle \theta, S, cf \rangle$ belongs to $Cc(C)$.

If the abstract cut flag acf of C has the value cut, then every clause that follows the clause c in the procedure pr is never executed for any input substitution θ satisfying β_{cut} and not satisfying β_{nocuts}. Thus, this information can be used to refine the execution of successive clauses. Clauses that follow a clause with a cut can be reexecuted with refined inputs (those that do not satisfy β_{cut} or those that satisfy one of the β_{nocuts}), such that more accurate cardinality information can be checked (see Section 6.4 and Section 6.5).

Abstract execution with cuts

The abstract algorithm `analyse_procedure` explained in Section 3.5 is modified for detecting whether a cut is green or not, and for keeping information about the execution of cuts inside a clause. A procedure is checked by executing its clauses from the last clause to the first clause, instead of the original top-down order, so that the analyser is able to maintain the set $SuccBs$ that contains the abstract sequences modelling the already executed clauses (i.e., the clauses that follow the currently analysed clause in the procedure). The availability of $SuccBs$ allows the checker to verify that a cut is green (see Section 4.2.2). The new algorithm of `analyse_procedure` is depicted in Figure F.1, page 268.

The abstract execution of a clause `analyse_clause`, introduced in Section 3.5, is refined as follows (the new abstract execution algorithm is depicted in Figure 4.1).

When the checker encounters a cut in the current clause, then the two sufficient conditions characterising green cuts are verified (see Section 4.2.2). This is performed by the new abstract operation $\text{CUT\_AI}(B_{k-1}, SuccBs) = \langle B_k, green\_cut \rangle$, where B_{k-1} is the abstract sequence corresponding to the program point before the execution of the cut. This operation computes the abstract sequence B_k corresponding to the program point after the cut, by restricting the number of solutions expressed in the E_{sol} component of B_{k-1} to be at most one. The boolean $green\_cut$ with the value $true$ implies that the cut is green. Note that the detection of exclusivity between abstract sequences, needed for detecting whether a cut is green, can be refined by considering the new abstract domains, and in particular, the new *failure* component of abstract sequences (see Section 6.3). In order to build the abstract sequence with cut information modelling the execution of the clause, the operation $\text{CUT\_FLAG}(B_{k-1})$ computes the abstract cut flag acf and the conditions of sure execution of the cut (β_{cut} and β_{nocuts}).

The abstract concatenation operation CONC, realised after the abstract execution of all the clauses of the procedure, is also modified to take into account the execution of cuts in clauses and to model accurately the concrete operation $\square$ between sequences (see Section 6.4).

PROCEDURE analyse_clause$(c, B, se, SBeh, SuccBs)$ =
   $\beta_{in} \leftarrow input(B)$
   $\langle acf, \beta_{cut}, \beta_{nocuts} \rangle \leftarrow \langle nocut, undef, undef \rangle$
   $B_0 \leftarrow$ EXTC(c, β_{in})
   for $k \leftarrow 1$ **to** s **do**
     if $l_k = !$
     then
        $\langle B_k, green\_cut \rangle \leftarrow$ CUT_AI$(B_{k-1}, SuccBs)$
        if $acf = nocut$
           $\langle acf, \beta_{cut}, \beta_{nocuts} \rangle \leftarrow$ CUT_FLAG(B_{k-1})
     else
       $\beta^k_{inter} \leftarrow$ RESTRG(l_k, B_{k-1})
       switch (l_k) **do**
         case $X_{i_1} = X_{i_2}$:
           $B^k_{aux} \leftarrow$ UNIF_VAR(β^k_{inter})
         case $X_{i_1} = f(X_{i_2}, \ldots, X_{i_m})$:
           $B^k_{aux} \leftarrow$ UNIF_FUNC(β^k_{inter}, f)
         case $q(X_{i_1}, \ldots, X_{i_m})$ **and** $q \neq p$:
           $\langle success_k, B^k_{aux} \rangle \leftarrow$ LOOKUP$(\beta^k_{inter}, q, SBeh)$
         case $p(X_{i_1}, \ldots, X_{i_n})$:
           $B^k_{aux} \leftarrow B$
           $success_k \leftarrow$ CHECK_TERM$(l_k, B_{k-1}, se) \wedge \beta^k_{inter} \leq \beta_{in}$
         case not(l):
           $\langle success_k, B^k_{aux}, sound\_neg \rangle \leftarrow$ NOT_AI$(\beta^k_{inter}, l_k, SBeh)$
       $B_k \leftarrow$ EXTG$(l_k, B_{k-1}, B^k_{aux})$
   if there exists k **in** $\{1, ..., s\}$ **such that**
     either $l_k ::= q(X_{i_1}, \ldots, X_{i_m}) \wedge \neg success_k$
     or $l_k ::= p(X_{i_1}, \ldots, X_{i_n}) \wedge \neg success_k$
     or $l_k ::=$ not$(l) \wedge \neg success_k$
    then $success \leftarrow false$
    else $success \leftarrow true$ **and** $B_{out} =$ RESTRC(c, B_s)
   return $\langle success, \langle B_{out}, acf, \beta_{cut}, \beta_{nocuts} \rangle \rangle$

Figure 4.1: Algorithm for the abstract execution of a clause with cut information and with negations.

Illustrating example: modelling execution of cuts

Consider the following procedure:

```
p(X,Y,Z,W) :- not(X=a), Y=b, !, Z=c, !, W=d.
p(X,Y,Z,W) :- Z=e, W=f, !.
p(X,Y,Z,W) :- X=a, W=g.
```

Assume that input X, Y, and Z are ground terms and that input W is any term. The abstract sequence with cut information $C_i = \langle B_i, acf_i, \beta^i_{cut}, \beta^i_{nocuts} \rangle$ models the execution of the ith clause as follows ($1 \le i \le 3$).

$$C_3 : \quad B_3 \quad : \quad \begin{array}{l} \texttt{in(X:ground,Y:ground,Z:ground,W:any)} \\ \texttt{ref(a,\_,\_,\_)} \\ \texttt{out(a,\_,\_,g)} \\ \texttt{sol(sol =< 1)} \end{array}$$

$$\begin{array}{l} acf_3 \quad : \quad nocut \\ \beta^3_{cut} \quad : \quad undef \\ \beta^3_{nocuts} \quad : \quad undef \end{array}$$

No cut is executed in the last clause ($acf_3 = nocut$). Furthermore, the input X must be the constant a for the execution of the third clause to succeed (see the ref component of B_3).

$$C_2 : \quad B_2 \quad : \quad \begin{array}{l} \texttt{in(X:ground,Y:ground,Z:ground,W:any)} \\ \texttt{ref(\_,\_,e,\_)} \\ \texttt{out(\_,\_,e,f)} \\ \texttt{sol(sol =< 1)} \end{array}$$

$$\begin{array}{l} acf_2 \quad : \quad weakcut \\ \beta^2_{cut} \quad : \quad \texttt{(X:ground,Y:ground,Z:e,W:any)} \\ \beta^2_{nocuts} \quad : \quad \{\} \end{array}$$

The cut in the second clause is a *weakcut*. It may be not executed. However, a necessary (but not sufficient) condition for its execution is expressed by the β^2_{cut} and β^2_{nocuts} components: the input argument Z must be the constant e.

$$C_1 : \quad B_1 \quad : \quad \begin{array}{l} \texttt{in(X:ground,Y:ground,Z:ground,W:any)} \\ \texttt{ref(\_,b,c,\_)} \\ \texttt{fail(a,\_,\_,\_)} \\ \texttt{out(a,b,c,d)} \\ \texttt{sol(sol =< 1)} \end{array}$$

$$\begin{array}{l} acf_1 \quad : \quad cut \\ \beta^1_{cut} \quad : \quad \texttt{(X:ground,Y:b,Z:ground,W:any)} \\ \beta^1_{nocuts} \quad : \quad \{\texttt{(X:a,Y:ground,Z:ground,W:any)}\} \end{array}$$

The leftmost cut in the first clause is surely executed ($acf_1 = cut$) if and only if input Y is the constant b (see component β^1_{cut}) and if input X is not the constant a (see component β^1_{nocuts}).

4.3 Disjunction and 'if then else'

4.3.1 Disjunctive constructs

Most Prologs allow the programmer to use the construct $g_1; g_2$ (where g_1 and g_2 are goals) to define disjunctions between literals inside a clause. For instance, consider the procedure `red_white_blue_list(Xs)` that tests whether `Xs` is a list whose elements are either `red`, `white` or `blue`.

```
red_white_blue_list([]).
red_white_blue_list([X|Xs]) :-
  (X=red; X=white; X=blue),
  red_white_blue_list(Xs).
```

Procedure 4.5 `red_white_blue_list(Xs)`

Consider that input `Xs` is a ground list, and see how the analyser proves the following specification:

```
red_white_blue_list/1
  in(Xs:ground list)
  sol(sol =< 1)
  sexpr(< Xs >)
```

Specification 4.5 `red_white_blue_list(Xs)`

The analyser does not abstractly execute Procedure 4.5, but instead another equivalent code, where the disjunctive goal (`X=red; X=white; X=blue`) has been replaced by a call to a new fresh subprocedure (not yet occurring in the program), namely `red_white_blue(X)`. The program variables occurring in the head of `red_white_blue(X)` are all the program variables occurring in the disjunction. Each clause of the new subprocedure corresponds to one part of the disjunctive goal. This syntactical source-to-source transformation yields the following procedure:

```
red_white_blue(red).
red_white_blue(white).
red_white_blue(blue).

red_white_blue_list([]).
red_white_blue_list([X|Xs]) :-
  red_white_blue(X),
  red_white_blue_list(Xs).
```

Procedure 4.6 `red_white_blue_list(Xs)`

The checker abstractly executes Procedure 4.6 instead of Procedure 4.5. Before the call to `red_white_blue(X)` in the second clause, the abstract sequence verified by the analyser is `B_before`:

```
B_before:
  ref([X:ground, Xs:ground list])
  out([X:ground, Xs:ground list], X:ground)
  sol(sol = 1)
```

At that program point, from the out part of B_before, the analyser detects that red_white_blue(X) is called when X is a ground term. Because there exists no formal specification for red_white_blue(X) (this part of code has been automatically generated by the analyser), the checker abstractly executes the sub-call with the input in(X:ground). This input corresponds to the abstract substitution β_{inter}^k in the abstract execution algorithm explained in Section 3.5.3. The analyser can infer the specification of predicates that are not recursive. The subprocedure is not a recursive one, so that the system is able to infer the following formal specification modelling the execution of red_white_blue(X) when input X is ground[1]:

```
red_white_blue/1
  in(X:ground)
  sol(sol =< 1)
```
Specification 4.6   red_white_blue(X)

The analyser then continues the abstract execution of Procedure 4.6 using the generated Specification 4.6, and is thus finally able to verify Specification 4.5.

4.3.2   'If Then Else' constructs

Most Prologs allow the programmer to use the constructs 'If Then' $(g_1 -> g_2)$ and 'If Then Else' $(g_1 -> g_2; g_3)$, where g_1, g_2 and g_3 are goals. For instance, consider the procedure substitute(X, Y, L1, L2) that describes the relation that holds iff L2 is the list L1 where each occurrence of X has been replaced by Y (the elements of L1 distinct from X are left unchanged in L2).

```
substitute(X,Y,[],[]).
substitute(X,Y,[H1|T1],[H2|T2]) :-
  (    X=H1
  ->   H2=Y
  ;    H2=X ),
  substitute(X,Y,T1,T2).
```
Procedure 4.7   substitute(X,Y,L1,L2)

In order to analyse such a code, the checker replaces the conditional goal by a call to a new fresh subprocedure that does not occur in the program, namely update(X, Y, H1, H2). The program variables occurring in the head of update are all the program variables occurring in the conditional goal.

---

[1] Specification 4.6 can be refined thanks to the new type system (see Section 5.2).

```
update(X,Y,H1,H2) :- X=H1, !, H2=Y.
update(X,Y,H1,H2) :- H2=X.

substitute(X,Y,[],[]).
substitute(X,Y,[H1|T1],[H2|T2]) :-
  update(X,Y,H1,H2),
  substitute(X,Y,T1,T2).
```
Procedure 4.8 `substitute(X,Y,L1,L2)`

Consider that inputs X and Y are ground terms, that input L1 is a ground list, and that input L2 is a variable. The system is able to check Procedure 4.8 according to the following formal specification.

```
substitute/4
  in(X:ground, Y:ground, L1:ground list, L2:var)
  out(_, _, _, ground list)
  srel(L1_in = L2_out)
  sol(sol = 1)
  sexpr(< L1 >)
```
Specification 4.7 `substitute(X,Y,L1,L2)`

The abstract sequence corresponding to the program point just before the call to `update(X,Y,H1,H2)` is B_before:

```
B_before:
  ref(X:ground, Y:ground,
      L1:[ground|ground list],
      L2:var)
  out(X:ground, Y:ground,
      L1:[H1:ground|T1:ground list],
      L2:[H2:var|T2:var],
      H1:ground, T1:ground list,
      H2:var, T2:var;
      noshare(<H2,T2>))
  sol(sol = 1)
```

Thus, `update(X,Y,H1,H2)` is called when X, Y, and H1 are ground terms, and when H2 is a variable. There exists no specification for the new subprocedure update. It has been automatically generated by the analyser. The checker executes `update(X,Y,H1,H2)` with input:

```
in(X:ground,Y:ground,H1:ground,H2:var)
```

The analyser generates and verifies the following specification:

```
update/4
   in(X:ground, Y:ground, H1:ground, H2:var)
   out(_, _, _, ground)
   sol(sol = 1)
```
Specification 4.8   update(X,Y,H1,H2)

The analyser has checked that the conditional part X=H1 of the construct is called with ground terms and that its execution is deterministic, such that the conditional construct is sound. The checker then continues the abstract execution of Procedure 4.8 by using Specification 4.8, and the verification succeeds.

As another example and similarly, the analyser can check that Procedure 4.9, which is the version of efface(X,T,TEff) using an 'If Then Else' construct, satisfies Specification 4.4.

```
efface(X,[H|T],TEff)  :-
   (   X = H
   ->  T = TEff
   ;   TEff = [H|TEffs]
       efface(X,T,TEffs)
   ).
```
Procedure 4.9   efface(X,T,TEff)

4.4   Dynamic predicates

This section discusses the treatment of dynamic predicates, and next sections discuss how the framework can be used to deal with meta-calls and dynamic scheduling. Dealing with such features allows the analyser to accept the full dialect of Prolog. Dealing with full Prolog is also one of the objectives of the preprocessor CiaoPP [66] (see, in particular, [18]).

In Prolog, programmers can use some extralogical features like dynamic predicates. The built-in assert/1 adds a new clause (the input argument) at the bottom of the corresponding procedure, and the built-in retract/1 (resp., retract_all/1) removes from some existing procedure the first clause (resp., all clauses) whose head unifies with the input argument. Usually, a procedure of name p and arity n that is used in such built-ins must be declared as a *dynamic* procedure with the directive :- dynamic p/n.

In the new framework, the user must specify the way a dynamic predicate can be called (at least one specification is attached to each dynamic predicate). The new flag dynamic is used in a formal specification to denote that the specification refers to a dynamic predicate. The built-ins assert/1 and retract/1 must also be specified by the user in order to describe what is the instantiation level of the input clauses that can be asserted or retracted during the execution. Usually, the analyser cannot prove the accurate number of solutions for a procedure using dynamic predicates, because new clauses can be dynamically inserted or removed from the database, such that the number of solutions can be modified. However, the system is able to check that every call to a dynamic predicate corresponds to the `in` part of one of its specifications. Also, the analyser is still able to verify accurately the procedures of the program that are not involved with dynamic predicates.

4.4.1 Illustrating example

As an example, consider the problem `hanoi(N,A,B,C,Moves)` resolving the 'Towers of Hanoi' puzzle. `Moves` is the sequence of moves required to move `N` disks from peg `A` to peg `B` using peg `C` as an intermediary according to the rules of the Towers of Hanoi puzzle. There are two rules. Only one disk can be moved at a time, and a larger disk can never be placed on top of a smaller disk. The number of disks `N` is represented as follows: `o` denotes zero, `s(o)` denotes one, `s(s(o))` denotes two, etc.

We provide here a solution of the Towers of Hanoi, inspired from [124]. Memoisation is used to speed up the program by storing the results of procedure calls for later reuse, rather than recomputing them at each invocation of the procedure. In this case, it consists in repeatedly solving subproblems moving the identical number of disks. The built-in `assert/1` is used to recall the moves made in solving each subproblem of moving a smaller number of disks. Later attempts to solve the subproblem can use the computed sequence of moves rather than recomputing them. In the last clause, the first recursive call to solve `hanoi` is remembered, and can be used by the second call to `hanoi`.

```
:- dynamic hanoi/5.

hanoi(o,A,B,C,[]).
hanoi(s(N),A,B,C,Moves) :-
    hanoi(N,A,C,B,Ms1),
    assert(hanoi(N,A,C,B,Ms1)),
    hanoi(N,C,B,A,Ms2),
    append(Ms1,[to(A,B)|Ms2],Moves).

test_hanoi(N,Pegs,Moves) :-
    hanoi(N,A,B,C,Moves), Pegs=[A,B,C].
```
Procedure 4.10 `hanoi(N,A,B,C,Moves)`

The program is tested with the predicate `test_hanoi(N,Pegs,Moves)`. The argument `N` is the number of disks; `Pegs` is the list of the three peg names; and `Moves` is the list of moves that must be made. Note that in order to take advantage of memoisation through the built-in `assert/1`, a general problem is solved first. Only when the solution is complete, and all built-ins `assert/1` have recorded their results, the peg names are instantiated.

The expected behaviour for the procedure `hanoi` is described by the following formal specification, which is tagged with the label `dynamic`:

```
dynamic hanoi/5
  in(N:ground,A:var,B:var,C:var,Moves:var;
     noshare(<A,B,C,Moves>))
  out(N:_,A:_,B:_,C:_,Moves:list;
     noshare(<A,B,C>))
```
Specification 4.9   `hanoi(N,A,B,C,D,Moves)`

In order to check the procedure `hanoi`, the user must provide the following specification for the built-in `assert/1`, which expresses the kind of clauses the built-in accepts.

```
assert/1
  in(Clause:hanoi(N:ground,A:var,B:var,C:var,
                  Moves:list);
     noshare(<A,B,C>))
  out(_; noshare(<A,B,C>))
  sol(sol = 1)
```
Specification 4.10   `assert/1`

4.4.2   Further extensions to the framework

The actual framework is inaccurate to prove termination and to prove cardinality information of a procedure using dynamic predicates. To remedy this problem, the following solution can be used. A dynamic predicate has several so-called *dynamic specifications*. Every such a specification has a special status - either *enabled* or *disabled* - such that only one of them is enabled at a time and can be used by the analyser. A dynamic specification can switch its status, by becoming enabled or disabled, during the abstract execution of the built-ins `assert/1` or `retract/1` (and more generally, during the execution of the procedures using such built-ins). To describe this behaviour, the formal specification language is enriched with a new tag `dynamic` inside the `in` or `out` parts of a specification, that lists the dynamic specifications that are currently activated (before or after the execution).

Consider for instance the following program:

```
:- dynamic memo/1.

p :- read(Y), assert(memo(Y)).
q :- retract_all(memo(_)).
test(X) :- p, memo(X), q.
```
Procedure 4.11   `p/0, q/0, test/1`

The procedure `p` reads a term `Y` and asserts it into the dynamic procedure `memo/1`. The user provides the following two dynamic specifications, identified by `memo[1]` and `memo[2]`, such that only one of them is enabled at a time of the execution.

```
dynamic memo[1]              dynamic memo[2]
   in(X:var)                    in(X:var)
   sol(sol = 0)                 sol(sol >= 1)
```
Specification 4.11 memo/1

The first specification describes the situation where there is currently no clause of memo/1 in the database constituting the program. The second specification describes the situation where memo/1 is composed of at least one clause.

The built-ins assert/1 and retract_all/1 can be specified as follows:

```
assert/1                         retract_all/1
   in(Clause:memo(any))             in(Clause:memo(var))
   out(_;dynamic(memo[2]))          out(_;dynamic(memo[1]))
   sol(sol = 1)                     sol(sol = 1)
```
Specification 4.12 assert/1, retract_all/1

Note the new flag dynamic in the out part of the specifications, that lists the new dynamic specifications that are enabled (the other ones are disabled). In particular, after the execution of a call to assert(memo(X)), then the second specification of memo/1 is enabled while the first one is disabled. The reverse case happens for the execution of retract_all(memo(_)).

The auxiliary input/output built-in can be specified as follows:

```
read/1
   in(X:var)
   sol(sol = 1)
```
Specification 4.13 read/1

The procedure p/0, q/0 and test/1 can be accurately specified and checked as follows:

```
p/0
   in()
   out(dynamic(memo[2]))
   sol(sol = 1)

q/0
   in()
   out(dynamic(memo[1]))
   sol(sol = 1)

test/1
   in(X:var)
   sol(sol >= 1)
```
Specification 4.14 p/0, q/0, test/1

In particular, the analyser is able to prove the sure success of the execution of test(X) when input X is a variable.

4.5 Higher-order predicates

A feature of Prolog is the equivalence of programs and data. Both can be represented by terms, and a term can be converted into a goal. For instance, the system predicate call(X), where X is a term, calls Prolog to solve the converted goal X. In practice, most Prolog implementations relax the restriction that the literals in the body of a clause must be non-variable terms. The *meta-variable facility* allows a variable to appear in the body of the goal. During the computation, by the time it is called, the variable must be instantiated to a term. It is then treated as usual. If the variable is not instantiated when it comes to be called, then an error is reported.

4.5.1 Illustrating example

The extended framework now accepts Prolog program using such meta-variable facility. For instance, Procedure 4.10 can be rewritten as follows.

```
:- dynamic hanoi/5.

lemma(P) :- P, assert(P).

hanoi(o,A,B,C,[]).
hanoi(s(N),A,B,C,Moves) :-
    lemma(hanoi(N,A,C,B,Ms1)),
    hanoi(N,C,B,A,Ms2),
    append(Ms1,[to(A,B)|Ms2],Moves).
```
Procedure 4.12   hanoi(N,A,B,C,Moves)

The higher-order procedure lemma(P) attempts to prove the goal P and, if successful, stores the result of the proof as a lemma. The formal specification of lemma is as follows:

```
lemma/1
    in(P:hanoi(N:ground,A:var,B:var,C:var,Moves:var);
        noshare(<A,B,C,Moves>))
    out(P:hanoi(N:ground,A:var,B:var,C:var,
                Moves:list);
        noshare(<A,B,C>))
```
Specification 4.15   lemma/1

The analyser is able to prove that the procedure lemma(P) satisfies Specification 4.15. In particular, before the call to the meta-variable P, the analyser can check that P is bound to a term of the form $hanoi(t_n, t_a, t_b, t_c, t_{moves})$, where t_n is a ground term, and where t_a, t_b, t_c, t_{moves} are distinct variables. Those argument terms satisfy the `in` part of Specification 4.9. So, that specification can be used and the abstract execution continues.

Together with Specification 4.10, the analyser is able to prove Specification 4.9 for Procedure 4.12.

4.5.2 Abstract execution with meta-calls

The abstract execution algorithm `analyse_clause` for verifying a clause in a procedure, depicted in Figure 4.1 is augmented in order to execute meta-calls. If the next literal l_k to be checked is a meta-variable, the framework executes the new abstract operation $\text{AI\_META\_CALL}(\beta_{inter}^k, l_k, SBeh) = \langle success_k, B_{aux}^k \rangle$, where β_{inter}^k is the output abstract substitution, restricted (and renamed) to the program variable l_k, of the abstract sequence B_{k-1} that is situated before the meta-call. The boolean $success_k$ is true if the meta-variable l_k is sufficiently instantiated in β_{inter}^k and corresponds to a specification inside the family of behaviours $SBeh$. If such a specification can be applied, then it is used to compute the abstract sequence B_{aux}^k, modelling the execution of the meta-call.

4.5.3 Further extensions

The actual framework is accurate when the frame attached to the meta-calls are known statically. It is more intricate to prove the procedures that perform meta-calls without knowing statically which procedure is attached to them.

For instance, consider the procedure `execute_goals(Ps)`, that executes every predicate belonging to the list `Ps`.

```
execute_goals([]).
execute_goals([P|Ps]) :- P, execute_goals(Ps).
```
Procedure 4.13 `execute_goals(Ps)`

In the basic framework, one can specify that procedure as follows:

```
execute_goals/1
  in(Ps:list)
  sexpr(< Ps >)
```
Specification 4.16 `execute_goals(Ps)`

The current framework is unable to check such a specification, because the frame of the meta-call `P` in the second clause is never known. A solution to this problem may consist in allowing the user to specify that the *type* of an argument of the procedure is a predicate satisfying some given specification, or, in the example `execute_goals(Ps)`, that the type of `Ps` is a list of predicates, each of them satisfying some general specification.

4.6 Dynamic scheduling

The first logic programming languages use a fixed scheduling rule, in which all atoms in a goal are processed left-to-right. Unfortunately, this means that programs written in a declarative style are not always operationally correct (see Section 2.1). With such a scheduling rule, a program only terminates when certain inputs are ground, and it can produce wrong results if negation as failure is used. For this reason, there has been widespread interest in a class of 'second generation' logic programming languages, such as NU-Prolog, SICstus-Prolog, Ciao, etc., that provide more flexible scheduling in which computation generally proceeds left-to-right, but in which some calls are dynamically 'delayed' until their arguments are sufficiently instantiated to allow the call to run correctly. Such dynamic scheduling overcomes the problems associated with traditional Prologs and their fixed scheduling. It allows the same program to have many different operational semantics as the operational behaviour depends on which arguments are supplied the query. Also, the treatment of negation as failure becomes sound, as negative calls are delayed until all arguments are ground. However, dynamic scheduling can yield in 'floundering', i.e., the program never produces a solution, since the conditions of the delay declarations are never satisfied. Furthermore, dynamic scheduling has a significant cost: goals, if affected by a delay declaration, must be checked to see whether they should delay or not. Upon variable binding, possibly delayed calls must be put in a 'pending' list, so that they are woken before the next goal to be executed. Space needs to be allocated for delayed goals until they are woken [20].

It is not easy to extend our abstract interpretation framework for traditional Prolog to a language with dynamic scheduling, as, in our framework, the fixed left-to-right scheduling rule is crucial to ensure correctness and termination. Frameworks for global analysis of logic programs with dynamic scheduling are proposed in [5, 92]. Even if we have not extended our framework to safely and accurately handle dynamic scheduling, it can be used to perform some optimisation, by eliminating delay conditions when it is not needed and/or producing reorderings in which dynamic scheduling is not needed any more, as it is done for instance in [117]. Such an optimisation technique could be integrated to our optimiser (see Chapter 9).

Chapter 5

Additional abstract domains – more expressive specifications

This chapter presents the new domains of abstract substitutions, which make formal specifications more expressive. Section 5.1 introduces the new component of linearity, that is instrumental for proving the occur-check freeness of unification. The basic framework considers a poor system of types (it is only accurate for describing lists and terms instantiable to a list). Section 5.2 extends the type system by defining new primitive types for handling numbers, and by allowing the user to declare its own parametric types. Instantiations of such parametric types, called *type expressions*, can be used in specifications. The basic framework only considers the list-length as the unique size measure that can be used in the srel and sol parts of a specification. Section 5.3 presents the new primitive norms and functions, and illustrates how the user can declare its own norms and functions.

All those improvements allow the user to describe more specialised behaviours, such that the analysis is more accurate.

5.1 Linearity

Section 5.1.1 illustrates the interest of the new domain of linearity for proving occur-check freeness of a program. Section 5.1.2 defines the new domain of linearity, that is integrated into the abstract tuple in abstract substitutions. Section 5.1.3 shows how the linearity component interacts with the other domains composing an abstract substitution. Finally, Section 5.1.4 formally describes how the checker proves that a unification is not subject to the occur-check.

5.1.1 Illustrating example

Consider Procedure 2.4 append(X1,X2,X3) when inputs X1 and X2 are any terms, X3 is a (possibly non-ground) list, and such that the three input arguments

do not share any variable. The behaviour of the procedure can be described by the
following formal specification:

```
append/3
    in(X1:any, X2:any, X3:list; noshare(<X1,X2,X3>))
    out(list, list, _)
    srel(X1_out+X2_out = X3_in)
    sol(sol =< X3_in+1)
    sexpr(< X3 >)
```
Specification 5.1 append(X1,X2,X3)

As expected, the analyser is able to check Specification 5.1, but it cannot prove
that the procedure is occur-check free. Several unifications performed during the
execution may indeed be subject to the occur-check. The checker abstractly executes the normalised version of Procedure 2.4:

```
append(X1, X2, X3):-₁ X1=[]₂, X3=X2₃ .₄
append(X1, X2, X3):-₅ X1=[X4|X5]₆, X3=[X4|X6]₇,
                              append(X5, X2, X6)₈ .₉
```

The abstract sequence computed after the first unification is B2:

```
B2:
    in(X1:any,X2:any,X3:list; noshare(<X1,X2,X3>))
    out(X1:[],X2:any,X3:list; noshare(<X2,X3>))
    sol(sol =< 1)
```

The next unification X3=X2 of the first clause is not occur-check free. Indeed, by
considering the out part of B2, the analyser knows that X2 and X3 do not share
a variable, that X2 is bound to any term, and that X3 is bound to any list. For instance, it may thus happen that X2 is bound to $[y, y]$ (where y is a standard variable)
and that X3 is bound to the list $[x, f(x)]$ (where x is a standard variable distinct
from y). The execution of X3=X2 without occur-check unifies x with $f(x)$, which
is operationally incorrect. In the second clause, the abstract sequence B5 is:

```
B5:
    in(X1:any,X2:any,X3:list,X4:var,X5:var,X6:var;
        noshare(<X1,X2,X3,X4,X5,X6>))
    out(X1:any,X2:any,X3:list,X4:var,X5:var,X6:var;
        noshare(<X1,X2,X3,X4,X5,X6>))
    sol(sol = 1)
```

The unification X1=[X4|X5] is occur-check free because, in the out part of B5,
X4 and X5 are two distinct variables that do not occur in X1. The next abstract
sequence B6 is computed:

```
B6:
  in(X1:any,X2:any,X3:list,X4:var,X5:var,X6:var;
     noshare(<X1,X2,X3,X4,X5,X6>))
  out(X1:[X4:any|X5:any],X2:any,X3:list,
      X4:any,X5:any,X6:var;
      noshare(<X1,X2,X3,X6>))
  sol(sol =< 1)
```

At that program point, X3 is any list, X4 is any term, and X6 is a variable. The unification X3=[X4|X6] is not occur-check free. For instance, X3 may be bound to $[f(x,x)]$ (where x is a standard term), X4 may be bound to $f(y,g(y))$ (where y is a standard variable distinct from x), and X6 is bound to z (where z is a standard variable distinct from x and y). In such a situation, the unification X3=[X4|X6] results in unifying y with $f(y)$, which is operationally unsound.

The correct code of append(X1,X2,X3) for Specification 5.1 would be:

```
append([], X2, X3) :-
  unify_with_occurs_check(X3, X2).
append([X4|X5], X2, X3) :-
  unify_with_occurs_check(X3, [X4|X6]),
  append(X5, X2, X6).
```

where the built-in unify_with_occurs_check(X,Y) is assumed to perform the unification between X and Y with the occur-check. Its formal specification is as follows[1]:

```
unify_with_occurs_check/2
  in(X:any, Y:any)
  out(X:_, X:_)
  sol(sol =< 1)
```

Specification 5.2 unify_with_occurs_check(X,Y)

The necessary conditions for detecting whether a unification is occur-check free have been investigated by many researchers (e.g., [6, 36]). An important property to be considered is the linearity of terms. A term is linear if each variable of the term occurs at most once in the term. Consider the unification X=Y. If either X or Y is linear and if X and Y do not share a variable, then the unification is occur-check free.

The language of formal specifications has been extended to allow the user to specify that an argument is linear. For instance, the user can now write the following specification for append:

---

[1]Specification 5.2 of the builtin unify_with_occurs_check(X,Y) is not as accurate as the abstract unification operations, namely UNIF_VAR and UNIF_FUNC (see Section 3.5.1 and [33, 53, 78, 80]). Therefore, the best way to abstraclty execute such a builtin is to use these abstract unification operations, but by disabling occur-check.

```
append/3
  in(X1:any, X2:any, X3:list;
     linear(X3);
     noshare(<X1,X2,X3>) )
  out(list, list, _)
  srel(X1_out+X2_out = X3_in)
  sol(sol =< X3_in+1)
  sexpr(< X3 >)
```
Specification 5.3   `append(X1,X2,X3)`

The new tag `linear` in the `in` part of Specification 5.3 describes that the input argument `X3` is bound to a linear term. Such a tag may also occur in the `ref` or in the `out` parts of a specification. The checker is able to prove that Procedure 2.4 respects Specification 5.3, and it proves that the procedure is occur-check free under those input conditions.

5.1.2   Definition of the new domain of linearity

The abstract tuple α of an abstract substitution $\beta = \langle sv, frm, \alpha \rangle$ has been extended with a new linearity component lin.

Definition 5.1

The *linearity* component lin specifies the set of terms that are surely linear. A term t is linear if each variable in $vars(t)$ occurs only once in t. For any set of indices I, we denote by Lin_I the set of all subsets of I, augmented with $\perp$. The semantics of an element $lin \in \mathrm{Lin}_I$ is given by the following concretisation function $Cc : \mathrm{Lin}_I \to 2^{T^I}$. If $lin = \perp$ then $Cc(lin) = \emptyset$. Otherwise,

$$Cc(lin) = \{ \langle t_i \rangle_{i \in I} \in T^I \mid \forall i \in I : i \in lin \Rightarrow t_i \text{ is a linear term} \}$$

In the rest of this document, $lin(i)$ denotes that the index i belongs to lin and $\neg lin(i)$ denotes that the index i does not belong to lin.

5.1.3   Cooperation between the linearity domain and the frame, mode and possible sharing domains

Together with the *frame*, the *mode*, and the *possible sharing* components of an abstract substitution, the *linearity* component allows us to deduce the actual linearity information.

Let $\beta = \langle sv, frm, \alpha : \langle mo, ty, ps, lin \rangle \rangle \in \mathrm{AS}_{D,I}$. For all $i, i_1, ..., i_m \in I$ such that $frm(i) = f(i_1, ..., i_m)$, the following equivalence holds:

$$lin(i) \Leftrightarrow \begin{cases} lin(i_k) & \forall 1 \leq k \leq m \\ \neg ps(i_k, i_l) & \forall 1 \leq k < l \leq m \end{cases}$$

This means that a compound term is linear if and only if its subterms are linear and do not share a variable between them. The subterms of a linear compound term forms a so-called *linear family* of terms.

Furthermore, each ground term or variable is linear, such that for all $i \in I$, $mo(i) \leq$ gv implies $lin(i)$, where gv denotes the 'ground or variable' mode.

5.1.4 Proving occur-check freeness of unification

The tool can prove the occur-check freeness of unification thanks to the cooperation between the frame, the mode, the possible sharing and the linearity components of abstract substitutions.

Let $B = \langle \beta_{in}, \beta_{ref}, \beta_{out} : \langle sv, frm, \langle mo, ty, ps, lin \rangle \rangle, ... \rangle$ be the abstract sequence corresponding to the program point situated just before a unification *unif*.

If the unification *unif* is of the form $X_i = X_j$, then it is occur-check free if one of the two following conditions holds:

- $mo(sv(X_i)) = mo(sv(X_j)) = \text{var}$
- $\neg ps(sv(X_i), sv(X_j)) \ \wedge \ (lin(sv(X_i)) \vee lin(sv(X_j)))$

If the unification *unif* is of the form $X_i = f(X_{i_1}, ..., X_{i_m})$, then it is occur-check free if the following condition is satisfied:

- $\neg ps(sv(X_i), sv(X_k)) \ (1 \leq k \leq m) \ \wedge \ (lin(sv(X_i)) \vee lin(f(X_{i_1}, ..., X_{i_m})))$

where

$$lin(f(X_{i_1}, ..., X_{i_m})) \Leftrightarrow \begin{cases} lin(sv(X_{i_k})) & \forall 1 \leq k \leq m \\ \neg ps(sv(X_{i_k}), sv(X_{i_l})) & \forall 1 \leq k < l \leq m \end{cases}$$

5.2 Types

The basic framework defines a simple type system (see Section 3.3.4): only lists, terms instantiable to a list, and unrestricted terms are considered. Consequently, the original analyser is only accurate for program using lists. This section presents the new type system that is integrated into the framework.

New primitive (or base) types have been defined to handle integers (int) and floats (float), as well as to represent unrestricted terms (ground for ground terms or any for possibly non-ground terms). Additionally, the user can declare its own parametric types. The type declarations are provided by the user besides the input program and the formal specifications to be verified. A type declaration defines a function which, given a set of terms that is associated to each type parameter, produces a new set of terms. The types that are used in formal specifications and that are assigned to each term and subterm of an abstract sequence are called *type expressions*. A type expression represents a set of (possibly non-ground) terms. Type expressions are not parametric: they are primitive types, or they are constructed by using the name of a parametric type declaration and by replacing the type parameters by primitive types or by other type expressions. There are an infinite number of type expressions.

Our type expressions can be related to the type graphs of G. Janssens and M. Bruynooghe [69] (see also A. Cortesi et al. [31]). As in such works, our type declarations and type expressions use the modes `ground` and `any` as primitive types. However, the mode `var` (denoting the set of all variables) is not defined as a primitive type. The authors of [69] have extended the notion of type graphs to integrate the mode `var` as a primitive type (such type graphs are called *integrated type graphs*). In our framework, modes (including `var`) are combined with types at the abstract substitution level. Note that types and modes are also combined with the other components of an abstract substitution (namely, the same-value, the frame, the possible sharing, and the linearity components, see Section 3.3). To the contrary of [69], the type expressions that are derived during our abstract execution are built on the primitive types and on the declared types only. So, every term in a substitution that cannot be described within a type declaration is approximated by the most accurate primitive type whose concretisation contains that term (e.g., `ground` or `any`). In our approach, the user has only to declare the types for which he is interested. When the type of a term cannot be described by a user-declared type, this means that the user does not want to have an accurate information about the type of that term, or this indicates that there is perhaps a bug in the program. Furthermore, in order to avoid combinatorial explosion problems arising in type graphs, the user is required to declare disjoint types (i.e., principal functors of two types must be distinct). These constraints (the user has to declare the types for which he want to maintain some accurate information, and two declared types must be disjoint) both greatly simplify the implementation of abstract operations on type expressions, making them accurate and efficient, in comparison with the complexity of abstract operations in [69] and in [31]. For instance, the least upper bound of type expressions (used for concatenating abstract sequences) and the greatest lower bound of type expressions (used for performing abstract unification between two (abstract) terms) are implemented without the need of any widening techniques as it is done in [31, 69].

The use of parametric type declarations and type expressions has also similarities with the type and mode system of Mercury [123]. In Mercury, the state of instantiation of a program variable at some program point is described by a so-called *instantiatedness tree*, which is the counterpart of a type expression in our framework (see Section 2.5.2 for details). Like in our system, an instantiatedness tree is built on primitive types and on parametric type declarations (provided by the user). Mode information is integrated in each node of such trees, denoting whether the (sub)term corresponding to that node is a *free* variable or is *bound* to some functor. In our system, the mode `var`, which corresponds to the Mercury mode *free*, is not a primitive type and cannot be used directly in type expressions.

However, the mode `any`, which denotes the set of any terms, can be used in our type expressions but is not available in Mercury.

Our parametric type declarations can also be related to regular types [48, 119], which are notably used in CiaoPP [66] (see Section 2.4.4 for details). As it is the case in CiaoPP, the constructors in a type declaration must be distinct (this restriction is also called the *principal functor restriction* in [31]). The types are thus *tuple-distributive*. I.e, if the concretisation of a type contains two terms with the same principal functor (for instance, $f(a, b)$ and $f(c, d)$), then necessarily, it contains terms with the same principal functor obtained by exchanging subterms of the two terms in the same argument positions (in this case, it contains also the terms $f(c, b)$ and $f(a, d)$).

The rest of this section is organised as follows. Section 5.2.1 shows the inaccuracies and the limitations of the type system of the basic framework. The main features of the new type system, which overcome the limitations of the basic framework, are illustrated in the next four sections: Section 5.2.2 presents the new *primitive types*, Section 5.2.3 gives some examples of *parametric type declarations* that are provided by the user, Section 5.2.4 illustrates the *type expressions* that are used into formal specifications, and Section 5.2.5 motivates the design of so-called *selection type expressions* that allows the analyser to concatenate abstract sequences accurately. Then, the next four sections formally provide: the syntax of parametric type declarations (Section 5.2.6), the denotation of such type declarations (Section 5.2.7), the syntax of type expressions (Section 5.2.8), and the denotation of type expressions (Section 5.2.9). The last sections present the main abstract operations that are performed on type expressions, which are used during the abstract execution: Section 5.2.10 presents the partial ordering over type expressions, Section 5.2.11 presents an algorithm that normalises type expressions, Section 5.2.12 and 5.2.13 implement the greatest lower bound and the least upper bound of type expressions, respectively.

5.2.1 Inaccuracies of the basic type system

This section shows some procedures for which the basic framework is unable to specify and verify an accurate behaviour due to the limited expressiveness of its type system. The analyser cannot prove the precise number of solutions (especially, the determinacy and the sure success of the execution) to a procedure call using numbers or structures other than lists.

Example 1: specifying `integer`

Test predicates like `integer(X)` cannot be accurately specified in the basic framework. The best way to specify it is as follows:

```
integer/1
  in(X:any)
  ref(ground)
  sol(sol =< 1)
```
Specification 5.4 `integer(X)`

It accepts any term as input and a condition for the sure success of the execution is that X is a ground term. The basic framework cannot specify that the procedure succeeds if and only if input X is an integer.

Example 2: specifying `colour_index`

Consider the procedure `colour_index(X,I)` that associates an integer I to a colour X (a colour is either `blue`, `red` or `white`).

```
colour_index(blue,1).
colour_index(red,2).
colour_index(white,3).
```
Procedure 5.1 `colour_index(X,I)`

When input X is a ground term, and when input I is a variable, the procedure can be specified as follows:

```
colour_index/2
  in(X:ground, I:var)
  out(_, ground)
  sol(sol =< 1)
```
Specification 5.5 `colour_index(X,I)`

The basic checker cannot specify and check that the procedure succeeds if and only if X is a colour, and it cannot specify that output I is an integer.

Example 3: specifying `flattree`

Consider the program `flattree(T,L)`. It describes a relation that holds iff L is the list of the elements of the binary tree T in prefix order.

```
flattree(void, []).
flattree(t(X,LT,RT), [X|Xs]) :-
  flattree(LT, LLT),
  flattree(RT, LRT),
  append(LLT, LRT, Xs).
```
Procedure 5.2 `flattree(T,L)`

This procedure can be used when input T is a ground binary tree and when input L is a variable. In the basic framework, the best way to specify this behaviour is as follows:

```
flattree/2
  in(T:ground, L:var)
  out(_, ground list)
  sol(sol =< 1)
```
Specification 5.6 flattree(T,L)

The input argument T has the mode ground and the type any. The basic framework cannot express that input T is a binary tree and the procedure does not surely succeed for any input ground term T.

A more general way for calling the procedure is when input T is bound to a binary tree that is not necessarily ground, and when input L is a variable that does not occur in T. The output L is then bound to a (possibly non-ground) list. In the basic framework, this kind of calls corresponds to the following formal specification:

```
flattree/2
  in(T:novar, L:var; noshare(<T,L>))
  out(_, list)
  sol(sol =< 1)
```
Specification 5.7 flattree(T,L)

The input binary tree T has the mode novar and the type any. In this case, the checker cannot prove that the two recursive literals are correctly called. In the second clause, after the unification between input argument T and the term t(X,LT,RT), the program variables X, LT, and RT have the mode any. Thus, the recursive literal flattree(LT,LLT) is called when LT is any term, and when LLT is a variable not occurring in LT. Because there is no specification corresponding to this kind of call, the verification of Specification 5.7 fails.

Example 4: specifying deriv

As another example, consider the procedure deriv(F,DF), where DF is the derivative of the expression F.

```
deriv(x, const(1)).
deriv(const(N), const(0)).
deriv(neg(F), neg(DF)) :-
      deriv(F,DF).
deriv(add(F,G), add(DF,DG)) :-
      deriv(F,DF),
      deriv(G,DG).
deriv(mult(F,G), add(mult(F,DG),mult(DF,G))) :-
      deriv(F,DF),
      deriv(G,DG).
deriv(sub(F,G), sub(DF,DG)) :-
      deriv(F,DF),
      deriv(G,DG).
deriv(div(F,G), div(sub(mult(G,DF),mult(F,DG)),
                    mult(G,G))) :-
      deriv(F,DF),
      deriv(G,DG).
```

Procedure 5.3   `deriv(F,DF)`

If we consider the situation where input F is an expression and DF is a variable, the best way to specify the behaviour of the procedure is as follows:

```
deriv/2
  in(F:ground,DF:var)
  out(_,ground)
  sol(sol =< 1)
```

Specification 5.8   `deriv(F,DF)`

With the basic framework, we can only specify that the input F is bound to a ground term (instead of an expression). The procedure does not surely succeed for any input ground term F.

5.2.2   Primitive types

We have extended the type system with primitive types to handle numbers, namely `int` and `float`. With such types, we are able to describe accurately the behaviour of the test predicate `integer(X)`, and Specification 5.4 can be refined as follows:

```
integer/1
  in(X:any)
  ref(int)
  sol(sol = 1)
```

Specification 5.9   `integer(X)`

The built-in `integer(X)` accepts any term as input. It is fully-deterministic if and only if X is an integer.

Definition 5.2

Formally, the set of primitive types, denoted by *TypePrim*, is {bottom, any, int, float, ground}. The semantics of a primitive type *tprim* ∈ *TypePrim* is given by the function $\mathcal{T}\!ype\mathcal{P}rim\,[\![tprim]\!]$ as follows:

$$\mathcal{T}\!ype\mathcal{P}rim : TypePrim \rightarrow 2^{\mathcal{T}}$$

$$
\begin{array}{rcl}
\mathcal{T}\!ype\mathcal{P}rim\,[\![\texttt{bottom}]\!] & = & \emptyset \\
\mathcal{T}\!ype\mathcal{P}rim\,[\![\texttt{any}]\!] & = & \mathcal{T} \\
\mathcal{T}\!ype\mathcal{P}rim\,[\![\texttt{int}]\!] & = & \{t \in \mathcal{T} \mid t \text{ is an integer}\} \\
\mathcal{T}\!ype\mathcal{P}rim\,[\![\texttt{float}]\!] & = & \{t \in \mathcal{T} \mid t \text{ is a float}\} \\
\mathcal{T}\!ype\mathcal{P}rim\,[\![\texttt{ground}]\!] & = & \{t \in \mathcal{T} \mid t \text{ is ground}\}
\end{array}
$$

The framework should be easily extended with other primitive types to make specifications more expressive. For instance, the primitive type num could be defined to denote numbers (either integers or floats), the type atom to denote atoms, the type char to denote characters, etc. Extending the set of primitive types will also improve the analysis accuracy. For instance, the least upper bound of int and float would be num (instead of ground).

5.2.3 Declaring parametric types

The new framework allows the user to declare its own types. For instance, one can define the type colour as follows, where blue, red, and white are the principal functors (i.e., the constructors). The principal functors of a type declaration must be distinct (this is called the *principal functor restriction* in [31]).

```
colour ::= blue | red | white
```
Type definition 5.1   colour

This user type can be used to refine Specification 5.5 as follows:

```
colour_index/2
   in(X:ground, I:var)
   ref(colour, _)
   out(_, int)
   sol(sol = 1)
```
Specification 5.10   colour_index(X,I)

Now, the checker is able to prove that the procedure colour_index(X,I) succeeds exactly once if and only if input X is a colour, and the output argument I has been instantiated to an integer.

The user can also declare parametric types. A parametric type defines a function which, given a set of terms that is associated to each type parameter, produces a new set of terms. For instance, the type list(T) denotes the set of lists whose elements are of type T and the type tree(T) defines the set of binary trees whose elements are of type T. The variable T is called the *type parameter*.

```
list(T) ::= [] | [T|list(T)]
```
Type definition 5.2 list(T)

```
tree(T) ::= void | t(T,tree(T),tree(T))
```
Type definition 5.3 tree(T)

A type for expressions terms that are used in Procedure 5.3 can also be defined as follows:

```
expr(T) ::= x
          |  const(T)
          |  neg(expr(T))
          |  add(expr(T),expr(T))
          |  sub(expr(T),expr(T))
          |  mult(expr(T),expr(T))
          |  div(expr(T),expr(T))
```
Type definition 5.4 expr(T)

5.2.4   Using type expressions in formal specifications

Type expressions are instantiations of parametric types: they are constructed from parametric type declarations by replacing the type parameters by primitive types or by other type expressions. A type expression denotes a set of (possibly non-ground) terms. Type expressions can be used directly into formal specifications. For instance, the type expression list(int) denotes the set of lists of integers; the type expression list(list(any)) denotes the set of lists whose elements are lists of any terms; the type expression tree(ground) denotes the set of binary trees whose elements are ground terms; etc.

With such type expressions, Specification 5.6 can be refined as follows, using the type definitions 5.2 and 5.3:

```
flattree/2
   in(T:tree(ground), L:var)
   out(_, list(ground))
   sol(sol = 1)
```
Specification 5.11 flattree(T,L)

The checker is able to verify that the procedure is fully-deterministic for any input ground binary tree and that L becomes a ground list.

More specialised behaviours can be specified: for instance, when the input T is a binary tree whose elements are lists of integers, then the new checker can check that output L becomes a list whose elements are lists of integers:

```
flattree/2
  in(T:tree(list(int)), L:var)
  out(_, list(list(int)))
  sol(sol = 1)
```
Specification 5.12 flattree(T,L)

Similarly, Specification 5.7 can be refined as follows:

```
flattree/2
  in(T:tree(any), L:var; noshare(<T,L>))
  out(_, list(any))
  sol(sol = 1)
```
Specification 5.13 flattree(T,L)

In this case, the procedure surely succeeds and the argument L is bound to a possibly non-instantiated list after the execution.

Similarly, the analyser can also check the procedure flattree2(T,L), which is another version of Procedure 5.2 (the call to append has been placed before the two recursive calls).

```
append(L1,L2,L3) :- [see Procedure 2.4]

flattree2(void, []).
flattree2(t(X,LT,RT), [X|Xs]) :-
  append(LLT, LRT, Xs),
  flattree2(LT, LLT),
  flattree2(RT, LRT).
```
Procedure 5.4 flattree2(T,L)

That procedure can be checked with respect to the following specification, which describes the other directionality of Specification 5.13.

```
flattree2/2
  in(T:var, L:list(ground))
  out(tree(ground), _)
  sol(sol >= 1)
```
Specification 5.14 flattree2(T,L)

Specification 4.5 of Procedure 4.5 can be refined as follows, using type definitions 5.1 and 5.2:

```
red_white_blue_list/1
  in(Xs:list(ground))
  ref(list(colour))
  sol(sol = 1)
  sexpr(< Xs >)
```
Specification 5.15 red_white_blue_list(Xs)

Similarly, Specification 5.8 of the procedure deriv(F,DF) can be refined as follows, using type definition 5.4:

```
deriv/2
   in(F:expr(int), DF:var)
   out(_, expr(int))
   sol(sol = 1)
```
Specification 5.16   `deriv(F,DF)`

5.2.5   Selection type expressions

This section illustrates a particular kind of type expressions, that we call *selection type expressions*. Selection type expressions are introduced to compute abstract sequence concatenation accurately. Abstract sequence concatenation is used to compute the global abstract sequence modelling the execution of a whole procedure that is composed of several clauses. This operation is defined in details in Section 6.4.

Consider again Procedure 5.1. The abstract sequences modelling each of the three clauses of `colour_index(X,I)` are B1, B2 and B3, respectively:

```
B1:
   ref(X:colour 'blue', I:var)
   out(_, int 1)
   sol(sol = 1)

B2:
   ref(X:colour 'red', I:var)
   out(_, int 2)
   sol(sol = 1)

B3:
   ref(X:colour 'white', I:var)
   out(_, int 3)
   sol(sol = 1)
```

After the abstract execution of the clauses, the checker has to concatenate the abstract sequences (see Section 6.4 and Appendix F for a detailed description of the abstract sequence operation). It first concatenates B2 and B3, yielding the abstract sequence B23 that models the execution of the last two clauses:

```
B23:
   ref(X:colour, I:var)
   out(_, int)
   sol(0 =< sol =< 1)
```

The ref part of B23 is the least upper bound of the ref parts of B2 and B3. In particular, by considering the input X, the upper bound of colour 'red' and colour 'white' is over approximated by the type colour. The type colour is not an exact upper bound of 'red' and 'white' because the colour 'blue' is also considered. Thus, the number of solutions has to be relaxed: the last two clauses may fail (when input X is bound to 'blue'). The checker then concatenates B1 and B23, yielding the abstract sequence B123:

```
B123:
    ref(X:colour, I:var)
    out(_, int)
    sol(0 =< sol =< 2)
```

The exclusivity between B1 and B23 cannot be proved because the frame information of the ref part of B23 has been lost. The abstract sequence B123 does not imply Specification 5.10, so that the verification fails.

To remedy this problem, we define a special kind of type expressions that considers some specific principal functors among the principal functors defined in the corresponding type declaration. Such type expressions are called *selection type expressions*, because they select some subset of the principal functors declared in their corresponding type definition. For instance, the 'selection type expression' (colour ('red'|'white')) denotes the set composed of the two terms red and white only (the principal functors red and white have been selected in the type definition of colour). As another example, the 'selection type expression' (tree ('t/3') (int)) denotes the set of non-empty binary trees whose elements are integers (the principal functor t/3 has been selected in the type definition of tree, and the type parameter has been instantiated to int).

With such type expressions, the analyser is now able to prove Specification 5.10. The abstract sequence B23, which is the result of the abstract concatenation of the last two clauses, is the following:

```
B23:
    ref(X:(colour ('red'|'white')), I:var)
    out(_, int)
    sol(sol = 1)
```

Finally, the abstract concatenation of B1 and B23 becomes:

```
B123:
    ref(X:(colour ('blue'|'red'|'white')), I:var)
    out(_, int)
    sol(sol = 1)
```

Because B123 is equal to Specification 5.10, the verification succeeds.

5.2.6   Well-formed type declarations

This section provides the abstract syntax of parametric type declarations, which are illustrated in Section 5.2.3, as well as additional conditions to have so-called *well-formed* type declarations. The denotation of well-formed type declarations is presented in Section 5.2.7.

Abstract syntax of type declarations

The abstract syntax for type declarations is depicted in Figure 5.1. The set of type declarations is denoted by *TypeDecls*.

tdecls	$\in$	*TypeDecls*			
tdef	$\in$	*TypeDef*	*tdecls*	::=	*tdef**
edef	$\in$	*ExprDef*	*tdef*	::=	*tn* T^* *prf**
T	$\in$	*TypeParam*	*prf*	::=	func f *edef**
prf	$\in$	*PrincipalFunctor*	*edef*	::=	T | *tprim* | *tedef*
f	$\in$	*FunctorName*	*tprim*	::=	bottom | any | ground |
tedef	$\in$	*TypeExprDef*			int | float
tn	$\in$	*TypeName*	*tedef*	::=	type *tn* *edef**
tprim	$\in$	*TypePrim*			

Figure 5.1: Abstract syntax of parametric type declarations.

In what follows, a type definition *tdef* whose name is *tn*, whose type parameters are $T_1, ..., T_n$ and whose declared principal functors are $prf_1, ..., prf_m$, is denoted by *tn* $(T_1, ..., T_n)$ $(prf_1|...|prf_m)$. For instance, the abstract syntax of Type Definition 5.3, denoting the set of binary trees of type T, is *tree* (T) $(prf_1|prf_2)$, where T is the type parameter, where prf_1 is the principal functor func *void*, where prf_2 is the principal functor func $t(T, tedef_2, tedef_3)$, where $tedef_2$ and $tedef_3$ are the same type expression definition type *tree*(T). The symbols func and type in the abstract syntax are used to distinguish principal functors (their associated name f is a constructor of a type) from type expression definitions (their associated name *tn* is the name of a type).

Well-formed type declarations

We impose some syntactic conditions over type declarations to obtain so-called *well-formed type declarations*. Let *tdecls* $\in$ *TypeDecls* be the set of user-declared type definitions, such that:

$$tdecls \quad ::= \quad tn_1 \ (T_1, ..., T_{n_1}) \ (\text{func } f_1^1 \ edefs_1^1|...|\text{func } f_{m_1}^1 \ edefs_{m_1}^1)$$
$$...$$
$$tn_r \ (T_1, ..., T_{n_r}) \ (\text{func } f_1^r \ edefs_1^r|...|\text{func } f_{m_r}^r \ edefs_{m_r}^r)$$

The type declarations *tdecls* are *well-formed* if the following properties hold:

- *Primitive Types Cannot Be Redefined.*
  For all $x \in \{1, ..., r\}$, $tn_x \notin TypePrim$.

- *Principal Functors Must Be Distinct Inside a Type Definition.*
  For all $x \in \{1, ..., r\}$, there is no $i, j \in \{1, ..., m_x\}$ ($i \neq j$) such that $f_i^x = f_j^x$. Due to this *principal functor restriction*, the types are tuple-distributive (see introduction of Section 5.2).

- *Type Parameters Must Be Distinct Inside a Type Definition.*
  For all $x \in \{1, ..., r\}$, $T_i \neq T_j$ ($i, j \in \{1, ..., n_x\}, i \neq j$).

- *Type Parameters Must Be Declared Inside a Type Definition.*
  For all $x \in \{1, ..., r\}$, the set of type parameters occurring in $(\texttt{func}\ f_1^x\ edefs_1^x | ... | \texttt{func}\ f_{m_x}^x\ edefs_{m_x}^x)$ is exactly the set of declared type parameters $\{T_1, ..., T_{n_x}\}$.

- *Parametric Types Must Be Disjoint.*
  For all $x, y \in \{1, ..., r\}$ ($x \neq y$), we have $tn_x \neq tn_y$. Moreover, there is no $i \in \{1, ..., m_x\}$ and no $j \in \{1, ..., m_y\}$ such that $f_i^x = f_j^y$. This condition simplifies the implementation of abstract operations over type expressions, notably the greatest lower bound (see Section 5.2.12) and the least upper bound (see Section 5.2.13) of type expressions.

In what follows, *TypeDecls* always denotes the set of *well-formed* type declarations.

5.2.7 Denotation of type declarations

The denotation of primitive types has been provided in Section 5.2.2 (*TypePrim*). In this section, we first define the denotation of expression definition (elements of *ExprDef*). Then, we give the denotation of principal functors (elements of *PrincipalFunctor*). Finally, we provide the denotation of type definitions and declarations.

Denotation of expression definitions

An expression definition is either a type parameter, or a primitive type, or a type expression definition. It is an argument of a principal functor in a type definition. It denotes a set of terms as follows. The semantics of an expression definition $edef \in ExprDef$ inside a type definition is given by the function $\mathcal{E}xprDef$:

$$\mathcal{E}xprDef : \quad ExprDef \rightarrow [TypeName \rightarrow (TypeParam \nrightarrow 2^T) \nrightarrow 2^T]$$
$$\rightarrow (TypeParam \nrightarrow 2^T) \nrightarrow 2^T$$

Let $\varphi : [TypeName \rightarrow (TypeParam \nrightarrow 2^T) \nrightarrow 2^T]$ be the function that provides the semantics of a type (a type denotes a set of terms), given the name of a type and the values of its actual parameters.
Let $\pi : TypeParam \nrightarrow 2^T$ be the function that maps each type parameter of the

current type definition to a set of terms.

Then $\mathcal{E}xpr\mathcal{D}ef\ [\![edef]\!]\ \varphi\ \pi$ is defined as follows:

$$\begin{array}{ll}
\mathcal{E}xpr\mathcal{D}ef\,[\![T]\!] & \varphi\ \pi = \pi(T) \\
\mathcal{E}xpr\mathcal{D}ef\,[\![tprim]\!] & \varphi\ \pi = \mathcal{T}ype\mathcal{P}rim\ [\![tprim]\!] \\
\mathcal{E}xpr\mathcal{D}ef\,[\![\texttt{type}\ tn(ed_1, ..., ed_n)]\!] & \varphi\ \pi = \varphi\ tn\ \{T_1 \mapsto ST_1, ..., T_n \mapsto ST_n\} \\
 & \textbf{where for all}\ i \in \{1, ..., n\}: \\
 & ST_i = \mathcal{E}xpr\mathcal{D}ef\ [\![ed_i]\!]\ \varphi\ \pi
\end{array}$$

Denotation of principal functors

The semantics of a principal functor $prf \in PrincipalFunctor$ inside a type definition is given by the function $\mathcal{P}r\mathcal{F}$:

$$\begin{aligned}
\mathcal{P}r\mathcal{F}:\quad &PrincipalFunctor \rightarrow [TypeName \rightarrow (TypeParam \nrightarrow 2^T) \nrightarrow 2^T] \\
&\rightarrow (TypeParam \nrightarrow 2^T) \nrightarrow 2^T
\end{aligned}$$

Let $\varphi : [TypeName \rightarrow (TypeParam \nrightarrow 2^T) \nrightarrow 2^T]$ be the function that provides the semantics of a type (a type denotes a set of terms), given its name and the values of its actual parameters.

Let $\pi : TypeParam \nrightarrow 2^T$ be the function that maps each type parameter of the current type definition to a set of terms.

Then $PrincipalFunctor\ [\![prf]\!]\ \varphi\ \pi$ is defined as follows:

$$\mathcal{P}r\mathcal{F}\ [\![\texttt{func}\ f(ed_1, ..., ed_n)]\!]\ \varphi\ \pi = \{f(t_1, ..., t_n) \in \mathcal{T} : t_k \in \mathcal{E}xpr\mathcal{D}ef\ [\![ed_k]\!]\ \varphi\ \pi\}$$

Denotation of type declarations

The semantics of type declarations $tdecls$, denoted by Φ_{tdecls}, is a function with the same signature as the function φ used in the two previous subsections (denotation of an expression definition and of a principal functor). The denotation of a type is a set of terms, given its name and the values of its actual parameters. The function Φ_{tdecls} is computed as a least fixpoint of a transformation $T_{[\![tdecls]\!]}$.

Let $tdecls \in TypeDecls$. The transformation $T_{[\![tdecls]\!]}$ building the semantics of the type declarations $tdecls$ has the following signature:

$$\begin{aligned}
T_{[\![tdecls]\!]}:\quad &[TypeName \rightarrow (TypeParam \nrightarrow 2^T) \nrightarrow 2^T] \\
&\rightarrow \\
&[TypeName \rightarrow (TypeParam \nrightarrow 2^T) \nrightarrow 2^T]
\end{aligned}$$

Assume that $tdecls$ is as follows:

$$\begin{aligned}
tdecls \quad ::= \quad &... \\
&tn\ (T_1, ..., T_n)\ (prf_1 | ... | prf_m) \\
&...
\end{aligned}$$

Let $\varphi : [TypeName \rightarrow (TypeParam \nrightarrow 2^T) \nrightarrow 2^T]$ be the function that provides the semantics of a type, given its name and the values of its actual parameters.

Let $\pi : TypeParam \nrightarrow 2^T$ be the function that maps each type parameter of the current type definition to a set of terms.

Then $T_{[\![tdecls]\!]}\ \varphi\ tn\ \pi$ is defined as the union of the denotation of the different parts of the type definition of tn:

$$T_{[\![tdecls]\!]}\ \varphi\ tn\ \pi = \bigcup_{1 \leq i \leq m} \mathcal{P}r\mathcal{F}\ [\![prf_i]\!]\ \varphi\ \pi$$

The semantics of a type declaration $tdecls \in TypeDecls$ is given by the function Φ_{tdecls}:

$$\Phi_{tdecls} : TypeName \rightarrow (TypeParam \nrightarrow 2^T) \nrightarrow 2^T$$

Φ_{tdecls} is defined as the least fixpoint of the transformation $T_{[\![tdecls]\!]}$:

$$\Phi_{tdecls} = \mu\ (T_{[\![tdecls]\!]})$$

5.2.8 Type expressions

This section provides the abstract syntax of type expressions, which are illustrated in Section 5.2.4 and Section 5.2.5. A type expression is either a primitive type or a 'selection type expression'. A 'selection type expression' is an instantiation of some user-given type definition $tdef$ (type parameters of $tdef$ are replaced by other type expressions, and a subset of the principal functors of $tdef$ is selected). The abstract syntax for type expressions is depicted in Figure 5.2. The set of type expressions is denoted by $TypeExpr$. The denotation of a type expression, which is a set of terms, is presented in Section 5.2.9.

f	$\in$	*FunctorName*	*texpr*	::=	$tprim \mid tsel$
tn	$\in$	*TypeName*	*tprim*	::=	$\texttt{bottom} \mid \texttt{any} \mid \texttt{ground} \mid$
texpr	$\in$	*TypeExpr*			$\texttt{int} \mid \texttt{float}$
tprim	$\in$	*TypePrim*	*tsel*	::=	$tn\ f^*\ texpr^*$
tsel	$\in$	*TypeSelect*			

Figure 5.2: Abstract syntax of type expressions.

Type expressions are constructed from the set of primitive types and from the well-formed type declarations (provided by the user). In what follows, a type selection expression $tsel$ is denoted by $tn\ (f_1|...|f_z)\ (texpr_1,...,texpr_n)$, where tn is the name of a parametric type definition $tdef$ of arity n, where $f_1,...,f_z$ are the selected functors (drawn from the set of principal functors defined in $tdef$), and where $texpr_1,...,texpr_n$ are the type expressions replacing the n type parameters of the type definition $tdef$. A type selection expression can also be denoted by $tn\ fs\ (texpr_1,...,texpr_n)$, where fs is the set of selected functors $\{f_1,...,f_z\}$.

5.2.9 Denotation of type expressions

A type expression denotes a set of terms. It is defined with respect to the semantics of the well-formed type declarations (provided by the user). Let $tdecls \in$

TypeDecls be the *well-formed* type declarations, and let $texpr \in TypeExpr$ be a type expression. Then the concretisation of $texpr$ with respect to $tdecls$ is provided by the function Cc:

$$Cc : (TypeExpr \times TypeDecls) \rightarrow 2^T$$

The concretisation is defined depending on the type expression is a primitive type or a selection type expression.

Primitive type expressions

Assume that $texpr \in TypePrim$. Then $Cc(texpr, tdecls) = TypePrim \ [\![texpr]\!]$, where the semantic function $TypePrim$ is defined in Section 5.2.2.

Selection type expressions

Assume that $texpr \in TypeSelect$ such that:

$$texpr \quad ::= \quad tn \ (f_1|...|f_m) \ (te_1, ..., te_n)$$

Then $Cc(texpr, tdecls)$ is defined as follows:

$$Cc(texpr, tdecls) = \bigcup_{1 \leq k \leq m} \left\{ t \in T \ \middle| \ \begin{array}{l} t \in \Phi_{tdecls} \ tn \ \{T_1 \mapsto ST_1, ..., T_n \mapsto ST_n\} \\ ST_i = Cc(te_i, tdecls), \forall i \in \{1, ..., n\} \\ f_k \text{ is the principal functor of } t \end{array} \right\}$$

where Φ_{tdecls} is the denotation of $tdecls$ (see Section 5.2.7).

In what follows and for the sake of clarity, and when no confusion is possible about the underlying type declaration $tdecls$, we simply write $Cc(texpr)$ instead of $Cc(te, tdecls)$.

Concretisation of the type component of an abstract substitution

We can now redefine the type component of an abstract substitution as follows (see Section 3.3.4).

Definition 5.3

The *type* component ty of the abstract tuple α in the abstract substitution β (in $AS_{D,I}$) is now defined as a total function that maps each index of the abstract substitution to its associated type expression, i.e., $ty : I \rightarrow TypeExpr$, such that $Cc(ty) = \{\langle t_i \rangle_{i \in I} \in T^I \mid t_i \in Cc(ty(i), tdecls)\}$.

5.2.10   Pre-ordering over type expressions

Let $te_1, te_2 \in TypeExpr$ be type expressions. The pre-ordering $\leq$ over type expressions can be depicted in Figure 5.3, where an arc between T_1 and T_2 with T_1 above T_2 means that $T_1 > T_2$. We use a dotted arc between the primitive type ground and a 'selection type expression', since a 'selection type expression' may be ground or not. The concretisation function Cc is monotonic w.r.t. $\leq$:

$$\forall te_1, te_2 \in TypeExpr : te_1 \leq te_2 \Rightarrow Cc(te_1) \subseteq Cc(te_2)$$

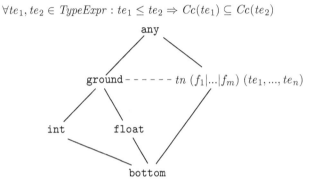

Figure 5.3: The pre-ordering relationship over type expressions.

The pre-ordering over type expressions is defined as follows:

$$te_1 \leq te_2$$
$$\Leftrightarrow$$

if $te_1 = te_2$ **then** *true*
else if $te_2 =$ any **then** *true*
else if $te_1 =$ bottom **then** *true*
else if $te_1 \in \{$int, float$\}$ and $te_2 =$ ground **then** *true*
else if $te_1 = tn_1\, fs_1\, (te_1^1, ..., te_{n_1}^1)$ **and** $te_2 =$ ground
    then $\forall k \in \{1, ..., n_1\} : te_k^1 \leq$ ground
else if $te_1 = tn\, fs_1\, (te_1^1, ..., te_n^1)$ **and**
    $te_2 = tn\, fs_2\, (te_1^2, ..., te_n^2)$
    then $fs_1 \subseteq fs_2 \wedge \forall k \in \{1, ..., n\} : te_k^1 \leq te_k^2$
else *false*

Examples

By considering the type definitions 5.2 and 5.3, we have:

list ([]/0) (bottom) $\leq$ list ([]/0|[|]/2) (int)
tree (t/3) (list ([]/0|[|]/2) (float)) $\leq$ tree (t/3) (any)

The first relation expresses that an empty list is included in the set of lists of integers. The second relation expresses that the set of non-empty binary trees whose elements are lists of floats is included in the set of non-empty binary trees whose elements are any terms. Note also that both left-hand side 'type selection expressions' are less than ($<$) the primitive type `ground`.

5.2.11   Normal type expressions

The relation $\leq$ over type expressions is a *pre-order*, i.e., it is reflexive and transitive, but not necessarily antisymmetric (two distinct type expressions can represent the same set of terms). For instance, the type expressions `list ([]) (any)`, `list ([]) (int)`, and `list ([]) (bottom)` denote the empty list. To make the $\leq$ relation a partial-ordering, and to simplify the implementation of abstract operations over type expressions, we implement an operation that *normalises* a type expression. Considering the set of all type expressions that have the same denotation, we only consider one representant of this set, called a *normal* type expression, that is the least (w.r.t. the $\leq$ ordering defined in previous section) type expression of this set. In the above-mentioned example, the type expression `list ([]) (bottom)` is used to represent an empty-list.

Definition of normal type expressions

A type expression *texpr* $\in$ *TypeExpr* is *normal* if for all *te* $\in$ *TypeExpr* such that $Cc(texpr) = Cc(te)$, we have that $texpr \leq te$.

Specification [normalisation]

Given a type expression, the operation NORMALISE is responsible to compute the corresponding *normal* type expression.

Let *te* $\in$ *TypeExpr*. The operation NORMALISE(*te*) returns a normal type expression *te'* $\in$ *TypeExpr* such that the following two properties are satisfied:

$$(1)\quad Cc(te') = Cc(te)$$

$$(2)\quad \left. \begin{array}{l} te'' \in \mathit{TypeExpr} \\ Cc(te'') = Cc(te) \end{array} \right\} \Rightarrow te' \leq te''$$

Examples

```
NORMALISE(list () (any))                     = bottom
NORMALISE(list ([]/0) (any))                 = list ([]/0) (bottom)
NORMALISE(list ([|]/2) (bottom))             = bottom
NORMALISE(list ([]/0 | [|]/2) (bottom)) = list ([]/0) (bottom)
```

We first define some syntactic functions used to capture relevant information from a well-formed type declaration. They are useful to formalise the normalisation operation of type expressions. Let $tdecls \in TypeDecls$ such that:

$$tdecls ::= tdef_1$$
$$\ldots$$
$$tdef_r$$

where, for all $x \in \{1, ..., r\}$, the type definition $tdef_x$ is of the form:

$$tdef_x ::= tn_x (T_1, ..., T_{n_x}) (prf_1^x | ... | prf_{m_x}^x)$$

and where, for all $x \in \{1, ..., r\}$ and for all $i \in \{1, ..., m_x\}$, the principal functor prf_i^x is of the form:

$$prf_i^x ::= \text{func } f_i^x \, edefs_i^x$$

Principal functor. Given a functor name, the mapping PrF provides the corresponding principal functor (of a type definition). Because type declarations are disjoint (the principal functors of two type definitions are distinct), there is at most one principal functor for a given functor name. It has the following signature:

$$\text{PrF} : (FunctorName \times TypeDecls) \nrightarrow PrincipalFunctor$$

For all $x \in \{1, ..., r\}$, for all $i \in \{1, ..., m_x\}$, we have:

$$\text{PrF}(f_i^x, tdecls) = prf_i^x$$

Type parameters. The mapping TParams provides the set of type parameters occurring in an expression definition, or in a principal functor, or in a type definition. It is defined as follows:

$$\text{TParams} : (ExprDef \cup PrincipalFunctor \cup TypeDef) \rightarrow 2^{TypeParam}$$

$$
\begin{aligned}
\text{TParams}(T) &= \{T\} \\
\text{TParams}(tprim) &= \emptyset \\
\text{TParams}(\text{type } tn(edef_1, ..., edef_n)) &= \bigcup_{1 \le i \le n} \text{TParams}(edef_i) \\
\text{TParams}(\text{func } f(edef_1, ..., edef_n)) &= \bigcup_{1 \le i \le n} \text{TParams}(edef_i) \\
\text{TParams}(tdef_x) &= \{T_1, ..., T_{n_x}\}
\end{aligned}
$$

Implementation [normalisation]

We can now implement the operation NORMALISE(te) as follows. If te is a primitive type, then it is already normalised. Otherwise, if te is a 'selection type expression', we first normalise its type expressions arguments, and then, we normalise it through the specialised operation `NORMALISE_2`.

$$\text{NORMALISE}(te) =$$

> **if** $te \in \mathit{TypePrim}$ **then return** te
> **else**
> > $te = tn\ fs\ (te_1, ..., te_n)$
> > **for all** $i \in \{1, ..., n\}$ **do** $te'_i = \text{NORMALISE}(te_i)$
> > **return** $\text{NORMALISE\_2}(tn\ fs\ (te'_1, ..., te'_n))$

Let $tsel \in \mathit{TypeSelect}$ be a selection type expression $tsel = tn\ fs\ (te'_1, ..., te'_n)$ where the te'_i's are normalised. Then the operation $\text{NORMALISE\_2}(te)$ normalises $tsel$ as follows:

$$\text{NORMALISE\_2}(tsel) =$$

> **if** $fs = \emptyset$ **then** bottom
> **else**
> > **if** $\exists f \in fs, \exists T_i \in \text{TParams}(\text{PrF}(f, tdecls)) : te'_i = \text{bottom}$
> > > **then** $\text{NORMALISE\_2}(tn\ (fs\backslash\{f\})\ (te'_1, ..., te'_n))$
> > **else if** $\exists j \in \{1, ..., n\} : te'_j \neq \text{bottom}$ **and**
> > > $\forall f \in fs, T_j \notin \text{TParams}(\text{PrF}(f, tdecls))$
> > > **then** $\text{NORMALISE\_2}(tn\ fs\ (te'_1, ..., te'_{j-1}, \text{bottom}, te'_{j+1}, ..., te'_n))$
> > **else** $tn\ fs\ (te'_1, ..., te'_n)$

5.2.12   Greatest lower bound of type expressions

We now define the greatest lower bound operation of type expressions. This operation computes a type expression te which is the *intersection* of the type expressions te_1 and te_2, in the sense that its denotation contains only those terms which belong to $Cc(te_1)$ and $Cc(te_2)$.

Note that the denotation of a type expression is *closed under substitution*. Given a type expression te, for each term t belonging to the concretisation of te, and for any substitution θ, then the term $t\theta$ belongs to the concretisation of te. This is due to the fact that only the primitive `any` in a type expression can cause the existence of non-ground terms in a denotation. Due to the substitution-closedness of the denotation of type expressions, the abstract interpretation of the unification builtin $=/2$ is based upon the intersection operation.

Specification [greatest lower bound]

Let $te_1, te_2 \in \mathit{TypeExpr}$ be normalised type expressions. The greatest lower bound of te_1 and te_2, denoted by $te_1 \sqcap te_2$, is a normal type expression such that $Cc(te_1 \sqcap te_2) = Cc(te_1) \cap Cc(te_2)$.

Implementation [greatest lower bound]

In the following, $i, j \in \{1, 2\}$ $(i \neq j)$.

$te_1 \sqcap te_2 =$

   if $te_i = te_j$ **then** te_i
   else if $te_i =$ bottom **then** bottom
   else if $te_i =$ any **then** te_j
   else if $te_i =$ int and $te_j =$ float **then** bottom
   else if $te_i \in \{$int, float$\}$ **and** $te_j =$ ground **then** te_i
   else if $te_i = tn_i \; fs_i \; (te_1^i, ..., te_{n_i}^i)$ **and** $te_j \in \{$int, float$\}$
      then bottom
   else if $te_i = tn_i \; fs_i \; (te_1^i, ..., te_{n_i}^i)$ **and** $te_j =$ ground
      then NORMALISE$(tn_i \; fs_i \; (te_1^i \sqcap$ ground$, ..., te_n^i \sqcap$ ground$))$
   else if $te_i = tn_i \; fs_i \; (te_1^i, ..., te_n^i)$ **and**
      $te_j = tn_j \; fs_j \; (te_1^j, ..., te_n^j)$ **and**
     then
        if $(tn_i \neq tn_j)$ **then** bottom
        else NORMALISE$(tn_i \; (fs_i \cap fs_j) \; (te_1^i \sqcap te_1^j, ..., te_n^i \sqcap te_n^j))$

Examples

Consider the following type definition:

```
foo(T,U) ::= a(T) | b(T,U) | c
```
Type definition 5.5 `foo(T,U)`

We illustrate the greatest lower bound of type expressions on the following examples:

$$\left(\begin{array}{l} \text{list }([]/0|[|]/2)\text{ (any) } \sqcap \\ \text{list }([]/0|[|]/2)\text{ (ground)} \end{array} \right) \quad = \quad \text{list }([]/0|[|]/2)\text{ (ground)}$$

$$\left(\begin{array}{l} \text{foo }(a/1|b/2)\text{ (int, any) } \sqcap \\ \text{ground} \end{array} \right) \quad = \quad \text{foo }(a/1|b/2)\text{ (int, ground)}$$

$$\left(\begin{array}{l} \text{foo }(a/1|b/2)\text{ (int, any) } \sqcap \\ \text{foo }(a/1|c/0)\text{ (ground, bottom)} \end{array} \right) \quad = \quad \text{foo }(a/1)\text{ (int, bottom)}$$

$$\left(\begin{array}{l} \text{foo }(a/1|c/0)\text{ (int, bottom) } \sqcap \\ \text{foo }(b/2|c/0)\text{ (float, ground)} \end{array} \right) \quad = \quad \text{foo }(c/0)\text{ (bottom, bottom)}$$

5.2.13 Least upper bound of type expressions

The least upper bound operation over the type expressions te_1 and te_2 computes a type expression te which is the *union* of the type expressions te_1 and te_2, in the sense that its denotation contains those terms which belong to $Cc(te_1)$ or $Cc(te_2)$.

This operation is needed for the implementation of the least upper bound of abstract substitutions (see [53, 80]). The least upper bound operation over abstract substitutions is itself used for the implementation of the abstract sequence concatenation (see Section 6.4).

Specification [least upper bound]

Let $te_1, te_2 \in TypeExpr$. The least upper bound of te_1 and te_2, denoted by $te_1 \sqcup te_2$, is such that $Cc(te_1 \sqcup te_2) \supseteq Cc(te_1) \cup Cc(te_2)$.

Implementation [least upper bound]

In the following, $i, j \in \{1, 2\}$ $(i \neq j)$.

$$te_1 \sqcup te_2 =$$

> **if** $te_i = te_j$ **then** te_i
> **else if** $te_i = $ bottom **then** te_j
> **else if** $te_i = tn\ fs_i\ (te_1^i, ..., te_n^i)$ **and**
> $\qquad te_j = tn\ fs_j\ (te_1^j, ..., te_n^j)$
> $\qquad\qquad$ **then** $tn\ (fs_i \cup fs_j)\ (te_1^i \sqcup te_1^j, ..., te_n^i \sqcup te_n^j)$
> **else if** $te_i, te_j \leq$ ground **then** ground
> **else** any

Examples

Considering Type Definition 5.5, can illustrate the least upper bound of type expressions on the following examples:

$$\begin{pmatrix} \texttt{list ([]/0) (bottom)} \ \sqcup \\ \texttt{list ([|]/2) (int)} \end{pmatrix} \quad = \quad \texttt{list ([]/0 | [|]/2) (int)}$$

$$\begin{pmatrix} \texttt{list ([|]/2) (float)} \ \sqcup \\ \texttt{list ([|]/2) (int)} \end{pmatrix} \quad = \quad \texttt{list ([|]/2) (ground)}$$

$$\begin{pmatrix} \texttt{foo (a/1) (any, bottom)} \ \sqcup \\ \texttt{foo (b/2) (int, float)} \end{pmatrix} \quad = \quad \texttt{foo (a/1 | b/2) (any, float)}$$

$$\begin{pmatrix} \texttt{foo (b/2) (any, float)} \ \sqcup \\ \texttt{foo (b/2) (int, any)} \end{pmatrix} \quad = \quad \texttt{foo (b/2) (any, any)}$$

$$\begin{pmatrix} \texttt{foo (b/2) (int, float)} \ \sqcup \\ \texttt{foo (b/2) (int, any)} \end{pmatrix} \quad = \quad \texttt{foo (b/2) (int, any)}$$

5.3 Norms

Automatic termination analysers typically measure the size of terms by applying norms which are mappings from terms to the natural numbers. The basic framework considers the list-length as the unique size measure for terms. The framework has thus been extended to handle other *norms* and *functions*. A *norm* defines a mapping from terms to the natural numbers, and a *function* defines a mapping from terms to the integers (possibly negative). Some primitive norms and functions are now predefined in the system. Furthermore, the user can declare its own norms and functions, which are associated to previously defined types. Several norms or functions can be attached to a single type. Such size measures are combined into the size components of an abstract sequence (i.e., into the srel and sol parts of a formal specification). This improvement increases the expressiveness of abstract sequences, as well as the accuracy of the global analysis.

Related tools also define norms to compute interargument size relations, which are instrumental for verifying or inferring the termination of a procedure (e.g., [27, 46, 86]). For instance, in TerminWeb, various norms can be combined [51], and the candidate norms for a term are provided on the basis of the (regular) type that is assigned to that term [15]. In CiaoPP [40], lower and upper-bound of sizes are computed and are instrumental to approximate some well-defined cost functions.

Section 5.3.1 describes the new primitive norms and functions that are integrated in our system. Section 5.3.2 illustrates how the user can declare its own norms and functions, which are associated to some defined types. Section 5.3.3 illustrates how combined norms and functions can be used in formal specifications.

5.3.1 Primitive norms and functions

The framework has been extended with the following primitive norms (mappings from terms to the natural numbers) and functions (mappings from terms to the integers). The *absolute* norm, denoted by (abs), maps any integer to its absolute value, and returns zero for non-integer terms. The *general* norm, denoted by (gen), counts the number of functors in a term.[2] It is defined recursively as follows for any term t:

$$(\text{gen})t \;=\; \begin{cases} 1 + (\text{gen})t_1 + ... + (\text{gen})t_n & \textbf{if } t = f(t_1, ..., t_n) \\ 1 & \textbf{if } t \text{ is a constant} \\ 0 & \textbf{otherwise} \end{cases}$$

The *integer* function, denoted by (int), returns the integer value for an integer term and returns zero for non-integer terms.

As an example, the *integer* function allows us to specify the arithmetic comparison = : = as follows.

---

[2]The *general* norm is identical to the *term-size* norm (see, e.g., [15]).

```
=:=/2
  in(X:int, Y:int)
  srel((int)X_ref = (int)Y_ref)
  sol(sol = 1)
```
Specification 5.17   =:=/2

Formal specification 5.17 expresses that the predicate X =:= Y surely succeeds if and only if the integer value of X equals the integer value of Y.[3] Constraints using functions are maintained in the *size relations* component srel, even if actually, they express relations between actual values (in the above example, they are relations between (possibly negative) integers).

5.3.2   Declaring norms and functions associated to types

Besides the input program, the formal specifications, and the type declarations, the user can also declare its own norms and functions. This section illustrates how this can be achieved. The list-length norm, called (list), can be declared recursively as follows:

```
(list) []    = 0
(list) [_|T] = 1+(list)T
```
Norm definition 5.1   (list)

The value of a norm is defined for every term. The norm value of a term which is not described in the corresponding definition is set to zero. So, regarding the above norm definition, the list-length of a term whose principal functor does not match with [] or [_|T] is zero.

Actually, the norm (list) is predefined in the system and users need not to redefine it. Other norms can be declared, depending on the application. For instance, the norm (elems), which is attached to a binary tree (Type Definition 5.3), returns the number of inner nodes of a binary tree:

```
(elems) void       = 0
(elems) t(_,LT,RT) = 1+(elems)LT+(elems)RT
```
Norm definition 5.2   (elems)

The user can also declare its own functions. For instance, the following function, called (intsum), refers to the integer sum of the elements of a binary tree:

```
(intsum) void       = 0
(intsum) t(I,LT,RT) = (int)I+(intsum)LT+(intsum)RT
```
Function definition 5.1   (intsum)

Note that several norms or functions can be declared for the same type.

---

[3]Note that the arithmetic comparison =:= can also be used when inputs are floats (the primitive type float can then be used in the specification). The framework should be extended to handle functions that map terms to non-integer values (in this case, the function (float) should map any float term to its value and any other term to zero).

5.3.3 Using norms and functions in formal specifications

The primitive and user-declared norms and functions can be combined into the size components of an abstract sequence. For instance, Procedure 5.2 can be specified (and checked) as follows, by using the `list` and `elems` norms:

```
flattree/2
  in(T:tree(ground), L:var)
  out(_, list(ground))
  srel( (elems)T_in = (list)L_out )
  sol(sol = 1)
```
Specification 5.18 `flattree(T,L)`

The `srel` component above expresses that the number of nodes of the input binary tree T is equal to the list-length of the output list L.

The following example shows a combination between primitive and declared functions. The predicate `sumtree(T,Sum)` holds iff Sum is the sum of the elements composing the integer binary tree T.

```
sumtree(void,0).
sumtree(t(X,L,R),Sum) :-
  sumtree(L,SL),
  sumtree(R,SR),
  Sum is X+SL+SR.
```
Procedure 5.5 `sumtree(T,Sum)`

When input T is a binary tree of integers and when Sum is a variable, then the procedure `sumtree(T,Sum)` can be specified (and verified) as follows.

```
sumtree/2
  in(T:tree(int),Sum:var)
  out(_,int)
  srel((intsum)T_in = (int)Sum_out)
  sol(sol = 1)
```
Specification 5.19 `sumtree(T,Sum)`

Chapter 6

More accurate analysis

This chapter presents some other improvements to the basic framework in order to make the analysis more accurate. More information is placed into abstract sequences, such that abstract operations become more precise. The implementation of the main abstract operations is presented, by considering the new components defined in the previous chapters. It results that more specialised behaviours can be specified and verified.

Section 6.1 introduces a new component in abstract sequences that describes the set of input terms that are left untouched (uninstantiated) during the execution. For instance, negations or test predicates like `nonvar/1` do not instantiate their arguments. In the basic framework, the `sexpr` tag in formal specifications describes the induction parameter, which is a linear expression in function of the size (list-length) of input terms. It is instrumental to prove the termination of the procedure. Section 6.2 extends this component to handle *sequences* of linear size expressions as induction parameters. This allows us to prove the termination of more programs. The sequence of linear expressions must decrease (according to the lexicographic ordering) through recursive calls. Now, combined norms and functions (introduced in Section 5.2) can be used inside the *size relations* and the *size expression* components of abstract sequences. This section also explains how to deal with the termination of procedures that are mutually recursive. Section 6.3 provides the implementation of the abstract operation that detects whether two abstract sequences are exclusive. This property is relevant for making the abstract concatenation accurate. Thanks to the *refined* input abstract substitution and the new *failure* components (introduced in Section 4.1.3), the analyser is able to perform optimal abstract concatenation. When there are more than two clauses in a procedure, the basic framework concatenates in sequence the abstract sequences modelling the execution of the clauses. However, this approach may be inaccurate. Section 6.4 presents how the checker realises an optimal solution for concatenating multiple abstract sequences, guided by the specification to be verified. Section 6.5 illustrates that a strategy of local reexecution is occasionally needed to refine the abstract information, thanks to the *refined* and *failure* input components of abstract sequences.

6.1   Untouched terms

This section introduces the new *untouched* component of abstract sequences that describes the set of terms that are left uninstantiated during the execution. First, Section 6.1.1 illustrates that the basic framework is inaccurate to model and to verify the execution of procedures that do not modify some of their arguments. Then, Section 6.1.2 provides the definition of the new component and illustrates how it can be used into formal specifications. Section 6.1.3 refines the pre-ordering relation between abstract sequences by considering the new untouched component. Finally, Section 6.1.4 presents how the *untouched* component is implemented in abstract sequences.

6.1.1   Inaccuracies of the basic framework

There exist many situations where the execution of a procedure does not modify some input terms, even if those input terms are not ground. For instance, consider the length procedure that computes the length N of the list L.

```
length([],0).
length([_|L],N)  :- length(L,N1), N is N1+1.
```
Procedure 6.1   length(L,N)

Examine the execution of length(L,N) when the input argument L is a (non necessarily ground) list and when the input N is a variable that does not occur in L. Clearly, L is exactly the same term before and after the execution. Up to now, the most accurate formal specification corresponding to the behaviour of length(L,N) in such a situation can be written as follows:

```
length/2
   in(L:list(any), N:var; noshare(<L,N>))
   out(list(any), int; srel((int)N >= 0))
   srel( (list)L_in = (int)N_out )
   sol(sol = 1)
   sexpr(< (list)L >)
```
Specification 6.1   length(L,N)

Among the executions described by Specification 6.1, some of them actually never happen. The output list L is a list of any term, and its elements have been possibly instantiated during the execution. Consider for instance the input substitution $\theta = \{L/[y_1, b, y_2, d], N/y_3\}$ where the program variable L is bound to a list $[y_1, b, y_2, d]$ (y_1 and y_2 are distinct standard variables, and b and d are constants), and where the program variable N is bound to a standard variable y_3 that is distinct from y_1 and y_2. The input substitution θ satisfies the conditions imposed by the in part of the specification, and the following substitution sequences satisfy the conditions imposed by Specification 6.1 (where a and c are constants):

$$S_1 = \; < \{L/[y_1, b, y_2, d], \; N/4\} >$$
$$S_2 = \; < \{L/[a, b, y_2, d], \; N/4\} >$$
$$S_3 = \; < \{L/[a, b, c, d], \quad N/4\} >$$
$$\ldots$$

Actually, only the first sequence S_1 is the exact description of the execution `length(L,N)` θ. The other sequences S_1 and S_2 are examples where the list L has been (partially) instantiated, and do not correspond to reality.

The fact that we are not able to express in the basic framework that terms are left uninstantiated during the execution can lead to some inaccuracies during the abstract execution, as it is illustrated in the following example. Consider the program `set_length(L)`, which accepts any linear non-empty list as input, of the form `[X|Ls]`, such that X is a variable. This procedure instantiates the first element of L (the variable X) to the length of L.

```
set_length(L) :-₁ length(L,N)₂, L=[N|Ls]₃ .₄
```
Procedure 6.2 `set_length(L)`

Ideally, we want to prove that this procedure is fully deterministic, that the output list L is still linear, and that the first element of output list L is the list-length of L. The expected formal specification is thus:

```
set_length/1
  in(L:[X:var|Ls:list(any)]; linear(L))
  out(L:[X:int|Ls:list(any)]; linear(L))
  srel( (int)X_out = (list)L_in )
  sol(sol = 1)
```
Specification 6.2 `set_length(L)`

The basic framework is unable to prove the sure success of the execution, and that output list L is linear. Before the call to `length(L,N)`, the abstract sequence B1 is as follows:

```
B1:
  in(L:[X:var|list(any)]; linear(L))
  out(L:[X:var|list(any)], N:var, Ls:var;
      linear(L); noshare(<L,N,Ls>))
  sol(sol = 1)
```

The abstract sequence B2 after the execution of the literal `length(N,L)` is:

```
B2:
    in(L:[X:var|list(any)]; linear(L))
    out(L:[X:any|list(any)], N:int, Ls:var;
        noshare(<L,Ls>))
    srel( (int)N_out = (list)L_in )
    sol(sol = 1)
```

Note that at this program point, X is any term instead of the expected variable. Furthermore, the analyser loses the information that L is a linear term. Indeed, at the view of Specification 6.1, nothing expresses that the list L has been left uninstantiated, such that it is impossible to have accurate information about the elements of L, and in particular about its first element X. This lack of accuracy has bad repercussions on the execution of the next unification L=[N|Ls]. The basic framework cannot prove that this unification surely succeeds, because N is an integer and L is a list of any terms (possibly non linear). The next abstract sequence B3 is thus:

```
B3:
    in(L:[X:var|list(any)]; linear(L))
    out(L:[X:int|Ls:list(any)], N:int, Ls:list(any))
    srel( (int)N_out=(list)L_in,
          (int)X_out=(int)N_out  )
    sol(sol =< 1)
```

such that Specification 6.1 cannot be checked: the linearity of the output list L and the sure success of the execution cannot be proved.

Also, negations and test predicates do not instantiate their input arguments. For instance, the formal specification of the built-in `nonvar/1` can be written as follows in the basic framework:

```
nonvar/1
    in(T:any)
    ref(novar)
    sol(sol = 1)
```
Specification 6.3   nonvar(T)

The above built-in accepts any term T at input, and succeeds only the input term is not a variable (this is described by the `ref` part of the specification). The specification expresses that at output, the term T is not a variable, but nothing express that the output T is the same term as the input T. Procedures using such test predicates cannot be checked accurately. For instance, consider the procedure `close(L)` that closes a possibly opened list. It uses the test predicates `var/1` and `nonvar/1`.

```
close(L)  :- var(L), L=[].
close(L)  :- nonvar(L), L=[].
close(L)  :- nonvar(L), L=[_|Ls], close(Ls).
```
Procedure 6.3 `close(L)`

A formal specification for `close` can be as follows:

```
close/1
  in(L:any)
  out(list(any))
  sexpr(< L >)
```
Specification 6.4 `close(L)`

The basic framework is unable to prove the termination of `close(L)`; it cannot check that the induction parameter decreases through the recursive call in the third clause. Indeed, the abstract sequence computed before the recursive call is `B_before`:

```
B_before:
  in(L:any)
  ref(L:[any|Ls:any])
  out(L:[any|Ls:any], Ls:any)
  srel( (list)L_ref = (list)Ls_ref+1
        (list)L_out = (list)Ls_out+1 )
  sol(sol = 1)
```

At that program point, the inequality `(list)Ls_out < (list)L_ref` does not hold into the `srel` part of `B_before`. No information tell us that L is untouched until that point, such that the list-length `L_ref` cannot be proved equal to the list-length `L_out`. It follows that Specification 6.4 cannot thus be proved.

6.1.2 Untouched component to model uninstantiated terms

The definition of abstract sequence is enhanced with a new abstract component that maintains the set of input terms that are untouched during the execution.

Definition 6.1

Formally, an abstract sequence B is now of the form $\langle \beta_{in}, \beta_{fails}, \beta_{ref}, U, \beta_{out}, E_{ref\_out}, E_{sol} \rangle$. The semantics of U is as follows. Let $\langle \theta, S \rangle \in Cc(B)$, as it is defined in Section 3.4.4. Let $\theta \in Cc(\beta_{ref})$ and such that $\theta \notin Cc(\beta_f)$, for all $\beta_f \in \beta_{fails}$. For all standard substitution σ such that $\theta\sigma \in Subst(S)$, we have that $i \in U$ implies $t_i\sigma = t_i$, where t_i is the term of θ that corresponds to the index i in β_{ref}, i.e., $\langle t_i \rangle_{i \in I_{ref}} = \text{DECOMP}(\theta, \beta_{ref})$.

The new optional tag `untouched` can be used in formal specifications. It contains the names of some input terms, and the analyser checks that such terms are untouched during the execution. For instance, Specification 6.1 can be extended as follows, where L is an untouched term:

```
length/2
    in(L:list(any), N:var; noshare(<L,N>))
    out(list(any), int; srel((int)N >= 0))
    untouched(L)
    srel( (list)L_in = (int)N_out )
    sol(sol = 1)
    sexpr(< L >)
```
Specification 6.5 length(L,N)

The checker verifies that the program length satisfies this specification, and the program set_length can be checked according to Specification 6.2. Actually, Specification 6.2 can be refined as follows, where the tail of L, i.e. Ls, is untouched.

```
set_length/1
    in(L:[X:var|Ls:list(any)]; linear(L))
    out(L:[X:int|Ls:list(any)]; linear(L))
    untouched(Ls)
    srel( (int)X_out = (list)L_in )
    sol(sol = 1)
```
Specification 6.6 set_length(L)

Similarly, the procedure list(L) called when the input L is list of any terms does not instantiate L.

```
list([]).
list([_|L]) :- list(L).
```
Procedure 6.4 list(L)

```
list/1
    in(L:list(any))
    untouched(L)
    sol(sol = 1)
    sexpr(< L >)
```
Specification 6.7 list(L)

Thanks to the new component, the exact behaviour of test predicates can be specified, like the following specification for nonvar/1:

```
nonvar/1
    in(T:any)
    ref(novar)
    untouched(T)
    sol(sol = 1)
```
Specification 6.8 nonvar(T)

The analyser is now able to verify the program `close(L)` according to Specification 6.4, and in particular, it proves the termination of its execution for any input terms.

6.1.3 Pre-ordering on abstract sequences with the untouched component

The pre-ordering relation $\leq$ between two abstract sequences has to be refined to consider the new untouched component. Let $B_1, B_2 \in \mathsf{ASeq}_D$. We have $B_1 \leq B_2$ if the conditions defined so far are satisfied (see Section 3.4.5 and Section 4.1.4), and if the following additional condition holds:

$$(*) \quad U^1 \supseteq tr^{>}_{ref}(U^2)$$

where $tr_{ref} : \beta^2_{ref} \rightarrow \beta^1_{ref}$ is the structural mapping between the refined components of B_2 and B_1.

This condition expresses that if a term in β^2_{ref} is untouched (i.e., its index belongs to the untouched component U_2 of B_2), then the corresponding term in β^1_{ref} must be untouched. The correspondence between indices is performed through the direct constrained mapping operation (see Section 3.4.2).

6.1.4 Implementation: fusion of indices into abstract sequences

Untouched terms are implemented by *sharing* the set of indices between the β_{ref} and β_{out} components of an abstract sequence. The indices both occurring in β_{ref} and in β_{out} denote the terms that are left uninstantiated during the execution of a goal. An untouched term X can therefore be modelled by the constraint $sv_{ref}(\mathtt{X}) = sv_{out}(\mathtt{X})$. More generally, equality constraints between any input and output terms can be expressed. So, the constraint $sv_{ref}(\mathtt{X1}) = sv_{out}(\mathtt{X2})$ means that *input* term X1 is equal to *output* term X2.

Definition 6.2

Technically, a *shared abstract substitution* β_{ref_out} with input domain D, with output domain D' ($D \subseteq D'$), and over the set of indices I, is defined as a tuple of the form $\langle sv_{ref}, sv_{out}, frm, \alpha \rangle$. The refined same-value component sv_{ref} belongs to $\mathsf{SV}_{D,I}$; the output same-value component sv_{out} belongs to $\mathsf{SV}_{D',I}$; the frame component frm belongs to FRM_I; and the abstract tuple α belongs to ALPHA_I.

A *shared abstract sequence* B_{shared} is a tuple of the form $\langle \beta_{in}, \beta_{fails}, \beta_{ref\_out}, E_{ref\_out}, E_{sol} \rangle$.

For instance, the shared abstract version corresponding to the abstract sequence in Figure 3.1 is depicted in Figure 6.1.

$$
\begin{aligned}
\beta_{in} \quad &: sv &&= \{\mathtt{X} \mapsto 1, \mathtt{L} \mapsto 2, \mathtt{Ls} \mapsto 3\} \\
&\ frm &&= \{\} \\
&\ mo &&= \{1 \mapsto \mathtt{var}, 2 \mapsto \mathtt{ground}, 3 \mapsto \mathtt{var}\} \\
&\ ty &&= \{1 \mapsto \mathtt{anylist}, 2 \mapsto \mathtt{list}, 3 \mapsto \mathtt{anylist}\} \\
&\ ps &&= \{(1,1),(3,3)\} \\
\beta_{fails} \quad &: \emptyset \\
\beta_{ref\_out} &: sv_{ref} &&= \{\mathtt{X} \mapsto 1, \mathtt{L} \mapsto 2, \mathtt{Ls} \mapsto 3\} \\
&\ sv_{out} &&= \{\mathtt{X} \mapsto 6, \mathtt{L} \mapsto 2, \mathtt{Ls} \mapsto 7\} \\
&\ frm &&= \{2 \mapsto [4|5]\} \\
&\ mo &&= \{1 \mapsto \mathtt{var}, 2 \mapsto \mathtt{ground}, 3 \mapsto \mathtt{var}, 4 \mapsto \mathtt{ground}, \\
&&&\quad\ 5 \mapsto \mathtt{ground}, 6 \mapsto \mathtt{ground}, 7 \mapsto \mathtt{ground}\} \\
&\ ty &&= \{1 \mapsto \mathtt{anylist}, 2 \mapsto \mathtt{list}, 3 \mapsto \mathtt{anylist}, 4 \mapsto \mathtt{any}, \\
&&&\quad\ 5 \mapsto \mathtt{list}, 6 \mapsto \mathtt{any}, 7 \mapsto \mathtt{list}\} \\
&\ ps &&= \{(1,1),(3,3)\} \\
&\ lin &&= \{1,2,3,4,5,6,7\} \\
E_{ref\_out} &: \{sz(7) = sz(5)\} \\
E_{sol} \quad &: \{\mathtt{sol} = sz(2)\}
\end{aligned}
$$

Figure 6.1: Shared abstract sequence corresponding to Specification 3.1 of the procedure `select(X,L,Ls)`.

Shared domains reduce the dimensions of the linear constraint systems since every untouched term is mapped onto a unique index variable. So there is no need to maintain an equality constraint between the input and output sizes of the term. Table 8.2 compares the average number of indices described in abstract sequences, without the sharing of indices (i.e., indices from β_{ref} + indices from β_{out}) and with the sharing of indices (i.e., indices from β_{ref_out}).

6.2   Termination

The new framework is able to prove termination of more programs. Section 6.2.1 illustrates the interest of combining norms and functions inside the E_{ref_out} and E_{sol} components of abstract sequences, as well as inside the `sexpr` part of specifications. Section 6.2.2 explains how the termination of mutually recursive procedures can be checked. Section 6.2.3 extends the `sexpr` part of specifications for handling *sequences* of linear expressions.

6.2.1   Combined norms in size relations between input/output terms

In Section 5.3, we have defined the new E_{ref_out} and E_{sol} components of an abstract sequence, where several norms and functions (primitive + user-declared) are

combined together to describe size relations between input/output terms and the
number of solutions in function of the size of input terms. The basic framework
defines the `sexpr` part of formal specifications as a linear expression in function
of the list-length of input terms. Now, we allow the user to use the new norms and
functions in the `sexpr` part.

For instance, Procedure 5.2 can be specified as follows:

```
flattree/2
  in(T:tree(ground), L:var)
  out(_, list(ground))
  srel( (elems)T_in = (list)L_out )
  sol(sol = 1)
  sexpr(< (gen)T >)
```
Specification 6.9 `flattree(T,L)`

In particular, the new analyser is able to prove that the procedure terminates,
by using the general norm (`gen`) of the first argument as induction parameter.

The primitive function (`int`) can also be used in the `sexpr` part of a specification. For instance, the behaviour of the procedure `factorial(N,F)`, that
computes the factorial F of an input positive integer N, can be described in Specification 6.10.

```
factorial(0,1).
factorial(N,F) :-
  N > 0,
  N1 is N-1,
  factorial(N1,F1),
  F is N*F1.
```
Procedure 6.5 `factorial(N,F)`

```
factorial/2
  in(N:int, F:var; srel((int)N >= 0))
  out(_, int)
  sol(sol = 1)
  sexpr(< (int)N >)
```
Specification 6.10 `factorial(N,F)`

Combined norms and functions are necessary to prove more intricate procedures, like the procedure `tree_list_tree(T,L)`:

```
append(L1,L2,L3)  :-  [see Procedure 2.4]
flattree(T,L)  :-     [see Procedure 5.2]
flattree2(T,L)  :-    [see Procedure 5.4]

tree_list_tree(void, []).
tree_list_tree(t(X,LT,RT), [X|L])  :-
    flattree(LT,La),
    flattree(RT,Lb),
    append(La,Lb,Lc),
    flattree2(T,Lc),
    tree_list_tree(T,L).
```
Procedure 6.6   `tree_list_tree(T,L)`

The `flattree(T,L)` and `flattree2(T,L)` predicates describe a rela-
tion that holds iff `L` is the list of the elements of the binary tree `T` in prefix order.
The `flattree(T,L)` procedure is used when input `T` is a binary tree and `L` is
a variable, whereas the `flattree2(T,L)` procedure is used when input `T` is a
variable and `L` is a list. The following specification can be written (and checked)
for the procedure `tree_list_tree`:

```
tree_list_tree
    in(T:tree(ground), L:var)
    out(_, list(ground))
    srel((elems)T_in = (list)L_out)
    sexpr(< (elems)T >)
```
Specification 6.11   `tree_list_tree(T,L)`

The new framework allows us to combine the user-declared norm (`elems`)
(type definition 5.2) and the primitive function (`int`) inside the `srel` component. The checker proves that the induction parameter, i.e., the number of elements
of the first argument which is a binary tree, is decreasing through the recursive call.

6.2.2   Checking termination of mutually recursive procedures

The basic framework is extended to deal with mutual recursive procedures. The
abstract operation CHECK_TERM performs a termination test based on the size expressions of all the procedures concerned by mutual recursion (the basic framework
uses only such a test for recursive procedures). So, if p and q are mutually recur-
sive procedures, if $\langle B_p, se_p \rangle \in Beh_p$ and if the execution of $\langle \theta, p \rangle$, where $\theta \in
Cc(input(B_p))$, uses a subcall $\langle \theta', q \rangle$, where θ' can be described by $\langle B_q, se_q \rangle \in
Beh_q$, we have to check (at the abstract level) that $se_q(\|\theta'X_1\|, ..., \|\theta'X_m\|) \leq
se_p(\|\theta X_1\|, ..., \|\theta X_n\|)$, where n and m are respectively the arities of p and q. This
test ensures that the mutually recursive procedures do not loop infinitely. In order
to use this method, we must analyse the program to find out all mutually recursive

procedures or, more precisely, all pairs of triplets $\langle\langle p, B_p, se_p\rangle, \langle q, B_q, se_q\rangle\rangle$ (with $\langle B_p, se_p\rangle \in Beh_p$ and $\langle B_q, se_q\rangle \in Beh_q$) describing procedure calls that may use subcalls described by the other one. The termination test CHECK_TERM is realised only when the triplets associated with the subcall and the head call are mutually recursive.

Consider for instance the mutually recursive procedures even and odd.

```
even([]).
even([_|T]) :- odd(T).

odd([_|T]) :- even(T).
```
Procedure 6.7 even(L), odd(L)

Those procedures can be specified as follows.

```
even/1
  in(L:list(any))
  untouched(L)
  sol(sol =< 1)
  sexpr(< (list)L >)

odd/1
  in(L:list(any))
  ref([_|_])
  untouched(L)
  sol(sol =< 1)
  sexpr(< (list)L >)
```
Specification 6.12 even(L), odd(L)

The analyser detects that the two procedures are mutually recursive. Because the induction parameter always decreases through the mutually recursive calls, the checker is able to verify the termination of the two procedures.

6.2.3 Induction parameters: sequences of linear expressions

The basic framework is extended to allow the user to provide a sequence of linear expressions as the induction parameter in the sexpr part of a formal specification. The analyser checks if this sequence of linear expressions decreases through (mutually) recursive subcalls, according to the lexicographic ordering. The implementation of CHECK_TERM using the sequences of linear expressions is implemented in [54].

For instance, consider the procedure ack (M, N, Val) that computes the Ackermann function for two input integers M and N.

```
ack(0,  N,  N1)  :- N1 is N+1.
ack(M1,  0,  Val)  :-
     M1>0, M is M1-1, ack(M, 1, Val).
ack(M1,  N1,  Val)  :-
     M1>0, N1 > 0, M is M1-1, N is N1-1,
        ack(M1, N, Val1), ack(M, Val1, Val).
```
Procedure 6.8   ack (M, N, Val)

A possible formal specification for the procedure ack (M, N, Val) is as follows.

```
ack/3
   in(M:int,N:int,Val:var;
       srel((int)M >= 0, (int)N >= 0))
   out(_,_,int)
   srel((int)Val_out >= (int)N_in+1)
   sol(sol = 1)
   sexpr(< (int)M, (int)N >)
```
Specification 6.13   ack (M, N, Val)

The analyser is able to prove the above specification, and it proves that the procedure terminates according to the sequence of expressions $\langle(\text{int})M, (\text{int})N\rangle$: at each recursive call, either the value of the first parameter is strictly less than the input M, or the value of the first parameter is equal to the input M and the second parameter's value is strictly less than the input argument N.

As another example, consider the two following mutually recursive procedures f / 3 and g / 4:

```
f([],Res,Res).
f([H|T],X,Res) :- g(T,X,[H|T],Res).

g(A,B,C,Res) :- f(A,[B|C],Res).
```
Procedure 6.9   f / 3, g / 4

They can be specified as follows, and the checker proves the termination of both procedures.

```
f/3
  in(Xs:list(ground),Acc:list(ground),Res:var)
  out(_,_,list(ground))
  sol(sol =< 1)
  sexpr(< (list)Xs, 0 >)

g/4
  in(A:list(ground), B:list(ground),
     C:list(ground), Res:var)
  out(_,_,_,list(ground))
  sol(sol =< 1)
  sexpr(< (list)A, 1 >)
```
Specification 6.14   f/3, g/4

A quite intricate example is the procedure special(Xs,Ys). This procedure builds pairs of lists (NewXs and NewYs) such that the sum of their length is less than the sum of the length of Xs and Ys.

```
append(L1,L2,L3)  :- [see Procedure 2.4]
length(L,N)  :-        [see Procedure 6.1]

maxlist(L1,L2,Lmax)  :- length(L1,N1),
                        length(L2,N2),
                        N1>=N2, !, Lmax=L1.
maxlist(L1,L2,L2).

special(Xs,Ys)  :- append(Xs,Ys,[_|Zs]),
                   append(NewXs,NewYs,Zs),
                   maxlist(Xs,NewXs,Xs),
                   special(NewXs,NewYs).
```
Procedure 6.10   special(Xs,Ys)

The procedure special(Xs,Ys) terminates and surely fails when it is called with two ground lists as input. This behaviour can be specified (and checked) by the following specification.

```
special/2
  in(Xs:list(ground), Ys:list(ground))
  sol(sol = 0)
  sexpr(< (list)Xs, (list)Ys >)
```
Specification 6.15   special(Xs,Ys)

```
maxlist/3
  in(L1:list(ground), L2:list(ground),
    Lmax:list(ground))
  srel( Lmax_out >= L1_in,
        Lmax_out >= L2_in,
        Lmax_out =< L1_in+L2_in )
  sol(sol =< 1)
  sexpr(< (list)L1 >)
```
Specification 6.16 `maxlist(L1,L2,Lmax)`

6.3 Exclusivity

Detecting that two abstract sequences are mutually exclusive is important to make the cardinality information more accurate, and in particular, to prove that the execution of a procedure is deterministic. Detecting exclusivity of abstract sequences is also relevant to prove that a cut is green at some position in the procedure (see Section 4.2). Section 6.3.1 recalls how the basic framework detects exclusivity through the operation EXCLUSIVE. In some situations that are illustrated in Section 6.3.2, the basic framework fails to detect the exclusivity of clauses. Section 6.3.3 provides the new implementation for detecting exclusivity of abstract sequences, by considering the new *failure* and *size relations* components of abstract sequences.

6.3.1 Detection of exclusivity in the basic framework

Specification [exclusivity]

Let B_1, B_2 be two abstract sequences that have the same β_{in} component. The abstract operation EXCLUSIVE(B_1, B_2) is responsible to check whether the two abstract sequences B_1 and B_2 are exclusive. If the operation returns true, then the following holds. Let $\theta \in Cc(\beta_{in})$. If $\langle \theta, S_1 \rangle \in Cc(B_1)$ and $\langle \theta, S_2 \rangle \in Cc(B_2)$ then either $S_1 = <>$ or $S_2 = <>$.

Implementation [exclusivity]

The basic framework implements the operation EXCLUSIVE(B_1, B_2) as follows:

$$\text{EXCLUSIVE}(B_1, B_2) \Leftrightarrow \beta_{ref}^1 \sqcap \beta_{ref}^2 = \bot$$

6.3.2 Inaccuracies of the basic framework

Example 1: Basic framework is unable to check determinacy of `merge`

Consider the procedure `merge(Xs,Ys,Zs)` that merges the two ordered lists of integers `Xs` and `Ys` into the ordered list `Zs`.

```
merge(Xs, [], Xs).
merge([], [Y|Ys], [Y|Ys]).
merge([X|Xs], [Y|Ys], [X|Zs]) :-
    X < Y, merge(Xs, [Y|Ys], Zs).
merge([X|Xs], [Y|Ys], [X,X|Zs]) :-
    X =:= Y, merge(Xs, Ys, Zs).
merge([X|Xs], [Y|Ys], [Y|Zs]) :-
    X > Y, merge([X|Xs], Ys, Zs).
```
Procedure 6.11   merge(Xs,Ys,Zs)

Assume that this procedure is called when input Xs and Ys are lists of integers and when input Zs is a variable. The expected formal specification can be described as follows.

```
merge/3
    in(Xs:list(int), Ys:list(int), Zs:var)
    out(_, _, list(int))
    srel( Xs_in+Ys_in = Zs_out )
    sol(sol = 1)
    sexpr(< (list)Xs+(list)Ys >)
```
Specification 6.17   merge(Xs,Ys,Zs)

The checker starts its verification analysis by executing each clause separately. Below, $ref i$ denotes the ref part of the abstract sequence modelling the execution of the ith clause of the procedure merge.

```
ref1(Xs:[X:int|list(int)],Ys:[],                      Zs:var)
ref2(Xs:[],                   Ys:[Y:int|list(int)],Zs:var)
ref3(Xs:[X:int|list(int)],Ys:[Y:int|list(int)],Zs:var)
ref4(Xs:[X:int|list(int)],Ys:[Y:int|list(int)],Zs:var)
ref5(Xs:[X:int|list(int)],Ys:[Y:int|list(int)],Zs:var)
```

Based on this information, the basic framework is able to check that the first two clauses are exclusive, and that they are exclusive with the last three clauses (the frame information is incompatible). However, the checker is unable to detect that the last three clauses are exclusive (they are abstractly identical). Thus, the analyser cannot prove Specification 6.17.

Example 2: Basic framework is unable to prove determinacy of delete

In Section 4.1.2, we have illustrated the inaccuracy of the basic framework for detecting the determinacy of procedures using negations. In particular, we have shown that the exclusivity between the first two clauses of Procedure 4.1 with respect to Specification 4.1 cannot be proved by relying only on the ref part of abstract sequences.

6.3.3   Improving the detection of exclusivity with the new domains

Example 1: Take into account the *size relations* component

In Section 5.3, abstract sequences and substitutions have been enhanced with a new *size relations* component, where several primitive and user-defined norms and functions are combined. The ref parts of the abstract sequences modelling the last three clauses of the procedure merge, enhanced with their related size component, are as follows:

```
ref3([X:int|list(int)], [Y:int|list(int)], Zs:var;
     srel((int)X+1 =< (int)Y) )
ref4([X:int|list(int)], [Y:int|list(int)], Zs:var;
     srel((int)X = (int)Y) )
ref5([X:int|list(int)], [Y:int|list(int)], Zs:var;
     srel((int)X >= (int)Y+1) )
```

Incompatibility between the above srel components implies that the last three clauses are exclusive to each other. Note that in this case, the srel components describe relations between actual integer values and not, strictly speaking, relations between sizes, since the primitive function (int) is used.[1] It follows that the determinacy of the whole procedure can be proved and Specification 6.17 is successfully checked.

Example 2: Take into account the *failure* component

As it is illustrated in Section 4.1.3, it is possible to detect that the first two clauses of the procedure delete are exclusive by considering the new *failure* component, which models the input substitutions leading to a sure failure of the execution.

Detection of exclusivity in the new framework

The new framework implements the operation EXCLUSIVE(B_1, B_2), specified in Section 6.3.1, by taking into account the input refined conditions (β_{ref}), the size components (E_{ref_out}), as well as the failure components (β_{fails}).

$$\text{EXCLUSIVE}(B_1, B_2) \Leftrightarrow \left(\begin{array}{l} \beta^1_{ref} \sqcap \beta^2_{ref} = \bot \\ \vee \quad tr_1^{>}(E^1_{ref\_out}) \sqcap tr_2^{>}(E^2_{ref\_out}) = \bot \\ \vee \quad \exists \beta_f \in \beta^1_{fails} \cup \beta^2_{fails} : (\beta^1_{ref} \sqcap \beta^2_{ref}) \leq \beta_f \end{array} \right)$$

where tr_i is the structural mapping between β^i_{ref} and $(\beta^1_{ref} \sqcap \beta^2_{ref})$ $(i = 1, 2)$.

---

[1] As described in Section 5.3.1, *functions* define mapping from terms to integer values. The framework should be extended to handle functions that map terms to non-integer values. For instance, the function (float) should map each float term to its value. If the procedure merge is called with input lists of floats, then the function (float) will be used in the srel components, so that exclusivity of clauses can be proved.

6.4 Abstract sequence concatenation

When a procedure is composed of several clauses, the abstract operation CONC is responsible to concatenate the abstract sequences modelling the execution of the clauses. If the procedure is not specified, the abstract concatenation is necessary to compute an abstract sequence modelling the execution of the whole procedure (for a given class of input calls, and provided that the analyser is able to derive the abstract sequences of the clauses). In the context of verification, the result of the concatenation is compared with the intended abstract sequence, i.e., with the formal specification provided by the user. If the result of the concatenation 'implies' ($\leq$, see Section 3.4.5) the formal specification, then the analyser succeeds to prove that the procedure meets its specification. Otherwise, the verification analysis fails. Thus, the operation used for concatenating abstract sequences is crucial, and it must be designed to compute accurate results. In particular, the operation must precisely compute the global number of solutions, including global input conditions for which the execution surely succeeds or fails.

The basic framework [78] proposes an implementation for concatenating two abstract sequences. That *binary abstract concatenation* uses actively the original aspects of the framework, especially the *input refined component* of abstract sequences (see Section 3.4.4) and the *constrained mappings* over the size components (see Section 3.4.2 and Appendix E). However, the implementation of the basic framework can be improved. For instance, it is not accurate when the procedure uses negation or cuts, and when the procedure uses structures other than lists. Also, when a procedure consists of more than two clauses, the basic framework concatenates all abstract sequences by repeatedly applying the binary concatenation (from the bottom to the top of the procedure). This strategy does not always find the optimal result, because other combinations of abstract sequences may provide more precise abstract results, for instance, by considering groups of exclusive clauses separately.

This section presents the new abstract sequence concatenation. The operation takes into account the new domains of abstract substitutions and abstract sequences, e.g., the type system (see Section 5.2), the size relations with combined norms (see Section 5.3), the untouched component (see Section 6.1), the failure component (see Section 4.1.3), as well as the abstract domain modelling the execution of cuts (see Section 4.2.3). The abstract concatenation operation illustrates the interest of putting together all the concepts introduced so far: those from the basic framework and those from the new extensions presented in this thesis. We provide several examples to show the benefits of each domain to obtain a precise implementation.

The key aspects of the new abstract operation are the detection of exclusivity of abstract sequences and the detection of the global sure success of the execution. The *detection of exclusivity* of abstract sequences (see Section 6.3) is needed to prove the determinacy and more generally, to refine the number of solutions by considering groups of clauses that are mutually exclusive. It allows us to decide whether the numbers of solutions of the abstract sequences must be summed, or if we need only to compute a least upper bound of the cardinality information. We can even better refine the global number of solutions, by splitting non-exclusive abstract sequences into smaller exclusive ones. An abstract sequence may be specialised by considering the refined and failure components of the other abstract sequences. All abstract domains of substitutions are relevant for the detection of exclusivity, especially, the new types and the size relations with combined norms. The *detection of sure success of execution* of the whole procedure requires a lot of attention. The refined (`ref`) and failure (`fail`) components of an abstract sequence inform us about the input conditions for which a clause (or a group of clauses) succeeds or fails. To prove that every input considered by the specification is covered and surely succeeds, we have to check whether the least upper bound of the refined conditions covers the considered input, and whether it is an *exact* upper bound. The failure components must also be taken into account, which complicates the implementation of the concatenation operation. The concatenation of more than two abstract sequences is performed by grouping together non-exclusive abstract sequences (abstract sequences belonging to different groups are exclusive). Different groups are treated separately (the concatenation is performed for each group), and then, the abstract results are merged (operation `MERGE`). In particular, this operation checks whether the sure success is preserved after having merged the abstract sequences. The computation of the exact least upper bound requires to find the best combination of the input refined components (the computation may be performed in another order than from bottom to top). To guarantee sure success, the operation also verifies that each failure component of each clause is covered by the refined component of another clause.

The abstract operation is complex and its formal implementation is provided in Appendix F. This section presents the operation on small examples of increasing complexity. We progressively introduce the benefits and the necessity of each domain. The rest of this section is organised as follows. Section 6.4.1 presents the binary abstract concatenation, without cut and without negation. The implementation of the basic framework is recalled, and several examples show that the input refined domains, as well as the new domains of abstract substitutions (e.g., types, norms) are important to get good accuracy. Section 6.4.2 describes the binary abstract concatenation, without cut but with negation. The interest of the failure component is illustrated. Section 6.4.3 describes the multiple abstract concatenation, without cut and without negation. Section 6.4.4 describes the multiple abstract concatenation, without cut and with negation. Section 6.4.5 describes what changes in the operation when the procedure uses cuts.

6.4.1   Binary abstract concatenation (without cut, without negation)

This section illustrates the *binary abstract concatenation* when the procedure does not use cut nor negation. We first recall how the binary abstract concatenation is implemented in the basic framework. Then, six examples are proposed. The first two examples are performed using the binary abstract concatenation of the basic framework: Example 1 is a case where the refined component is not needed, and Example 2 shows that the refined component is instrumental to prove the exclusivity of clauses. The last four examples show the limitations of the basic framework and how we overcome those limitations by using the new abstract domains. Example 3 shows the benefit of having the new type system for proving the sure success of the execution, Example 4 and Example 5 illustrate the interest of considering size relations for the detection of exclusivity. Example 6 shows the interest of decomposing non-exclusive abstract sequences into exclusive and non-exclusive specialised abstract sequences, in order to refine the global number of solutions.

Abstract concatenation in the basic framework

The implementation of the binary concatenation CONC of abstract sequences B_1 and B_2 is recalled in Appendix F.3. The operation uses several auxiliary operations over abstract substitutions and over size components (e.g., (exact) least upper bound, greatest lower bound, constrained mappings), which are formally defined in the appendix. The operation works as follows. First, it performs the greatest lower bound of the input refined components ($\beta_{glb} = \text{GLB}(\beta^1_{ref}, \beta^2_{ref})$). If β_{glb} is equal to $\bot$, then the two clauses are exclusive, such that the global number of solutions is the least upper bound (operation $\sqcup$ over size components) of E^1_{sol} and E^2_{sol}. Otherwise, the global number of solutions is the least upper bound of E^1_{sol}, E^2_{sol}, and the 'sum' of the two solutions components (operation $\text{SUM\_SOL}(\overline{E}^1_{sol}, \overline{E}^2_{sol})$), where $\overline{E}^i_{sol}$ is the constrained mapping projection of E^i_{sol} over the indices of β_{glb}, $i = 1, 2$). The global sure success is preserved if the least upper bound of β^1_{ref} and β^2_{ref} is exact (computed though the operation $\langle \beta'_{ref}, exact \rangle = \text{EXT\_LUB}$, with the boolean $exact$ implies that the least upper bound is exact). Otherwise, the number of solutions is relaxed, and may be equal to zero. The accuracy of the operation depends especially on the ability to detect the exclusivity of abstract sequences (and then, to sum or not the number of solutions) and to detect if the least upper bound of the refined components is exact (and then, to preserve or not the sure success). The final output substitution β'_{out} and the size relations E'_{ref_out} are computed through the least upper bound operations.

Example 1: the input refined conditions are sometimes non-necessary

Consider the following procedure p_1/2.

```
p_1(X,Y)  :- X=a,  q_1(Y).
p_1(X,Y)  :- X=b,  q_2(Y).
```

Assume that the predicates q_1/1 and q_2/1 are specified as follows.

```
assume q_1                    assume q_2
   in(Y:var)                     in(Y:var)
```

```
out(ground)                          out(ground)
sol(sol = 1)                         sol(sol = 2)
```

Consider the class of input calls in(X:var,Y:var;noshare(<X,Y>)). The abstract sequences modelling the first and second clauses are B1 and B2, respectively.

```
B1:                                  B2:
   in(X:var,Y:var;                      in(X:var,Y:var;
       noshare(<X,Y>))                      noshare(<X,Y>))
   sol(sol = 1)                         sol(sol = 2)
```

The two abstract sequences above are not exclusive: both surely succeed for the same input (in this case, the in and ref parts are identical). Thus, the final number of solutions E'_{sol} is the result of summing the two solutions components of B_1 and B_2 through the operation SUM_SOL(E^1_{sol}, E^2_{sol}). The result of the concatenation, which models the execution of the whole procedure p_1, is thus:

```
p_1
   in(X:var, Y:var; noshare(<X,Y>))
   out(ground, ground)
   sol(sol = 3)
```

Example 2: the input refined conditions are instrumental to detect exclusivity

Consider now the class of input calls in(X:ground,Y:var) for the same procedure p_1/2. If we do not consider the input refined components of abstract sequences, then the two abstract sequences B1 and B2 (modelling the execution of the two clauses) are as follows:

```
B1:                                  B2:
   in(X:ground,Y:var)                   in(X:ground,Y:var)
   sol(sol =< 1)                        sol(sol =< 2)
```

The sure success cannot be guaranteed. Furthermore, the exclusivity between the clauses cannot be checked, because the two input refined components ref (which are equal to the in component) are equal, so that the concatenation operation sums the number of solutions, yielding the following inaccurate abstract sequence.

```
p_1
   in(X:ground, Y:var)
   out(_, ground)
   sol(sol =< 3)
```

If we now consider the input refined components, then the abstract sequences B1 and B2 are more accurate (they contain information about the sure success and the sure failure of the execution).

```
B1:                                   B2:
  in(X:ground,Y:var)                    in(X:ground,Y:var)
  ref(a,var)                            ref(b,var)
  sol(sol = 1)                          sol(sol = 2)
```

The two clauses are exclusive because $\text{GLB}(\beta_{ref}^1, \beta_{ref}^2)$ is equal to $\bot$. However, the least upper bound of the two refined components is not exact $(\text{EXT\_LUB}(\beta_{ref}^1, \beta_{ref}^2) = \langle(\text{X}:\textbf{ground}, \text{Y}:\textbf{var}), \textit{false}\rangle)$. Thus, the final abstract sequence is as follows (it is more accurate than without considering the β_{ref} components, but the sure success is still not verified).

```
p_1
  in(X:ground, Y:var)
  out(_, ground)
  sol(sol =< 2)
```

Removing the limitations of the basic framework

Example 3: the new type systems allows us to check sure success

The new domain of types allows us to improve the detection of sure success. Consider again the previous example, and assume that the type ab is declared as follows:

```
    ab ::= a | b
```

Type definition 6.6   ab

Now, the least upper bound between β_{ref}^1 and β_{ref}^2 becomes (X:ab,Y:var), which is an exact union. The sure success is thus preserved, and we obtain the optimal abstract sequence:

```
p_1
  in(X:ground, Y:var)
  ref(ab, _)
  out(_, ground)
  sol(1 =< sol =< 2)
```

Example 4: the new norms allows us to detect exclusivity

Consider the predicate minimum(X,Y,Z) which holds iff Z is the minimum of X and Y.

```
minimum(X,Y,X) :- X =< Y.
minimum(X,Y,Y) :- X > Y.
```

Consider the class of input calls in(X:int,Y:int,Z:var). The following two abstract sequences B1 and B2 model the execution of the first and second clauses, respectively.

```
B1:                                    B2:
  in(X:int,Y:int,Z:var)                  in(X:int,Y:int,Z:var)
  out(_, _, int)                         out(_, _, int)
  srel((int)X_ref =< (int)Y_ref)  srel((int)X_ref>(int)Y_ref)
  sol(sol = 1)                           sol(sol = 1)
```

The basic implementation considers only the input refined components to detect exclusivity. In this case, $\beta_{glb} = \mathrm{GLB}(\beta^1_{ref}, \beta^2_{ref})$ is not equal to $\perp$, so that the number of solutions of the two clauses is summed, yielding the following imprecise abstract sequence:

```
minimum
   in(X:int,Y:int,Z:var)
   out(_, _, int)
   sol(1 =< sol =< 2)
```

As already illustrated in Section 6.3.3, the new framework takes into account the size components (projected on the indices of the β_{glb} by constrained mappings) to detect exclusivity of abstract sequences. In this case, the two size relations are incompatible ($E^1_{sol} \sqcap E^2_{sol} = \perp$), and the final (and more accurate) abstract sequence is thus:

```
minimum
   in(X:int,Y:int,Z:var)
   out(_, _, int)
   sol(sol = 1)
```

Example 5: new types and new norms allow us to prove more general relations

This example is introduced to illustrate that we can prove more general relations between the size of the input terms and the number of solutions thanks to refined input components, types and norms. For instance, consider the following procedure p_2/2.

```
p_2(X,Y) :- X=a(Z), q_1(Z,Y).
p_2(X,Y) :- X=b(Z), q_2(Z,Y).
```

We assume the following formal specifications for q_1/2 and q_2/2:

```
assume q_1                     assume q_2
   in(Z:ground, Y:var)            in(Z:ground, Y:var)
   ref(list(int), _)             ref(list(float), _)
   sol(sol = (list)Z_in)         sol(sol = 2 * (list)Z_in)
```

We assume the following type declaration for ab/2:

```
ab(Ta,Tb) ::= a(list(Ta)) | b(list(Tb))
```
Type definition 6.7   ab/2

We assume the following norm declaration (ab), which is associated to the type ab/2:

```
(ab) a(L) = (list)L
(ab) b(L) = (list)L
```
Norm definition 6.3   ab/2

With those information, the analyser can prove the following formal specification:

```
p_2
  in(X:ground, Y:var)
  ref(ab(int,float), _)
  sol((ab)X_ref =< sol =< 2 * (ab)X_ref)
```

In the rest of the discussion, we stick to simpler examples because we focus on problems that are specific to the abstract sequence concatenation.

Example 6: decomposing abstract sequences allows us to refine cardinality

The last example of this section illustrates another inaccuracy of the binary operation CONC that is implemented in the basic framework, and how we modify it to obtain better results. Consider the procedure append(X1,X2,X3):

```
append([],X2,X2).
append([X4|X5],X2,[X4|X6]) :- append(X5,X2,X6).
```

Consider the class of input calls where X1 and X2 are two distinct variables and where X3 is a ground list. The analyser is able to derive the following two abstract sequences B1 and B2, which correspond to the execution of the two clauses:

```
B1:
  in(X1:var,X2:var,X3:list(ground); noshare(<X1,X2>))
  out(list(ground),list(ground),_)
  sol(sol = 1, (list)X3_ref >= 0)

B2:
  in(X1:var,X2:var,X3:list(ground); noshare(<X1,X2>))
  ref(_,_,[ground|list(ground)])
  out([ground|list(ground)],list(ground),_)
  sol(sol = (list)X3_ref, (list)X3_ref >= 1)
```

The sol component describes the number of solutions in function of the size of input terms. It is defined on the set of indices occurring in the ref component (plus the special variable sol denoting the number of solutions). The first clause surely succeeds exactly once, for any input list X3 (the list-length of input X3 is greater than or equal to zero). The second clause surely succeeds if and only if the third argument X3 is a non-empty list (X3_ref >= 1). The number of solutions is exactly the list-length of X3.

The two clauses are not exclusive, so that the global number of solutions is computed as the upper bound of E^1_{sol}, and E^2_{sol}, and the sum of E^1_{sol} and E^2_{sol} when input X3 is a non-empty list (sol=(list)X3_ref+1,(list)X3_ref>=1). The upper bound is computed as the convex hull of polyhedra [7, 120], and is thus (1 =< sol =< (list)X3_ref+1). The sure success is preserved because the least upper bound of β^1_{ref} and β^2_{ref} is exact (it is equal to β^1_{ref}). The final abstract sequence is thus:

```
append
    ref(X1:var,X2:var,X3:list(ground);
        noshare(<X1,X2>))
    sol(1 =< sol =< (list)X3_ref+1)
```

To obtain a more accurate cardinality information, one can compute the global number of solutions in a different way, by decomposing the two non-exclusive abstract sequences B_1 and B_2 into a set of specialised abstract sequences: two with exactly the same refined components (they are not exclusive and the number of solutions is summed), and two other that are exclusive with the others. The final abstract sequence modelling the whole procedure is obtained by making a union.

For the append example, we can compute, from B1 and B2, the two abstract sequences which are surely exclusive. This is performed by removing from one abstract sequence the refined component of the other (through the operation DIFFERENCE(B_i, β^j_{ref}), $i = 1, 2, j = 1, 2, i \neq j$):

```
DIFFERENCE(B1,ref2):                 DIFFERENCE(B2,ref1):
  ref(X1:var,X2:var,                   ref(bottom)
      X3:[];                           sol(sol = 0)
      noshare(<X1,X2>))
  sol(sol = 1, (list)X3_ref = 0)
```

The first abstract sequence describes the conditions for which only the first clause succeeds. When X3 is an empty list, then the first clause succeeds exactly once, and the second clause fails. The second abstract sequence is empty: this comes from the fact that the refined component of B_2 is less than the refined component of B_1. If the second clause succeeds, then the first clause succeeds too.

We can compute also, from B1 and B2, the two abstract sequences that are not exclusive. This is performed by intersecting the two refined input components (through the operation INTER(B_i, β^j_{ref}), $i = 1, 2, j = 1, 2, i \neq j$):

```
INTER(B1,ref2):                      INTER(B2,ref1):
  ref(X1:var,X2:var,                   ref(X1:var,X2:var,
      X3:[ground|list(ground)];          X3:[ground|list(ground)];
      noshare(<X1,X2>))                  noshare(<X1,X2>))
  sol(sol = 1)                         sol(sol = (list)X3_ref)
```

The above two abstract sequences have a common input refined component (the input X3 is a non-empty list). A specialised concatenation is performed (through the specialised operation CONC1, see Appendix F.5):

```
CONC1(INTER(B1,ref2),INTER(B2,ref1)):
  ref(X1:var,X2:var,X3:[ground|list(ground)];
      noshare(<X1,X2>))
  sol(sol = (list)X3_ref+1)
```

Finally, the abstract operation MERGE computes the final abstract sequence, by merging the two exclusive abstract sequences DIFFERENCE(B1,ref2) and CONC1(INTER(B1,ref2),INTER(B2,ref1)). In particular, the least upper bound of (sol=1,(list)X3_ref=0) and (sol=(list)X3_ref+1, (list)X3_ref>=1) is (sol=(list)X3_ref+1,(list)X3_ref>=0). The final abstract sequence modelling the procedure append is thus the expected one:

```
append
  ref(X1:var,X2:var,X3:list(ground);
      noshare(<X1,X2>))
  sol(sol = (list)X3_ref+1)
```

The new implementation of the binary concatenation of abstract sequences can then be summarised as follows (see Appendix F for more details). The operation $\text{CONC}(B_1, B_2)$ computes a set of exclusive abstract sequences SB as follows.

1. Compute $\beta_{glb} = \text{GLB}(\beta_{ref}^1, \beta_{ref}^2)$. If $\beta_{glb} = \perp$ then $SB = \{B_1, B_2\}$.

2. Otherwise, compute $B_1^{inter} = \text{INTER}(B_1, \beta_{ref}^2)$ and $B_2^{inter} = \text{INTER}(B_2, \beta_{ref}^1)$. The abstract sequence B_1^{inter} is a specialisation of B_1, where its refined component β_{ref}^1 is intersected with the refined component β_{ref}^2 of B_2. The resulting abstract sequences B_1^{inter} and B_2^{inter} have the same refined components, and are thus non-exclusive (they represent the executions for which both clauses succeed).

3. Then, compute $B_{12}^{inter} = \text{CONC1}(B_1^{inter}, B_2^{inter})$ (the sure success is preserved and no constraints sol=0 is added in B_{12}^{inter}).

4. Then, compute $B_1^{excl} = \text{DIFFERENCE}(B_1, \beta_{ref}^2)$ and $B_2^{excl} = \text{DIFFERENCE}(B_2, \beta_{ref}^1)$. The abstract sequence B_1^{excl} is a specialisation of B_1, where the refined component β_{ref}^2 of B_2 is removed from the refined component β_{ref}^1 of B_1. Thus, B_1^{excl} denotes the executions for which only the first clause succeeds, and B_2^{excl} denotes the executions for which only the second clause succeeds.

5. SB is the set $\{B_{12}^{inter}, B_1^{excl}, B_2^{excl}\}$.

After that, the operation MERGE(SB) merges the set of exclusive abstract sequences SB. That operation performs least upper bounds over the components of abstract sequences (in particular, it does not sum the number of solutions) and it is responsible to check the sure success (by detecting whether the least upper bound of the input refined conditions is an exact union). If the least upper bound of the refined components is not exact, then the number of solutions must be relaxed (the global number of solutions may be equal to zero). The reason comes from the meaning (concretisation) of the refined component of abstract sequences. A refined component denotes necessary conditions for sure success, such that any input calls that do not satisfy the refined component surely fail. So, if the upper bound of the refined component β_{ref}^1 and β_{ref}^2 is not exact, then it contains some input calls that do not belong to the concretisation of β_{ref}^1 and β_{ref}^2, so that the execution surely fails (the sure success is not preserved, and a constraint sol=0 must be added in the global cardinality component).

6.4.2   Binary abstract concatenation (without cut, with negation)

This section now considers the binary abstract concatenation for procedures that use negations. In Section 4.1, we propose a *failure* component of abstract sequences, which allows us to model accurately the execution of negation. The new binary abstract operation takes into account this component, which allows the analyser to gain in accuracy with respect to the detection of exclusivity and of the sure success.

Inaccuracies of the basic framework

The following example shows the inaccuracy of the basic framework to detect exclusivity and sure success without the failure component.

Example 7: the basic framework cannot detect exclusivity and sure success

Consider the following procedure p_3/2:

```
p_3(X,Y) :- X=a, q_1(Y).
p_3(X,Y) :- not(X=a), q_2(Y).
```

We assume the same formal specifications as before for q_1/1 and q_2/1 (see Example 1). Consider the class of input calls in(X:ground,Y:var). In the basic framework, the abstract sequences modelling the execution of the first and second clause are B1 and B2, respectively:

```
B1:                          B2:
   ref(X:a,Y:var)               ref(X:ground,Y:var)
   sol(sol = 1)                 sol(sol =< 2)
```

The sure success of the second clause (when X $\neq$ a) cannot be modelled. Furthermore, the exclusivity of the two clauses cannot be proved ($\text{GLB}(\beta_{ref}^1, \beta_{ref}^2) = \beta_{ref}^1 \neq \perp$), so that the final number of solutions is the sum of E_{sol}^1 and E_{sol}^2. The inaccurate final abstract sequence for the whole procedure is:

```
p_3
    ref(X:ground,Y:var)
    sol(sol =< 3)
```

Binary abstract concatenation with the failure components

We reconsider Example 7 by taking into account the *failure* component of abstract sequences. This implies a modification of the algorithm proposed in the previous section for the detection of exclusivity and sure success. Thanks to the failure component, the abstract sequence B2 is more accurate:

```
B1:                          B2:
    ref(X:a,Y:var)               ref(X:ground,Y:var)
    sol(sol = 1)                 fail(a,  var)
                                 sol(sol = 2)
```

The two clauses are exclusive because the refined component β_{ref}^1 is equal to the failure component β_{fail}^2. Consequently, a least upper bound is performed over the number of solutions, yielding (1=<sol<=2). The sure success is preserved because the least upper bound of the 'refined minus fails' components of B1 and B2 is exact. To prove it, we remove the failure components of some abstract sequences that are covered by the refined component of other abstract sequences. In this case, the failure component of B2 is contained in the input refined component of B1, so that the failure component is covered. Having removed the failure component, we still have to check that the least upper bound of the two refined components is exact, which is the case. The final abstract sequence is thus:

```
p_3
    in(X:ground, Y:var)
    out(_, ground)
    sol(1 =< sol =< 2)
```

6.4.3 Multiple abstract concatenation (without cut, without negation)

This section deals with procedures that are composed of more than two clauses. Example 8 shows the interest of grouping together the clauses that are non-exclusive. The groups are concatenated separately, and then, the resulting abstract sequences are merged (operation MERGE). Example 9 illustrates how the concatenation is performed inside a group of non-exclusive abstract sequences. We reuse the idea of Section 6.4.1, i.e., we decompose the abstract sequences in pieces that have identical refined components or are exclusive. The abstract sequence modelling the group is then computed through the operation MERGE. Afterwards, Example 10 shows how the MERGE procedure computes the global sure success, by performing an knapsack algorithm for computing the exact upper bound of more than two refined components.

Example 8: groups of non-exclusive clauses

Consider the following procedure p_4/1, which is composed of five clauses:

```
p_4(X):- X = a.
p_4(X):- X = b.
p_4(X):- X = a.
p_4(X):- X = b.
p_4(X):- X = a.
```

Assume that the type ab is declared (Type Definition 6.6). Consider the class of input calls in(X:ground). In the basic framework, the concatenation is performed in sequence (from the bottom to the top of the procedure). It begins to concatenate B4 and B5, then it concatenates the result with B3, and so on. The intermediate results are depicted below.

```
CONC(B4,B5):                CONC(B3,CONC(B4,B5)):
  ref(X:ab)                   ref(X:ab)
  sol(sol = 1)                sol(1 =< sol =< 2)

CONC(B2,CONC(B3,CONC(B4,B5))):
  ref(X:ab)
  sol(1 =< sol =< 3)

CONC(B1,CONC(B2,CONC(B3,CONC(B4,B5)))):
  ref(X:ab)
  sol(1 =< sol =< 4)
```

A better cardinality information can be checked by grouping together non-exclusive clauses (actually, their corresponding abstract sequence). If two abstract sequences do not belong to the same group, they are exclusive. The composition of such groups is performed by using the operation EXCLUSIVE described in Section 6.3. In this example, thanks to the refined component, we can consider two mutually exclusive groups (each of them contains non-exclusive abstract sequences): the group {B1,B3,B5} and the group {B2,B4}.

Each group is abstractly concatenated, which gives:

```
GROUP[B1,B3,B5]:            GROUP[B2,B4]:
  ref(a)                      ref(b)
  sol(sol = 3)                sol(sol = 2)
```

These two abstract sequences are merged (MERGE), and we obtain the following final abstract sequence, which gives a more accurate cardinality information than before:

```
p_4
  in(X:ground)
  ref(ab)
  sol(2 =< sol =< 3)
```

Example 9: decomposing abstract sequences inside a non-exclusive group

This example illustrates how to deal with a non-exclusive group. Consider this procedure p_5/1.

```
p_5(X):- X = a.
p_5(X).
p_5(X):- X = b.
```

Consider the class of input calls in(X:ground). The abstract sequences B1, B2 and B3 corresponding to the execution of the three clauses are as follows:

```
B1:                 B2:                 B3:
  ref(a)              ref(ground)        ref(b)
  sol(sol = 1)        sol(sol = 1)       sol(sol = 1)
```

The three clauses belong to the same non-exclusive group, because the first and the third clauses are non-exclusive with the second clause. In the basic framework, the result of the concatenation is:

```
CONC(B1,CONC(B2,B3)):
  in(X:ground)
  sol(1 =< sol =< 3)
```

The new implementation allows us to obtain more accurate results. We split the non-exclusive sequences into pieces that are non-exclusive (they have the same refined elements and failure components), and pieces that are exclusive by construction. We can consider that the latter pieces are exclusive (even if they are not exclusive formally) because their common elements have been put in the sequences with the same input refined components.

In this example, the abstract sequences B1, B2 and B3 are decomposed into Ba, Bb, Bab as follows (using the DIFFERENCE and INTER operations).

```
Ba:                 Bb:                 Bab:
  ref(a)              ref(b)             ref(ground)
  sol(sol = 2)        sol(sol = 2)       fail(a)
                                         fail(b)
                                         sol(sol = 1)
```

The above exclusive abstract sequences are merged through the operation MERGE, yielding the final abstract sequence:

```
p_5
  in(X:ground)
  sol(1 =< sol =< 2)
```

Example 10: using a knapsack algorithm for proving the global sure success

Consider the following procedure p_6, which is composed of four exclusive clauses (in the context of the class of input calls in(X:ground)).

```
p_6(X)  :- X=f(a).
p_6(X)  :- X=g(b).
p_6(X)  :- X=f(b).
p_6(X)  :- X=g(a).
```

We assume that the types fg/1 and ab/0 are declared as follows.

```
fg(T) ::= f(T) | g(T)
ab ::= a | b
```

Type definition 6.8   fg/1, ab/0

In the basic framework, the concatenation is performed from the bottom to the top of the procedure. In particular, the global least upper bound of the input refined components is computed as $\mathrm{LUB}(\beta_{ref}^1, \mathrm{LUB}(\beta_{ref}^2, \mathrm{LUB}(\beta_{ref}^3, \beta_{ref}^4)))$. The global least upper bound is considered exact only if each of the intermediate least upper bounds are exact. In this case, the $\mathrm{LUB}(\beta_{ref}^3, \beta_{ref}^4)$ is (X:fg(ab)), which is not an exact union of β_{ref}^3 and β_{ref}^4. It follows from this computation that the sure success cannot be proved:

```
p_6
  in(X:ground)
  ref(fg(ab))
  sol(sol =< 1)
```

To solve this problem, we try to find the best combination between the abstract sequences to compute (if it is possible) an *exact* least upper bound of their input refined components. A knapsack algorithm tries to find a combination between the input refined components such that each operation LUB computes an exact upper bound, and such that the global upper bound is exact. In this case, the winning computation is $\mathrm{LUB}(\mathrm{LUB}(\beta_{ref}^1, \beta_{ref}^3), \mathrm{LUB}(\beta_{ref}^2, \beta_{ref}^4))$. It results that the sure success is preserved, and the final abstract sequence modelling the whole procedure is optimal:

```
p_6
  in(X:ground)
  ref(fg(ab))
  sol(sol = 1)
```

6.4.4 Multiple abstract concatenation (without cut, with negation)

When a procedure uses negations, the abstract sequences may contain failure components. This situation may also occur when the procedure does not use explicitly of negation, but when it calls a procedure whose specification contains information about its failing executions.

In such a situation, the multiple abstract concatenation is performed in the same way than in the previous sections. With the failure components, we can detect more situations of exclusivity, which is important to build the exclusive groups of clauses. Section 6.3 illustrates how such a detection of exclusivity may benefit from the failure component (operation EXCLUSIVE): if the refined component of a clause is included in a failure component of another clause, then the two clauses are exclusive.

Example 11: procedure with negation

Consider the following procedure p_7/3

```
p_7(X, Y, Z):- X = a.
p_7(X, Y, Z):- not(X = a), not(Y = b).
p_7(X, Y, Z):- not(X = a), Y = b, Z = c.
p_7(X, Y, Z):- not(X = a), Y = b, not(Z = c).
```

Consider the class of input calls in (X:ground,Y:ground,Z:ground). The abstract sequences modelling the clauses are:

```
B1:
  ref(X:a,Y:ground,Z:ground)
  sol(sol = 1)
B2:
  ref(X:ground,Y:ground,Z:ground)
  fail(X:a,Y:ground,Z:ground)
  fail(X:ground,Y:b,Z:ground)
  sol(sol = 1)
B3:
  ref(X:ground,Y:b,Z:c)
  fail(X:a,Y:ground,Z:ground)
  sol(sol = 1)
B4:
  ref(X:ground,Y:b,Z:ground)
  fail(X:a,Y:ground,Z:ground)
  fail(X:ground,Y:b,Z:c)
  sol(sol = 1)
```

The analyser is able to detect that the clauses are mutually exclusive. Thus, each abstract sequence constitutes a separate group. The first clause is exclusive with the others because the refined component β^1_{ref} of B1 is contained in the failure components of B2, B3 and B4. The third and fourth clauses are exclusive with the second clause because their input refined component β^3_{ref} and β^3_{ref} are contained in the failure component of B2. Finally, the last two clauses are exclusive because the refined component of B3 is included in the failure component of B4.

Because the abstract sequences are exclusive, we can apply the operation MERGE to merge those abstract sequences. The detection of the global sure success, and the computation of the global refined conditions and failure components are performed as follows.

To check whether the global sure success is preserved, the analyser checks (1) if the least upper bound of the input refined components is exact, and (2) if each failure component of an abstract sequence is covered by another abstract sequence. As before (see Example 10), the analyser applies a knapsack algorithm in order to find (if possible) a suitable combination of the abstract sequences to compute an exact upper bound of the input refined components. In this case, several combinations are possible to compute an exact upper bound, for instance, $\mathrm{LUB}(\mathrm{LUB}(\mathrm{LUB}(\beta^1_{ref}, \beta^2_{ref}), \beta^3_{ref}), \beta^4_{ref})$ is exact. A failure component is covered by another clause if it is included in the refined component of that clause, and such that it is exclusive with the failure components of that clause. Each time the analyser detects that a failure component is covered, then it removes it from the corresponding abstract sequence, and it tries to check whether other failure components are covered. If all the failure components can be removed, then the global non-failure input condition is the least upper bound of the refined components.

In this example, the failure component fail(X:a,Y:ground,Z:ground) of B2, B3 and B4 is covered by the first clause, because it is included in β^1_{ref} of B1 (and no failure component is attached to B1). We can thus remove that component in the last B2, B3 and B4:

```
B1:  ref(X:a,Y:ground,Z:ground)

B2:  ref(X:ground,Y:ground,Z:ground)
     fail(X:ground,Y:b,Z:ground)

B3:  ref(X:ground,Y:b, Z:c)

B4:  ref(X:ground,Y:b, Z:ground)
     fail(X:ground,Y:b,Z:c)
```

Now, the failure component fail(X:ground,Y:b,Z:c) of the last clause is covered, because it is included in β^3_{ref}. By removing this component, we obtain:

```
B1:  ref(X:a,Y:ground,Z:ground)

B2:  ref(X:ground,Y:ground,Z:ground)
     fail(X:ground,Y:b,Z:ground)
```

```
B3: ref(X:ground,Y:b, Z:c)

B4: ref(X:ground,Y:b, Z:ground)
```

The last remaining failure component, `fail(X:ground,Y:b,Z:ground)`, is included in the input refined component of B4, which has no more failure component. Thus, we can remove it from the abstract sequence B2. There is no more failure elements, and the least upper bound of the input refined components is exact, such that the sure success is preserved. This allows the MERGE operation to compute the final abstract sequence modelling the whole procedure p_7:

```
p_7
   in(X:ground,Y:ground,Z:ground)
   sol(sol = 1)
```

6.4.5   Multiple abstract concatenation (with cut)

This section illustrates the abstract concatenation operation when the procedure uses cuts. It approximates the concrete concatenation □ of substitution sequences with cut information (see Section 4.2.1). The principle of the abstract concatenation is the same as before, except that the number of solutions of a clause using a cut is not summed with the number of solutions of its subsequent clauses (instead of, a least upper bound is performed). The implementation is provided in Appendix F.5.

We recall the notion of *abstract sequence with cut information*, which models the execution of a clause using cuts (see Section 4.2.3 for more details). An abstract sequence with cut information C is a tuple of the form $\langle B, acf, \beta_{cut}, \beta_{nocuts} \rangle$, where B is an abstract sequence, acf is the abstract cut information in $\{nocut, cut, weakcut\}$, β_{cut} is an abstract substitution, and β_{nocuts} is a set of abstract substitutions. β_{cut} and β_{nocuts} are defined only if $acf \in \{cut, weakcut\}$. If $acf = nocut$ then no cut is executed for any input θ. If $acf = cut$ then a cut is surely executed if and only if the input substitution θ satisfies the conditions of β_{cut} and does not satisfy the conditions imposed by the abstract substitutions β_{nocuts}. If $acf = weakcut$ then the β_{cut} and β_{nocuts} components impose necessary (but not sufficient) conditions for the sure execution of a cut.

Example 12: procedure with cuts

Consider the procedure p_8/2.

```
p_8(X,Y)  :- X=0, !, Y=a.
p_8(X,Y)  :- q(X,Y).
```

Assume the following formal specification for q/2.

```
q
   in(X:int,Y:var; srel((int)X >= 0))
   out(_, ground)
   sol(sol = (int)X_in)
```

Consider that input X is an non-negative integer and that input Y is a variable. The execution of the first clause is modelled by the abstract sequence with cut information $C_1 = \langle B_1, cut, \beta_{cut}^1, \emptyset \rangle$, where B_1 and β_{cut}^1 are as follows:

```
B1:
   ref(X:0, Y:var)              beta_cut(X:0, Y:var)
   sol(sol = 1)
```

The execution of the second clause is described by the abstract sequence B_2.

```
B2:
   ref(X:int, Y:var; srel((int)X >= 0))
   sol(sol = (int)X_ref)
```

The second clause is surely not executed for the inputs described by β_{cut}^1. So, the abstract sequence B_2 can be refined by DIFFERENCE(B_2, β_{cut}^1), where the β_{cut}^1 is removed from the refined component of B_2:

```
DIFFERENCE(B2,cut1):
   ref(X:int, Y:var; srel((int)X >= 1))
   sol(sol = (int)X_ref, (int)X_ref >= 1)
```

Thanks to the above abstract sequence, we know that the second clause is executed only if input X is greater or equal to one, and so that it surely succeeds. Afterwards, the operation MERGE merges the abstract sequences B_1 and DIFFERENCE(B_2, β_{cut}^1) by performing a least upper bound of their components. The sure success is preserved because the upper bound of the refined components is an exact union. The final abstract sequence is thus:

```
p_8:
   ref(X:int, Y:var; srel((int)X >= 0))
   sol(1 =< sol =< (int)X_ref)
```

In Chapter 8, we present our experimental results of the checker. The abstract sequence concatenation allows the system to check precise cardinality information of procedures (including the determinacy, sure success, sure failure). All the procedures and formal specifications verified by the checker are also available in [55].

6.5 Reexecution

6.5.1 Inaccuracies of the basic framework

The basic analyser performs a single pass during the abstract execution. It realises a form of forward/backward abstract interpretation. The backward step consists in maintaining in each program point the input conditions that ensure the sure success of the execution until that point. Such conditions are placed into the `ref` component of abstract sequences. This is realised locally, i.e., during the abstract execution of the literal and during the abstract extension of the goal (operation EXTG). This strategy works fine on a lot of examples, but there exist some situations where it does not suffice.

For instance, assume that a procedure, called `do_something`, is associated with the following two formal specifications.

```
do_something/2
   in(G:ground, Res:var)
   out(_, ground)
   sol(sol =< 1)
```
Specification 6.18 `do_something(G,Res)`

```
do_something/2
   in(G:list(ground), Res:var)
   out(_, ground)
   sol(sol = 1)
```
Specification 6.19 `do_something(G,Res)`

Specification 6.18 is more general (but less accurate) than Specification 6.19. Those specifications express that the procedure `do_something(G,Res)` is deterministic when input G is a ground term, and that it is fully deterministic when input G is a ground list.

Consider now the procedure `do_something_list(G,Res)` that calls the procedure `do_something` and then, tests whether G is a list.

```
list(L)  :-  [see Procedure 6.4]
```

```
do_something_list(G,Res) :-₁
   do_something(G,Res)₂, list(G)₃ .₄
```
Procedure 6.12 `do_something_list(G,Res)`

The specification of the subprocedure `list` is as follows.

```
list/1
   in(L:ground)
   ref(list(ground))
   sol(sol = 1)
```
Specification 6.20 `list(L)`

The expected specification for do_something_list(G, Res) is that it accepts any ground term G as input, and that it is fully-deterministic iff G is a ground list. This behaviour can be described as follows.

```
do_something_list/2
    in(G:ground, Res:var)
    ref(list(ground), _)
    out(_, ground)
    sol(sol = 1)
```

Specification 6.21   do_something_list(G, Res)

The basic framework cannot prove the sure success of the execution. Before the call to do_something(G, Res), the abstract sequence B1 is:

```
B1:
    in(G:ground, Res:var)
    out(G:ground, Res:var)
    sol(sol = 1)
```

After the call to do_something(G, Res), the abstract sequence B2 is computed using Specification 6.18:

```
B2:
    in(G:ground, Res:var)
    out(G:ground, Res:ground)
    sol(sol =< 1)
```

After the execution of list(G), at the view of Specification 6.20, the abstract sequence B3, is computed (backward information is captured in the ref component).

```
B3:
    in(G:ground, Res:var)
    ref(G:list(ground), Res:var)
    out(G:list(ground), Res:ground)
    sol(sol =< 1)
```

The sure success of the execution is not checked such that Specification 6.21 is not verified. However, at the view of the ref part of B3, we know that a necessary condition for the sure success of the execution is that G is a ground list.

6.5.2   Abstract reexecution with refined input

It is possible to make the analysis more accurate by reexecuting the whole clause with the ref part of B4 as input (B4 is identical to B3). The analyser is then able to prove Specification 6.21.

Before the call do_something(G, Res), the abstract sequence B1 becomes:

```
B1:
  in(G:list(ground), Res:var)
  out(G:list(ground), Res:var)
  sol(sol = 1)
```

Using now the more specific Specification 6.19, the checker computes the more precise abstract sequence B2:

```
B2:
  in(G:list(ground), Res:var)
  out(G:list(ground), Res:ground)
  sol(sol = 1)
```

The literal `list(G)` obviously succeeds in that case, and thus, because no refinement is computed, the sure success is proved and Specification 6.21 is verified.

Note that the abstract execution of `do_something_list(G,Res)` succeeds if the call `list(G)` is before the call `do_something(G,Res)`.

The interest for abstract reexecution has been illustrated in previous work [81]. When performing abstract interpretation like the one of GAIA [80], the tables maintaining the abstract information can be updated and refined each time a more specialised call, not yet recorded in the tables, is encountered.

Chapter 7

Implementation issues

In this chapter, we discuss the development effort concerning the coding of the analyser described so far (the verifier). Section 7.1 gives information about the structure of the Java classes and packages of the checker. Section 7.2 presents how the analyser is interfaced with a polyhedral library in order to maintain the linear constraints between the size of (input/output) terms, and such that operations can be performed on such systems of (in)equations. Section 7.3 lists the warning messages that can be generated by the checker when the verification analysis fails. Such warning messages are useful to debug an operationally incorrect code with respect to some specification. Information about how to use the system is provided in Appendix I.

7.1   Hierarchy of Java packages and classes

Most of the data structures are the simple translation of the abstract domains. Table 7.1 shows how the Java code is organised, by providing the hierarchy of the Java packages of the checker. The analyser is composed of 23 packages and 147 classes. There are 33586 lines of code. The analyser distribution is available at the website http://www.info.ucl.ac.be/~gobert.

Typically, there exists a Java file for each abstract domain defined so far. For instance, the domains of abstract substitutions and abstract sequences are implemented in the files ASubst.java and ASeq.java (they are depicted in Figure 7.1 and Figure 7.2, respectively). Each abstract operation is implemented by a corresponding Java method (only their signatures are shown). Note that the two size components E_{ref_out} and E_{sol} of an abstract sequence have been merged into a single one, namely $E_{ref\_out\_sol}$, which is implemented in the file ERefOutSol.java.

Package	Sub-Package	Description	Cl	NCSS
parsing		Parsers of programs, of type and norm declarations, and of specifications (in JavaCC)	14	10290
program		Program representation and normalisation: procedures, clauses, literals	13	1208
src		Information provided in the source file		
	srctype	User type declarations	8	566
	srcnorm	User norm declarations	4	262
	srcspec	Formal specification representation and normalisation	6	1782
adom		Abstract domains and operations		
	norm	Primitive and user norms	5	349
	asubst	Abstract substitutions	5	3900
	asubst.sv	Same-value component	1	169
	asubst.frm	Frame component	3	459
	asubst.alpha	Abstract tuple component	3	1196
	asubst.alpha.mode	Mode component	3	815
	asubst.alpha.type	Type component	13	2186
	asubst.alpha.ps	Possible sharing component	1	547
	asubst.alpha.lin	Linearity component	1	245
	aseq	Abstract sequences	1	3139
	aseq.sizes	Size component interfaced with PPL	14	2056
	abeh	Abstract behaviours	3	293
annotation		Annotated procedures and clauses	6	672
execution		Abstract execution of the checker	5	1167
exception		Execution warning messages	10	68
mystructure		Basic data structures	28	2217
Total			147	33586

Table 7.1: Java packages of the checker. The number of classes (**Cl**) and the number of non commenting source statements (**NCSS**) have been measured by JavaNCSS Ant Task.

```
public class ASubst {
  private SV sv;            //the same-value component
  private FRM frm;          //the frame component
  private ATuple alpha;     //the abstract tuple component

  public static ASubst GLB(ASubst b1, ASubst b2) {...}
  public static ASubst LUB(ASubst b1, ASubst b2) {...}
  public static boolean EXT_LUB(ASubst b1, ASubst b2,
                                ASubst lub) {...}

  (...)
}
```

Figure 7.1: File `ASubst.java` implementing an abstract substitution.

```
public class ASeq {
  //components
  private ASubst beta_in;
  private Vector beta_fails;
  private ASharedSubst beta_ref_out;
  private ERefOutSol e_ref_out_sol;

  //abstract operations
  public static boolean LEQ(ASeq B1,ASeq B2) {...}
  public static ASeq EXTC(Clause c,ASubst beta) {...}
  public static ASeq RESTRC(Clause c,ASeq B) {...}

  public static ASubst RESTRG(Literal l,ASeq B) {...}
  public static ASeq EXTG(Literal l,ASeq B1,ASeq B2) {...}

  public static BehP LOOKUP(ASubst beta,
                            Predicate p,
                            SBeh sbeh) {...}
  public static boolean CHECK_TERM(Literal l,
                                   ASeq B,
                                   LinExpr[] se) {...}
  public static ASeq UNIF_VAR(ASubst beta) {...}
  public static ASeq UNIF_FUNC(ASubst beta,
                               Functor f) {...}
  public static ASeq NOT_AI(Literal l,
                            ASubst beta,
                            SBeh sbeh) {...}
  public static boolean EXCLUSIVE(ASeq B1, ASeq B2) {...}
  public static ASeq CONC(ASeq B1, ASeq B2) {...}

  (...)
}
```

Figure 7.2: File `ASeq.java` implementing an abstract sequence.

7.2 Interface with a polyhedral library through the Java Native Interface

Data structures and operations for the size components have been implemented using the Parma Polyhedra Library PPL [8]. This library (written in C and C++) is interfaced with the analyser (written in Java) through the Java Native Interface (JNI). The Java Native Interface is a programming framework that allows Java code running in the Java virtual machine to call and be called by native applications and libraries written in other languages, such as C and C++. This integration has been realised with the help of Gustavo Ospina [111, 112].

The interface of the analyser with the PPL library is depicted in Figure 7.3.

Java side	JNI	C side
E.java		CPoly.c
ERefOutSol.java		global.h, c
ATuple.java $\leftrightarrow$ Sizes.java $\leftrightarrow$ CPoly.java $\leftrightarrow$ CPoly.h $\leftrightarrow$		matrix.h, c
ASubst.java		function.h, c
ASeq.java		jniaux.h, c
		polyhedron.h, c
$\updownarrow$		$\updownarrow$
Other components		PPL library (C++)
of the analyser		

Figure 7.3: Architecture of the analyser: interface with PPL through JNI.

7.2.1 Java-C interface

The C structure polyhedron is defined in the file global.h and is depicted in Figure 7.4.

```
typedef struct POLY {
        int dim;
        int * vars;
        ppl_Polyhedron_t ppl_ph;
    } *polyhedron;
```

Figure 7.4: Polyhedron type structure (defined in the C side).

The type polyhedron is a pointer to a structure POLY. It is composed of an array vars of dim integers that are the identifiers of the variables of the constraints system, and of course, it contains a reference to the effective PPL polyhedron ppl_ph (defined in the PPL library) whose dimension is equal to dim.

The files CPoly.java and CPoly.h are depicted in Figure 7.5 and Figure 7.6, respectively.

```
public class CPoly {
  static {
    System.loadLibrary("ppl");
    try {CPoly.poly_initialize();}
    catch (CPolyException pe)
    { System.out.println("Cannot initialise the PPL library");
      System.exit(-1); } }

  private int cpoly; // the pointer to the polyhedron

  static native void poly_initialize() throws CPolyException;
  static native void poly_finalize();
  static native int poly_newPolyhedron(int[] vars,ConSys conSys)
        throws CPolyException;
  static native void poly_deletePolyhedron(int ph)
        throws CPolyException;
  static native int[] poly_getVars(int ph)
        throws CPolyException;
  static native ConSys poly_getConSys(int ph)
        throws CPolyException;
  static native boolean poly_isEmptyZPolyhedron(int ph)
        throws CPolyException;
  static native boolean poly_equals(int ph1, int ph2)
        throws CPolyException;
  static native boolean poly_leq(int ph1,int ph2)
        throws CPolyException;
  static native boolean poly_disjoint(int ph1, int ph2)
        throws CPolyException;
  static native void poly_addConstraint(int ph, Constraint c)
        throws CPolyException;
  static native void poly_restrict(int ph, int[] IntI)
        throws CPolyException;
  static native void poly_extend(int ph, int[] IntI)
        throws CPolyException;
  static native int poly_union(int ph1, int ph2)
        throws CPolyException;
  static native int poly_intersection(int ph1, int ph2)
        throws CPolyException;
  static native int poly_dcm(int ph1,int[] tr12,int[] I2)
        throws CPolyException;
  static native int poly_icm(int ph2,int[] tr12,int[] I1)
        throws CPolyException;

  protected void finalize() throws Throwable {
    try {CPoly.poly_deletePolyhedron(this.cpoly);}
    catch (CPolyException pe) {}
    finally {super.finalize();}
  }
}
```

Figure 7.5: File CPoly.java: interface at the Java side.

```
#include <jni.h>

JNIEXPORT void JNICALL Java_CPoly_poly_initialize
  (JNIEnv *, jclass);
JNIEXPORT void JNICALL Java_CPoly_poly_finalize
  (JNIEnv *, jclass);
JNIEXPORT jint JNICALL Java_CPoly_poly_newPolyhedron
  (JNIEnv *, jclass, jintArray, jobject);
JNIEXPORT void JNICALL Java_CPoly_poly_deletePolyhedron
  (JNIEnv *, jclass, jint);
JNIEXPORT jintArray JNICALL Java_CPoly_poly_getVars
  (JNIEnv *, jclass, jint);
JNIEXPORT jobject JNICALL Java_CPoly_poly_getConSys
  (JNIEnv *, jclass, jint);
JNIEXPORT jboolean JNICALL Java_CPoly_poly_isEmptyZPolyhedron
  (JNIEnv *, jclass, jint);
JNIEXPORT jboolean JNICALL Java_CPoly_poly_equals
  (JNIEnv *, jclass, jint, jint);
JNIEXPORT jboolean JNICALL Java_CPoly_poly_leq
  (JNIEnv *, jclass, jint, jint);
JNIEXPORT jboolean JNICALL Java_CPoly_poly_disjoint
  (JNIEnv *, jclass, jint, jint);
JNIEXPORT void JNICALL Java_CPoly_poly_addConstraint
  (JNIEnv *, jclass, jint, jobject);
JNIEXPORT void JNICALL Java_CPoly_poly_restrict
  (JNIEnv *, jclass, jint, jintArray);
JNIEXPORT void JNICALL Java_CPoly_poly_extend
  (JNIEnv *, jclass, jint, jintArray);
JNIEXPORT jint JNICALL Java_CPoly_poly_difference
  (JNIEnv *, jclass, jint, jint);
JNIEXPORT jint JNICALL Java_CPoly_poly_union
  (JNIEnv *, jclass, jint, jint);
JNIEXPORT jint JNICALL Java_CPoly_poly_intersection
  (JNIEnv *, jclass, jint, jint);
JNIEXPORT jint JNICALL Java_CPoly_poly_dcm
  (JNIEnv *, jclass, jint, jintArray, jintArray);
JNIEXPORT jint JNICALL Java_CPoly_poly_icm
  (JNIEnv *, jclass, jint, jintArray, jintArray);
```

Figure 7.6: File CPoly.h: interface at the C side (automatically generated by JavaCC).

The file CPoly.java contains the signatures of the native methods that correspond to the operations over the polyhedra (e.g., test for emptiness, intersection, union, direct and inverse constrained mappings, etc.). The private integer field cpoly is the reference to a C polyhedron that has been allocated by the C side of the analyser (the memory is managed differently by the Java side and by the C side of the analyser). The first time the class CPoly is called by the analyser, the static bloc of the class is executed, where the PPL library is loaded and initialised.

Memory is automatically garbage collected in Java, but this is not the case in C. The memory used by the C polyhedron must be explicitly deallocated each time the garbage collector is called for freeing an object CPoly. So, the method finalize has been overridden and executes the native method poly_deletePolyhedron(cpoly).

The C counterparts of CPoly.java are the header file CPoly.h and the implementation file CPoly.c. The signatures of the methods are automatically generated by JNI. The arguments of the methods contains references to the Java environment JNIEnv, which is useful to pass Java arguments in methods, and to recover or create new Java objects.

7.2.2 At the C side

The total number of C code lines is approximately 2507 (excluding preprocessor directives). The C files CPoly.c and polyhedron.c implement the native methods. For instance, consider the implementation of the union between two polyhedra. The methods are depicted in Figure 7.7 (for the file CPoly.c) and in Figure 7.8 (for the file polyhedron.c).

```
JNIEXPORT jint JNICALL Java_CPoly_poly_union
  (JNIEnv * env, jclass cls, jint ph1, jint ph2)
{
  polyhedron poly1 = (polyhedron) ph1;
  polyhedron poly2 = (polyhedron) ph2;
  polyhedron convexhull;

  if (poly_convex_hull(poly1, poly2, &convexhull) == FAIL)
  {
    jthrow_polyhedron_exception(env, "Convex hull fails");
    return (jint) NULL;
  }
  return (jint) convexhull;
}
```

Figure 7.7: Part of the file CPoly.c: implementation of the union operation.

The two most intricate operations over polyhedra are the direct and inverse constrained mapping operations, that have been introduced in Section 3.4.2. The interested reader can find their implementation in Appendix E.

```
int poly_convex_hull(polyhedron ph1, polyhedron ph2,
                     polyhedron *res)
{
  if (poly_have_same_domain(ph1, ph2)==FAIL)
    return FAIL;
  if (poly_copy(ph1, res)==FAIL)
    return FAIL;
  if (ppl_Polyhedron_poly_hull_assign((*res)->ppl_ph,
                                      ph2 >ppl_ph) < 0)
    return FAIL;
  return SUCCESS;
}
```

Figure 7.8: Part of the file `polyhedron.c`: implementation of the union operation. The method `ppl_Polyhedron_poly_hull_assign` is provided by
the PPL library.

7.2.3   At the Java side

At the Java side, the class E (implementing the size component E of an abstract
tuple α of an abstract substitution β) and the class ERefOutSol (describing the
systems of constraints E_{ref_out} and E_{sol} of an abstract sequence B) use the Java
object Sizes. The class Size interacts with the class CPoly and contains the
abstract operations that are specific to size relations. It is responsible for translating
each variable $(nn)sz(i)$ of the size constraints (where nn is a norm name and i is
an index occurring in the abstract substitution β or in the abstract sequence B),
into its corresponding integer identifier in the array vars of a C polyhedron.
The file Sizes.java is depicted in Figure 7.9.

7.2.4   Dimensions of the polyhedra

Polyhedral operations are costly in terms of space and of time consumption. They
are usually exponential in terms of the dimensions of the polyhedra. The number of
indices occurring in abstract sequences has been reduced thanks to the untouched
component of abstract sequences (see Section 6.1). The polyhedral dimensions can
be also reduced by maintaining size constraints only for indices that are leaves of
the frame component (i.e., indices that have no associated frame).

```
public class Sizes {

  private Indices I;      //set of indices

  private NormI_2_Vars A; //translation between (nn)sz(i)
                          //and identifiers in polyhedron

  private CPoly cpoly;    //polyhedron whose domain
                          //is image(A)

  public boolean isEmpty() {...}
  public ConSys getConSys() {...}
  public void addConstraint(Constraint c) {...}
  public static boolean leq(Sizes E1,Sizes E2) {...}
  public static Sizes LUB(Sizes E1,Sizes E2) {...}
  public static Sizes GLB(Sizes E1,Sizes E2) {...}
  public void restrict(Indices newI) {...}
  public void extend(Indices newI) {...}
  public static Sizes dcm(Sizes E1,I2I tr12,Indices I2){...}
  public static Sizes icm(Sizes E2,I2I tr12,Indices I1){...}
  (...)
}
```

Figure 7.9: File `Sizes.java`: implementation of the size components.

7.3 Abstract debugging: generating informative warning messages

Table 7.2 describes the warning messages that can be generated by the checker when the abstract execution of a clause or a procedure fails. Such messages can help to programmer to debug its program. It is important to stress that the analysis errors listed below actually are warning messages. They are potential but not sure errors. Indeed, the verification process may fail because the abstract interpretation analysis has been inaccurate. In order to obtain more details about a verification failure, the user can read the output reports generated by the system, that contain the abstract sequences (written in the syntax of formal specifications) verified at each program point.

Type	Subtype	Description of the exception (warning)
LEQ		some clause does not imply specification
	`ref_sv`	ref same-value component cannot be verified
	`out_sv`	out same-value component cannot be verified
	`ref_frm`	ref frame component cannot be verified
	`out_frm`	out frame component cannot be verified
	`ref_mo`	ref mode component cannot be verified
	`out_mo`	out mode component cannot be verified
	`ref_ty`	ref type component cannot be verified
	`out_ty`	out type component cannot be verified
	`ref_ps`	ref possible sharing component cannot be verified
	`out_ps`	out possible sharing component cannot be verified
	`ref_lin`	ref linearity component cannot be verified
	`out_lin`	out linearity component cannot be verified
	`ref_srel`	size relations between ref terms cannot be verified
	`out_srel`	size relations between out terms cannot be verified
	`ref_out_srel`	size relations between ref and out terms cannot be verified
	`ref`	ref component cannot be verified
	`fails`	fails components cannot be verified
	`untouched`	untouched component cannot be verified
TERM		termination cannot be proved
		(size expression does not decrease)
	`term_rec`	size expression does not decrease (recursive call)
	`term_mutrec`	size expression does not decrease (mutual recursive call)
LOOKUP		no specification cannot be safely applied to subcall
SOL		cardinality information cannot be verified
	`sf`	sure failure cannot be proved
	`ss_subproc`	sure success cannot be proved (subprocedure may fail)
	`ss_fails`	sure success cannot be proved (fails component not identical)
	`ss_ref`	sure success cannot be proved (ref component not identical)
	`ss_fails_ref`	sure success cannot be proved (union of ref/fails components not exact)
	`det_excl`	determinacy cannot be proved (clauses are non-exclusive)
	`det_subproc`	determinacy cannot be proved (subprocedure is not deterministic)
	`sol`	cardinality information cannot be proved
CUT		cut are possibly red (some solutions may be discarded)
	`red_cut_det`	execution before cut is not deterministic
	`red_cut_excl`	successive clause are not exclusive before the cut point
OCF		occur-check freeness of unification cannot be verified
	`ocf_global`	some unification are not occur-check free (possibly in subprocedures)
	`ocf_local`	some unification (local to the predicate) are not occur-check free
META		a meta-call is not sufficiently instantiated

Table 7.2: Warning messages generated by the checker when the verification fails.

Chapter 8

Experimental results of the checker

This chapter presents the experimental results performed on the checker. Section 8.1 evaluates the improvements on the basic framework presented in the previous chapters. Section 8.2 reports on the checker analysis time. The set of benchmarks that has been verified by the analyser is described. Section 8.3 evaluates the minimal information to be specified in order to prove a specific operational property.

8.1 Comparing the basic and extended frameworks

Table 8.1 evaluates the improvements performed on the basic framework in order to check more programs and to make the abstract analysis more accurate. The table considers the following extensions: the ability to use primitive types and norms and to declare new types and norms (**Types/Norms**), the modelling of untouched terms (**Untch**), the proof of termination (**Term**), the detection of exclusivity between clauses (**Excl**), the multiple abstract concatenation (**Conc**), and the treatment of negations and cuts (**Not/Cut**). The symbol '×' means that the corresponding improvement is useful for checking successfully the program. So, without that improvement, the basic framework is unable to check the specification whose identifier is provided in the column **BehNb**: $x.y$ defines Chapter x, Section y. The symbol '-' means that the basic framework does not need the corresponding improvement to check the procedure according to the specification.

Procedure	BehNb	Types/Norms (§5.2, §5.3)	Untch (§6.1)	Term (§6.2)	Excl (§6.3)	Conc (§6.4)	Not/Cut (§4.1), (§4.2)
select	3.1	-	-	-	-	×	-
select	3.2	-	-	-	-	×	-
append	3.3	-	-	-	-	-	-
append	3.4	-	-	-	-	-	-
append	3.5	-	-	-	-	×	-

Procedure	BehNb	Types/Norms (§5.2, §5.3)	Untch (§6.1)	Term (§6.2)	Excl (§6.3)	Conc (§6.4)	Not/Cut (§4.1), (§4.2)
append3	3.6	-	-	-	-	-	-
append3bis	3.7	-	-	-	-	-	-
reverse	3.8	-	-	-	-	-	-
reverse_acc	3.9	-	-	-	-	-	-
delete	4.1	-	-	-	×	×	×
member	4.3	-	-	-	×	-	×
efface	4.4	-	-	-	-	-	×
substitute	4.7	-	-	-	-	-	×
red_white_blue_list	5.15	×	-	-	-	-	-
red_white_blue	4.6	×	-	-	-	-	-
substitute	4.7	-	-	-	-	-	-
update	4.8	-	-	-	-	-	×
colour_index	5.10	×	-	-	×	×	-
flattree2	5.14	×	-	×	-	-	-
sumtree	5.19	×	-	×	-	-	-
deriv	5.16	×	-	×	-	×	-
sumtree	5.19	×	-	-	-	-	-
length	6.5	-	×	-	-	-	-
set_length	6.6	-	×	-	-	-	-
close	6.4	-	×	-	-	×	-
list	6.7	-	×	-	-	-	-
flattree	6.9	×	-	×	-	-	-
factorial	6.10	×	-	×	×	-	-
tree_list_tree	6.11	×	-	×	-	-	-
ack	6.13	×	-	×	-	×	-
even, odd	6.12	-	-	×	-	-	-
f, g	6.14	-	-	×	-	-	-
special	6.15	-	-	×	-	-	-
maxlist	6.16	-	-	-	-	-	×
merge	6.17	×	-	-	×	×	-

Table 8.1: Evaluation of the improvements to the basic framework.

As explained in Section 6.1, the untouched component U of an abstract sequence B is implemented by sharing the indices of the β_{ref} and β_{out} components. Table 8.2 compares the average number of indices per abstract sequence, between the basic framework (where indices are not shared) and the extended framework (where untouched indices are merged). For every procedure defined in this document, the number of indices is computed at each program point of the procedure. The following notations are used to describe the input part of the specification (column **Input**): 'a' denotes any, 'g' denotes the mode ground, 'v' denotes the mode var, 'i' denotes the type int, 'l' denotes the type expression list(any), 't' denotes the type expression tree(any). The execution time of abstract operations depends on the number of indices occurring in the abstract sequence. On average, there are 1.61 times less indices in the extended framework than in the basic one.

Program	Input	Separated Indices (basic abstract sequence)	Fusioned Indices (shared abstract sequence)
ack	(i,i,v)	10.7	7.83
append	(lg,lg,v)	8.43	5
append	(l,l,v)	8.43	5
append	(v,v,lg)	8.43	5.57
append	(a,a,l)	8.14	5.57
append3	(lg,lg,lg,v)	9	5.33
append3bis	(v,v,v,lg)	9	6.33
delete	(lg,g,v)	8.45	5
deriv	(g,v)	10.13	7.21
do_something_list	(g,v)	4	2.33
efface	(g,lg,a)	10	6
efface	(g,a,lg)	9	5.86
efface2	(v,lg,a)	10.71	6.71
odd	(l)	5.33	3
odd	(l)	5.33	3
factorial	(i,v)	8.5	6.67
f	(lg,lg,v)	7.5	4.17
g	(lg,lg,lg,v)	9	5.33
flattree	(tg,v)	9.67	6.56
flattree2	(v,lg)	8.89	6.78
list	(g)	4	2.2
list	(l)	4	2.2
minimum	(i,i,v)	5.33	3
close	(a)	3.2	2.2
length	(l,v)	8.44	5.56
set_length	(l)	7.33	5
merge	(li,li,v)	12.54	7.58
red_white_blue	(g)	2	1
red_white_blue_list	(lg)	4.33	2.33
color_index	(g,v)	4	2.33
member	(g,lg)	6.83	3.67
remove_red	(lg,v)	7	4.25
reverse	(lg,v)	5	3.33
reverse	(l,v)	5	3.67
reverse_acc	(lg,v,lg)	8.43	4.86
reverse_acc	(l,v,l)	8.43	5.43
select	(v,lg,v)	10	6.17
select	(g,v,lg)	9	6
maxlist	(lg,lg,lg)	7.78	4.89
special	(lg,lg)	8.29	6.57
substitute	(g,g,lg,v)	11.38	6.88
update	(g,g,g,v)	7.4	3.8
sumtree	(ti,v)	10.7	7.1
tree_list_tree	(tg,v)	11.73	8.45

Table 8.2: Average number of indices in abstract sequences.

8.2 Checker analysis time

All tests of the checker have been realised on a Pentium III of 1.5 GHz with 1GB of RAM. The machine runs under Linux Suse and is equipped with JDK 1.5.0 and the Parma Polyhedra Library PPL 0.9 [7].

Procedures from this document

Table 8.3 shows the execution analysis time for verifying the procedures of this document encountered so far. The name of the procedure is given in the column **Program**. We use the following notations to describe the input part of the specification (column **Input**): 'a' denotes any, 'g' denotes the mode ground, 'v' denotes the mode var, 'i' denotes the type int, 'l' denotes the type expression list(any), 't' denotes the type expression tree(any). The analysis can be performed when the Parma Polyhedra Library [8] is enabled (column **PPL**) or when it is disabled (column **NoPPL**). If the polyhedra library is disabled, then the cardinality properties and the termination are not proved. Execution analysis time is given in seconds.

All benchmarks tested on the checker

Table 8.4 shows the average analysis execution time for programs drawn from [3, 13, 45, 124] and from the Internet. The column **Bench** gives the name of the benchmark. All benchmarks (procedures and specifications) are available at the website http://www.info.ucl.ac.be/~gobert. For each benchmark, the column ♯**Pr** gives the number of procedures and the column ♯**Beh** gives the number of formal specifications verified by the analyser. The average number of clauses per procedure is shown in the column ♯**Cl/Pr**. The average analysis execution time for a pair procedure/specification is given in the column **PPL** (when the Parma Polyhedra Library [8] is enabled) and in the column **NoPPL** (when the polyhedra library is disabled). Execution time is given in seconds.

Program	Input	PPL	NoPPL
ack	(i,i,v)	1.81	0.46
append	(lg,lg,v)	0.82	0.16
append	(l,l,v)	0.51	0.1
append	(v,v,lg)	0.65	0.2
append	(a,a,l)	0.76	0.16
append3	(lg,lg,lg,v)	1.04	0.25
append3bis	(v,v,v,lg)	1.02	0.2
delete	(lg,g,v)	1.24	0.26
deriv	(g,v)	2.86	0.9
do_something_list	(g,v)	0.37	0.23
efface	(g,lg,a)	0.89	0.36
efface	(g,a,lg)	0.67	0.21
efface2	(v,lg,a)	0.97	0.22
odd	(l)	0.71	0.19
odd	(l)	0.71	0.19
factorial	(i,v)	0.74	0.22
f	(lg,lg,v)	0.71	0.19
g	(lg,lg,lg,v)	0.71	0.19
flattree	(tg,v)	1.92	0.36
flattree2	(v,lg)	1.47	0.27
list	(g)	0.23	0.13
list	(l)	0.37	0.06
minimum	(i,i,v)	0.63	0.1
close	(a)	0.44	0.14
length	(l,v)	0.79	0.19
set_length	(l)	0.99	0.24
merge	(li,li,v)	5.14	0.78
red_white_blue	(g)	0.17	0.08
red_white_blue_list	(lg)	0.54	0.13
color_index	(g,v)	0.18	0.04
member	(g,lg)	0.54	0.22
remove_red	(lg,v)	1.39	0.39
reverse	(lg,v)	0.87	0.17
reverse	(l,v)	0.82	0.28
reverse_dl	(lg,v,lg)	0.71	0.09
reverse_dl	(l,v,l)	0.71	0.23
select	(v,lg,v)	1.68	0.37
select	(g,v,lg)	0.68	0.22
maxlist	(lg,lg,lg)	1.19	0.32
special	(lg,lg)	2.76	0.67
substitute	(g,g,lg,v)	1.28	0.23
update	(g,g,g,v)	0.4	0.11
sumtree	(ti,v)	1.29	0.29
tree_list_tree	(tg,v)	4.61	0.92
Mean		1.11	0.27

Table 8.3: Procedures from this document: analysis execution time.

Bench	♯Pr	♯Beh	♯Cl/Pr (mean)	PPL (mean)	NoPPL (mean)
list	97	207	2.1	0.464	0.081
difflist	17	18	1.8	0.521	0.177
matrix	18	37	2.2	0.936	0.165
tree [124]	21	35	2.2	1.540	0.250
arithmetics	42	58	2.7	0.551	0.089
programs	65	70	1.9	0.912	0.290
deville [45]	14	25	2.2	0.809	0.178
lecharlier	9	9	2.3	0.203	0.055
gobert	36	44	1.7	0.165	0.042
bratko [13]	121	152	2.0	0.801	0.183
terminweb [27]	36	51	2.1	0.555	0.105
cTI [96]	26	26	1.6	0.884	0.174
plumer	40	52	1.9	0.865	0.150
cut	6	6	2.5	1.088	0.163
negation	40	42	1.7	0.169	0.045
Mean				0.698	0.143

Table 8.4: All benchmarks checked by the analyser: analysis execution time.

8.3 Specifying operational properties

The way a user specifies a procedure depends on the purpose of the verification. One can be interested in proving only termination, or occur-check freeness, or determinacy of the procedure, for some input context. There exist several ways to specify a procedure, and a specification can be more or less accurate. This section shows what is the minimal information to be specified in order to prove a specific operational property for a given 'use' of the procedure. It gives an idea of which domain is responsible for proving the determinacy, the sure success, the termination or the occur-check freeness. The 'use' of a procedure corresponds to the `in` part of a specification. For a given operational property to be checked and for a given 'use' of a procedure, we will only consider the most general `in` parts of specifications, i.e., those that describe the biggest set of input substitutions corresponding to the given 'use' and such that the analyser is able to prove the operational property. There may be several specifications corresponding to a 'use'.

The following tables illustrate the formal specifications that can be expressed (and checked by the analyser) when we are interesting in proving only a specific operational property of a program. The operational properties that are considered here are: determinacy (Table 8.5), full determinacy (Table 8.6), sure success (Table 8.7), termination (Table 8.8), and occur-check freeness (Table 8.9). For each operational property to be checked, only the minimal formal specifications are provided (i.e., only the necessary parts of the specifications are given).

The name of the program is given in the column **Program**, where (Pr. $x.y$) means that the program is defined in Chapter x, Section y of this document. The column **Use** provides informal information about the way the main procedure of the program is used. Each argument is associated with a symbol. The symbol '+' (resp. '-') means that the argument is used as an input (resp. as an output). The formal specifications, corresponding to the most general use of the program, are shown in the column **Minimal specifications**.

Proving determinacy

The `sol` component allows us to express the determinacy. For most examples, an argument used as input ('+') has the mode `ground` and an argument used as an output ('-') has the most general mode `any`. Other kinds of deterministic specifications can be expressed thanks to the new polymorphic type system presented in Section 5.2: an input argument needs not to be completely instantiated. For instance, the input argument of the procedure `flattree` may be a (possibly non ground) binary tree, which is expressed by the type expression `tree(any)`. Sometimes, it is necessary to specify the `out` part of a specification, as it is the case for the program `flattree`. Without this output information, the analyser cannot verify that the call to `append` corresponds to a well-known deterministic specification.

Program	Use	Minimal specifications to prove determinacy
append (Pr. 2.4)	(+,-,-)	```append in(ground,any,any) sol(sol =< 1)``` ------- ```append in(list(any),any,any) sol(sol =< 1)```
flattree (Pr. 5.2)	(+,-)	```flattree append in(ground,any) in(ground,ground,any) out(_,ground) out(_,_,ground) sol(sol =< 1) sol(sol =< 1)``` ------- ```flattree append in(tree(any),any) in(list(any), out(_,list(any)) list(any),any) sol(sol =< 1) out(_,_,list(any)) sol(sol =< 1)```
delete (Pr. 4.1)	(+,+,-)	```delete in(ground,ground,any) sol(sol =< 1)```
deriv (Pr. 5.3)	(+,-)	```deriv in(ground,any) sol(sol =< 1)```
close (Pr. 6.3)	(-)	```close var nonvar in(any) in(any) in(any) sol(sol=<1) ref(var) ref(nonvar) sol(sol=<1) sol(sol=<1)```

Table 8.5: Minimal specifications for proving determinacy.

Proving full determinacy

To express that a procedure is fully deterministic, we write sol=1 in the sol component of specifications. The ref component is useful to refine the set of input substitutions that lead to a sure success of the execution. Of course, all the conditions of the ref part can be directly put into the in part of specifications, such that the in and ref parts are equal. But in that case, the resulting specifications are less general (in the sense that they accept as input only those for which the procedure is fully deterministic). The new type system allows us to describe accurately the full determinacy for procedures using structures other than lists. For instance, the procedure deriv(F,DF) accepts any ground term F as input and it is fully deterministic if and only if F is an expression (type expression expr(ground)). When an input argument is not completely instantiated, it is often necessary to specify that it does not share a variable with the other arguments through the noshare tag in the in part or in the ref part of a specification. Note the interest of the type anylist in the specification of the procedure close: this procedure is fully deterministic for any input that can be instantiated to a list, and it fails for any other input.

Program	Use	Minimal specifications to prove full determinacy

append (Pr. 3.2)	(+,-,-)	`append`
		`  in(A:ground,B:any,C:var; noshare(<B,C>))`
		`  ref(list(ground),_,_)`
		`  sol(sol = 1)`
		`append`
		`  in(A:list(any),B:any,C:var; noshare(<B,C>))`
		`  ref(_,_,_; noshare(<A,C>))`
		`  sol(sol = 1)`

flattree (Pr. 5.2)	(+,-)	`flattree              append`
		`  in(ground,var)        in(list(ground),`
		`  ref(tree(ground),_)       list(ground),var)`
		`  out(_,list(ground))   out(_,_,list(ground))`
		`  sol(sol = 1)          sol(sol = 1)`
		`                                append`
		`flattree                in(A:list(any),`
		`  in(T:tree(any),L:var)     B:list(any),C:var)`
		`  ref(_,_;noshare(<T,L>)) ref(_,_,_;`
		`  out(_,list(any))          noshare(<A,C>))`
		`  sol(sol = 1)            out(_,_,list(any))`
		`                          sol(sol = 1)`

delete (Pr. 4.1)	(+,+,-)	`delete`
		`  in(ground,ground,var)`
		`  ref(list(ground),_,_)`
		`  sol(sol = 1)`

deriv (Pr. 5.3)	(+,-)	`deriv`
		`  in(ground,any)`
		`  ref(expr(ground),_)`
		`  sol(sol = 1)`

close (Pr. 6.3)	(-)	`close            var           nonvar`
		`  in(any)         in(any)       in(any)`
		`  ref(anylist)    ref(var)      ref(nonvar)`
		`  sol(sol = 1)    sol(sol = 1)  sol(sol = 1)`

Table 8.6: Minimal specifications for proving full determinacy.

Proving sure success

All the examples of Table 8.6 (full determinacy) obviously belong to Table 8.7 (sure success). The specification of `select` corresponding to the use (-,+,-) shows the interest of the *frame* component in the `ref` part. The procedure surely succeeds if and only if the input list is a non-empty list. Note that the analyser can check more accurate cardinality information than the one expressed in the table: the exact number of solutions for the procedure `select(X,L,Ls)` for that use is the list-length of the input list L (see Specification 3.1).

Program	Use	Minimal specifications to prove sure success
All programs/specifications from Table 8.6		
append (Pr. 3.2)	(-,-,+)	```append in(A:var,B:var,C:any; noshare(<A,B,C>)) sol(sol >= 1)```
flattree2 (Pr. 5.4)	(-,+)	```flattree2 in(T:var,L:list(any); noshare(<T,L>)) sol(sol >= 1)``` ```append in(A:var,B:var, C:list(any); noshare(<A,B,C>)) out(list(any), list(any),_) sol(sol >= 1)```
select (Pr. 3.1)	(-,+,-)	```select in(X:var,L:list(any),Ls:var; noshare(<X,L,Ls>)) ref(_, [_|_], _) sol(sol >= 1)```
select (Pr. 3.1)	(-,-,+)	```select in(X:any,L:var,Ls:list(any); noshare(<X,L,Ls>)) sol(sol >= 1)```

Table 8.7: Minimal specifications for proving sure success.

Proving termination

Table 8.8 shows the minimal information that must be specified to prove termination of a procedure. The induction parameters are explicitly given in the specifications. We illustrate the interest of the new type and norm system. The induction parameter for programs using other structures than lists are composed of user-defined norms, like (elems) for the second specification of the procedure flattree. When an input term has no specific type, the general primitive norm (gen) is automatically chosen by the checker, like in the specification of deriv. To prove termination of the program flattree2, the srel part of the subprocedure append must be specified. Without this information, the analyser is unable to check that the induction parameter decreases through recursive call. Even if the srel part does not occur in most specifications of Table 8.8, the *size relations* component is used in abstract sequences to check that the induction parameter decreases. This component interacts with the frame components of abstract substitutions. Note that termination of the procedure close can be proved only if we put the untouched part in the specification of nonvar. A further extension to the framework should be to automatically discover the induction parameter when it is not available.

Program	Use	Minimal specifications to prove termination

delete (Pr. 4.1)	(+,-,-)	`delete`
		`  in(Xs:ground,X:any,Zs:any)`
		`  sexpr(< (gen)Xs >)`

deriv (Pr. 5.3)	(+,-)	`deriv`
		`  in(F:ground,DF:any;`
		`  sexpr(< (gen)F >)`

close (Pr. 6.3)	(-)	`close` `nonvar`
		`  in(L:any)      var      in(X:any)`
		`  sexpr(< (list)L >)  in(any)  ref(novar)`
		`                               untouched(X)`

flattree (Pr. 5.2)	(+,-)	`flattree                   append`
		`  in(T:ground,L:any)      in(A:ground,B:ground,C:any)`
		`  out(_,ground)            out(_,_,ground)`
		`  sexpr(< (gen)T >)        sexpr(< (gen)A >)`
		--- --- --- --- ---
		`flattree                 append`
		`  in(T:tree(any),L:any)    in(A:list(any),B:list(any),`
		`  out(_,list(any))           C:any)`
		`  sexpr(< (elems)T >)      out(_,_,list(any))`
		`                           sexpr(< (list)A >)`

flattree2 (Pr. 5.4)	(-,+)	`                         append`
		`flattree2                  in(A:any,B:any,C:list(any))`
		`  in(T:any,L:list(any))  out(list(any),list(any),_)`
		`  sexpr(< (list)L >))    srel(A_out+B_out=C_in)`
		`                           sexpr(< (list)C >)`

select (Pr. 3.1)	(-,+,-)	`select`
		`  in(X:any,L:ground,Ls:any)`
		`  sexpr(< (gen)L >)`
		--- --- ---
		`select`
		`  in(X:any,L:list(any),Ls:any)`
		`  sexpr(< (list)L >)`

select (Pr. 3.1)	(-,-,+)	`select`
		`  in(X:any,L:any,Ls:ground)`
		`  sexpr(< (gen)Ls >)`
		--- --- ---
		`select`
		`  in(X:any,L:any,Ls:list(any))`
		`  sexpr(< (list)Ls >)`

Table 8.8: Minimal specifications for proving termination.

Proving occur-check freeness

The analyser does not need to maintain the *size relations* components when the
only purpose of the verification is to prove that the unifications are occur-check
free. Thus, the operations over polyhedra can be disabled. The main domains
of interest for proving occur-check freeness are the modes, the linearity and the
possible sharing between terms. Note that the procedure `close` is occur-check
free for any input any term (possibly non linear).

Program	Use	Minimal specifications to prove occur-check freeness
append (Pr. 3.2)	(-,-,-)	```append in(A:any,B:any,C:any; noshare(<A,C>,<B,C>); linear(C))``` ⸺⸺⸺⸺ ```append in(A:any,B:any,C:any; noshare(<A,B,C>); linear(A,B))```
delete (Pr. 4.1)	(-,-,-)	```delete in(Xs:any,X:any,Zs:any; noshare(<Xs,X,Zs>); linear(Xs))```
deriv (Pr. 5.3)	(-,-)	```deriv in(F:any,DF:any; noshare(<F,DF>); linear(DF))```
close (Pr. 6.3)	(-)	```close var nonvar in(any) in(any) in(any)```
flattree (Pr. 5.2)	(-,-)	```flattree append in(T:any,L:any; in(A:any,B:any,C:any; noshare(<T,L>)) noshare(<A,C>,<B,C>); linear(L)) linear(C))```
flattree2 (Pr. 5.4)	(-,-)	```flattree2 append in(T:any,L:any; in(A:any,B:any,C:any; noshare(<T,L>)) noshare(<A,B,C>); linear(T)) linear(A,B))```
select (Pr. 3.1)	(-,-,-)	```select in(X:any,L:any,Ls:any; noshare(<X,L,Ls>); linear(X,Ls))``` ⸺⸺⸺⸺ ```select in(X:any,L:any,Ls:any; noshare(<X,L>,<L,Ls>); linear(L))```

Table 8.9: Minimal specifications for proving occur-check freeness.

Program	Pg	Input	Lin	Noshare	Ocf
member	58	(a,g)	-	-	yes
		(a,l)	1	(1,2)	yes
prefix	59	(a,g)	-	-	yes
		(a,l)	1	(1,2)	yes
suffix	59	(a,g)	-	-	yes
		(a,l)	1	(1,2)	yes
append	60	(g,g,a)	-	-	yes
		(l,l,a)	3	(1,3),(2,3)	yes
naive_reverse	62	(g,a)	-	-	yes
		(l,a)	2	(1,2)	yes
acc_reverse	62	(g,a)	-	-	yes
		(l,a)	2	(1,2)	yes
acc_reverse	62	(g,g,a)	-	-	yes
		(l,a,a)	3	(1,3),(2,3)	yes
delete	67	(g,g,a)	-	-	yes
		(g,g,a)	2	-	yes
select	67	(g,g,a)	-	-	yes
		(g,g,a)	3	-	yes
ins_sort	70	(g,a)	-	-	yes
insert	70	(g,g,a)	-	-	yes
tree_member	73	(a,g)	-	-	yes
		(a,t)	-	-	yes
isotree	74	(g,g)	-	-	yes
substitute	75	(g,g,g,a)	-	-	yes
pre_order	76	(g,a)	2	-	yes
		(t,a)	2	(1,2)	yes
in_order	76	(g,a)	2	-	yes
		(t,a)	2	(1,2)	yes
post_order	76	(g,a)	2	-	yes
		(t,a)	2	(1,2)	yes
polynomial	79	(g,g)	-	-	yes
derivative	80	(g,g,a)	-	-	yes
hanoi	82	(g,g,g,g,a)	-		yes
append_dl	285	(gl,a,gl,gl,a,a)	-	-	yes
		(a,a,a,a,a,a)	2,5,6	(1,2,3,4,5,6)	yes
flatten_dl	286	(gl,gl)	-	-	yes
flatten_dl	286	(g,g,a)	-	-	yes
flatten	287	(g,a)	2	-	yes
flatten	287	(g,a,a)	3	(2,3)	yes
reverse_dl	288	(gl,a)	-	-	yes
reverse_dl	288	(gl,a,gl)	-	-	yes
quicksort	289	(gl,gl)	-	-	yes
quicksort_dl	289	(gl,gl,a)	-	-	yes
partition	70	(gl,g,a,a)	3,4	(3,4)	yes
dutch	290	(gl,a)	-	-	yes
distribute	290	(gl,a,a,a)	-	-	yes
dutch_dl	291	(gl,a)	2	-	no
distribute_dls	291	(gl,a,a,a,a,a)	Specification. 8.1		yes

Table 8.10: Occur-check freeness detection for the programs proposed in [6]. The column **Pg** refers to the page where the program is defined in the book of Sterling and Shapiro [124].

Table 8.10 reports on the detection of occur-check freeness of programs proposed in [6]. The column **Program** gives the name of the program and the column **Pg** refers to the page of the book of Sterling and Shapiro [124] where the program is defined. The column **Input** is the in part of the specification. To make this table more shorter, the following notations are used. 'a' denotes the mode any, 'g' denotes the mode ground, 'l' denotes the type expression list(any) (list of any terms), 't' denotes the type expression tree(any) (binary tree of any terms). The columns **Lin** and **Noshare** describe the linear and noshare parts of the specification, respectively (arguments are identified by their positions). The occur-check freeness of every program in Table 8.10 can be proved (column **Ocf**), except for the procedure dutch_dl(Xs,RWBs), where RWBs is the list of elements of Xs ordered by colour: red, then white, finally blue. The code of this procedure, using difference-lists, is as follows (Page 291 in [124]).

```
dutch_dl(Xs,RWBs)
        :- distribute_dls(Xs,RWBs,WBs,WBs,Bs,Bs,[]).

distribute_dls([red(X)|Xs],
               [red(X)|Rs],Rs1,
               Ws,Ws1,
               Bs,Bs1)
        :- distribute_dls(Xs,Rs,Rs1,Ws,Ws1,Bs,Bs1).
distribute_dls([white(X)|Xs],
               Rs,Rs1,
               [white(X)|Ws],Ws1,
               Bs,Bs1)
        :- distribute_dls(Xs,Rs,Rs1,Ws,Ws1,Bs,Bs1).
distribute_dls([blue(X)|Xs],
               Rs,Rs1,
               Ws,Ws1,
               [blue(X)|Bs],Bs1)
        :- distribute_dls(Xs,Rs,Rs1,Ws,Ws1,Bs,Bs1).
distribute_dls([],
               Rs,Rs,
               Ws,Ws,
               Bs,Bs).
```
Procedure 8.1   dutch_dl(Xs,RWBs)

The subprocedure distribute_dls(Xs,Rs,Rs1,Ws,Ws1,Bs,Bs1) is such that Rs-Rs1, Ws-Ws1, Bs-Bs1 are difference-lists of red, white, and blue elements of the list Xs, respectively. The analyser is able to check that the procedure distribute_dls is occur-check free with respect to the following specification:

```
distribute_dls/7
   in(Xs:list(ground),
      Rs:any,  Rs1:any,
      Ws:any,  Ws1:any,
      Bs:any,  Bs1:any;
      linear(<Rs,Ws,Bs>);
      noshare(<Rs1,Rs>,<Ws1,Rs>,<Bs1,Rs>,
              <Rs1,Ws>,<Ws1,Ws>,<Bs1,Ws>,
              <Rs1,Bs>,<Ws1,Bs>,<Bs1,Bs>) )
   sol(sol =< 1)
   sexpr(< (list)Xs >)
```
Specification 8.1 `distribute_dls(Xs,Rs,Rs1,Ws,Ws1,Bs,Bs1)`

The analyser cannot verify that the procedure `dutch_dl` is occur-check free when input `Xs` is a ground list and `RWBs` is bound to a linear term. Indeed, in such a situation, the subcall to `distribute_dls` does not satisfy the `in` part of Specification 8.1. A relaxed version of the specification for `distribute_dls` must thus be written, by removing the `linear` and `noshare` tags. In this case, the subprocedure is no more occur-check free.

Note that the system is unable to check Specification 8.2 for procedure `dutch_dl`, expressing that, after the execution, `RWBs` is a ground list whose size is the same as the one of `Xs`. The reason is that difference-lists cannot be modelled accurately in the current framework of the analyser. The checker cannot capture that, as soon as `Bs` becomes ground, then `WBs` becomes ground, and then `RWBs` finally becomes ground.

```
dutch_dl/2
   in(Xs:list(ground),RWBs:any; linear(RWBs))
   out(_,list(ground))
   srel(Xs_in = RWBs_out)
   sol(sol =< 1)
```
Specification 8.2 `dutch_dl(Xs,RWBs)`

8.4 Comparison with TerminWeb

TerminWeb [27] performs inference of termination, which generalises termination checking. With termination inference, annotations such as the parameter induction have not to be provided by the user. In our system, the ability to explicitly specify decreasing size-expressions is maintained since it is sometimes desirable that the user can provide such information to the system.

Table 8.11 shows the programs proposed in the TerminWeb website whose termination can be successfully proved by our analyser. The induction parameter is given in the column **Induction parameter**. The analysis execution time, expressed in seconds, is provided in the column **PPL**.

Program	Input	Induction parameter	PPL
average	(g,g,v)	2*(nat)X1+(nat)X2	2,052
minsort	(g,v)	(list)X1	0,420
min1	(v,g)	-	0,213
min2	(g,v,g)	(list)X3	0,418
min	(g,g,v)	-	0,252
remove	(g,g,v)	(list)X2	0,467
perm_a	(g,v)	(list)X1	0,646
perm_b	(g,v)	(list)X1	0,498
rotate	(g,v)	-	0,076
log2	(g,v)	(gen)X1	0,193
log2	(g,g,v)	(gen)X1	0,641
half	(g,v)	(gen)X1	0,523
log2_bis	(g,v)	-	0,228
log2_bis	(g,g,g,v)	(gen)X1+(gen)X2	0,785
small	(v)	-	0,116
small	(g)	-	0,092
loop	(g,g,g)	(gen)X2	0,240
loop_bis	(g,g,g)	(gen)X3	0,173
interleave	(g,g,v)	(list)X1+(list)X2	0,455
app3_a	(g,g,g,v)	-	0,122
app3_b	(g,g,g,v)	-	0,114
append3	(g,g,g,v)	-	0,109
append3backwards	(v,v,v,g)	-	0,183
reach	(a,a,g,g)	(list)X4	1,315
fluc	(g,g)	(gen)X1+(gen)X2	0,558
f	(g,g,v)	$\langle$ (list)X1, 0 $\rangle$	0,305
g	(g,g,g,v)	$\langle$ (list)X1, 1 $\rangle$	0,101
p	(g,g,g,v)	(list)X1+(list)X2+(list)X3	1,336
f2bis	(g,g,v)	(list)X1+(list)X2	0,753
f2	(g,g,v)	(list)X1+(list)X2	0,837
f3	(g,g,v)	(list)X2	0,660
g3	(g,g,v)	(list)X1	0,426
ways	(g,g,v)	$\langle$ (list)X2,(gen)X1 $\rangle$	2,164
ways_b	(g,g,v)	$\langle$ (list)X2,(gen)X1 $\rangle$	2,191
Mean			0.578

Table 8.11: Termination of programs proposed at the TerminWeb website:
http://www.cs.bgu.ac.il/~mcodish/TerminWeb.

8.5 Comparison with Mercury

Table 8.12 compares what can be specified and checked by the analyser and by Mercury [123]. The table only gives the specifications that can be described in Mercury. So, only fully-instantiated terms as input, and free variable as output are considered. Our system can describe more behaviours, and can be more accurate. For instance, the procedure `append(X1,X2,X3)` where inputs `X1` and `X2` are two lists of any terms (possibly non-linear and that may share variables in common), and where input `X3` is any term cannot be executed in Mercury (it is rejected by the Mercury compiler). Our analyser can prove that this call to the procedure terminates and is deterministic (at most one solution).

Note that Mercury is not always able to detect (semi)determinacy if the procedures are written in the usual Prolog style. However, if an equivalent code is written with explicit 'If Then Else' constructs or with so-called *switch*, then Mercury may check the intended determinacy information. A switch goal is rather like a C's switch statement and consists of a set of alternatives testing a given variable against different possible values it might have. Mercury will generate very efficient code for them, using a lookup-table or hashtable. For instance, consider the procedure `efface(X,T,TEff)` described in Section 2.2, page 14, written in the usual style of Prolog:

```
efface(X,[X|T],TEff).
efface(X,[H|T],[H|TEff]) :-
    not(X=H), efface(X,T,TEff).
```

Mercury cannot prove that the above procedure is semideterministic when input `X` is a ground term, input `T` is a ground list, and input `TEff` is a variable. However, Mercury is able to prove that the following equivalent code is semideterministic, which uses the 'If Then Else' construct (this code is similar to Procedure 4.9, page 94):

```
:- pred efface(T,list(T),list(T)).
:- mode efface(in,in,out) is semidet.
efface(X,[H|T],TEff) :-
    if X = H
    then
      T = TEff
    else
      TEff = [H|TEffs],
      efface(X,T,TEffs).
```

Program Specifications in the analyser	Types and modes annotations in Mercury
append	
in(X1:list(ground),X2:list(ground),X3:var) sol(sol = 1) in(X1:var,X2:var,X3:list(ground); noshare(<X1,X2>)) sol(sol = X3_in+1)	:- pred append(list(T),list(T),list(T)). :- mode append(in,in,out) is det. :- mode append(out,out,in) is multi.
select	
in(X1:var,X2:list(ground),X3:var; noshare(<X1,X3>)) ref(_, [_|_], _) sol(sol = X2_ref) in(X1:ground,X2:var,X3:list(ground)) sol(sol = X3_in+1)	:- pred select(T,list(T),list(T)). :- mode select(out,in,out) is nondet. :- mode select(in,out,in) is multi.
efface	
in(X1:ground,X2:list(ground),X3:ground) sol(sol =< 1) in(X1:ground,X2:list(ground),X3:var) sol(sol =< 1) in(X1:var,X2:list(ground),X3:var) sol(sol =< X2_in)	:- pred efface(T,list(T),list(T)). :- mode efface(in,in,in) is semidet. :- mode efface(in,in,out) is nondet. :- mode efface(out,in,out) is nondet.
merge	
in(X1:list(int),X2:list(int),X3:var) sol(sol = 1)	:- pred merge(list(int),list(int),list(int)). :- mode merge(in,in,out) is nondet.
factorial	
in(X1:int,X2:var) sol(sol =< 1)	:- pred factorial(int,int). :- mode factorial(in,out) is nondet.
flattree	
in(X1:tree(ground),X2:var) sol(sol = 1)	:- pred flattree(tree(T),list(T)). :- mode flattree(in,out) is det.
flattree2	
in(X1:var,X2:list(ground)) sol(sol >= 1)	:- pred flattree(tree(T),list(T)). :- mode flattree(out,in) is multi.

Table 8.12. Comparison between the analyser and Mercury

Part II

Automated optimisation by source-to-source transformations

Chapter 9

Prolog code optimisation

9.1 Motivations

In Prolog, code optimisation is essential to get a program that is efficient in terms of execution time and memory utilisation so that it can compete with other operational programming languages. Optimising techniques like indexing and cut insertion allow the programmer to control efficiently the operational execution of Prolog [1, 131]. Alas, making a Prolog program more efficient by transforming its source code, without modifying its operational semantics, is a difficult task. It requires the programmer to have a clear understanding of how the Prolog compiler works, and in particular, of the effects of impure features. Adding control information is tricky and error-prone. For an non-expert programmer, it is difficult to ensure that the optimised code with control information produces exactly the same solutions as the original one. Furthermore, writing a program with impure features breaks the declarative nature of Prolog, and the optimised code is not as readable as a declarative code.

Instead of compelling a programmer to become an expert in Prolog for writing efficient code by himself, it is desirable to automate the optimisation process. This is for instance the point of view of Deville's methodology, which separates the declarative and the operational aspects during the construction of a program in Prolog [45]. Starting from a declaratively correct program (written in pure logic, without control information), a specialised Prolog code is derived by safely applying some source-to-source transformations. However, in Deville's methodology, the derivation of an efficient code from a logic description is not automated.

In this part of the thesis, we present the implementation of an optimiser of Prolog that automates the generation of specialised procedures for specific classes of calls.[1] Classes of calls are described by formal specifications. The optimiser is intended for two application contexts. In the first context, optimisations are applied to programs that are declaratively correct, i.e., whose operational semantics complies with their declarative meaning. Given a formal specification and a declar-

---

[1]A preliminary version of this chapter has been presented at WLPE'2007 [58].

atively correct Prolog code, the optimiser produces code that an expert programmer in Prolog would have written, as in Deville's approach. In the second application context, the optimiser accepts any Prolog code as input. The input code may have unclear or no declarative meaning, and it may contain cuts and other non logical features. The optimiser is used for specialising such (impure) code. Source-to-source transformations are applied to such code, and it is guaranteed that the generated code computes the same answer substitutions sequences as the original one, given the user formal specification.

Automatic optimisation is a major concern when implementing a logic language that is completely declarative. The programmer concentrates on the declarative aspects and the optimiser is responsible to add control. This is, for example, the view of Debray and Warren who suggest that a Prolog programmer should not use the cut, and that cuts should be automatically inserted at compile-time [39]. Our optimiser is also similar to the Mercury compiler, which automatically determines the order of literals in clauses and chooses one of three execution models (deterministic, semi-deterministic, or non-deterministic) [123], depending on the determinacy information. Similarly to the Mercury compiler, our optimiser takes advantage of the type, mode and determinacy information to generate efficient code. However, the language accepted by our optimiser is more general than Mercury (the full expressiveness of Prolog is accepted, with general unifications). Our optimiser produces impure Prolog code as output, while Mercury produces C code. Our optimiser is also related to the CiaoPP preprocessor, which can perform many different optimisations on Prolog code [66]. These are state-of-the art optimisations, such as partial evaluation and automatic parallelisation, that are less intended than ours to be used in the context of optimising declarative programs.

The way a Prolog code is written - e.g., the order of clauses, the order of literals in a clause, the use of cuts or negations - influences its efficiency. To increase the efficiency of a declaratively correct program, some criteria are necessary to characterise which procedure is more efficient than another one. Looking at the operational semantics and the execution model of Prolog [1, 131], one can list several important efficiency factors. A code is more efficient than another if its clauses contain less literals, if the clause heads are instantiated as much as possible (explicit unifications are removed), if it uses cuts instead of negations, if a cut is executed as soon as possible (at a leftmost position in a clause), if its clauses have a long deterministic prefix, etc. Code transformations can be chosen to obtain code that meets such efficiency criteria. Unfortunately, different criteria may be redundant or conflicting when they are applied together - e.g., inserting cuts and enabling indexing. To select which transformations to apply and in which order to perform them, some heuristics are needed. In that sense, our optimiser is similar to an expert system: we define a list of heuristics and we construct a system that implements them by detecting conflicts and making choices.

The abstract interpretation framework that is at the core of this thesis has been shown especially adequate to design and justify all optimisation steps that are presented later on. Particularly, the notion of abstract sequence allows us to straightforwardly formalise all conditions that must be checked to safely perform the code transformations. Although most of such application conditions are undecidable in general, our abstract domains are powerful enough to decide them in many situations.

The rest of this chapter is organised as follows. Section 9.2 presents characteristics that a Prolog procedure should have to be efficient in terms of space utilisation and execution time. Section 9.3 illustrates the benefits of the optimiser. One specialised version is generated for each pair of procedure/specification. Section 9.4 describes the strategy for choosing which transformations to apply on a procedure and in which order to combine them to generate efficient code. Our abstract interpretation framework is used to verify sufficient conditions to apply the source-to-source transformations safely. Section 9.5 illustrates the strategy on the `efface` procedure. Finally, Section 9.6 presents the experimental evaluation of the optimiser results.

9.2 Characterisation of an optimal procedure

This section presents some characteristics that an optimal procedure should have. This characterisation justifies the choice of specific source-to-source transformations. To characterise an efficient procedure, we use the criteria proposed by Yves Deville, which are independent from a specific Prolog implementation [45], and we look at the Warren Abstract Machine, which allows us to understand how the memory is managed and how Prolog code is compiled into instructions of Warren's virtual machine [1, 131]. Efficiency concerns execution time and space utilisation. In the Warren Abstract Machine of Prolog, the memory space is divided in several data structures. The heap (or global stack) is used to store the constructed terms (references, structures, constants), the trail maintains information about the references that must be freed during backtracking, the local stack contains the clauses' environment frames and choice point frames (the presence of a choice point frame prevents the deallocation of environment frames allocated before on the stack), and the Push Down List is used to compute the general unification between two terms. We characterise an optimal procedure according to the following efficiency criteria:

- *Tail recursive procedure.* A procedure is tail recursive if the recursive call is the last operation of the procedure, either in the last clause of the procedure or in a clause that contains a cut. Last call optimisation is implemented in Warren's Abstract Machine, such that the environment frame is deallocated *before* executing the last call. If the topmost frame on the stack is the current environment and not the current choice-point, its space can be reused in the next stack allocation. This slows down growth of the local stack considerably. On the other hand, if the top of the stack is a choice point, last call optimisation does not have immediate effect on the stack due to environment protection. In the case where the last call of the last rule is a recursive call, the stack does not grow at all, reusing over and over the exact same space for successive environment frames of the procedure, resulting in an iterative loop.

- *Longest deterministic prefix in clauses.* With such a characteristic, multiple answer substitutions are only generated by the suffixes of the clauses. If a failure occurs during the execution of the deterministic prefix, then the clause will fail immediately. Thus, this decreases the execution time.

- *Small bodies.* Less memory space and less execution time are needed for executing small bodies. In particular, a chain rule (a clause containing only one literal in the body) does not allocate any environment frame on the local stack, which is not the case for deep rules (with more than one literal in the body). Code transformations aiming to remove useless or redundant literals in bodies are thus relevant for making the code efficient.

- *Cuts.* Generally, cuts reduce the space utilisation as well as the global execution time. The effect of executing the cut in a clause is to prune the search tree, by removing all the choice points that were created on the local stack for the clause execution. The effect of cut is also the deallocation of environment frames that were protected by the choice points. Placing a cut at a *leftmost* position in a clause allows us to commit the cut quicker, so that the subsequent clauses are no more selected. Note that a *neck* cut (situated just after the symbol ': –' in the clause) is more efficient than *deep* cuts (placed away in the clause). The presence of a deep cut in a rule that would otherwise be a chain rule (e.g., a :- b, ! .) makes it a deep rule requiring environment allocation. However, this is not the case when a neck cut occurs in a rule that would otherwise be a chain rule. A neck cut does not make such a rule a deep rule, even though it might be construed as having two body goals. Furthermore, inserting a green cut may allow the possible removal of test literals or negation in subsequent clauses. Such a cut becomes *red* as soon as the test literal is suppressed. The operational semantics of the resulting program is equivalent to the declarative semantics of the initial program (however, the resulting program is no longer declarative, since it contains a red cut).

- *No explicit unifications.* Placing unifications at the beginning of the bodies is useful to instantiate the clause heads and subcalls, and to suppress these equality literals. That supports the construction of small bodies.

The optimiser performs source-to-source transformations to augment the efficiency of a Prolog code in the context of a formal specification, with the objective to construct a code that meets the above characteristics. Our experimental results show that optimisation mainly concerns the local stack utilisation (see Section 9.6).

efface1 in(X:ground,T:list(ground),TEff:var) sol(sol =< 1)	`efface1(X, [X	T], T) :- !.` `efface1(X, [H	T], [H	TEff]) :-` ` efface1(X, T, TEff).`
efface2 in(X:ground,T:list(ground),TEff:any) sol(sol =< 1)	`efface2(X, [X	T], TEff) :- !, T=TEff.` `efface2(X, [H	T], [H	TEff]) :-` ` efface2(X, T, TEff).`
efface3 in(X:ground,T:any,TEff:list(ground)) sol(sol =< (list)TEff_in+1)	`efface3(X, [H	T], [H	TEff]) :-` ` not(X=H), efface3(X, T, TEff).` `efface3(X, [X	T], T).`
efface4 in(X:var,T:list(ground),TEff:any; noshare(<X,TEff>)) sol(sol =< (list)T_in)	`efface4(X, [H	T], [H	TEff]) :-` ` efface4(X, T, TEff), not(X=H).` `efface4(X, [X	T], T).`

Figure 9.1: Multiple specialisation of the procedure `efface/3`.

9.3 Benefits of the optimiser: a first example

The input of the optimiser consists of any Prolog procedure with a formal specification. The optimiser is designed to be useful mostly when the input procedure is declaratively correct (i.e., it has a declarative meaning and its operational meaning fits its declarative meaning as in Deville's approach [45]). Such a procedure does not contain any impure features. Nevertheless, the optimiser accepts arbitrary Prolog procedures, possibly with impure features, even if the optimisation of impure code is normally less rewarding than the optimisation of pure declarative code. Given a procedure and a formal specification, the optimiser generates a specialised version of the procedure for the context of the formal specification. The output procedure may contain impure features, but it is guaranteed to produce the same solutions as the original code.

For instance, consider the predicate `efface(X,T,TEff)`, seen in Section 2.2, that holds iff X is an element of the list T and if TEff is the list T without the first occurrence of X in T.[2] Assume that the input Prolog code is the following.

```
efface(X,[H|T],[H|TEff]) :- efface(X,T,TEff), not(X=H).
efface(X,[X|T],T).
```

The above code is declaratively and operationally correct for several directionalities. Figure 9.1 depicts the specialised versions generated by the optimiser for the corresponding formal specifications.

We have tested the programs on a 1.5 GHz Pentium; 1GB RAM; Linux Suse; SWI-Prolog v 5.4.6 [132]. The local stack is allowed to grow until 2048000 B. Table 9.1 compares the execution of the original code and the specialised code

---

[2]This example is borrowed from [45].

efface1. Several tests have been performed with input lists of various lengths. The table shows that the original code is less efficient than the specialised one in terms of execution time and local stack usage. The specialised code uses a constant amount of local stack (independently of the size of the input list), while we yield a local stack error if we try to execute the original code with an input list of length 25000. The speedup increases according to the size of the input: for instance, the optimised code needs 3.61 times less execution time for an input list of size 10000.

Input	Execution Time			Used Local Stack	
list	efface	efface1		efface	efface1
size	(ms)	(ms)	(sdup)	(B)	(B)
100	71	25	2.84	8508	108
1000	693	225	3.09	84108	108
10000	8176	2264	3.61	840108	108
25000	ERROR	5633	-	ERROR	108

Table 9.1: Efficiency comparison of efface and efface1. The program is executed 1000 times, when X is a ground term, T is a ground list, and TEff is a variable.

Similarly, Table 9.2 compares the execution of the original code efface and the generated version efface2. Several tests have been performed by considering executions that succeed and that fail, and by varying the length of the input list T. Table 9.3 compares the execution of the original code efface and the generated version efface3. The specialised version uses less local stack, and the speedup drastically increases according to the size of the input TEff.

Success	Input	Execution Time			Used Local Stack	
of	list	efface	efface2		efface	efface2
execution	size	(ms)	(ms)	(sdup)	(B)	(B)
no	100	41	23	1.83	8508	156
no	1000	380	194	1.96	84108	156
no	10000	4268	1893	2.25	840108	156
no	25000	ERROR	4715	-	ERROR	156
yes	100	115	26	4.39	8508	156
yes	1000	689	221	3.11	84108	156
yes	10000	7334	2207	3.32	840108	156
yes	25000	ERROR	5527	-	ERROR	156

Table 9.2: Efficiency comparison of efface and efface2. The program is executed 1000 times. Several tests are performed, depending on whether the execution fails or succeeds, and depending on the list-length of T.

Success of execution	Input list size	Execution Time			Used Local Stack	
		efface (ms)	efface3 (ms)	(sdup)	efface (B)	efface3 (B)
no	100	377	10	39.00	8508	192
no	1000	26770	63	422.68	84108	192
no	25000	ERROR	1397	-	ERROR	192
yes	100	1290	77	16.75	8508	4308
yes	200	4999	190	26.31	16908	8508
yes	500	30700	806	38.07	42108	21108
yes	25000	ERROR	1306670	-	ERROR	840108

Table 9.3: Efficiency comparison of `efface` and `efface3`. The program is executed 1000 times. All solutions are computed. Several tests are performed, depending on whether the execution fails or succeeds, and depending on the list-length of `TEff`.

9.4 Strategy to apply source-to-source transformations

This section presents the strategy used by the optimiser (which code transformations are applied and in which order) so that the final code satisfies "as much as possible" the efficiency criteria presented in Section 9.2. The input procedure is assumed to be correct with respect to its formal specification. As said previously, we do not require that the input procedure has a declarative meaning. Prolog extralogical features are accepted (e.g., cuts, meta-calls, dynamic predicates), provided that the checker of Part I is accurate enough to handle them (see Chapter 4). Given a formal specification and a procedure, the optimiser applies a number of code transformations in a fixed order. These transformations include normalisation, clause and literal reordering, cut insertion, removal of redundant literals, and denormalisation. The optimiser guarantees that the code transformations are safe, i.e., the generated code produces the same solutions as the original one, for any input substitution satisfying the `in` part of the formal specification. In particular, code transformations that are applied by the optimiser do not introduce non-termination. The output of each step (except the last one) is an annotated procedure completely similar to the annotated procedure that should be produced by the checker if it was applied to the transformed code and the formal specification. The abstract information is useful to detect sufficient conditions for ensuring a safe application of the code transformations. The strategy of the optimiser is mainly motivated by the objective of inserting cuts at positions that allow the optimiser to remove as much negated and test literals as possible.

The conditions for applying a code transformation can be expressed in terms of the length of the answer substitutions sequence, computed from the execution of a literal, or a goal, or a clause, or a procedure. In general, such application conditions are not decidable, but they can be detected in a significant number of

situations, thanks to our abstract interpretation framework. We define the following
properties, in the context of some input substitution (the terminology of [45] is
used):

- The procedure pr, or the clause c, or the prefix of a clause g, or the literal
  after the execution of the goal g is **deterministic** iff their sequence of answer
  substitutions has *at most one* computed answer substitution;

- The procedure pr, or the clause c, or the prefix of a clause g, or the literal
  after the execution of the goal g is **fully deterministic** iff their sequence of
  answer substitutions has *one and only one* answer substitution;

- The procedure pr, or the clause c, or the prefix of a clause g, or the literal
  after the execution of the goal g **surely succeeds** iff their sequence of answer
  substitutions has *at least one* answer substitution;

- The literal l is a **test literal** after the execution of the goal g if it is not a cut,
  it is deterministic, and it does not instantiate any variable;

- Two clauses c_1 and c_2 (with the same arity n) are **exclusive** iff either the
  execution of c_1 fails, or the execution of c_2 fails, or both executions of c_1
  and c_2 fail. The same definition applies for exclusivity of two prefixes of
  clauses of same arity.

We classify the transformations into two categories. Transformations in the
first category have to consider the procedure globally. Transformations in the second category deal with each program clause independently of the other clauses.
The category of each code transformation will be explicitly specified (*'procedure'*
or *'clause'*). The specialised code is derived by applying nine steps in the following
order.

Step A) Syntactic normalisation and code annotation [*'clause'*]

The first step consists of applying the checker of Part I to the procedure and the
formal specification. The objective is not to verify the input procedure since it is
assumed to be correct with respect to the specification, but the annotating abstract
information provided by the checker is needed by the optimiser to safely apply
the code transformations. The result of the checker is a normalised procedure
(see Section 3.2.1 and Appendix G.2), annotated with abstract sequences at each
program point (see Appendix G.3).

Note that, in practice, two situations may happen: either, the procedure has
been previously verified with respect to the specification, so that the optimiser can
retrieve and reuse the annotated code without recomputing it (see Appendix I);
otherwise, the procedure has not yet been verified with respect to this specification,
so that the checker is actually executed. In the later case, the verification may
possibly fail. In such a situation, the optimisation process is aborted.

Step B) Removing green cuts [*'procedure'*]

At this step, the optimiser safely removes green cuts occurring in the procedure (if any). This code transformation depends on the order of the clauses. A cut is removed from a clause if the sequence of literals before the cut in the clause is deterministic (i.e., succeeds at most once) and exclusive with the subsequent clauses. It may seem strange to remove cuts from the procedure to be optimised since cuts are supposed to improve efficiency. However, the presence of cuts prevents the optimiser from performing clause reordering. Thus, we remove green cuts to increase opportunities for clause reordering. Cuts are re-inserted later on and, hopefully, at better positions (Step F).

The optimiser looks at each cut position and detects whether the cut can be removed. For each abstract sequence B corresponding to the program point situated just before a cut, the optimiser removes the cut if the E_{sol} component of B implies `sol=<1`, and if B is exclusive with the output abstract sequence of each subsequent clause, as it is explained in detail in Section 6.3.

Step C) Clause reordering [*'procedure'*]

At this step, the optimiser reorders the clauses of the procedure, so that the clauses containing negated literals and recursive calls are placed at the bottom of the procedure. The motivation of such a heuristic is to obtain tail recursive procedures, and to suppress negation (Step G) after the future insertion of cuts at top of the procedure (Step F). For instance, the benefits of making a procedure tail recursive is illustrated in Table 9.7 (for the `suffix` procedure), and the benefits of putting the clauses with negation at the bottom of a procedure, followed by the removal of such a negation by the safe introduction of a cut is illustrated in Table 9.1 (for the `efface` procedure).

The optimiser splits the procedure in groups of clauses that are consecutive, that do not contain cuts, that are deterministic (the E_{sol} component of the output abstract sequence B of the clauses implies `sol=<1`), and that are mutually exclusive (see Section 6.3). For each group, the optimiser reorders the clauses inside the group according to the following priority order: 1) clauses without negation are placed at the top of the group (first the clauses without recursive call, and then those with recursive call), and 2) clauses with negation are placed at the bottom of the group (first the clauses without recursive call, and then those with recursive call). If several clauses contain negations, then the optimiser sorts them by placing those having a greater number of negations after the others. Note that the optimiser preserves the order of groups inside the procedure.

Step D) Semantic normalisation [*'clause'*]

At this step, the optimiser performs a finer normalisation of the procedure, by exploiting the abstract information annotating each program point. Semantic normalisation increases the number of positions where a cut could be inserted and, in particular, it allows the optimiser to insert a cut as soon as possible.

The optimiser *introduces new unifications* in a clause, *simplifies* unifications, and *decomposes* unifications that may fail. The key idea is to introduce new program variables in the clause so that each index i of the β_{out} component of the abstract sequence corresponding to any intermediate program point has (is identified by) at least one program variable X_j. Maintaining this invariant ensures that all the structural information is made explicit as early as possible in the clause. Some unifications can also be removed because they are redundant with other unifications introduced beforehand. The rules of semantic normalisation are provided in Appendix G.5.

Introducing new unifications in a clause. To show the benefit on introducing new unifications, let us consider the following program:

```
p(X1,X2)  :- q(X1,X2).
p(X1,X2)  :- not(X1=f(X3)), X2=b.
```

Assume that the procedure is called when X1 is ground and X2 is a variable, and suppose that the formal specification (abstract sequence) attached to the execution of q(X1) is:

```
q(X1)
   in(X1:ground,X2:var)
   ref(X1:f(_),_)
```

Then, the refined component modelling the sure execution of the call q(X1) is explicitly expressed by inserting the new unification X1=f(X3) before the call:

```
p(X1,X2)  :- X1=f(X3), q(X1,X2).
p(X1,X2)  :- not(X1=f(X3)), X2=b.
```

Later on, the optimiser will be able to insert a cut after the new unification (Step F), and to remove the negation of the second clause (Step G).

Simplifying unifications. The optimiser simplifies each unification of a clause, depending on its form ($X = Y$ or $X = f(X_1, ..., X_n)$), and on the abstract information attached to the program variables at the program point situated just before the unification. For each unification in the clause, the optimiser looks at the same-value sv and the frame frm components of the β_{out} part of the abstract sequence situated just before the unification. Suppose that the unification is $X = Y$. If the terms bound to X and Y have the same value (i.e., $sv(X) = sv(Y)$) then the unification is safely removed. If they have an identical pattern (i.e., $frm(sv(X)) = f(i_1, ..., i_n)$ and $frm(sv(Y)) = f(j_1, ..., j_n)$) then the unification is replaced by $X_1 = Y_1, ..., X_n = Y_n$, where $X_1, ..., X_n, Y_1, ..., Y_n$ are the program variables attached to the indices $i_1, ..., i_n, j_1, ..., j_n$ in β_{out}. If only the frame of X

is known (i.e., $frm(sv(X)) = f(i_1, ..., i_n)$ and $frm(sv(Y))$ is undefined) then the original unification is replaced by $Y = f(X_1, ..., X_n)$, where $X_1, ..., X_n$ are the program variables attached to the indices $i_1, ..., i_n$ in β_{out}. Similar simplifications are performed by the optimiser for unifications of the form $X = f(X_1, ..., X_n)$.

Decomposing unifications. Unifications that may fail are decomposed into equivalent ones. For each unification of the form $X = f(X_1, ..., X_n)$, the optimiser looks at the abstract sequence modelling the execution of the unification. The optimiser detects that the unification does not surely succeed if the β_{in} and β_{ref} components are not identical, and if the E_{sol} component does not imply `sol=1`. If so, the unification is decomposed and replaced by the following equivalent ones: $X = f(Y_1, ..., Y_n), X_1 = Y_1, ..., X_n = Y_n$, where $Y_1, ..., Y_n$ are new program variables that do not occur in the clause.

Step E) Move unification and negation forwards [*'clause'*]

At this step, the optimiser advances unifications and negations at the beginning of the bodies.[3] The deterministic prefixes of the resulting clauses become longer, which is often a characteristic of efficient code. Also, because unifications and negations are often responsible for making a clause exclusive with subsequent ones, this allows the optimiser to insert a cut as soon as possible in a clause (Step F). Another interest of putting unifications at the beginning of clauses is the future instantiation of the clause heads and the suppression of those equality literals (Step I).

This step is performed by the optimiser for each clause, independently from the other ones. Consider the following clause

$$p(X_1, ..., X_n) : - Unifs_0, call_1, Unifs_1, call_2, ..., call_r, Unifs_r.$$

where $Unifs_k$ is a sequence (possibly empty) of unifications and negations $(0 \leq k \leq r)$, and where $call_i$ is a literal that is not a unification nor a negation $(1 \leq i \leq r)$. The optimiser analyses the clause from right to left. At each step i (from r to 1), it advances unifications and negations from the sequence $Unifs_i$ to the end of the sequence $Unifs_{i-1}$. The checker recomputes the abstract sequences annotating the program points related to the moved unifications.

---

[3]We use the terminology *forwards propagation* of [45] to denote that unifications are propagated at the beginning of the bodies of the clauses. Other work uses the terminology *backpropagation bindings* [2].

The application conditions for moving a unification or a negation before a call depend on the form of the call (either a procedure call or a cut):

Moving a unification before a procedure call.

We first define the notion of *logicalness* of a procedure w.r.t. its specification.[4] Informally, a procedure is unlogic if it has a different behaviour when unifications are moved before the procedure. In what follows, the execution of a goal g with input substitution θ is denoted by $g\theta$. A procedure p/n is logic with respect to the in part of its specification iff, for any substitution θ and any unification *unif*, the execution of $(p(X_1, ..., X_n), unif)\theta$ and of $(unif, p(X_1, ..., X_n))\theta$ produces the same answer substitution sequence, provided that the call to $p(X_1, ..., X_n)$ in both goals satisfies the in part of the specification. Logicalness and unlogicalness of a procedure is described in formal specifications by the tags `logic` or `unlogic` respectively (if it is not specified, the procedure is logic by default).

Let B be the abstract sequence situated just before the procedure call, let B_{call} be the specification attached to the procedure call, and let *unif* be a unification from the block of unifications situated after the procedure call. The optimiser proceeds as follows for deciding whether the unification can be moved before the procedure call.

If the parameters of the procedure call and of the unification *unif* do not share a variable in the β_{out} component of B, then the unification is safely moved before the call, since the unification does not modify the input pattern of the procedure call.

Otherwise, the optimiser uses the checker to execute the unification *unif* at the position B (the input abstract substitution of the unification is computed from the abstract substitution β_{out} of B, restricted to the program variables occurring in *unif*). Let B_{aux} be the freshly computed abstract sequence situated just after the unification *unif*. The optimiser then verifies that the specification of the procedure call B_{call} can still be applied (the restriction of the output component of B_{aux} on the variables of the procedure call must satisfy the in part of the specification B_{call}). If the specification cannot be applied, the unification is not moved forwards. If the specification can be applied, the optimiser moves the unification before the procedure call if the procedure is *logic* w.r.t. the in part of its specification (i.e., the tag `logic` is attached to the specification B_{call}).

For instance, the test predicate `var/1` is specified as follows.

```
unlogic var/1        logic var/1          logic var/1
  in(X:any)            in(X:var)            in(X:novar)
  ref(var)             untouched(X)         sol(sol = 0)
  untouched(X)         sol(sol = 1)
  sol(sol = 1)
```

---

[4]The *logicalness* property is similar to the notion of *binding insensitivity* of an atom [2]. A binding-sensitive predicate is characterised by having a different success or failure behaviour if bindings are moved before the predicate.

The `var/1` builtin used in the context of the first specification is clearly unlogic. The second specification considers the test-predicate when it is used with a variable as input, so that the predicate surely succeeds. In that context, any unification that does not change the context of the call (i.e., `var/1` is still called with a variable) can be safely placed before the builtin. Similarly, the test-predicate is logic when its input is not a variable (in that case, the builtin surely fails).

For instance, consider the goal `var(X),X=Y`. Assume that input X is any term and that Y is a ground term. In such a case, the first specification is used to model the execution of `var(X)`. The procedure only succeeds if the input X is a variable. The builtin used in such a situation is *unlogic*, so that the unification cannot be moved forwards. Indeed, the execution of `var(X),X=Y` may succeed (it succeeds if X is a variable), although the execution of `X=Y,var(X)` surely fails. Now, assume that input X and Y are two variables. In such a situation, the second specification is used to model the execution of the call to `var(X)`. In this case, the unification can be safely placed before the test predicate, since the procedure is *logic* in such a situation, and because the unification `X=Y` executed before the test predicate is such that X remains a variable (so that the call to `var(X)` still satisfies the `in` part of the second specification).

Moving a unification before a cut.

At this step, cuts are red (green cuts were removed in Step B). So, only fully deterministic literals can be moved before a red cut, so that the input conditions for which a cut is executed are not modified. A unification is moved before a cut if the unification is fully deterministic (i.e., surely succeeds) when it is executed just before the cut. Let B be the abstract sequence situated just before the cut. The optimiser applies the checker to derive the abstract sequence B_{unif}, modelling the execution of the unification whose abstract input is restricted from the β_{out} component of B. If the β_{in} and β_{ref} components of B_{unif} are equal, and if the E_{sol} component of B_{unif} implies `sol=1`, then the optimiser moves the unification before the cut.

Moving a negation before a procedure call.

A negated literal is moved before a procedure call if it remains sound when it is executed before the call (i.e., if its arguments are ground). The optimiser checks that the modes attached to the program variables occurring in the negated literals are ground in the β_{out} component of the abstract sequence situated just before the procedure call.

More technical details about this step are provided in Appendix G.6.

Step F) Leftmost green cut insertion ['*procedure*']

During this step, the optimiser inserts a green cut at the leftmost position possible of each clause (except for the last clause). The previous steps have transformed the code so that cuts can be placed as soon as possible. A cut is inserted at a position in a clause only if the sequence of literals before that position is deterministic and exclusive with subsequent clauses.

The optimiser analyses each position of a clause from left to right, until the first program point (if any), where the following conditions hold: the E_{sol} component of the abstract sequence B annotated at that position implies sol=<1, and if B is exclusive with the output abstract sequence of each subsequent clause, as it is performed with precision in Section 6.3. No cut is inserted in a clause if no such position can be discovered. This step is detailed in Appendix G.7.

For instance, consider the procedure p(X1,X2) presented in Step D, when input X1 is a ground term and X2 is a variable. The cut is inserted just after the first unification, since the refined component of the abstract sequence at that position is equal to the failure component of the second clause (X1:f(ground),X2:var):

```
p(X1,X2)  :- X1=f(X3),  !,  q(X1,X2).
p(X1,X2)  :- not(X1=f(X3)),  X2=b.
```

Note that placing a cut at a leftmost position in a clause depends on the order of literals, and especially on the order of unifications. For instance, consider the following procedure:

```
p2(X1,X2)  :- X1=f(X3,X4),  X3=a,  X4=b,  X2=c.
p2(X1,X2)  :- X1=f(X3,X4),  X2=d,  not(X4=b).
```

If input X1 is a ground term and X2 is any term, then the leftmost cut will be placed after the unification X4=b in the first clause. However, switching the unifications X3=a and X4=b allows the optimiser to insert a cut much more quickly:

```
p2(X1,X2)  :- X1=f(X3,X4),  X4=b,  !,  X3=a,  X2=c.
p2(X1,X2)  :- X1=f(X3,X4),  X2=d,  not(X4=b).
```

Step G) Move cut backwards ['*clause*']

At this step, the optimiser moves every cut backwards (we use the terminology of [45]). Unifications and calls that are fully deterministic (i.e., succeed exactly once) are moved before the cut. This does not modify the input conditions for which the cut is surely executed, so that the transformed procedure still computes the same solutions as before. This code transformation has the advantage of putting more unifications at the beginning of the clauses. It also avoids useless backtracking, since a cut is surely executed after the computation of the first (and unique) solution of such a (fully deterministic) literal.

This step is performed by the optimiser for each clause, independently from the other ones. Consider the following clause that contains a cut at some position

$$p(X_1, ..., X_n) : -...,!, Unifs_i, call_{i+1}, Unifs_{i+1}, ..., call_r, Unifs_r.$$

where $Unifs_k$ is a (possibly empty) sequence of unifications $(i \leq k \leq r)$, and where $call_k$ is a literal that is not a unification $(i + 1 \leq k \leq r)$. The optimiser advances the maximum of unifications from $Unifs_i$ before the cut (see Step E). A unification is moved forwards if its execution (with abstract input that is restricted from the abstract sequence situated just before the cut) is fully deterministic (i.e., succeeds exactly once). If not every unification from $Unifs_i$ can be placed before the cut, then this step stops. Otherwise, the optimiser continues with the procedure call $call_{i+1}$. If $call_{i+1}$ is a cut, then the optimiser simply removes it. Otherwise, the optimiser checks if the procedure call $call_{i+1}$ is fully deterministic, so that it can be placed before the cut: the E_{sol} component of the formal specification attached to the procedure call must imply sol=<1, and the restriction (onto program variables of $call_{i+1}$) of the output abstract substitution situated just before the cut must imply (i.e., be less or equal to) the refined component of the formal specification attached to the procedure call.

Step H) Remove redundant literals [*'procedure'*]

At this step, the optimiser removes redundant test literals. A literal is called a test literal if it is deterministic, does not instantiate its arguments, and has no side-effects. A test literal is redundant (can be removed) if it is fully deterministic at this position in the clause. The removal of a redundant test literal corresponds to the notion of *abstract execution* defined in [115, 118]. Removing test literals obviously increases the efficiency. Furthermore, it also reduces the size of the clause body. Note that during the semantic normalisation the optimiser has already simplified (or removed) some unifications (Step D).

The optimiser detects that a literal is a test predicate by looking inside the abstract sequence modelling the execution of the literal: the E_{sol} component must imply sol=<1, and every index in the β_{ref} component must belong to the untouched component. A test literal in a clause is redundant (and is thus safely removed from the clause) if it is fully deterministic (i.e., surely succeeds) with respect to the abstract input of the clause (i.e., the in part of the formal specification of the analysed procedure), or if the execution of some cut in previous clauses prevents the literal to fail. This step is detailed in Appendix G.8.

Removing test literals that are fully deterministic.

For each test literal, let B_{lit} be the abstract sequence modelling its execution at that program point. The optimiser checks whether the E_{sol} component of B_{lit} implies sol=1, and if the restriction (onto the program variables of the literal) of the output abstract substitution situated just before the literal implies (i.e., is less than) the β_{ref} component of B_{lit}.

For instance, consider the $minimum(X,Y,Z)$ procedure:

```
minimum(X,Y,Z)  :-  integer(X),  integer(Y),  X=<Y,  Z=X.
minimum(X,Y,Z)  :-  Y<X,  Z=Y.
```

where the formal specification for the test predicate $integer/1$ is:

```
unlogic integer/1
  in(T:any)
  ref(int)
  untouched(X)
  sol(sol = 1)
```

Let the class of input calls for $minimum$ be $in(X:int,Y:int,Z:var)$. Then, the first two test predicates are safely removed, since the type of X and Y in the output abstract substitution situated before the builtins is int, which is equal to the ref part of the specification of $integer/1$.

Removing test literals due to the execution of a cut.

An annotated clause contains information about the input conditions for which a cut is surely executed in the clause (the abstract cut information acf and the β_{cut} abstract substitution, see Section 4.2.3). If the abstract cut information acf is cut, then a cut is surely executed in the clause for any input substitutions satisfying the β_{cut} component. Thus, subsequent clauses are not executed for such input conditions. A test literal in a clause is safely removed if the E_{sol} component of the abstract sequence modelling the literal execution implies $sol=1$, and if there exists some β_{cut} in a previous clause such that the failure component attached to the test literal implies (i.e., is less than) β_{cut}.

Typically, the execution of cuts allows the suppression of arithmetic comparisons and negations, as illustrated by the following example. Consider the following version of $minimum$ (when input X and Y are integers and Z is any term):

```
minimum(X,Y,Z)  :-  X=<Y,  !,  Z=X.
minimum(X,Y,Z)  :-  Y<X,  Z=Y.
```

The arithmetic comparison Y<X of the second clause can be safely removed, since the failure component attached to Y<X is:

```
fail(Y:int,X:int; srel((int)X =< (int)Y))
```

which is equivalent to the β_{cut} component of the first clause.

Step I) Denormalisation [*'clause'*]

The code generated until the previous step is still normalised (with possibly added cuts). Thus, it remains inefficient. The last step of the optimiser consists of applying the reverse transformation. The denormalisation suppresses explicit unifications, and instantiates the clause heads and subcalls as much as possible. This reduces the number of literals in a clause. Denormalisation rules are provided in Appendix G.9.

Indexing.   Currently, the strategy of the optimiser does not take indexing into account. Indexing is a technique to deterministically select a clause (or a group of clauses) to execute, based on the structure of input terms and on the instantiation of clause heads of the procedure (see, e.g., [1, 20]). It avoids (or limits) the creation of choice points. Indexing must be enabled on 'good' candidate keys: an argument's position is a good candidate if the principal functors of every head at that position are distinct. Indexing a procedure on good candidate keys is generally more efficient than inserting cuts. In Section 9.6, we illustrate the benefits of indexing (on the `deriv` procedure), and we explain how the optimiser strategy could be extended to choose whether indexing must be enabled or disabled.

Delay declarations.   Currently, the strategy of the optimiser does not take delay declarations into account (see Section 4.6). The strategy of the optimiser could be extended, by eliminating delay conditions when it is not needed (at each program point, one can check if the delay conditions are satisfied or not, thanks to the abstract information that is contained in each abstract sequence) and/or producing reorderings in which dynamic scheduling is not needed any more, as it is done for instance in [117].

9.5   Illustration of the optimiser strategy

We illustrate the optimisation strategy presented in the previous section. We show the optimisation process for the procedure `efface(X,T,TEff)` in the context of the first three formal specifications of Section 9.3. Let us recall the original code, and the specifications:

```
efface(X,[H|T],[H|TEff]) :- efface(X,T,TEff), not(X=H).
efface(X,[X|T],T).

efface1
  in(X:ground,T:list(ground),TEff:var)
  sol(sol =< 1)

efface2
  in(X:ground,T:list(ground),TEff:any)
  sol(sol =< 1)
```

```
efface3
  in(X:ground,T:any,TEff:list(ground))
  sol(sol =< (list)TEff_in+1)
```

Step A) Syntactic normalisation and code annotation

The first step of the optimiser consists of syntactically translating the original procedure into an equivalent normalised code. The checker annotates every program
point with an abstract sequence (we do not show the annotations explicitly).[5]

```
efface(X1,X2,X3)    :-   X2=[X4|X5],  X3=[X4|X6],
                          efface(X1,X5,X6),  not(X1=X4).
efface(X1,X2,X3)    :-   X2=[X1|X3].
```

Step B) Removing green cuts

In this example, the procedure contains no cuts, so that we continue to the next step.

Step C) Clause reordering

The first clause contains a negation, which is a good candidate to be removed later
on (after having inserted some cut). The optimiser reorders the clauses only for the
first two specifications, since the procedure is deterministic in such contexts. The
third version is left unchanged. The generated code for efface1 (or efface2)
is thus:

```
efface1(X1,X2,X3)    :-   X2=[X1|X3].
efface1(X1,X2,X3)    :-   X2=[X4|X5],  X3=[X4|X6],
                          efface1(X1,X5,X6),  not(X1=X4).
```

Step D) Semantic normalisation

During this step, the following code is generated for efface1 (and for efface2):

```
efface1(X1,X2,X3)    :-   X2=[X4|X5],  X4=X1,  X5=X3.
efface1(X1,X2,X3)    :-   X2=[X4|X5],  X3=[X4|X6],
                          efface1(X1,X5,X6),  not(X1=X4).
```

In the first clause, the previous unification X2=[X1|X3] has been decomposed
and replaced by three more elementary unifications: the initial unification suc-
ceeds if X2 is a non-empty list (i.e., X2=[X4|X5]), and if its first element is X1
(i.e., X4=X1), and if its tail is X3 (i.e., X5=X3). Now, the resulting clause is
composed of more literals, so that more positions are possible for inserting a cut
(see Step F). Note that the last clause is not normalised semantically because no
cut will be inserted there.

---

[5]The annotated code for the first specification of efface is provided in Appendix I, on page 332.

Step E) Move unification and negation forwards

In this example, all unifications are already at the beginning of the clauses. However, the negation of the second clause can be advanced before the recursive call, since it remains sound (its arguments are ground). The generated code at this step is thus as follows:

```
efface1(X1,X2,X3)    :-   X2=[X4|X5], X4=X1, X5=X3.
efface1(X1,X2,X3)    :-   X2=[X4|X5], X3=[X4|X6],
                          not(X1=X4), efface1(X1,X5,X6).

efface3(X1,X2,X3)    :-   X2=[X4|X5], X3=[X7|X6], X7=X4,
                          not(X1=X4), efface3(X1,X5,X6).
efface3(X1,X2,X3)    :-   X2=[X1|X3].
```

Step F) Leftmost green cut insertion

The objective of this step is to insert leftmost green cuts in every clause, except in the last clause. In our example, no cut can be inserted for efface3, since the two clauses are not exclusive in that context. For the efface1 and efface2 versions, the optimiser inserts a green cut after the unification X4=X1, because the sequence of literals before that unification is deterministic and exclusive with the second clause. The generated code with the cut is:

```
efface1(X1,X2,X3)    :-   X2=[X4|X5], X4=X1, !, X5=X3.
efface1(X1,X2,X3)    :-   X2=[X4|X5], X3=[X4|X6],
                          not(X1=X4), efface1(X1,X5,X6).
```

Note that if we had not performed semantic normalisation (Step D), then the cut would have been placed at the end of the first clause. In the next step, the cut will be moved backwards, by advancing literals that are fully deterministic only.

Step G) Move cut backwards

The objective of this step is to obtain the longest deterministic prefix before executing a cut in a clause. An inserted cut is moved backwards by passing literals that are fully deterministic before the cut. For the version efface1, the cut is moved backwards the unification X5=X3, since the unification is fully deterministic (at that point, X3 is a variable). However, for the version efface2, the cut must stay in place, because the unification X5=X3 does not surely succeed (at that point, X5 is a ground list and X3 is any term). The resulting codes are thus:

```
efface1(X1,X2,X3)    :-   X2=[X4|X5], X4=X1, X5=X3, !.
efface1(X1,X2,X3)    :-   X2=[X4|X5], X3=[X4|X6],
                          not(X1=X4), efface1(X1,X5,X6).

efface2(X1,X2,X3)    :-   X2=[X4|X5], X4=X1, !, X5=X3.
efface2(X1,X2,X3)    :-   X2=[X4|X5], X3=[X4|X6],
                          not(X1=X4), efface2(X1,X5,X6).
```

Step H) Remove redundant literals

The analyser is able to capture the input conditions for which a cut is *surely* executed. This information is used to refine the input conditions of the successive clauses. This allows the optimiser to remove some literals which become useless (e.g., negation, test predicates, arithmetic built-ins). In our example, for the versions efface1 and efface2, the cut is surely executed when the first element of input list X2 is the input X1. The second clause is thus surely not executed for that input. In particular, the negation surely succeeds and can therefore be suppressed safely:

```
efface1(X1,X2,X3)    :-   X2=[X4|X5], X4=X1, X5=X3, !.
efface1(X1,X2,X3)    :-   X2=[X4|X5], X3=[X4|X6],
                          efface1(X1,X5,X6).


efface2(X1,X2,X3)    :-   X2=[X4|X5], X4=X1, !, X5=X3.
efface2(X1,X2,X3)    :-   X2=[X4|X5], X3=[X4|X6],
                          efface2(X1,X5,X6).
```

Step I) Denormalisation

The last step consists of instantiating the clause heads and removing the unifications. The following three specialised codes for efface are thus finally generated:

```
efface1(X1,[X1|X2],X2) :- !.
efface1(X1,[X4|X2],[X4|X3]) :- efface1(X1,X2,X3).

efface2(X1,[X1|X2],X3) :- !, X2=X3.
efface2(X1,[X4|X2],[X4|X3]) :- efface2(X1,X2,X3).

efface3(X1,[X4|X2],[X4|X3]):-not(X1=X4),efface3(X1,X2,X3).
efface3(X1,[X1|X2],X2).
```

Note that the above specialised codes are identical to the ones that are derived by applying manually Deville's methodology [45].

Major remark.   All steps in the algorithm above are necessary to obtain the desirable efficient code. For instance, consider the second specification efface2, and assume that we do not perform the semantic normalisation (i.e., we bypass Step D). Then, the green cut will be inserted at the very end of the first clause. In such a situation, if X1 is equal to the first element of X2, then the cut is not surely executed, since the unification of X3 and the tail of X2 may fail. So, it results that the negation of the second clause is not redundant and it will not be removed during Step H.

9.6 Experimental evaluation of the optimiser

The optimiser has been tested on some classical programs, borrowed from [3, 45, 124] and from the Internet. The source programs, the formal specifications, the generated specialised codes, and the efficiency tests are available at *http://www.info.ucl.ac.be/~gobert*. The tests have been realised on a 1.5 GHz Pentium, 1 GB RAM, Linux Suse, with SWI-Prolog v 5.4.6 [132]. This section summarises our experimental results.[6]

Checker and optimiser execution time. Table 9.4 summarises the checker (Step A) and optimiser (Step B to Step I) execution time of 109 pairs of procedures/specifications. Time is expressed in second. The average analysis time is 6.05 sec.

	Step A	Step B-C-D	Step E-F-G-H	Step I	Total
mean	2.46	2.92	0.62	0.05	6.05
max	17.75	23.35	6.26	0.27	36.62
min	0.08	0.06	0.01	0.00	0.15

Table 9.4: Summary of the checker and optimiser execution time.

Tests on speedup. Table 9.5 reports on execution time speedup, defined as the ratio between the execution time spent for the source program and for the specialised program. A speedup greater than (resp. less than) one means that the specialised code is more (resp. less) efficient than the source code. We consider 57 procedures and 109 specifications (some procedures have several specifications, because they are multidirectional). The benchmark *all* is composed of 187 efficiency tests (there is at least one efficiency test for each specification of a procedure). The benchmark *det* is a subset of the benchmark *all*. It contains only the efficiency tests for the deterministic procedures. The benchmark *ss* contains the efficiency tests for the procedures that surely succeed. The benchmark *det+ss* contains the efficiency tests for the deterministic procedures that surely succeed. The benchmark *not* contains the efficiency tests for the procedures that contain negation. The benchmark *arith* contains the efficiency tests for the procedures that contain arithmetic comparison. The results reported on Table 9.5 depend on the choice of the efficiency tests. It is impossible to perform tests that include every situation in the context of a directionality. We have tried to make sufficiently general tests for each directionality. By default, SWI-Prolog enables indexing on the first argument position of each procedure. Note that the optimiser strategy that we have implemented (see Section 9.4) does not consider indexing. We have thus performed two kinds of efficiency tests: when indexing is enabled (for both the original and the specialised

---

[6]Appendix H contains detailed tables on the efficiency tests.

versions), and when indexing is disabled (for both the original and the specialised versions). When indexing is enabled (**Default indexing**), the mean speedup ranges from 1.32 to 3.11, the maximal speedup is 33.5 and the minimum speedup is 0.67. When indexing is disabled (**No indexing**), the speedup is slightly better: considering the benchmark *all*, the mean speedup is 1.83, the maximal speedup is 36, and the minimum speedup is 0.91. The best speedup is obtained for procedures that contain negation (benchmark *not*). This is not surprising, since the optimiser strategy has been designed to safely remove redundant negations after cut insertion.

| Efficiency tests | Execution Speedup (Specialised w.r.t. User code) | | | | | |
| | Default indexing | | | No indexing | | |
	Mean	Max	Min	Mean	Max	Min
187 *all*	1.8	33.5	0.67	1.83	36	0.91
140 *det*	1.67	33.5	0.67	1.68	31.9	0.91
54 *ss*	1.52	8.11	0.9	1.5	8.06	1
47 *det+ss*	1.6	8.11	0.9	1.57	8.06	1
55 *not*	3.11	33.5	0.94	3.09	36	0.95
78 *arith*	1.32	2.5	0.9	1.32	2.5	0.95

Table 9.5: Execution time speedup between source codes and specialised codes generated by the optimiser: 187 efficiency tests distributed out of 57 predicates and 109 formal specifications.

When indexing is enabled, from the 187 efficiency tests, we obtain a speedup for 170 tests, and a slight slowdown for 17 tests. When indexing is disabled, we obtain a speedup for 177 tests, and a slight slowdown for 10 tests only. The reasons of a slowdown can be explained as follows. The insertion of a cut may generate time overhead, especially if it does not allow us to suppress some redundant test literals in subsequent clauses. There are more situations of slowdown when indexing is enabled than when indexing is disabled. The effect of indexing is to avoid the creation of a choice point on the local stack, although the effect of a cut is to remove a choice point from the local stack. These two techniques are thus redundant. Executing a cut when indexing is enabled may be useless, since no choice point has to be deallocated. However, the two techniques should be combined, since we can still insert leftmost cuts inside groups of clauses where indexing has no effect.

The efficiency results depend on the way the source code is written. For all the benchmarks reported in Table 9.5, the original program was written in the usual Prolog style (i.e., not normalised). The optimiser can take as input programs that are normalised, like the ones that are derived in Deville's methodology [45]. Table 9.6 reports on the same efficiency tests with syntactic normalised programs as initial source code. For such inputs, when indexing is enabled, we obtain a mean speedup of 3.57, a maximal speedup of 64, and a minimal speedup of 0.73.

Efficiency tests		Execution Speedup (Specialised w.r.t. Syntactic Normalised code)					
		Default indexing			No indexing		
		Mean	Max	Min	Mean	Max	Min
187	*all*	3.57	64	0.73	3.38	61	1
140	*det*	3.54	64	0.73	3.28	61	1
54	*ss*	3.12	8.64	1	2.79	8.65	1
47	*det+ss*	3.29	8.64	1	2.9	8.65	1
55	*not*	5.3	64	1.38	5.13	61	1.33
78	*arith*	2.63	4.9	0.73	2.57	6	1

Table 9.6: Execution time speedup between syntactic normalised source codes and specialised codes generated by the optimiser: 187 efficiency tests distributed out of 57 predicates and 109 formal specifications.

Benefits of denormalisation. Denormalisation suppresses explicit unifications, and instantiates the clause heads and subcalls as much as possible (Step I, see Section 9.4). This code transformation reduces the number of literals in a clause, and it increases the number of situations where indexing can be applied. We have experimentally tested that the denormalisation process never generates a slowdown when it is applied just after the syntactic normalisation (Step A). Each original code has been syntactically normalised, and immediately after, it has been denormalised: the mean speedup is 1.04 and the minimal speedup is 1.

Tests on local stack utilisation. We compare the local stack utilisation of the source and specialised code of 57 procedures (see Appendix H.3 for details). The efficiency tests have been performed when indexing was enabled on the first argument position and when indexing was disabled. When indexing is enabled, the maximal amount of local stack used during the execution of the generated code is either reduced (for 33 procedures), or identical (for 11 procedures), or slightly increased (for 13 procedures) w.r.t. the maximal amount of local stack used during the execution of the source code. Furthermore, 17 specialised procedures use a constant amount of local stack (this is the case for only 9 original procedures). When indexing is disabled, the maximal amount of local stack used during the execution of the generated code is either reduced (for 46 procedures), or identical (for 9 procedures), or slightly increased (for 2 procedures) w.r.t. the maximal amount of local stack used during the execution of the source code. Furthermore, 17 specialised procedures use a constant amount of local stack (this is the case for only 4 original procedures).

The reason for which some specialised programs need a larger amount of local stack space is as follows. During the optimiser strategy, cuts are inserted at a leftmost position (Step F), and then, cuts are moved backwards (Step G). After denormalisation (Step I), it may thus happen that some cut is not situated just after the symbol : – (such a cut is called a *deep* cut). The execution of a deep cut requires environment allocation on the local stack. In particular, a rule of the form a : – ! , b . requires no environment allocation, whereas a rule of the form a : –b, ! . requires environment allocation (even if it would be a chain rule without the cut). A specialised code containing deep cuts may thus use more local stack space than an original code (without cuts).

Tail recursive procedure: an example.   Clause reordering (Step C) may allow us to obtain a tail recursive program (see Section 9.2). For instance, consider the following input code for the predicate suffix(Xs,Ys) that holds iff Xs is a suffix of the list Ys.

```
suffix(Xs,[Y|Ys])  :- suffix(Xs,Ys).
suffix(Xs,Xs).
```

Consider that the input Xs and Ys are ground lists. In that case, the predicate is deterministic. Note that indexing has not effect here, since the first argument is a program variable in both clauses heads. The optimiser generates the following code (the clauses have been reordered and a cut has been inserted in the basic clause):

```
suffix(Xs,Xs)  :- !.
suffix(Xs,[Y|Ys])  :- suffix(Xs,Ys).
```

Input	Execution Time			Used Local Stack	
list	suffix	suffix (reordered)		suffix	suffix (reordered)
length	(ms)	(ms)	(sdup)	(B)	(B)
500	50	50	1.00	36108	176
1000	200.33	199.33	1.01	360108	176
25000	ERROR	7933.67	-	ERROR	176

Table 9.7: Efficiency comparison of suffix(Xs,Ys) (clause reordering). The program is executed 10 times, when Xs and Ys are ground lists. Tests were performed by varying the list-length of input Xs.

Table 9.7 compares the two versions of suffix. The second version is more efficient than the original code in terms of local stack utilisation. In the first version, the local stack increases, since a choice point is created each time the recursive clause is called (the choice point is deallocated only when the second clause is called). In particular, there is a local stack overflow if we try to execute the first version with an input list Xs of 25000 elements. However, the second version uses a constant amount of local stack: a choice point is pushed on the local stack each time the basic clause is executed, but it is immediately deallocated after the success of that clause (the execution of the cut removes the choice point) or after the failure of that clause (deallocation of the choice point is the first WAM instruction of the second clause, since it is the last clause of the procedure).

Indexing: an example. Currently, the strategy of the optimiser does not take indexing into account. Indexing a procedure on good candidate keys is generally more efficient than inserting cuts. As an example, consider the procedure deriv(F,DF) (Procedure 5.3, page 110), in the context of Specification 5.16: input F is a ground expression, and input DF is a variable. Our optimiser generates the following code, with inserted cuts (the procedure is fully deterministic):

```
deriv(x, const(1)) :- !.
deriv(const(_), const(0)) :- !.
deriv(neg(F), neg(DF)) :-
      deriv(F,DF), !.
deriv(add(F,G), add(DF,DG)) :-
      deriv(F,DF),
      deriv(G,DG), !.
deriv(mult(F,G), add(mult(F,DG),mult(DF,G))) :-
      deriv(F,DF),
      deriv(G,DG), !.
deriv(sub(F,G), sub(DF,DG)) :-
      deriv(F,DF),
      deriv(G,DG), !.
deriv(div(F,G), div(sub(mult(G,DF),mult(F,DG)),
                    mult(G,G))) :-
      deriv(F,DF),
      deriv(G,DG).
```

Table 9.8 compares the specialised code (with cut, but without indexing) with respect to the original code (without cut, but indexed on its first argument). The specialised code is less efficient than the original code (slowdown from 0.84 to 0.86), and uses a greater amount of local stack.

Input	Execution Time			Used Local Stack	
size	deriv (indexed) (ms)	deriv (cut) (ms)	(sdup)	deriv (indexed) (B)	deriv (cut) (B)
12	259	301	0.86	780	1184
13	260	305	0.85	836	1268
14	261	310	0.84	892	1352

Table 9.8: Efficiency comparison of deriv(F,DF) with and without indexing. The program is executed 1000 times. Input size denotes the depth of the input expression F.

The optimiser should be extended to take indexing into account in its strategy. Enabling indexing by default, as it is done in SWI-Prolog, is not the best solution. We must define some heuristics, based on the abstract information, to choose whether indexing has to be enabled or not, and if so, to choose on which good candidate keys indexing must be enabled. A position is a good candidate for indexing a procedure if it is sufficiently discriminating, i.e., if most clause heads of the procedure are instantiated to a different principal functor at that argument position. It may happen that inserting leftmost cuts becomes redundant (or generates time overhead) if indexing is enabled. However, the two approaches (indexing and leftmost cut insertion) can be combined, since we can still insert leftmost cuts in groups of clauses that cannot be deterministically selected by the index.

Conclusion and perspectives

Chapter 10

Conclusion and perspectives

10.1 Context of this thesis

The major difficulty of programming in Prolog is that the declarative and operational semantics of Prolog do not coincide. The gap between the two semantics makes difficult the implementation of declaratively and operationally correct Prolog programs, as well as their optimisation. Lots of researches have been realised to obtain systematic methodologies or automated tools for checking and optimising Prolog programs. We can quote the following work. Y. Deville proposes a methodology to construct reliable and efficient code, based on a specification and a safe application of code transformations [45]. Deville's methodology is not automated, however. Several frameworks exist to verify specific operational properties (e.g., occur-check freeness [36], termination [27]). The proposed frameworks are heterogeneous and are not always implemented and validated, so that it is not easy to combine them into a single global environment. CiaoPP is a global environment that is composed of a lot of analyses devoted to verification and optimisation [66]. However, the framework of CiaoPP is not completely unified as in our approach. The Mercury language is another approach to remove the conflict existing between the declarative and the operational semantics, which restricts the class of accepted logic programs and compels the user to write declarations besides his program [123].

In this thesis, we have designed, implemented and validated a static analyser of Prolog programs that is able to integrate state-of-the art techniques, in a unified abstract interpretation framework.

10.2 Contributions of this thesis

We have completely implemented the framework proposed in [78] and we have validated it. We have shown its power and its flexibility to design complex and integrated analyses. This framework is conceptually more attractive than other fragmentary approaches. The main novelty of this framework is the notion of *abstract sequence*, which abstracts the 'concrete' semantic notion of *sequence of answer substitutions*. This allows us to integrate many several analyses that are usually done separately. Abstract sequences are composed of several domains to collect desirable information, including relations between the input and output sizes of terms, termination, input conditions about the success or the failure of the execution, and the number of solutions to a call. The desirable operational properties of a procedure are described by so-called *formal specifications* and are provided by the user. The abstract execution is compositional. It does not perform any fixpoint. It analyses a subcall in a procedure by relying on the formal specifications provided by the user. One can thus analyse a program where some parts of its code are unavailable but where the formal specifications are available. The framework is generic since it is based on the domain Pat($\mathcal{R}$) [33, 80], so that we did not need to modify everything in the framework to add or to refine abstract domains.

However, the paper [78] is only theoretical and is incomplete in several respects, as not all introduced abstract operations are completely defined. Moreover, this paper only describes the main principles of the verifier. It does not address optimisation issues nor the support of declarative program construction. Its treatment of types and norms is simplified as it only considers lists and the list norm. Also, it does not consider the cut or negation as failure that both require non trivial extensions to the framework. Modularity issues are not taken into account. We have thus extended and improved the basic framework along the following lines:

- *Handling full Prolog.* The framework now accepts features that make Prolog more expressive (negation as failure, disjunctive and if-then-else constructs), as well as extralogical features (cut, meta-call, and dynamic predicates). New domains and new abstract operations have been implemented to model such features.

- *Extending expressiveness.* An abstract domain for linearity is added in abstract substitutions. It allows us to describe more kinds of calls to a procedure, and to prove the occur-check freeness of programs. We define a type language to describe and to analyse more accurately the behaviours of programs using structures other than lists. The user is now able to declare its own (parametric) types, as well as norms attached to them. The possibility to combine several norms (user-defined and primitive norms) into the inter-argument sizes relations is useful for proving termination.

- *Improving accuracy of the analysis.* A domain of untouched terms has been designed, which is useful to analyse with precision the behaviour of procedure using test predicates. Termination analysis has been extended to deal with mutually recursive procedures, and to allow the user to declare sequence of expressions as induction parameter. The system proves the termination of a procedure by checking that the induction parameter decreases through (mutually) recursive calls, according to the lexicographic order. We also improve the design of the concatenation of abstract sequences, which computes the abstract sequence modelling the behaviour of a procedure composed of several clauses.

- *Modularity.* The input program can be decomposed in modules. Each module is analysed separately, by importing the public formal specifications of the modules. The SWI-Prolog library has been specified (e.g., test predicates, arithmetic built-ins).

We have implemented and validated two applications, showing the interest and the precision of the framework.

- *The checker* verifies any Prolog program (possibly without any declarative semantic) with respect to some intended operational properties (expressed in formal specifications). The checker annotates each program point with an abstract sequence. If the analysis succeeds, the programmer can be more confident in its code, since it is guaranteed that the formal specification holds for the code. Otherwise, the checker generates error or warning messages that can help the programmer to debug its program. If the input program has a declarative meaning, the verification of operational properties (termination, determinacy, occur-check freeness, soundness of negation as failure, green cuts) ensures that the declarative and operational semantics agree.

- *The optimiser* specialises a Prolog code with respect to a formal specification, by applying safe code transformations. Such code transformations include clause and literal reordering, cut insertion, removal of redundant literals, and denormalisation. The input code must meet a formal specification. The optimiser first executes the checker to verify sufficient conditions to apply the code transformations safely, based on the abstract information annotating each program point. We have defined a strategy to choose which transformations to apply and in which order. Usually, the specialised code generated by the optimiser has no-longer a declarative meaning, but it is guaranteed that its operational semantic agree with the declarative semantic of the input program (in the context of the specification). The optimiser can be used as an implementation and an automation of the last step of Deville's methodology.

10.3 Perspectives and further work

In this thesis, we have extended, improved, and evaluated our abstract interpretation framework. Our experiments with the checker and the optimiser have shown encouraging results. A lot of work remain to do however, as we discuss it now.

10.3.1 Abstract interpretation framework

Inference of specifications.   Our tool relies on information provided by the programmer although some or all of this information could be inferred automatically. Asking the programmer for such information may allow the tool to prove the correctness of more difficult programs and to find more programming mistakes. However, this task may appear to be too cumbersome for the programmer. It should be desirable to have a system where procedures may be specified, partially specified, or not specified at all. Two solutions exist to deal with unspecified procedures. A first solution consists of 'guessing' a formal specification for the procedure, and trying to verify it. Another solution is to implement a fixpoint algorithm, extending the one in [79], and including the definition of widening operators for the abstract domains.

Refinement of specifications.   The analysis relies on the specification provided by the user to abstractly execute a procedure call. It may happen that the output abstract sequence derived during the analysis of a procedure (i.e., the result of the abstract concatenation) is more precise than the formal specification provided by the user. In such a case, the derived abstract information should be used by the checker for proving other procedures, instead of relying only on the (less precise) user-given specifications.

Proving non-termination.   The current framework is designed to prove that a procedure terminates. It should be extended for proving sure non-termination, as well as for proving that a predicate has an infinite number of solutions (see, for instance, [79]).

Extending the type system.   Several improvements should be realised on the type system, to augment the expressiveness and precision of the analysis.

The set of primitive types should be extended. For instance, a new primitive type `var`, denoting the set of all variables, will allow the user to describe more precise types, like a list of variables `list(var)`. Note that such a type system with variables subsumes the modes. However, the abstract unification over such types is more difficult, since it cannot be implemented as a greatest lower bound.

The basic framework defines the type `anylist`, which denotes the set of terms that are instantiable to a list. Such 'instantiable types' are necessary to support Deville's methodology (such types are used in preconditions of specifications). For instance, the type `anylist` is useful to describe and to accurately analyse a predicate like `close/1`, which closes a possibly open list. Type expressions in the new framework should be extended to express such 'instantiable terms'. For instance, a type expression of the form `*any* tree(int)` will denote the set of terms that are instantiable to a tree of integers.

Type expressions are currently not expressive enough to describe special structures like difference lists. To remedy this problem, one can define the concept of 'indexed type declarations' and 'indexed type expressions'. An index in such declarations and expressions denotes a specific term, as an index in an abstract substitution represents a term in the concrete substitution. For instance, the indexed type declaration `list(T,i) ::= i | [T|list(T,i)]`, where `T` is the type variable and `i` is an index representing a specific term t_i, denotes lists of type `T`, ending with the term t_i. Given such a type declaration, the difference list `A-B` should be described by specifying `A` and `B` with `A:list(any,B)` and `B:any`.

The formal specifications are currently not polymorphic. It should be interesting to allow the user to write parametric type expressions (with type variables) in specifications. Specifications that use such parametric type expressions represent families of non-polymorphic specifications. These should be interpreted as infinite sets of specifications (without type variables). To deal with such non-polymorphic specifications, we should extend the framework according to the following two directions. In the first direction, no attempt should be done to prove the correctness of the procedure with respect to a polymorphic specification as a whole. Verification should be done on demand when a specific instance of the specification is needed. This extension is easy since it does not require to modify the basic algorithms of the analyser. Notice that a procedure could be correct for some instances of the specification but incorrect for other ones. The most ambitious direction will be to prove the correctness against a polymorphic specification as a whole but we currently have no precise clue of the difficulty of doing so. (It is probably more difficult than the Mercury case.)

10.3.2 Full Prolog

The framework analyses with precision the execution of negations of the form `not(X=Y)` and `not(X=f(X1,...,Xn))`. However, the current analyser cannot always prove accurate cardinality information of procedures using negation of the form `not(p(X1,...,Xn))`. Explicit information about the success or failure of such negation should be maintained during the analysis. Also, extralogical features should be analysed more accurately. The specification of an higher-order predicate should be extended so that the user can express that an argument of a procedure is a predicate that satisfies some given specification. Such information can be used during the abstract analysis, when the meta-call is executed. The treatment of dynamic predicates should be improved, by integrating new abstract domains that take the state of the database into account.

10.3.3   Checker

The readability of the checker output reports and warning messages can be improved. Also, the checker execution time can be improved. The analysis could be parametrised according to the operational properties that must be checked. Not every abstract domain has to be enabled during the analysis of a procedure with respect to its specification. For instance, if one is not interested in proving termination and cardinality of a procedure, then the sizes components of abstract sequences should be disabled during the analysis.

10.3.4   Optimiser

The current strategy of the optimiser can be improved in many ways.

Firstly, indexing has to be taken into account. We must define some heuristics to choose whether indexing must be enabled, and if so, to choose the good candidate keys. It may happen that inserting a leftmost cut becomes redundant if indexing is enabled. However, the two approaches (indexing and leftmost cut insertion) can be combined, since we can still insert leftmost cuts in groups of clauses where indexing has no effect.

Our strategy of clause reordering can be refined. The current framework only reorders clauses inside groups of consecutive clauses that are deterministic and mutually exclusive. One should consider also non-consecutive groups of clauses that are mutually exclusive and deterministic. Also, we should imagine to reorder such groups of clauses between them, and not only reorder clauses inside a group. Furthermore, the priority that we apply for sorting the clauses inside a group can be improved. For instance, if the clause reordering transformation places a clause with negation at the bottom of the procedure, one may decide to keep or to modify this ordering later on, depending on whether the negated literals have been effectively removed or not. If the negated literals have not been removed, then one can try another more interesting clause reordering.

To reduce the optimiser execution time, the semantic normalisation should be performed only if necessary. Indeed, this step is particularly time consuming, since the annotation of the semantically normalised clause (which contains more literals and more variables) must be recomputed.

Other strategies and code transformations of the optimiser should be investigated. For instance, instead of placing leftmost cut, one can try to insert rightmost cut, or leftmost and rightmost cut insertion, or even more cuts. Other techniques of partial evaluation like folding and unfolding could be also integrated in the strategy. Also, it should be interesting to reorder literals in a clause according to some information about the (space or time) complexity of the literals, so that literals with a high complexity are placed after literals with a smaller complexity. Such an information about complexity should be user-given or inferred like it is done in CiaoPP [110].

It should also be desirable to allow the user to parametrise the optimisation, so that he can decide which strategies to enable, or in which order to apply the code transformations.

10.3.5 Support of Deville's methodology

Our checker and optimiser can be used to support Deville's methodology. The third step of the methodology is automated. The checker verifies that a Prolog code respects intended operational properties, so that the gap between the declarative and operational semantics is reduced. The optimiser automates the derivation of specialised code by safe application of code transformations. However, the previous step in the methodology is not yet implemented. It consists of deriving an operationally correct Prolog code (for some given directionality), starting from a logical description (expressed in logic). Assuming a set of formal specifications, our abstract interpretation framework should be used to derive such a correct code, by trying to find one or several orderings of the literals and clauses of a procedure that ensure that all potential solutions to a call are actually computed.

As another extension, our system should be used to automatically generate multidirectional code. Some heuristics must be defined to choose which efficient codes to execute depending on the instantiation of the arguments. For instance, a multidirectional code for the `efface/3` procedure should be generated as follows (the specialised codes `efface1`, `efface3` and `efface4` are provided in Figure 9.1, page 203):

```
efface(X, T, TEff) :-
    var(TEff), !, efface1(X, T, TEff).
efface(X, T, TEff) :-
    var(X), !, efface3(X, T, TEff).
efface(X, T, TEff) :-
    efface4(X, T, TEff).
```

10.4 Towards an 'ideal' environment

We have experimented the difficulty of designing an 'ideal' programming environment. It is not obvious to determine the best solution for such an environment. Should it be a preprocessor that integrates all the analyses devoted to verification and optimisation (as in the spirit to the CiaoPP system), or should it be an environment used for declarative program construction with explicit specifications, similarly to Mercury but applicable to Prolog programs using general unification? The last approach, which could be supported by our integrated framework, would amount to define a new 'purely declarative' language, where we use pure Prolog procedures (without cuts and extralogical predicates) as our declarative descriptions, which means that we abstract from Prolog computation rule and depth-first search strategy. This amounts to say that the order of literals and clauses in a procedure is irrelevant. The environment will then automatically transform the declarative descriptions into efficient Prolog procedures by means of a number of well-controlled transformations (like it is done by our optimiser). Can we integrate the two approaches? These questions remain open. Answering these questions will allow us to remove the word '*towards*' in the title of our thesis.

Bibliography

[1] Hassan Aït-Kaci. *Warren's abstract machine: a tutorial reconstruction.* MIT Press, Cambridge, MA, USA, 1991.

[2] Elvira Albert, Germán Puebla, and John P. Gallagher. Non-leftmost Unfolding in Partial Evaluation of Logic Programs with Impure Predicates. In *LOPSTR*, pages 115–132, 2005.

[3] Krzysztof R. Apt. *From logic programming to Prolog.* Prentice-Hall, Inc., Upper Saddle River, NJ, USA, 1996.

[4] Krzysztof R. Apt and Roland N. Bol. Logic Programming and Negation: A Survey. *Journal of Logic Programming*, 19/20:9–71, 1994.

[5] Krzysztof R. Apt and Ingrid Luitjes. Verification of logic programs with delay declarations. In *Algebraic Methodology and Software Technology*, pages 66–90, 1995.

[6] Krzysztof R. Apt and Alessandro Pellegrini. On the Occur-Check-Free PROLOG Programs. *ACM Transactions on Programming Languages and Systems*, 16(3):687–726, May 1994.

[7] R. Bagnara, P. H. Hill, and E. Zaffanella. *User's Manual.* http://www.cs.unipr.it/ppl, March 2006.

[8] Roberto Bagnara, Elisa Ricci, Enea Zaffanella, and Patricia M. Hill. Possibly Not Closed Convex Polyhedra and the Parma Polyhedra Library. In *SAS '02: Proceedings of the 9th International Symposium on Static Analysis*, pages 213–229, Madrid, Spain, 2002. Springer-Verlag.

[9] R. Barbuti and R. Giacobazzi. A Bottom-up Polymorphic Type Inference in Logic Programming. *Science of Computer Programming*, 19(3), 1990.

[10] Roberto Barbuti, Paolo Mancarella, Dino Pedreschi, and Franco Turini. Intensional Negation of Logic Programs: Examples and Implementation Techniques. In *TAPSOFT '87: Proceedings of the International Joint Conference on Theory and Practice of Software Development, Volume 2: Advanced*

Seminar on Foundations of Innovative Software Development II and Colloquium on Functional and Logic Programming and Specifications (CFLP), pages 96–110, London, UK, 1987. Springer-Verlag.

[11] Roberto Barbuti, Paolo Mancarella, Dino Pedreschi, and Franco Turini. A transformational approach to negation in logic programming. *J. Log. Program.*, 8(3):201–228, 1990.

[12] C. Braem, B. Le Charlier, S. Modart, and P. van Hentenryck. Cardinality analysis of Prolog. In *ILPS '94: Proceedings of the 1994 International Symposium on Logic programming*, pages 457–471, Cambridge, MA, USA, 1994. MIT Press.

[13] Ivan Bratko. *Prolog (3rd ed.): programming for artificial intelligence.* Addison-Wesley Longman Publishing Co., Inc., Boston, MA, USA, 2001.

[14] Maurice Bruynooghe. A practical framework for the abstract interpretation of logic programs. *J. Log. Program.*, 10(2):91–124, 1991.

[15] Maurice Bruynooghe, Michael Codish, John P. Gallagher, Samir Genaim, and Wim Vanhoof. Termination analysis of logic programs through combination of type-based norms. *ACM Trans. Program. Lang. Syst.*, 29(2):10, 2007.

[16] F. Bueno, D. Cabeza, M. Carro, M. Hermenegildo, P. López-García, and G. Puebla. The Ciao Prolog System. Reference Manual. The Ciao System Documentation Series - TR CLIP3/97.1, School of Computer Science, Technical University of Madrid (UPM), August 1997.

[17] Francisco Bueno, María García de la Banda, and Manuel Hermenegildo. Effectiveness of abstract interpretation in automatic parallelization: a case study in logic programming. *ACM Trans. Program. Lang. Syst.*, 21(2):189–239, 1999.

[18] Francisco Bueno, Daniel Cabeza Gras, Manuel V. Hermenegildo, and Germán Puebla. Global Analysis of Standard Prolog Programs. In *European Symposium on Programming*, pages 108–124, 1996.

[19] Francisco Bueno, Pedro López-García, and Manuel V. Hermenegildo. Multivariant Non-failure Analysis via Standard Abstract Interpretation. In *FLOPS*, pages 100–116, 2004.

[20] Mats Carlsson. Freeze, Indexing, and Other Implementation Issues in the WAM. In *ICLP*, pages 40–58, 1987.

[21] D. Chan. Constructive negation based on the complete database. In R.A. Kowalski and editors K.A. Bowen, editors, *Proceedings of the 5th International Conference and Symposium on Logic Programming (ICSLP'88)*, pages 111–125, Seattle, Washington, September 1988. MIT Press.

[22] David Chan. An Extension of Constructive Negation and its Application in Coroutining. In *NACLP*, pages 477–493, 1989.

[23] K.L. Clark. Negation as failure. In H. Gallaire and J. Minker, editors. Logic and databases. 293-322 Plenum Press., 1978.

[24] M. Codish, D. Dams, and E. Yardeni. Derivation and safety of an abstract unification algorithm for groundness and aliasing analysis. In K. Furukawa, editor, *Proceedings of the Eight International Conference on Logic Programming (ICLP'91)*, Paris, France, June 1991. MIT Press.

[25] M. Codish, A. Mulkers, M. Bruynooghe, M. García de la Banda, and M. Hermenegildo. Improving abstract interpretations by combining domains. In *PEPM '93: Proceedings of the 1993 ACM SIGPLAN symposium on Partial evaluation and semantics-based program manipulation*, pages 194–205, New York, NY, USA, 1993. ACM Press.

[26] Michael Codish, Kim Marriott, and Cohavit Taboch. Improving Program Analyses by Structure Untupling. *The Journal of Logic Programming*, 43(3):251–263, 2000.

[27] Michael Codish and Cohavit Taboch. A Semantic Basis for the Termination Analysis of Logic Programs. *The Journal of Logic Programming*, 41(1):103–123, 1999.

[28] A. Colmerauer, H. Kanoui, R. Pasero, and P. Roussel. Un système de communication homme-machine en francais. Groupe de Recherche en I.A., Université d'Aix-Marseille, 1973.

[29] Alain Colmerauer and Philippe Roussel. The birth of Prolog. *History of programming languages—II*, pages 331–367, 1996.

[30] J. Correas, G. Puebla, M. Hermenegildo, and F. Bueno. Experiments in Context-Sensitive Analysis of Modular Programs. In *15th International Symposium on Logic-based Program Synthesis and Transformation (LOPSTR'05)*, number 3901 in LNCS, pages 163–178. Springer-Verlag, April 2006.

[31] A. Cortesi, B. Le Charlier, and P. Van Hentenryck. Type analysis of Prolog using type graphs. *Journal of Logic Programming*, 23(3):237-278, June 1995.

[32] Agostino Cortesi, Gilberto Filé, and William H. Winsborough. Optimal Groundness Analysis Using Propositional Logic. *J. Log. Program.*, 27(2):137–167, 1996.

[33] Agostino Cortesi, Baudouin Le Charlier, and Pascal Van Hentenryck. Combinations of abstract domains for logic programming: open product and

generic pattern construction. *Science of Computer Programming*, 38(1–3):27–71, 2000.

[34] Patrick Cousot and Radhia Cousot. Abstract Interpretation: A Unified Lattice Model for Static Analysis of Programs by Construction or Approximation of Fixpoints. In *POPL*, pages 238–252, 1977.

[35] Patrick Cousot and Rahida Cousot. Abstract interpretation and application to logic programs. *J. Log. Program.*, 13(2-3):103–179, 1992.

[36] Lobel Crnogorac, Andrew D. Kelly, and Harald Søndergaard. A Comparison of Three Occur-Check Analysers. In *SAS*, pages 159–173, 1996.

[37] Philip W. Dart and Justin Zobel. A Regular Type Language for Logic Programs. In *Types in Logic Programming*, pages 157–187. Pfenning, editor, 1992.

[38] Danny De Schreye and Stefaan Decorte. Termination of Logic Programs: The Never-Ending Story. *J. Log. Program.*, 19/20:199–260, 1994.

[39] S. K. Debray and D. S. Warren. Towards Banishing the Cut from Prolog. *IEEETSE*, 16(3):335–349, March 1990.

[40] Saumya Debray, Pedro López-García, Manuel Hermenegildo, and Nai-Wei Lin. Lower bound cost estimation for logic programs. In *ILPS '97: Proceedings of the 1997 international symposium on Logic programming*, pages 291–305, Cambridge, MA, USA, 1997. MIT Press.

[41] Saumya K. Debray. Static inference of modes and data dependencies in logic programs. *ACM Trans. Program. Lang. Syst.*, 11(3):418–450, 1989.

[42] Saumya K. Debray, P. López García, Manuel Hermenegildo, and N.-W. Lin. Estimating the Computational Cost of Logic Programs. In Baudouin Le Charlier, editor, *Proceedings of the First International Static Analysis Symposium*, pages 255–265. Springer Verlag, 1994.

[43] Saumya K. Debray, Pedro López-García, and Manuel V. Hermenegildo. Non-Failure Analysis for Logic Programs. In *ICLP*, pages 48–62, 1997.

[44] Saumya K. Debray and David Scott Warren. Automatic Mode Inference for Logic Programs. *Journal of Logic Programming*, 5(3):207–229, 1988.

[45] Yves Deville. *Logic programming: systematic program development*. Addison-Wesley Longman Publishing Co., Inc., Boston, MA, USA, 1990.

[46] J. Fischer. *Termination analysis for Mercury using convex constraints.* Honours report, Department of Computer Science and Software Engineering, The University of Melbourne, 2002.

[47] J. P. Gallagher. Tutorial on specialisation of logic programs. In *PEPM '93: Proceedings of the 1993 ACM SIGPLAN symposium on Partial evaluation and semantics-based program manipulation*, pages 88–98, New York, NY, USA, 1993. ACM.

[48] J.P. Gallagher and D.A. de Waal. Fast and Precise Regular Approximations of Logic Programs. In Pascal Van Hentenryck, editor, *Proceedings of the Eleventh International Conference on Logic Programming*, pages 599–613. The MIT Press, 1994.

[49] M. Garcia de la Banda, M. Hermenegildo, M. Bruynooghe, V. Dumortier, G. Janssens, and W. Simoens. Global Analysis of Constraint Logic Programs. *ACM Transactions on Programming Languages and Systems*, 18(5):564–614, September 1996.

[50] Samir Genaim and Michael Codish. Inferring Termination Conditions for Logic Programs using Backwards Analysis. In R. Nieuwenhuis and A. Voronkov, editors, *Proceedings of the Eighth International Conference on Logic for Programming, Artificial Intelligence and Reasoning*, volume 2250 of *Lecture Notes in Artificial Intelligence*, pages 681–690. Springer-Verlag, December 2001.

[51] Samir Genaim, Michael Codish, John P. Gallagher, and Vitaly Lagoon. Combining Norms to Prove Termination. In *VMCAI*, pages 126–138, 2002.

[52] Thomas W. Getzinger. The Costs and Benefits of Abstract Interpretation-driven Prolog Optimization. In *SAS '94: Proceedings of the First International Static Analysis Symposium on Static Analysis*, pages 1–25, London, UK, 1994. Springer-Verlag.

[53] François Gobert. Automated verification of Prolog programs: an implementation. Mémoire de maîtrise en informatique. Facultés Notre-Dame de la Paix. Namur. 146 pages., 2003.

[54] François Gobert. Checking Cardinality and Termination of Logic Programs by Abstract Interpretation. Diplôme d'études approfondies: DEA interuniversitaire en Informatique. Université Catholique de Louvain. 124 pages., 2005.

[55] François Gobert. Website of the analyser. Distribution sources, documentation, and benchmarck are publicly available at http://www.info.ucl.ac.be/~gobert, 2007.

[56] François Gobert and Baudouin Le Charlier. A System to check Operational Properties of Logic Programs. AFADL'07 conference. Namur. 2007.

[57] François Gobert and Baudouin Le Charlier. Un système vérifiant des propriétés opérationelles de programmes logiques. Soumis au numéro spécial de Technique et Science Informatique. AFADL 2007.

[58] François Gobert and Baudouin Le Charlier. Source-to-source optimizing transformations of Prolog programs based on abstract interpretation. WLPE. Porto., 2007.

[59] F. Henderson, Z. Somogyi, and T. Conway. *Determinism analysis in the Mercury compiler*, In Australian Computer Science Conference, pages 337–346, 1996.

[60] Jean Henrard and Baudouin Le Charlier. FOLON: An Environment for Declarative Construction of Logic Programs. In *PLILP*, pages 217–231, 1992.

[61] M. Hermenegildo, F. Bueno, D. Cabeza, M. Garcia de la Banda, P. López-García, and G. Puebla. The CIAO Multi-Dialect Compiler and System: An Experimentation Workbench for Future (C)LP Systems. Special volume on Parallelism and Implementation of Logic and Constraint Logic Programming. Nova Science Publishers, Inc, 1999.

[62] M. Hermenegildo and The Ciao Development Team. A Tutorial on Program Development and Optimization using the Ciao Preprocessor. Technical University of Madrid (UPM), January 2006.

[63] M. Hermenegildo and The Ciao Development Team. Why Ciao? An Overview of the Ciao System's Design Philosophy. Num. CLIP7/2006.0, 6 pages, Technical University of Madrid (UPM), December 2006.

[64] M. Hermenegildo, R. Warren, and S. Debray. Global Flow Analysis as a Practical Compilation Tool. *Journal of Logic Programming*, 13(4):349-367,1992.

[65] Manuel V. Hermenegildo. A Documentation Generator for (C)LP Systems. In *CL '00: Proceedings of the First International Conference on Computational Logic*, pages 1345–1361, London, UK, 2000. Springer-Verlag.

[66] Manuel V. Hermenegildo, Germán Puebla, Francisco Bueno, and Pedro López-García. Integrated program debugging, verification, and optimization using abstract interpretation (and the Ciao system preprocessor). *Sci. Comput. Program.*, 58(1-2):115–140, 2005.

[67] Manuel V. Hermenegildo, Germán Puebla, Kim Marriott, and Peter J. Stuckey. Incremental Analysis of Logic Programs. In *International Conference on Logic Programming*, pages 797–811, 1995.

[68] Patricia Hill and John Lloyd. *The Gödel programming language.* MIT Press, Cambridge, MA, USA, 1994.

[69] G. Janssens and M. Bruynooghe. Deriving descriptions of possible values of program variables by means of abstract interpretation. *J. Log. Program.*, 13(2-3):205–258, 1992.

[70] N.D. Jones and H. Søndergaard. A semantic-based framework for the abstract interpretation of Prolog. In S. Abramsky and C. Hankin, editors, *Abstract Interpretation of Declarative Languages*, chapter 6, pages 123-142. Ellis Horwood Limited, 1987.

[71] Neil D. Jones, Carsten K. Gomard, and Peter Sestoft. *Partial evaluation and automatic program generation.* Prentice-Hall, Inc., Upper Saddle River, NJ, USA, 1993.

[72] T. Kanomori and K. Horiuchi. Type inference in Prolog and its application. In *Proc. 9th IJCAI*, pages 704-709, 1985.

[73] R. Kowalski. *Logic for Problem Solving.* North Holland, Amsterdam, 1979.

[74] R.A. Kowalski. Predicate logic as programming language. In *Proc IFIP*, pages 569–574, Amsterdam, 1974.

[75] V. Lagoon, F. Mesnard, and P. Stuckey. *Termination analysis with types is more accurate*, In C. Palamidessi, editor, Logic Programming, 19th International Conference on Logic Programming, pages 254–269. Springer Verlag, 2003.

[76] B. Le Charlier, K. Musumbu, and P. Van Hentenryck. A generic abstract interpretation algorithm and its complexity analysis. In K. Furukawa, editor, *Proceedings of the Eighth International Conference on Logic Programming (ICLP'91)*, Paris, France, June 1991. MIT Press.

[77] Baudouin Le Charlier and Pierre Flener. On the Desirable Link Between Theory and Practice in Abstract Interpretation (Extended Abstract). In *Static Analysis Symposium*, pages 379–387, 1997.

[78] Baudouin Le Charlier, Christophe Leclère, Sabina Rossi, and Agostino Cortesi. Automated Verification of Prolog Programs. *Journal of Logic Programming*, 39(1-3):3–42, 1999.

[79] Baudouin Le Charlier, Sabina Rossi, and Pascal Van Hentenryck. Sequence-based abstract interpretation of Prolog. *TPLP*, 2(1):25–84, 2002.

[80] Baudouin Le Charlier and Pascal Van Hentenryck. Experimental evaluation of a generic abstract interpretation algorithm for PROLOG. *ACM Trans. Program. Lang. Syst.*, 16(1):35–101, 1994.

[81] Baudouin Le Charlier and Pascal van Hentenryck. Reexecution in abstract interpretation of Prolog. *Acta Inf.*, 32(3):209–253, 1995.

[82] C. Leclère. *On the design of some operations to combine domains for abstract interpretation.* PhD thesis, University of Namur (Belgium), 2004.

[83] C. Leclère and B. Le Charlier. Two dual abstract operations to duplicate, eliminate, equalize, introduce and rename place-holders occurring inside abstract descriptions. Research Paper RR-96-028, University of Namur, Belgium, September 1996.

[84] Chin Soon Lee. *Program Termination Analysis and Termination of Offline Partial Evaluation.* PhD thesis, University of Western Australia, August 2002.

[85] M. Leuschel and M. Bruynooghe. Logic program specialisation through partial deduction: Control issues. *Theory and Practice of Logic Programming*, 2(4&5):461–515, July & September 2002.

[86] Naomi Lindenstrauss, Yehoshua Sagiv, and Alexander Serebrenik. TermiLog: A System for Checking Termination of Queries to Logic Programs. In *Computer Aided Verification*, pages 444–447, 1997.

[87] J. W. Lloyd. *Foundations of logic programming; (2nd extended ed.).* Springer-Verlag New York, Inc., New York, NY, USA, 1987.

[88] John W. Lloyd and John C. Shepherdson. Partial Evaluation in Logic Programming. *J. Log. Program.*, 11(3&4):217–242, 1991.

[89] Pedro López-García, Francisco Bueno, and Manuel V. Hermenegildo. Determinacy Analysis for Logic Programs Using Mode and Type Information. In *LOPSTR*, pages 19–35, 2004.

[90] Lunjin Lu and Andy King. Determinacy Inference for Logic Programs. In *ESOP*, pages 108–123, 2005.

[91] K. Marriott and H. Søndergaard. Semantics-based dataflow analysis of logic programs. In G. Ritter, editor, *Information Processing'89*, pages 601-606, San Francisco, Californa, 1989.

[92] Kim Marriott, María José García de la Banda, and Manuel Hermenegildo. Analyzing Logic Programs with Dynamic Scheduling. In *20th Annual ACM Conf. on Principles of Programming Languages*, pages 240–253, January 1994.

[93] Kim Marriott, María José García de la Banda, and Manuel Hermenegildo. Analyzing logic programs with dynamic scheduling. In *POPL '94: Proceedings of the 21st ACM SIGPLAN-SIGACT symposium on Principles of programming languages*, pages 240–253, New York, NY, USA, 1994. ACM.

[94] Kim Marriott and Harald Søndergaard. Precise and Efficient Groundness Analysis for Logic Programs. *ACM Letters on Programming Languages and Systems*, 2(1-4):181–196, March–December 1993.

[95] C.S. Mellish. Abstract Interpretation of Prolog Programs. In S.Abramsky and C. Hankin, editors, *Abstract Interpretation of Declarative Languages*, chapter 8, pages 181-198. Ellis Horwood Limited, 1987.

[96] Frédéric Mesnard and Ulrich Neumerkel. Applying Static Analysis Techniques for Inferring Termination Conditions of Logic Programs. In *SAS '01: Proceedings of the 8th International Symposium on Static Analysis*, pages 93–110, London, UK, 2001. Springer-Verlag.

[97] Robin Milner. A proposal for standard ML. In *LFP '84: Proceedings of the 1984 ACM Symposium on LISP and functional programming*, pages 184–197, New York, NY, USA, 1984. ACM Press.

[98] Juan José Moreno-Navarro and Susana Muñoz-Hernández. How to Incorporate Negation in a Prolog Compiler. *Lecture Notes in Computer Science*, 1753:124–140, 2000.

[99] A. Mulkers. *Deriving Live Data Structures in Logic Programs by Means of Abstract Interpretation*. PhD thesis, Departement of Computer Science, Katholieke Universiteit Leuven, Belgium, 1991.

[100] Anne Mulkers, William Winsborough, and Maurice Bruynooghe. Analysis of shared data structures for compile-time garbage collection in logic programs. *Logic programming*, pages 747–762, 1990.

[101] Susana Muñoz-Hernández, Juan José Moreno-Navarro, and Manuel V. Hermenegildo. Efficient Negation Using Abstract Interpretation. In *LPAR '01: Proceedings of the Artificial Intelligence on Logic for Programming*, pages 485–494, London, UK, 2001. Springer-Verlag.

[102] K. Musumbu. *Interprétation Abstraite de Programmes Prolog*. PhD thesis, University of Namur (Belgium), September 1990.

[103] K. Muthukumar and M. Hermenegildo. *Determination of Variable Dependence Information at Compile-Time Through Abstract Interpretation*. North American Conference on Logic Programming, pages 166-189, MIT Press, October 1989.

[104] K. Muthukumar and M. Hermenegildo. Combined Determination of Sharing and Freeness of Program Variables through Abstract Interpretation. In Koichi Furukawa, editor, *Proceedings of the Eighth International Conference on Logic Programming*, pages 49–63, Paris, France, 1991. The MIT Press.

[105] K. Muthukumar and Manuel V. Hermenegildo. Compile-Time Derivation of Variable Dependency Using Abstract Interpretation. *Journal of Logic Programming*, 13(2,3):315–347, 1992.

[106] Alan Mycroft and Richard A. O'Keefe. A polymorphic type system for PROLOG. *Artif. Intell.*, 23(3):295–307, 1984.

[107] Lee Naish. *Negation and control in Prolog*. Springer-Verlag New York, Inc., New York, NY, USA, 1986.

[108] Lee Naish. Negation and Quantifiers in NU-Prolog. In *Proceedings of the Third International Conference on Logic Programming*, pages 624–634, London, UK, 1986. Springer-Verlag.

[109] Lee Naish. An introduction to MU-Prolog. Technical Report 82/2, Department of Computer Science, University of Melbourne, Melbourne, Australia, March 1982 (Revised July 1983).

[110] J. Navas, E. Mera, P. López-García, and M. Hermenegildo. User-Definable Resource Bounds Analysis for Logic Programs. In *23rd International Conference on Logic Programming (ICLP 2007)*, LNCS. Springer-Verlag, September 2007.

[111] Gustavo Ospina. Un cadre conceptuel pour l'interopérabilité des langages de programmation. PhD thesis, Université catholique de Louvain, February 2007.

[112] Gustavo Ospina, François Gobert, and Baudouin Le Charlier. An Experiment in Programming Language Interoperability: Using a C Polyhedra Library with a Java Application. Université catholique de Louvain. Département d'Ingénierie Informatique. 2005.

[113] G. Puebla, J. Correas, M. Hermenegildo, F. Bueno, M. García de la Banda, K. Marriott, and P. J. Stuckey. A Generic Framework for Context-Sensitive Analysis of Modular Programs. In M. Bruynooghe and K. Lau, editors, *Program Development in Computational Logic, A Decade of Research Advances in Logic-Based Program Development*, number 3049 in LNCS, pages 234–261. Springer-Verlag, August 2004.

[114] G. Puebla, M. Hermenegildo, and J. P. Gallagher. An Integration of Partial Evaluation in a Generic Abstract Interpretation Framework. In *Proceedings of PEPM'99, The ACM SIGPLAN Workshop on Partial Evaluation and Semantics-Based Program Manipulation, ed. O. Danvy, San Antonio*, pages 75–84. University of Aarhus, Dept. of Computer Science, January 1999.

[115] Germán Puebla, Elvira Albert, and Manuel V. Hermenegildo. Abstract interpretation with specialized definitions. In *SAS*, pages 107–126, 2006.

[116] Germán Puebla, Francisco Bueno, and Manuel V. Hermenegildo. An Assertion Language for Constraint Logic Programs. In *Analysis and Visualization Tools for Constraint Programming*, pages 23–62, 2000.

[117] Germán Puebla, Maria J. Garcia de la Banda, Kim Marriott, and Peter J. Stuckey. Optimization of Logic Programs with Dynamic Scheduling. In *International Conference on Logic Programming*, pages 93–107, 1997.

[118] Germán Puebla and Manuel V. Hermenegildo. Abstract Multiple Specialization and Its Application to Program Parallelization. *Journal of Logic Programming*, 41(2-3):279–316, 1999.

[119] Huseyin Saglam and John P. Gallagher. Approximating Constraint Logic Programs Using Polymorphic Types and Regular Descriptions. Technical Report CSTR-95-017, Department of Computer Science, University of Bristol, July 1995.

[120] Alexandeer Schrijver. *Theory of linear and integer programming*. John Wiley & Sons, Inc., New York, NY, USA, 1986.

[121] Zoltan Somogyi. A system of precise modes for logic programs. In E. Shapiro, editor, *Proceedings of the Third International Conference on Logic Programming (ICLP'86)*, volume 225 of *LNCS*, pages 769-787, London, England, July 1986. Springer-Verlag.

[122] Zoltan Somogyi and al. Mercury Library Reference Manual. Version 0.13.1. The University of Melbourne. 2005.

[123] Zoltan Somogyi, Fergus Henderson, and Thomas Conway. The Execution Algorithm of Mercury, an Efficient Purely Declarative Logic Programming Language. *Journal of Logic Programming*, 29(1-3):17–64, 1996.

[124] L. Sterling and E. Shapiro. *The Art of Prolog, Advanced Programming Techniques. Second Edition*. The MIT Press, Cambridge, Massachusetts. London., 1994.

[125] Peter J. Stuckey. Constructive Negation for Constraint Logic Programming. In *LICS*, pages 328–339, 1991.

[126] A. Taylor. Removal of Dereferencing and Trailing in Prolog Compilation. In *Proceedings of the Sixth International Conference on Logic Programming (ICLP'89)*, Lisbon, Portugal, June 1989. MIT Press.

[127] Pascal Van Hentenryck, Agostino Cortesi, and Baudouin Le Charlier. Evaluation of the Domain Prop. *J. Log. Program.*, 23(3):237–278, 1995.

[128] Peter Van Roy, Per Brand, Denys Duchier, Seif Haridi, Martin Henz, and Christian Schulte. Logic programming in the context of multiparadigm programming: the Oz experience. *Theory and Practice of Logic Programming*, 2003.

[129] Peter Van Roy and Alvin M. Despain. High-Performance Logic Programming with the Aquarius Prolog Compiler. *Computer*, 25(1):54–68, 1992.

[130] Claudio Vaucheret and Francisco Bueno. More Precise Yet Efficient Type Inference for Logic Programs. In *SAS '02: Proceedings of the 9th International Symposium on Static Analysis*, pages 102–116, London, UK, 2002. Springer-Verlag.

[131] David H. D. Warren. An Abstract Prolog Instruction Set. Technical Report 309, AI Center, SRI International, 333 Ravenswood Ave., Menlo Park, CA 94025, Oct 1983.

[132] Jan Wielemaker. SWI-Prolog 5.6 Ref. Manual. University of Amsterdam. *http://www.swi-prolog.org*, 2006.

[133] Eyal Yardeni and Ehud Shapiro. A Type System for Logic Programs. *Journal of Logic Programming*, 10(2):125–153, 1991.

Appendix A

Table of procedures

Procedure number	Name	Page number
6.5	factorial	139
6.6	tree_list_tree	140
6.7	even, odd	141
6.8	ack	142
6.9	f, g	142
6.10	special	143
6.11	merge	145
6.12	do_something_list	165

Appendix B

Table of formal specifications

Appendix C

Full Prolog abstract syntax accepted by the analyser

Figure C.1 depicts the abstract syntax of the full Prolog accepted by the checker.

$$
\begin{array}{llll}
P & \in & Programs & \\
pr & \in & Procedures & \\
c & \in & Clauses & \\
h & \in & Heads & \\
g & \in & Goals & \\
l & \in & Literals & \\
b & \in & Builtins & \\
p & \in & Procedure Names & \\
t & \in & Program\,Terms & \\
X & \in & Program\,Variables & \\
f & \in & Functor Names &
\end{array}
$$

$$
\begin{array}{lcl}
P & ::= & pr \mid pr\ P \\
pr & ::= & c \mid c\ pr \\
c & ::= & h \text{ :- } g. \\
h & ::= & p(t, \dots, t) \\
g & ::= & <> \\
& \mid & g, l \\
& \mid & g, (g; g) \\
& \mid & g, (g\text{->}g) \\
& \mid & g, (g\text{->}g; g) \\
l & ::= & p(t, \dots, t) \mid X \mid b \mid \mathtt{not}(g) \\
b & ::= & t = t \mid \text{!} \\
t & ::= & X \mid f(t, \dots, t)
\end{array}
$$

Figure C.1: Abstract syntax of Prolog programs

Appendix D

Abstract syntax of formal specifications

Figure D.1 and Figure D.2 report on the syntactic categories and the abstract grammar of formal specifications.

spec	$\in$	*Specification*	*z*	$\in$	*Integer*
p	$\in$	*ProcedureName*	*float*	$\in$	*Float*
seq	$\in$	*Sequence*	*consys*	$\in$	*ConSys*
subst	$\in$	*Substitution*	*ineq*	$\in$	*Inequality*
arg	$\in$	*Argument*	*linexpr*	$\in$	*LinExpr*
A	$\in$	*ArgName*	*tagconsys*	$\in$	*TagConSys*
mode	$\in$	*Mode*	*tagineq*	$\in$	*TagInequality*
tn	$\in$	*TypeName*	*taglinexpr*	$\in$	*TagLinExpr*
texpr	$\in$	*TypeExpr*	*solconsys*	$\in$	*SolConSys*
tprim	$\subseteq$	*TypePrim*	*solineq*	$\in$	*SolInequality*
tsel	$\in$	*TypeSelect*	*sollinexpr*	$\in$	*SolLinExpr*
frame	$\in$	*Frame*	*szA*	$\in$	*SizeArgName*
f	$\in$	*FunctorName*	*sztagA*	$\in$	*SizeTagArgName*
c	$\in$	*Constant*	*szsolA*	$\in$	*SizeSolArgName*
			norm	$\in$	*NormName*

Figure D.1: Syntactical categories for formal specifications.

253

$$
\begin{array}{lll}
spec & ::= & \texttt{p} \quad seq \\
& & \texttt{sexpr} \; linexpr^* \\[6pt]
seq & ::= & \texttt{in} \quad subst \\
& & \texttt{fails} \; subst^* \\
& & \texttt{ref} \quad subst \\
& & \texttt{out} \quad subst \\
& & \texttt{untouched} \; A^* \\
& & \texttt{srel} \quad tagconsys \\
& & \texttt{sol} \quad solconsys \\[6pt]
subst & ::= & \texttt{bottom} \mid arg^* \\
& & \quad\quad\quad \texttt{noshare} \, (A, A)^* \\
& & \quad\quad\quad \texttt{linear} \; A^* \\
& & \quad\quad\quad \texttt{srel} \quad consys \\[6pt]
arg & ::= & A{:}\; mode \; texpr \; frame \\[6pt]
mode & ::= & \texttt{ground} \mid \texttt{noground} \mid \texttt{var} \mid \texttt{novar} \mid \texttt{gv} \mid \texttt{ngv} \mid \texttt{any} \\
texpr & ::= & tprim \mid tsel \\
tprim & ::= & \texttt{bottom} \mid \texttt{any} \mid \texttt{ground} \mid \texttt{int} \mid \texttt{float} \\
tsel & ::= & tn \; f^* \; texpr^* \\
frame & ::= & \texttt{?} \mid f(arg_1, ..., arg_n) \mid c \mid z \mid \texttt{float} \\[6pt]
consys & ::= & ineq^* \\
ineq & ::= & linexpr \; (\texttt{=<} \mid \texttt{=}) \; 0 \\
linexpr & ::= & z(+z * szA)^* \\[6pt]
tagconsys & ::= & tagineq^* \\
tagineq & ::= & taglinexpr \; (\texttt{=<} \mid \texttt{=}) \; 0 \\
taglinexpr & ::= & z(+z * sztagA)^* \\[6pt]
solconsys & ::= & solineq^* \\
solineq & ::= & sollinexpr \; (\texttt{=<} \mid \texttt{=}) \; 0 \\
sollinexpr & ::= & z(+z * szsolA)^* \\[6pt]
szA & ::= & (norm) \; A \\
sztagA & ::= & (norm) \; A\_\texttt{ref} \mid (norm) \; A\_\texttt{out} \\
szsolA & ::= & \texttt{sol} \mid (norm) \; A\_\texttt{ref}
\end{array}
$$

Figure D.2: Abstract syntax of specifications.

Appendix E

Constrained mappings over the size relations: implementation

This appendix describes the implementation of the constrained mappings over the size components (see Section 3.4.2). They allow us to manipulate indices in the size components of abstract sequences. Section E.1 recalls the two primitive operations on polyhedra, namely RESTRICT and EXTEND. Section E.2 and Section E.3 present the direct and inverse constrained mappings, respectively.

E.1 Primitive operations on polyhedra

The implementation of the two following primitive operations on polyhedra can be found in [7, 120].

Operation RESTRICT$(E_1, I_2) = E_2$

Let $E_1 \in \text{Sizes}_{I_1}$, and $I_2 \subseteq I_1$. This operation computes $E_2 \in \text{Sizes}_{I_2}$, by restricting the set of constraints in E_1 to the variables in I_2. In the sense of the concretisation function, the following property holds:

$$\langle n_i \rangle_{i \in I_1} \in Cc(E_1) \Leftrightarrow \langle n_i \rangle_{i \in I_2} \in Cc(E_2)$$

Operation EXTEND$(E_1, I_2) = E_2$

Let $E_1 \in \text{Sizes}_{I_1}$, and $I_2 \supseteq I_1$. This operation computes $E_2 \in \text{Sizes}_{I_2}$, by extending the set of constraints in E_1 to the variables in I_2. In the sense of the concretisation function, the following property holds:

$$\langle n_i \rangle_{i \in I_1} \in Cc(E_1) \Leftrightarrow \langle n_i \rangle_{i \in I_2} \in Cc(E_2)$$

E.2   Direct Constrained Mapping

Operation $tr^>(E_1) = E_2$

Specification:
Let $E_1 \in \text{Sizes}_{I_1}$ and $tr : I_1 \rightarrow I_2$ be a (possibly partial) function. This operation computes the *direct constrained mapping* over the size component E_1, and is denoted $tr^>(E_1)$. More precisely, $tr^>(E_1)$ returns $E_2 \in \text{Sizes}_{I_2}$, such that the following relation holds:

$$\left. \begin{array}{l} \langle n_i^1 \rangle_{i \in I_1} \in Cc(E_1) \\ n_i^1 = n_{tr(i)}^2 \ (\forall i \in dom(tr)) \end{array} \right\} \Rightarrow \langle n_i^2 \rangle_{i \in I_2} \in Cc(E_2)$$

The implementation is as follows. We distinguish four cases.

Case 1.
    If $E_1 = \bot$ then $E_2 = \bot$.

Case 2.
    If $I_2 \subseteq I_1$ and $tr_{/I_2}$ is the identity function then $E_2 = \text{RESTRICT}(E_1, I_2)$.

Case 3.
    If $I_1 \subseteq I_2$ and tr is the identity function over I_1 (in that case, tr is a total function) then $E_2 = \text{EXTEND}(E_1, I_2)$.

Case 4.
    Otherwise, let $I_a = dom(tr)$ and $I_b = codom(tr)$.
    Let $E_a = \text{RESTRICT}(E_1, I_a)$; it consists of a system of m linear (in)equations:

$$A_a \cdot \overline{sz}_a \leq \overline{b}$$

where A_a is a $m \times |I_a|$ matrix, $\overline{sz}_a$ is a column vector of variables $\{sz(i)\}_{i \in I_a}$, and $\overline{b}$ is a column vector of m integers.
Construct the $|I_a| \times |I_b|$ matrix T from tr as follows:

$$T = (\tau_{i,j})_{i \in I_a, j \in I_b}$$

where

$$\tau_{i,j} = \begin{cases} 1 & \textbf{if } tr(i) = j \\ 0 & \textbf{otherwise.} \end{cases}$$

Compute the product $A_b = A_a.T$, which is a $m \times |I_b|$ matrix. Let E_b be consisting of the system of linear equations and inequalities:

$$A_b \cdot \overline{sz}_b \leq \overline{b}$$

where $\overline{sz}_b$ is a column vector of variables $\{sz(i)\}_{i \in I_b}$. The result of the operation is $E_2 = \text{EXTEND}(E_b, I_2)$.

E.3   Inverse Constrained Mapping

Operation $tr^<(E_2) = E_1$

Specification:
Let $E_2 \in \text{Sizes}_{I_2}$ and $tr : I_1 \rightarrow I_2$ be a (possibly partial) function. This operation computes the *inverse constrained mapping* over the size component E_2, and is denoted $tr^<(E_2)$. More precisely, $tr^<(E_2)$ returns $E_1 \in \text{Sizes}_{I_1}$, such that the following relation holds:

$$\left. \begin{array}{l} \langle n_i^2 \rangle_{i \in I_2} \in Cc(E_2) \\ n_{tr(i)}^2 = n_i^1 \ (\forall i \in dom(tr)) \end{array} \right\} \Rightarrow \langle n_i^1 \rangle_{i \in I_1} \in Cc(E_1)$$

The implementation is as follows. We distinguish three cases.

Case 1.
   If $E_2 = \bot$ then $E_1 = \bot$.

Case 2.
   If $I_1 \subseteq I_2$ and $tr_{/I_1}$ is the identity function (in that case, tr is a total function) then $E_1 = \text{RESTRICT}(E_2, I_1)$.

Case 3.
   Otherwise, let $I_a = dom(tr)$ and $I_b = codom(tr)$.
   Let $E_b = \text{RESTRICT}(E_2, I_b)$; it consists of a system of m linear (in)equations:

$$A_b \cdot \overline{sz}_b \leq \overline{b}$$

where A_b is a $m \times |I_b|$ matrix, $\overline{sz}_b$ is a column vector of variables $\{sz(i)\}_{i \in I_b}$, and $\overline{b}$ is a column vector of m integers.
Construct the $|I_b| \times |I_a|$ matrix T_{inv} from tr as follows:

$$T_{inv} = (\tau_{i,j})_{i \in I_b, j \in I_a}$$

where

$$\tau_{i,j} = \left\{ \begin{array}{ll} 1 & \textbf{if } j = min\{j_k \in I_a \mid tr(j_k) = i\} \\ 0 & \textbf{otherwise.} \end{array} \right.$$

Each row of T contains at most one 1.
Compute the product $A_a = A_b.T_{inv}$, which is a $m \times |I_a|$ matrix.
Consider the set

$$S = \{(j_1, j_2) \in I_a \times I_a \mid j_1 \neq j_2 \text{ and } tr(j_1) = tr(j_2)\}.$$

Let us enumerate the elements of S as: $(j_1^1, j_2^1), (j_1^2, j_2^2), \ldots, (j_1^{|S|}, j_2^{|S|})$.
Consider the $|S| \times |I_a|$ matrix A_{aux} defined by:

$$A_{aux} = (\gamma_{i,j})_{i \in \{1, \ldots, |S|\}, j \in I_a}$$

such that for all $i \in \{1, \ldots, |S|\}$,

$$\gamma_{i,j} = \begin{cases} 1 & \textbf{if } j = j_1^i \\ -1 & \textbf{if } j = j_2^i \\ 0 & \textbf{otherwise.} \end{cases}$$

Consider also the column vector $\bar{b}_{aux}$ of $|S|$ 0's.
Let E_a be consisting of the system of linear equations and inequalities:

$$\begin{aligned} A_a \cdot \overline{sz}_a &\leq \bar{b} \\ A_{aux} \cdot \overline{sz}_a &= \bar{b}_{aux} \end{aligned}$$

where $\overline{sz}_a$ is a column vector of variables $\{sz(i)\}_{i \in I_a}$. The result of the operation is $E_1 = \text{EXTEND}(E_a, I_1)$.

Appendix F

Abstract sequence concatenation: implementation

This appendix describes the implementation of the abstract sequence concatenation, which is informally presented in Section 6.4. Section F.1 formally specifies the auxiliary abstract operations over the abstract substitutions. Section F.2 presents the operation SUM_SOL over sizes components, which is used to concatenate two abstract sequences that are non-exclusive. Section F.3 recalls the implementation of the binary abstract operation of the basic framework [78]. Section F.4 specifies two auxiliary operations of abstract sequences that are instrumental to decompose non-exclusive abstract sequences into non-exclusive and exclusive abstract sequences. Section F.5 presents the two main abstract operations: the concatenation operation CONC and the operation MERGE. Finally, Section F.7 presents the abstract execution algorithm of a procedure, using the new abstract concatenation.

F.1 Auxiliary abstract operations on abstract substitutions

In this section, we provide the specification of the auxiliary abstract operation over abstract substitutions, namely the greatest lower bound GLB, the least upper bound LUB, and the exact least upper bound EXT_LUB. The implementation can be found in [53, 54, 80].

Operation $\mathrm{GLB}(\beta_1, \beta_2) = \langle \beta', tr_1, tr_2 \rangle$.

Let $\beta_1, \beta_2 \in \mathrm{AS}_D$ be two abstract substitutions over the same domain. This operation returns an abstract substitution $\beta' \in \mathrm{AS}_D$ such that $\beta' \leq \beta_1$, $\beta' \leq \beta_2$ and $Cc(\beta_1) \cap Cc(\beta_2) = Cc(\beta')$; and it returns the two associated structural mappings $tr_1 : \beta_1 \to \beta'$ and $tr_2 : \beta_2 \to \beta'$.

Operation $\mathrm{LUB}(\beta_1, \beta_2) = \langle \beta', tr_1, tr_2 \rangle$.

Let $\beta_1, \beta_2 \in \mathrm{AS}_D$ be two abstract substitutions over the same domain. This operation returns an abstract substitution $\beta' \in \mathrm{AS}_D$ such that $\beta_1 \leq \beta'$, $\beta_2 \leq \beta'$ and $Cc(\beta_1) \cup Cc(\beta_2) \subseteq Cc(\beta')$; and it returns the two associated structural mappings $tr_1 : \beta' \to \beta_1$ and $tr_2 : \beta' \to \beta_2$.

Operation $\mathrm{EXT\_LUB}(\beta_1, \beta_2) = \langle \beta', tr_1, tr_2, exact \rangle$.

Let $\beta_1, \beta_2 \in \mathrm{AS}_D$ be two abstract substitutions over the same domain. This operation returns an abstract substitution $\beta' \in \mathrm{AS}_D$ such that $\beta_1 \leq \beta'$, $\beta_2 \leq \beta'$ and $Cc(\beta_1) \cup Cc(\beta_2) \subseteq Cc(\beta')$; it returns the two associated structural mappings $tr_1 : \beta' \to \beta_1$ and $tr_2 : \beta' \to \beta_2$; and it returns a boolean *exact* which satisfies the implication $exact \Rightarrow Cc(\beta_1) \cup Cc(\beta_2) = Cc(\beta')$.

F.2   Auxiliary abstract operations on sizes components

Let B_1 and B_2 be two abstract sequences that are not exclusive. The number of solutions of the concatenation sequence of B_1 and B_2 is the result of summing the E_{sol} components of the two abstract sequences. The operation SUM_SOL over the sizes components is used to express the length of a sequence obtained by concatenating two other sequences. Formally, the operation is specified and implemented as follows.

Operation $\mathrm{SUM\_SOL}(E_{sol}^1, E_{sol}^2) = E_{sol}'$.
Let $E_{sol}^1, E_{sol}^2 \in \mathtt{Sizes}_{I+\{sol\}}$. The operation $\mathrm{SUM\_SOL}(E_{sol}^1, E_{sol}^2)$ returns $E_{sol}' \in \mathtt{Sizes}_{I+\{sol\}}$ such that:

$$\left. \begin{array}{l} (n_i^k)_{i \in I+\{sol\}} \in Cc(E_{sol}^k)\ (k=1,2) \\ n_i^1 = n_i^2 = n_i\ (i \in I) \\ n_{sol} = n_{sol}^1 + n_{sol}^2 \end{array} \right\} \Rightarrow (n_i)_{i \in I+\{sol\}} \in Cc(E_{sol}').$$

Implementation.
Let sol_1 and sol_2 be two new variables.

$$E_{sol}' = tr_{sol}^{<}(E_{sol}^1[sol \mapsto sol_1] \sqcap E_{sol}^2[sol \mapsto sol_2] \sqcap \{[\![sol = sol_1 + sol_2]\!]\})$$

where $tr_{sol} : I + \{sol\} \to I + \{sol, sol_1, sol_2\}$ is the canonical injection, and $E_{sol}^i[sol \mapsto sol_i]$ is the set of (in)equations obtained by syntactically replacing every occurrence of sol by sol_i in E_{sol}^i.

F.3 Binary abstract concatenation in the basic framework

Operation $\text{CONC}(B_1, B_2) = B'$.
Let $B_1, B_2 \in \text{ASeq}_D$ such that $input(B_1) = input(B_2) = \beta_{in}$. This operation returns an abstract sequence $B' \in \text{ASeq}_D$ such that:

$$\left.\begin{array}{c} \langle \theta, S_1 \rangle \in Cc(B_1) \\ \langle \theta, S_2 \rangle \in Cc(B_2) \end{array}\right\} \Rightarrow \langle \theta, S_1 :: S_2 \rangle \in Cc(B').$$

Implementation.
The operation $\text{CONC}(B_1, B2)$ computes $B' = \langle \beta'_{in}, \beta'_{ref}, \beta'_{out}, E'_{ref\_out}, E'_{sol} \rangle$ as follows:

$$\beta'_{in} = \beta_{in}$$
$$\langle \beta'_{ref}, tr^1_{ref}, tr^2_{ref}, exact \rangle = \text{EXT\_LUB}(\beta^1_{ref}, \beta^2_{ref})$$
$$\langle \beta'_{out}, tr^1_{out}, tr^2_{out} \rangle = \text{LUB}(\beta^1_{out}, \beta^2_{out})$$
$$E'_{ref\_out} = (tr^1_{ref} + tr^1_{out})^< (E^1_{ref\_out}) \sqcup (tr^2_{ref} + tr^2_{out})^< (E^2_{ref\_out})$$

$$E'_{sol} = \begin{cases} \begin{array}{l} (tr^1_{ref} + \{sol \mapsto sol\})^< (E^1_{sol}) \sqcup \\ (tr^2_{ref} + \{sol \mapsto sol\})^< (E^2_{sol}) \sqcup \\ (tr_{int} + \{sol \mapsto sol\})^< (\text{SUM\_SOL}(\overline{E}^1_{sol}, \overline{E}^2_{sol})) \end{array} & \text{if } exact \\[20pt] \begin{array}{l} (tr^1_{ref} + \{sol \mapsto sol\})^< (E^1_{sol}) \sqcup \\ (tr^2_{ref} + \{sol \mapsto sol\})^< (E^2_{sol}) \sqcup \\ (tr_{int} + \{sol \mapsto sol\})^< (\text{SUM\_SOL}(\overline{E}^1_{sol}, \overline{E}^2_{sol})) \sqcup \\ tr^>_{sol}(\llbracket sol = 0 \rrbracket) \end{array} & \text{if } \neg exact \end{cases}$$

where

$$\langle \bullet, tr^1_{int}, tr^2_{int} \rangle = \text{GLB}(\beta^1_{ref}, \beta^2_{ref})$$

$$\overline{E}^1_{sol} = (tr^1_{int} + \{sol \mapsto sol\})^> (E^1_{sol})$$
$$\overline{E}^2_{sol} = (tr^2_{int} + \{sol \mapsto sol\})^> (E^2_{sol})$$

and $tr_{sol} : \{sol\} \to I'_{ref} + \{sol\}$ is the canonical injection. The structural mappings tr^k_{ref}, tr^k_{int} $(k = 1, 2)$ and tr_{int} satisfy the following commutative diagram:

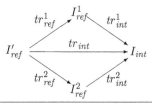

F.4   Difference and intersection operations

Operation $\text{DIFFERENCE}(B_1, \beta_2) = B'$. **We write also** $B' = B_1 \backslash \beta_2$.

Let $B_1 \in \text{ASeq}_D$ and $\beta_2 \in \text{AS}_D$. This operation returns an abstract sequence $B' \in \text{ASeq}_D$ such that $Cc(B') \supseteq Cc(B_1) \backslash \{\langle \theta, \_ \rangle \mid \theta \in Cc(\beta_2)\}$.

Operation $\text{INTER}(B_1, \beta_2) = B'$. **We write also** $B' = B_1 \sqcap \beta_2$.

Let $B_1 \in \text{ASeq}_D$ and $\beta_2 \in \text{AS}_D$. This operation returns an abstract sequence $B' \in \text{ASeq}_D$ such that $Cc(B') = Cc(B_1) \cap \{\langle \theta, \_ \rangle \mid \theta \in Cc(\beta_2)\}$.

F.5   New abstract concatenation

Abstract concatenation of non-exclusive sequences

The operation CONC1 approximates the concatenation operation '::' of finite substitution sequences. It applies on abstract sequences that have the same input refined components and the same input failure components.

Operation $\text{CONC1}(B_1, B_2) = B'$.

Let $B_1, B_2 \in \text{ASeq}_D$ with the same input components (β_{in}) and the same refined input components (β_{ref}) and the same failure components (β_{fails}). The operation $\text{CONC1}(B_1, B_2)$ returns an abstract sequence B' from ASeq_D such that:

$$\left. \begin{array}{l} \langle \theta, S_1 \rangle \in Cc(B_1) \\ \langle \theta, S_2 \rangle \in Cc(B_2) \end{array} \right\} \Rightarrow \langle \theta, S_1 :: S_2 \rangle \in Cc(B')$$

Implementation.

Let $B_i = \langle \beta_{in}, \beta_{ref}, \beta_{fails}, U^i, \beta_{out}^i, E_{ref\_out}^i, E_{sol}^i \rangle$ $(i = 1, 2)$.

Then, $\text{CONC1}(B_1, B_2)$ returns $\langle \beta_{in}, \beta_{ref}, \beta_{fails}, U', \beta_{out}', E_{ref\_out}', E_{sol}' \rangle$, where:

$$\begin{aligned} \beta_{out}' &= \beta_{out}^1 \sqcup \beta_{out}^2 \\ U' &= U^1 \cap U^2 \\ E_{ref\_out}' &= (tr_{ref} + tr_{out}^1)^<(E_{ref\_out}^1) \sqcup (tr_{ref} + tr_{out}^2)^<(E_{ref\_out}^2) \\ E_{sol}' &= \text{SUM\_SOL}(E_{sol}^1, E_{sol}^2) \end{aligned}$$

and where tr_{ref} is the identity mapping over I_{ref}, and $tr_{out}^i : \beta_{out}' \rightarrow \beta_{out}^i$ is the structural mapping between β_{out}' and β_{out}^i $(1 \leq i \leq 2)$.

Multiple abstract sequence concatenation

The operation CONC approximates the concatenation operation $\square$ of substitution sequences (defined in Section 4.2), by considering the abstract cut information. It applies on an abstract sequence with cut information C_1 and a set of exclusive abstract sequences SB_2. In the following, $Cc(SB)$ is defined by $\bigcup_{B \in SB} Cc(B)$.

Operation $\text{CONC}(C_1, SB_2) = SB'$.
Let $C_1 \in \text{ASeqC}_D$ and $SB_2 \in 2^{\text{ASeq}_D}$ such that $Cc(input(C_1)) = Cc(input(SB_2))$. The operation $\text{CONC}(C_1, SB_2)$ returns a set of abstract sequences SB' in 2^{ASeq_D} such that:

$$\left. \begin{array}{l} \langle \theta, S_1, cf \rangle \in Cc(C_1) \\ \langle \theta, S_2 \rangle \in Cc(SB_2) \end{array} \right\} \Rightarrow \langle \theta, \langle S_1, cf \rangle \square S_2 \rangle \in Cc(SB')$$

Implementation.
$SB' = \text{CONC}(B_1, SB_2)$ is defined as follows.
We assume that $B_i = \langle \beta_{in}^i, \beta_{ref}^i, \beta_{fails}^i, ... \rangle$ $(i = 1, 2)$.

1. Let assume that $C_1 = \langle B_1, acf, \beta_{cut}, \beta_{nocuts} \rangle$ and $SB_2 = \{B_2\}$.

    (a) Suppose that $acf = cut$. In this case, we define

    $$\begin{aligned} SB' &= \{B_2 \backslash \beta_{cut}\} \\ &\cup \bigcup_{\beta_f^c \in \beta_{nocuts}} (B_2 \sqcap \beta_f^c) \\ &\cup \{B_1 \sqcap \beta_{cut} \backslash \beta_{nocuts}\} \end{aligned}$$

    (b) Suppose that $acf = weakcut$. In this case, we define

    $$SB' = \{B_2\} \cup \{B_1 \sqcap \beta_{cut} \backslash \beta_{nocuts}\}$$

    (c) Suppose that $acf = nocut$. In this case, we define

    $$SB' = SB_a \cup SB_b \cup SB_c \cup SB_d \cup SB_e$$

    where:

    $$\begin{aligned} SB_a &= \{B_1 \backslash \beta_{ref}^2\} \\ SB_b &= \{B_2 \backslash \beta_{ref}^1\} \\ SB_c &= \bigcup_{\beta_f^2 \in \beta_{fails}^2} (B_1 \sqcap \beta_f^2) \\ SB_d &= \bigcup_{\beta_f^1 \in \beta_{fails}^1} (B_2 \sqcap \beta_f^1) \\ SB_e &= \{\text{CONC1}(B_1 \sqcap \beta_{ref}^2 \backslash \beta_{fails}^2 \ , \ B_2 \sqcap \beta_{ref}^1 \backslash \beta_{fails}^1)\} \end{aligned}$$

2. In the general case, we define

$$SB' = \bigcup_{B \in SB_2} \text{CONC}(C_1, \{B\})$$

Remark. We extend the definition of CONC when the second argument is an empty set, i.e., $\text{CONC}(C_1, \{\}) = \{B_1\}$, where $C_1 = \langle B_1, acf, \beta_{cut}, \beta_{nocuts} \rangle$.

F.6   The operation MERGE

The operation MERGE is responsible to fusion the set of exclusive abstract sequences SB resulting from the CONC operation into a single abstract sequence that approximates SB.

In the next, a so-called *refined/failed component* RF denotes the pair $\langle \beta_{ref}, \beta_{fails} \rangle$ of an abstract sequence. The concretisation of RF, denoted by $Cc(RF)$, is defined as $Cc(\beta_{ref}) \backslash Cc(\beta_{fails})$. A set of refined/failed components is denoted by SRF. The concretisation of SRF, denoted by $Cc(SRF)$, is defined by $\bigcup_{RF \in SRF} Cc(RF)$.

We first define the auxiliary operations REMOVE_FAIL, EXT_LUB_RF, LUB_RF and MULTI_EXT_LUB_RF. Then, the specification and implementation of MERGE is provided.

Check if failure components are covered by other refined/failed components

---

Operation REMOVE_FAIL(SRF) = SRF'.

Let SRF be a set of refined/failed components. The operation REMOVE_FAIL(SRF) tries to remove useless failed components from SRF, resulting in a set of refined/failed components SRF' that has still the same concretisation, i.e., $Cc(SRF) = Cc(SRF')$.

Implementation.
Assume that $SRF = \{\langle \beta_{ref}^1, \beta_{fails}^1 \rangle, ..., \langle \beta_{ref}^r, \beta_{fails}^r \rangle\}$. Construct the sequence of intermediate sets of refined/failed components $SRF^0, ..., SRF^k, ...$ as follows.

1. $SRF^0 = SRF$.

2. Assume given SRF^k. Suppose that there exists $i, j \in \{1, ..., r\}$ with $i \neq j$ such that $\exists \beta_f^i \in \beta_{fails}^i$ for which $\beta_f^i \leq \beta_{ref}^j$ and $\beta_f^i \sqcap \beta_f^j = \bot$, for all $\beta_f^j \in \beta_{fails}^j$. Then SRF^{k+1} is defined by:
   $\{\langle \beta_{ref}^1, \beta_{fails}^1 \rangle, ..., \langle \beta_{ref}^i, \beta_{fails}^i \backslash \{\beta_f^i\} \rangle, ..., \langle \beta_{ref}^r, \beta_{fails}^r \rangle\}$.

3. Otherwise, $SRF' = SRF^k$.

Binary exact upper bound of input refined/failed components

Operation EXT_LUB_RF$(RF_1, RF_2) = \langle RF', exact \rangle$.

Let RF_1 and RF_2 be two refined/failed components. The operation
EXT_LUB_RF(RF_1, RF_2) returns a tuple of the form $\langle RF', exact \rangle$ such that:

$$Cc(RF_1) \cup Cc(RF_2) \subseteq Cc(RF')$$

If the boolean $exact$ has the value $true$ then we have an exact upper bound, i.e.,

$$Cc(RF_1) \cup Cc(RF_2) = Cc(RF')$$

Implementation.
Assume that $RF_1 = \langle \beta_{ref}^1, \beta_{fails}^1 \rangle$ and $RF_2 = \langle \beta_{ref}^2, \beta_{fails}^2 \rangle$. The operation
EXT_LUB_RF(RF_1, RF_2) returns $\langle \langle \beta_{ref}', \beta_{fails}' \rangle, exact \rangle$ as follows.

$$\begin{aligned}
\langle \beta_{ref}', exact_{ref} \rangle &= \text{EXT\_LUB}(\beta_{ref}^1, \beta_{ref}^2) \\
\beta_{fails}' &= F_{a,1} \cup F_{a,2} \cup F_b \cup F_{c,1} \cup F_{c,2} \\
exact &= exact_{ref} \wedge exact_{fails}
\end{aligned}$$

where the sets of abstract substitutions $F_{a,1}, F_{a,2}, F_b, F_{c,1}, F_{c,2}$ and the boolean
$exact_{fails}$ are defined as follows (in the next, $i, j \in \{1, 2\}$ and $i \neq j$).

$$\begin{aligned}
F_{a,i} &= \{\beta_f^i \in \beta_{fails}^i \mid \beta_f^i \sqcap \beta_{ref}^j = \bot\} \\
F_b &= \{\beta_f^i \sqcap \beta_f^j \mid \beta_f^i \in \beta_{fails}^i, \beta_f^j \in \beta_{fails}^j\} \\
F_{c,i} &= \{\beta_{diff}^i \mid \langle \beta_{diff}^i, true \rangle \in DIFF_i\} \\
exact_{diff} &= |F_{c,1}| = |DIFF_1| \wedge |F_{c,2}| = |DIFF_2|
\end{aligned}$$

where $DIFF_i$ is defined by:

$$DIFF_i = \left\{ \text{EXT\_DIFF}(\beta_f^i, \beta_{ref}^j) \left| \begin{array}{l} \beta_f^i \in \beta_{fails}^i \\ \forall \beta_f \in F_{a,1} \cup F_{a,2} \cup F_b : \beta_f^i \not\leq \beta_f \end{array} \right. \right\}$$

where the operation EXT_DIFF$(\beta_1, \beta_2) = \langle \beta', exact_{diff} \rangle$ computes the difference between the two abstract substitutions, i.e., $Cc(\beta_1) \backslash Cc(\beta_2) \subseteq Cc(\beta')$,
and the boolean $exact_{diff}$ is true implies that $Cc(\beta_1) \backslash Cc(\beta_2) = Cc(\beta')$.

If we are not interested with the $exact$ boolean, we can use the operation
LUB_RF$(RF_1, RF_2) = RF'$, where $\langle RF', _ \rangle = $ EXT_LUB_RF(RF_1, RF_2). This
operation is extended to finite sequences of refined/failed components as follows:

$$\begin{aligned}
\text{LUB\_RF}(<>) &= \langle \bot, \emptyset \rangle \\
\text{LUB\_RF}(< RF >) &= RF \\
\text{LUB\_RF}(< RF_1, ..., RF_r >) &= \text{LUB\_RF}(RF_1, \text{LUB\_RF}(< RF_2, ..., RF_r >))
\end{aligned}$$

Multiple exact upper bound: a knapsack algorithm

Operation `MULTI_EXT_LUB_RF`$(SRF) = \langle RF', exact \rangle$.

Let SRF be a set of refined/failed components. The operation `MULTI_EXT_LUB_RF`(SRF) computes the least upper bound of the elements of the set SRF. It returns a tuple $\langle RF', exact \rangle$, where RF' is such that:

$$Cc(SRF) \subseteq Cc(RF')$$

and where the boolean $exact$ is such that $exact = true$ implies that RF' is an exact upper bound of SRF, i.e.,

$$Cc(SRF) = Cc(RF')$$

Implementation.

Assume that $SRF = \{RF_1, ..., RF_r\}$.
Consider the following sets of refined/failed components $ExtLubs_I$, defined for any subset I of $\{1, ..., r\}$:

$$ExtLubs_{\{i\}} = \{RF_i\}(1 \leq i \leq r)$$

$$ExtLubs_I = \left\{ RF \left| \begin{array}{l} \langle RF, true \rangle = \texttt{EXT\_LUB\_RF}(RF_x, RF_y) \\ RF_x \in ExtLubs_X, RF_y \in ExtLubs_Y \\ I = X \cup Y, |X|, |Y| \geq 1 \end{array} \right. \right\}$$

Then, the operation `MULTI_EXT_LUB_RF`(SRF) computes $\langle RF', exact \rangle$ as follows:

$$\langle RF', exact \rangle = \begin{cases} \langle RF, true \rangle & \textbf{if } RF \in ExtLubs_{\{1,...,r\}} \\ \langle \texttt{LUB\_RF}(< RF_1, ..., RF_r >), false \rangle & \textbf{otherwise} \end{cases}$$

In practice, we apply a dynamic programming technique to construct the sets $ExtLubs_I$, which are built in a 'top-down' way.

Abstract merging

The operation MERGE fusions a set of exclusive abstract sequences SB into a unique abstract sequence that approximates $Cc(SB)$. In particular, this operation is responsible to detect if the global sure success is guaranteed: it removes the failure components (through the operation REMOVE_FAIL), and it tries to find the best combination to compute an exact upper bound of the input refined components (through the knapsack algorithm MULTI_EXT_LUB_RF).

Operation MERGE$(SB) = B'$.

Let $\beta_{in} \in \mathrm{AS}_D$ and $SB \in 2^{\mathrm{ASeq}_D}$ such that $Cc(\beta_{in}) = Cc(input(SB))$. The operation MERGE$(\beta_{in}, SB)$ returns an abstract sequence B' in ASeq_D such that $Cc(SB) \subseteq Cc(B')$.

Implementation.

Assume that $SB = \{B_1, ..., B_r\}$. Let $SRF = \{\langle \beta_{ref}^1, \beta_{fails}^1 \rangle, ..., \langle \beta_{ref}^r, \beta_{fails}^r \rangle\}$ be the set of refined/failed components of $B_1, ..., B_r$. We assume that B_i is of the form $\langle \beta_{in}^i, \beta_{ref}^i, \beta_{fails}^i, \beta_{out}^i, U^i, E_{ref\_out}^i, E_{sol}^i \rangle$. The operation MERGE$(\beta_{in}, SB)$ computes $B' = \langle \beta_{in}', \beta_{ref}', \beta_{fails}', \beta_{out}', U', E_{ref\_out}', E_{sol}' \rangle$ as follows.

$$
\begin{aligned}
\beta_{in}' &= \beta_{in} \\
\langle \langle \beta_{ref}', \beta_{fails}' \rangle, exact \rangle &= \text{MULTI\_EXT\_LUB\_RF(REMOVE\_FAIL}(SRF)) \\
\beta_{out}' &= \text{LUB}(\{\beta_{out}^1, ..., \beta_{out}^r\}) \\
U' &= \bigcap_{1 \le i \le r} {tr_{ref}^i}^< (U^i) \\
E_{ref\_out}' &= \bigsqcup_{1 \le i \le r} (tr_{ref}^i + tr_{out}^i)^< (E_{ref\_out}^i) \\
E_{sol}' &= \begin{cases} E_{sol}^* & \textbf{if } exact = true \\ E_{sol}^* \sqcup \{[\![sol = 0]\!]\} & \textbf{otherwise} \end{cases}
\end{aligned}
$$

where $tr_{ref}^i : \beta_{ref}' \to \beta_{ref}^i$ and $tr_{out}^i : \beta_{out}' \to \beta_{out}^i$ $(1 \le i \le r)$ and where

$$
E_{sol}^* = \bigsqcup_{1 \le i \le r} (tr_{ref}^i + \{sol \mapsto sol\})^< (E_{sol}^i)
$$

F.7   Checking a procedure w.r.t. a specification

Let $pr ::= c_1...c_r$ be a procedure whose name is p. Let $Beh_p = \langle B : \langle \beta_{in}, ... \rangle, se \rangle$ be the abstract behaviour to be checked for that procedure. Let $SBeh$ be the set of abstract behaviours (i.e., specifications) corresponding to each procedure in the program. The algorithm execution of the procedure is depicted in Figure F.1. The clauses are abstractly executed from the bottom to the top of the procedure. The execution of each clause c_i is modelled by an abstract sequence with cut information C_i. After the execution of the clause c_i, the abstract sequence concatenation is realised through the operation CONC, by maintaining the set of exclusive abstract sequences SB_i that models the execution of the clauses $c_i, ..., c_r$. The result of the global concatenation of all the clauses is SB_1. This set is merged through the operation MERGE$(\beta_{in}, SB_1) = B_{out}$. The verification analysis succeeds if the global abstract sequence B_{out} imposes the same or more constraints than B, i.e., if B_{out} is less or equal than B.

```
PROCEDURE analyse_procedure(p, B, se, SBeh) =
    SB_{r+1} ← {}
    for i = r to 1 do
        ⟨success_i, C_i⟩ ← analyse_clause(c_i, B, se, SBeh, SB_{i+1})
        SB_i ← CONC(C_i, SB_{i+1})
    if there exists k ∈ {1, ..., r} such that ¬success_k
        then success ← false
        else B_out ← MERGE(β_in, SB_1)
             success ← (B_out ≤ B)
    return success
```

Figure F.1: Algorithm for the abstract execution of a procedure with cuts. The procedure p, of the form $c_1...c_r$, is checked according to the abstract behaviour $\langle B, se \rangle$ and the family of behaviours $SBeh$.

Note that we do not need to compute the concatenation (i.e., the abstract sequence B_{out}) completely. Instead of, we can verify that each abstract sequence in the set SB_1 implies the conditions described by the formal specification B. The global sure success can be proved by computing an exact upper bound of the refined components of the abstract sequences in SB_1.

Appendix G

Source-to-source transformations

This appendix describes the implementation of the source-to-source transformations performed by the optimiser presented in Section 9.4. Given a procedure and a formal specification, the code transformations are safely applied in deterministic order. At each step of the strategy, the optimiser guarantees that the transformed code produces the same solutions than the original one, for any input substitution satisfying the `in` part of the considered specification. The optimiser uses the abstract information provided by the checker to verify the application conditions.

The rest of this appendix is organised as follows. Section G.1 defines the equivalence of clauses and of procedures. Section G.2 presents the syntactic rules for normalising a Prolog procedure. Section G.3 recalls the output of the checker: annotated clauses and procedures. Section G.4 describes how abstract sequences are used to detect the operational properties needed to ensure the safe application of the code transformations (detecting determinacy, full determinacy, exclusivity, untouched terms). The next sections describe the source-to-source transformations applied by the optimiser: semantic normalisation (Section G.5), moving unifications forwards (Section G.6), leftmost green cut insertion (Section G.7), removing redundant literals (Section G.8), and denormalisation (Section G.9).

G.1 Equivalence of clauses and of procedures

Equivalence of clauses. Let c_1 and c_2 be two clauses in the program P_1 and P_2 respectively, with the same arity n. Let θ be a program substitution with domain $\{X_1, ..., X_n\}$. Then, c_1 and c_2 are *equivalent* for the program substitution θ iff they produce the same answer substitution sequence and the same cut flag for the input θ, i.e., $\langle \theta, c_1 \rangle \mapsto_{P_1} \langle S, cf \rangle$ and $\langle \theta, c_2 \rangle \mapsto_{P_2} \langle S, cf \rangle$. This will be denoted by $\langle c_1, P_1 \rangle \equiv_\theta \langle c_2, P_2 \rangle$.

Equivalence of procedures. Let pr and pr' be two procedures in the program P and P' respectively, with the same arity n, and whose names are p and p' respectively. Let θ be a program substitution with domain $\{X_1, ..., X_n\}$. Procedures pr

and pr' are *equivalent* for the program substitution θ iff they produce the same answer substitution sequence for the input θ, i.e., $\langle \theta, p \rangle \mapsto_P S$ and $\langle \theta, p' \rangle \mapsto_{P'} S$. This will be denoted by $\langle pr, P \rangle \equiv_\theta \langle pr', P' \rangle$.

G.2   Syntactic normalisation

The following operation syntactically normalises a clause.

SYN_NORM$(c, P) = \langle c', NewProcs \rangle$
Input: - a Prolog clause c in the program P
Output: - a normalised clause c'
          - a set of new (non-normalised) Prolog procedures $NewProcs$ that
          do not occur in P and that are called by c'
          - $\langle c, P \rangle \equiv_\theta \langle c', P' \rangle$, for any input substitution θ (P' is the pro-
          gram $P \cup NewProcs$ where c is replaced by c')

The following rules take as input a Prolog clause c in the context of a program P, and generate an equivalent Prolog clause c' and a (possibly empty) set of new procedures $NewProcs$ that do not occur in P but are used by c'.

$$\mathbf{R1}\left[\frac{c ::= p(t_1, ..., t_i, ..., t_n) \,\text{:-}\, g}{c' ::= p(t_1, ..., X, ..., t_n) \,\text{:-}\, {-}X = t_i, g}\right]$$
$$\mathbf{if} \begin{cases} X \text{ is a program variable that does not occur in } c \\ t_i \notin Program\,Variables \text{ or } \exists i : i \neq j \wedge t_i = t_j \end{cases}$$

$$\mathbf{R2}\left[\frac{c ::= h \,\text{:-}\, ..., q(t_1, ..., t_i, ..., t_n), ...}{c' ::= h \,\text{:-}\, ..., X = t_i, q(t_1, ..., X, ..., t_n), ...}\right]$$
$$\mathbf{if} \begin{cases} X \text{ is a program variable that does not occur in } c \\ t_i \notin Program\,Variables \text{ or } \exists i : i \neq j \wedge t_i = t_j \end{cases}$$

$$\mathbf{R3}\left[\frac{c ::= h \,\text{:-}\, ..., f(t_1, ..., t_n) = X, ...}{c' ::= h \,\text{:-}\, ..., X = f(t_1, ..., t_n), ...}\right]$$

$$\mathbf{R4}\left[\frac{c ::= h \,\text{:-}\, ..., X = f(t_1, ..., t_i, ..., t_n), ...}{c' ::= h \,\text{:-}\, ..., Y = t_i, q(t_1, ..., Y, ..., t_n), ...}\right]$$
$$\mathbf{if} \begin{cases} Y \text{ is a program variable that does not occur in } c \\ t_i \notin Program\,Variables \text{ or } X = t_i \text{ or } \exists i : i \neq j \wedge t_i = t_j \end{cases}$$

$$\mathbf{R5}\left[\frac{c ::= h \,\text{:-}\, ..., g(u_1, ..., u_m) = f(t_1, , ..., t_n), ...}{c' ::= h \,\text{:-}\, ..., X = g(u_1, ..., u_m), X = f(t_1, ..., t_n), ...}\right]$$
$$\mathbf{if} \begin{cases} X \text{ is a program variable that does not occur in } c \end{cases}$$

$$\mathbf{R6}\left[\frac{c ::= h \,\text{:-}\, ..., \text{not}(f(t_1, ..., t_n) = X), ...}{c' ::= h \,\text{:-}\, ..., \text{not}(X = f(t_1, ..., t_n)), ...}\right]$$

$$\textbf{R7} \left[\begin{array}{l} c ::= h \colon -..., \mathtt{not}(g), ... \\ \hline c' ::= h \colon -..., \mathtt{not}(q(X_1, ..., X_m)), ... \\ NewProcs ::= \{q(X_1, ..., X_m)\colon -g.\} \end{array} \right]$$

$$\textbf{if} \left\{ \begin{array}{l} g \text{ is not a normalised literal} \\ q \text{ is a new procedure name that does not occur in program } P \\ X_1, ..., X_m \text{ are program variables occurring in } g \end{array} \right.$$

The operation $\mathtt{SYN\_NORM}(c, P)$ is implemented as follows:

$$\begin{array}{l} c' = c \\ NewProcs = \emptyset \\ \textbf{while } \exists \text{ rule } \mathbf{R} \in \{\mathbf{R1}, ..., \mathbf{R7}\} \text{ that can be applied to } c' \textbf{ do} \\ \quad \langle c', NewProcs' \rangle = \mathbf{R}(c', P \cup NewProcs) \\ \quad NewProcs = NewProcs \cup NewProcs' \\ \text{rename the program variables occurring in } c' \text{ by } \mathtt{X1}, ..., \mathtt{Xm} \\ \textbf{return } \langle c', NewProcs \rangle \end{array}$$

G.3 Code annotation by the checker

This section recalls the result of the checker presented in Part I: annotated clauses and annotated procedures, with cut information (defined in Section 3.5.4 and Section 4.2.3).

Annotated Clauses. Let c be a normalised clause in program P of the form $h \colon -l_1, ..., l_s.$, let D be the set of all variables occurring in the head of c, let D' be the set of all variables occurring in c, and let β_{in}^c be an abstract substitution whose domain is D. An *annotated clause* of the clause c with input β_{in}^c, denoted by $\tilde{c}$, is a construct of the form:

$$(\beta_{in}^c)h \colon -(B_0)\tilde{l}_1, (B_1)...,(B_{s-1})\tilde{l}_s(B_s).\langle B_c, acf, \beta_c^{cut}, \beta_{nocuts}^c \rangle$$

where

- B_i is an abstract sequence with $dom_{in}(B_i) = D$ and $dom_{out}(B_i) = D'$, for all i in $\{0, ..., s\}$.
- $\tilde{l}_i$ is a tuple of the form $\langle l_i, \beta_{l_i}^{inter}, B_{l_i}, \beta_{l_i}^{sf} \rangle$, for all i in $\{1, ..., s\}$, where:
  l_i is a literal whose parameters are $X_{i_1}, ..., X_{i_r}$;
  $\beta_{l_i}^{inter}$ is an abstract substitution whose domain is $\{X_1, ..., X_r\}$;
  B_{l_i} is an abstract sequence whose input and output domain is $\{X_1, ..., X_r\}$;
  $\beta_{l_i}^{sf}$ is an abstract substitution whose domain is D.
- B_c is an abstract sequence $\langle \beta_{in}^c, ... \rangle$ with $dom_{in}(B_c) = dom_{out}(B_c) = D$.
- acf is the abstract cut information, belonging to $\{nocut, cut, weakcut\}$.

- β_c^{cut} is an abstract substitution whose domain is D.
- β_c^{nocuts} is a set of abstract substitutions whose domain is D.

Safe Approximation of Clauses. An annotated clause $\tilde{c}$ is a *safe approximation* of c if the following conditions hold. Let $\theta \in Cc(\beta_{in}^c)$. Consider the execution of the clause $\langle\theta, c\rangle \mapsto_P \langle S, cf\rangle$; the execution of the prefixes of the clause $\langle\theta, (l_1, ..., l_i), c\rangle \mapsto_P \langle S_i, cf_i\rangle$ $(0 \le i \le s)$; and the execution of the literals after the execution of a goal $\langle\theta_{\tau,i}, l_i\rangle \mapsto_P S_{\tau,i}$ $(1 \le i \le s)$, where τ in $Subst(S_{i-1})$, $X_{i_1}, ..., X_{i_r}$ are the parameters of l_i, and $\theta_{\tau,i} = \{X_1/X_{i_1}\tau, ..., X_r/X_{i_r}\tau\}$. Then, the following conditions imposed on θ, S, cf, S_i's, $\theta_{\tau,i}$'s and $S_{\tau,i}$'s must be satisfied:

- $\langle\theta, S\rangle \in Cc(B_c)$;
- $\langle\theta, S_i\rangle \in Cc(B_i)$, for all i in $\{0, ..., s\}$;
- $\theta_{\tau,i} \in Cc(\beta_{l_i}^{inter})$, for all i in $\{1, ..., s\}$ and $\tau \in Subst(S_{i-1})$;
- $\langle\theta_{\tau,i}, S_{\tau,i}\rangle \in Cc(B_{l_i})$, for all i in $\{1, ..., s\}$ and $\tau \in Subst(S_{i-1})$;
- For all i in $\{1, ..., s\}$, $\theta \notin Cc(\beta_{l_i}^{sf}) \Rightarrow \forall \tau \in Subst(S_{i-1}), S_{\tau,i} \ne <>$;
- If $acf = nocut$ then no cut is executed for any input θ, i.e., $cf = nocut$;
- If $acf = cut$ then a cut is surely executed if and only if the input substitution θ satisfies the conditions of β_{cut} and does not satisfy the conditions imposed by the abstract substitutions β_{nocuts}, i.e.,

$$\left.\begin{array}{l}\theta \in Cc(\beta_{cut}) \\ \theta \notin Cc(\beta_{nocuts})\end{array}\right\} \Leftrightarrow cf = cut;$$

- If $acf = weakcut$ then the β_{cut} and β_{nocuts} components impose necessary (but not sufficient) conditions for the sure execution of a cut, i.e.,

$$cf = cut \Rightarrow \left\{\begin{array}{l}\theta \in Cc(\beta_{cut}) \\ \theta \notin Cc(\beta_{nocuts})\end{array}\right.$$

Annotated Procedures. Let pr be a procedure whose name is p, whose arity is n, and that is composed of the clauses $c_1...c_r$. Let $B_{pr} = \langle\beta_{in}^{pr}, ...\rangle$ be an abstract sequence whose input and output domain is $\{X_1, ..., X_n\}$. An annotated procedure of pr (in the context of B_{pr}), denoted by $\tilde{pr}$, is the pair $\langle B_{pr}, < \tilde{c}_1, ..., \tilde{c}_r >\rangle$, where $\tilde{c}_k$ is an annotated clause of c_k with input β_{in}^{pr} $(1 \le k \le r)$.

Safe Approximation of Procedures. An annotated procedure $\tilde{pr}$ is a *safe approximation* of pr if the following conditions hold. For all $\theta \in Cc(\beta_{in}^{pr})$, consider the execution of the procedure $\langle\theta, p\rangle \mapsto_P S$. Then we have $\langle\theta, S\rangle \in Cc(B_{pr})$, and the annotated clause $\tilde{c}_k$ is a safe approximation of the clause c_k $(1 \le k \le r)$.

Code annotation. Given a normalised procedure pr, and given an abstract sequence B_{pr} (a specification of pr), the checker performs the abstract execution of pr, and annotates it with abstract information at each program point, through the operation ANNOTATE:

ANNOTATE$(pr, B_{pr}) = \tilde{pr}$
Input: - a normalised procedure pr of arity n
               - an abstract sequence B_{pr}, whose input and output domain is
               $\{X_1, ..., X_n\}$
Output: - an annotated procedure $\tilde{pr}$ of pr in the context of B_{pr}, that *safely*
               approximates the execution of pr for every input in $Cc(\beta_{in}^{pr})$

The abstract operation ANNOTATE(c, β_{in}) annotates the clause c with abstract input β_{in}:

ANNOTATE$(c, \beta_{in}) = \tilde{c}$
Input: - a normalised clause c of arity n
               - an abstract substitution β_{in}, whose domain is $\{X_1, ..., X_n\}$
Output: - an annotated clause $\tilde{c}$ of c with input β_{in}, that *safely approxi-*
               mates the execution of c for every input in $Cc(\beta_{in})$

The abstract operation ANNOTATE$((l_i, ..., l_j), B_{i-1})$ annotates the goal $l_i, ..., l_j$, where the input abstract substitution is the β_{out} component of B_{i-1}:

ANNOTATE$((l_i, ..., l_j), B_{i-1}) = (B_{i-1})\tilde{l}_i, (B_i)..., \tilde{l}_j(B_j)$
Input: - a normalised goal $l_i, ..., l_j$
               - an abstract sequence B_{i-1} whose output domain contains the
               program variables occurring in $l_i, ..., l_j$
Output: - an annotated goal $(B_{i-1})\tilde{l}_i, (B_i)..., \tilde{l}_j(B_j)$ that *safely approxi-*
               mates the execution of $l_i, ..., l_j$ for every input in $Cc(\beta_{out}^{i-1})$

G.4   Using the checker to verify operational properties

This section describes some auxiliary abstract operations over abstract substitutions β, abstract sequences B, and annotated literals $\tilde{l}$. They are used to check operational properties at some program point in a procedure, so that the code transformations described in the next sections can be safely applied.

Distinct variables. Let Vs be a set of program variables, and let β be an abstract substitution such that $Vs \subseteq dom(\beta)$. If the operation **distinct_variables**(Vs, β) returns true, then for any $X_1, X_2 \in Vs$ $(X_1 \neq X_2)$, the terms $X_1\theta$ and $X_2\theta$ are two distinct variables, for all $\theta \in Cc(\beta)$.

No-sharing. Let Vs_1 and Vs_2 be two sets of program variables, and let β be an abstract substitution such that $Vs_1 \cup Vs_2 \subseteq dom(\beta)$. If the operation no_share(Vs_1, Vs_2, β) returns true, then for each $X_1 \in Vs_1$ and $X_2 \in Vs_2$, the terms $X_1\theta$ and $X_2\theta$ do not share a variable, for all $\theta \in Cc(\beta)$.

Occur-check freeness. Let *unif* be a unification and let β be an abstract substitution such that $pvars(unif) \subseteq dom(\beta)$. If occur_check_free($unif, \beta$) returns true, then the unification $unif\theta$ is not subject to the occur-check, for all $\theta \in Cc(\beta)$. See implementation details in Section 5.1.4.

Untouched terms. Let $\tilde{l} = \langle l, \beta_l^{inter}, B_l, \beta_l^{sf} \rangle$ be an annotated literal. The operation **untouched**($\tilde{l}$) returns the set of program variables occurring in the literal l that are untouched during the execution of l. Let $\beta_l^{inter} = \langle sv_{int}, frm_{int},$ $\langle mo_{int}, ... \rangle \rangle$, $B_l = \langle \beta_{in}^l, \beta_{ref}^l, \beta_{fails}^l, U^l, ... \rangle$, and $\beta_{ref}^l = \langle sv_{ref}, ... \rangle$. Then, the operation **untouched**($\tilde{l}$) returns the set

$$\{X_{i_k} \in pvars(l) \mid mo(sv_{int}(X_k)) = \texttt{ground} \vee sv_{ref}(X_k) \in U^l\}.$$

Determinacy.

---

deterministic(B) = *bool*

Specification:
Let B an abstract sequence.
If *bool* is *true* then for all $\langle \theta, S \rangle \in Cc(B)$, we have $0 \leq |S| \leq 1$

Implementation:
deterministic(B) $\Leftrightarrow E_{sol} \Rightarrow \{[\![sol \leq 1]\!]\}$

---

deterministic($\tilde{l}$) = *bool*

Specification:
Let $\tilde{l} = \langle l, \beta_l^{inter}, B_l, \beta_l^{sf} \rangle$, and $B_l = \langle \beta_{in}^l, \beta_{ref}^l, \beta_{fails}^l, ... \rangle$.
If *bool* is *true* then we have:

$$\left. \begin{array}{l} \theta \in Cc(\beta_l^{inter}) \\ \langle \theta, S \rangle \in Cc(B_l) \end{array} \right\} \Rightarrow 0 \leq |S| \leq 1$$

Implementation:

$$\textbf{deterministic}(\tilde{l}) \Leftrightarrow \left(\begin{array}{l} \qquad \textbf{deterministic}(B_l) \\ \vee \quad \beta_l^{inter} \sqcap \beta_{ref}^l = \bot \\ \vee \quad \exists \beta_f \in \beta_{fails}^l : \beta_l^{inter} \leq \beta_f \end{array} \right)$$

Full determinacy.

> **fully_deterministic**$(B) = bool$
>
> *Specification:*
> Let B an abstract sequence. If *bool* is *true* then for all $\langle \theta, S \rangle \in Cc(B)$, we have $|S| = 1$
>
> *Implementation:*
> **fully_deterministic**$(B) \Leftrightarrow \left(\begin{array}{c} \beta_{in} = \beta_{ref} \wedge \beta_{fails} = \emptyset \wedge \\ E_{sol} \Rightarrow \{[\![sol = 1]\!]\} \end{array} \right)$

> **fully_deterministic**$(\tilde{l}) = bool$
>
> *Specification:*
> Let $\tilde{l}$ be an annotated literal of the form $\langle l, \beta_l^{inter}, B_l, \beta_l^{sf} \rangle$. If *bool* is *true* then we have:
>
> $$\left. \begin{array}{c} \theta \in Cc(\beta_l^{inter}) \\ \langle \theta, S \rangle \in Cc(B_l) \end{array} \right\} \Rightarrow |S| = 1$$
>
> *Implementation:*
> $$\begin{array}{c} \textbf{fully\_deterministic}(\tilde{l}) \\ \Longleftrightarrow \\ \textbf{fully\_deterministic}(B_l) \end{array}$$
> $$\text{or} \quad \left(\begin{array}{l} \beta_l^{inter} \leq \beta_{ref}^l \\ \wedge \quad \forall \beta_f \in \beta_{fails}^l : \beta_l^{inter} \sqcap \beta_f = \bot \\ \wedge \quad E_{sol}^l \Rightarrow \{[\![sol = 1]\!]\} \end{array} \right)$$

Exclusivity.

> **exclusive**$(B, Bs) = bool$
>
> *Specification:*
> Let B an abstract sequence, and let Bs be a set of abstract sequences. If *bool* is *true* then, for all $B' \in Bs$, we have:
>
> $$\left. \begin{array}{c} \langle \theta, S \rangle \in Cc(B) \\ \langle \theta, S' \rangle \in Cc(B') \end{array} \right\} \Rightarrow S = <> \text{ or } S' = <>$$
>
> *Implementation:*
> See Section 6.3

G.5   Semantic normalisation

The following operation performs a finer normalisation of a clause, based on the abstract information annotating each program point.

$\text{SEM\_NORM}(\tilde{c}) = \tilde{c}'$

Input: - an annotated clause $\tilde{c}$ with abstract input β_{in}^c (in the program P)

Output: - an annotated clause $\tilde{c}'$, where unifications of c are simplified and decomposed in c', and where new unifications have been inserted in c', making the pattern abstract information explicit in c'

           - $\langle c, P \rangle \equiv_\theta \langle c', P' \rangle$ for any $\theta \in Cc(\beta_{in}^c)$ (P' is the program P where c is replaced by c')

The following rules take as input an annotated clause $\tilde{c}$, and generate an equivalent clause c'.

Introducing new unifications in a clause. At each program point, the optimiser ensures that every index in the β_{out} components of an abstract sequence is attached to a program variable in the clause.

$$\mathbf{R8} \left[\frac{\tilde{c} ::= (\beta_{in})h : - \dots \ \tilde{l}_{i-1}, (B_{i-1})\tilde{l}_i, (B_i)\tilde{l}_{i+1}, \dots}{c' ::= h : - \dots, l_i, X = f(Y_1, \dots, Y_m), l_{i+1}, \dots} \right]$$

$$\mathbf{if} \begin{cases} X \text{ is a program variable in } c \\ \exists i : 0 \le i \le s \text{ such that } frm_{out}^i(sv_{out}^i(X)) = f(i_1, \dots, i_m) \\ \text{There is no unification of kind } X = f(\dots) \text{ in } c \\ Y_1, \dots, Y_m \text{ do not occur in } c \end{cases}$$

Simplifying unifications. The optimiser simplifies each unification of a clause, depending on its form ($X = Y$ or $X = f(X_1, \dots, X_n)$), and on the abstract information attached to the program variables at the program point situated just before the unification. We provide rules for unifications of the form $X = Y$ only.

$$\mathbf{R9} \left[\frac{\tilde{c} ::= (\beta_{in})h : - \dots \ \tilde{l}_{i-1}, (B_{i-1})\tilde{l}_i, (B_i)\tilde{l}_{i+1}, \dots}{c' ::= h : - \dots, l_{i-1}, l_{i+1}, \dots} \right]$$

$$\mathbf{if} \begin{cases} \text{The literal } l_i \text{ is of the form } X = Y \\ sv_{out}^{i-1}(X) = sv_{out}^{i-1}(Y) \end{cases}$$

$$\mathbf{R10}\left[\frac{\tilde{c} ::= (\beta_{in})h : -... \ \tilde{l}_{i-1}, (B_{i-1})\tilde{l}_i, (B_i)\tilde{l}_{i+1}, ...}{c' ::= h : -..., l_{i-1}, X_1 = Y_1, ..., X_n = Y_n, l_{i+1}, ...}\right]$$

$$\text{if} \begin{cases} \text{The literal } l_i \text{ is of the form } X = Y \\ frm_{out}(sv_{out}^{i-1}(X)) = f(i_1, ..., i_n) \\ frm_{out}(sv_{out}^{i-1}(Y)) = f(j_1, ..., j_n) \\ X_1, ..., X_n, Y_1, ..., Y_n \text{ are the program variables attached to the} \\ \text{indices } i_1, ..., i_n, j_1, ..., j_n \text{ in } \beta_{out}^{i-1} \end{cases}$$

$$\mathbf{R11}\left[\frac{\tilde{c} ::= (\beta_{in})h : -... \ \tilde{l}_{i-1}, (B_{i-1})\tilde{l}_i, (B_i)\tilde{l}_{i+1}, ...}{c' ::= h : -..., l_{i-1}, Y = f(X_1, ..., X_n), l_{i+1}, ...}\right]$$

$$\text{if} \begin{cases} \text{The literal } l_i \text{ is of the form } X = Y \\ frm_{out}(sv_{out}^{i-1}(X)) = f(i_1, ..., i_n) \\ frm_{out}(sv_{out}^{i-1}(Y)) = undef \\ X_1, ..., X_n \text{ are the program variables attached to the indices} \\ i_1, ..., i_n \text{ in } \beta_{out}^{i-1} \end{cases}$$

Decomposing unifications. Unifications that may fail are decomposed into equivalent ones. For each unification of the form $X = f(X_1, ..., X_n)$, the optimiser looks at the abstract sequence modelling the execution of the unification.

$$\mathbf{R12}\left[\frac{\tilde{c} ::= (\beta_{in})h : -... \ \tilde{l}_{i-1}, (B_{i-1})\tilde{l}_i, (B_i)\tilde{l}_{i+1}, ...}{c' ::= h : -..., l_{i-1}, X_{i_0} = f(Y_1, ..., Y_m), Y_1 = X_{i_1}, ..., Y_m = X_{i_m}, l_{i+1}, ...}\right]$$

$$\text{if} \begin{cases} \text{The literal } l_i \text{ is of the form } X_{i_0} = f(X_{i_1}, ..., X_{i_m}) \\ Y_1, ..., Y_m \text{ do not occur in } c \\ \neg\mathbf{fully\_deterministic}(\tilde{l}_i) \\ \neg\mathbf{distinct\_variables}(\{X_{i_1}, ..., X_{i_m}\}, \beta_{out}^{i-1}) \end{cases}$$

The operation SEM_NORM($\tilde{c}$) is implemented as follows:

$$\tilde{c}' = \tilde{c}$$
while $\exists$ rule $\mathbf{R} \in \{\mathbf{R8}, \mathbf{R9}, \mathbf{R10}, \mathbf{R11}, \mathbf{R12}\}$ that can be applied to $\tilde{c}'$ **do**
$\quad c' = \mathbf{R}(\tilde{c}')$
$\quad \tilde{c}' = \text{ANNOTATE}(c', \beta_{in}^c)$
return $\tilde{c}'$

G.6   Moving unification forwards

The following operation checks whether a unification can be placed before a procedure call:

ADV_UNIF_CALL$(B, call, unif) = bool$
Input: - a literal $call$ that is a procedure call in the program P (not a
    negation nor a cut)
    - a unification $unif$
    - an abstract sequence B with $pvars(unif) \subseteq dom_{out}(B)$ and
    $pvars(call) \subseteq dom_{out}(B)$
    - P the contextual program
Output: - if $bool$ is $true$ then, for all $\langle \theta, S \rangle \in Cc(B)$, for every $\theta' \in$
    $Subst(S)$, the queries $(call, unif)\theta'$ and $(unif, call)\theta'$ produce
    the same answer substitution sequence

---

let $call ::= q(X_{i_1}, ..., X_{i_m})$
let $B ::= \langle \beta_{in}, ..., \beta_{out}, ... \rangle$
let $beh_q ::= \langle B_q, sexpr_q, logic_q \rangle$ be the abstract behaviour attached to q
let $(B)unif(B_{aux}) = $ ANNOTATE$(unif, B)$
let $\beta_{call}^{inter} = $ RESTRG$(call, B_{aux})$ ['restriction of a goal', see Section 3.5.1]

$$\textbf{return} \left(\begin{array}{l} \beta_{call}^{inter} \leq \beta_{in}^{q} \\ \wedge \quad \textbf{occur\_check\_free}(unif, \beta_{out}) \\ \wedge \quad logic_q \vee \textbf{no\_share}(pvars(unif), pvars(call), \beta_{out}) \end{array} \right)$$

The code transformation that move unification forwards in a clause is as follows:

ADV_UNIF$(\tilde{c}) = \tilde{c}'$
Input: - an annotated clause $\tilde{c}$ with abstract input β_{in}^c (in the program P)
Output: - c' is the clause c where the unifications of c have been moved
    forwards as much as possible
    - $\tilde{c}'$ is an annotated clause of c'
    - $\langle c, P \rangle \equiv_\theta \langle c', P' \rangle$ for any $\theta \in Cc(\beta_{in}^c)$ (P' is the program P
    where c is replaced by c')

The clause c can be viewed as follows:

$$h : - Unifs_0, call_1, Unifs_1, ..., Unifs_{r-1}, call_r, Unifs_r.$$

where $Unifs_k$ is a sequence (possibly empty) of unifications ($0 \leq k \leq r$), and
where $call_i$ is a literal that is not a unification ($1 \leq i \leq r$).

let B_i be the abstract sequence before $call_i$ in $\tilde{c}$ $(1 \leq i \leq r)$
for $i = r$ **to** 1 **do**
   let $Unifs_i ::= unif_1, ..., unif_z$
   for $k = z$ **to** 1 **do**
$$advance = \begin{cases} \textbf{fully\_deterministic}(unif_k, B_i) & \text{if } call_i \text{ is a cut} \\ \textbf{no\_share}(pvars(call_i), pvars(unif_k), \beta_{out}^i) & \text{if } call_i \text{ is a negation} \\ \texttt{ADV\_UNIF\_CALL}(B_i, call_i, unif_k) & \text{otherwise} \end{cases}$$
   if $advance$
     $(B_i)\widetilde{unif}_k(B_i') = \texttt{ANNOTATE}(unif_k, B_i)$
     $B_i = B_i'$
     $Unifs_i = Unifs_i$ where $unif_k$ has been removed
     $Unifs_{i-1} = Unifs_{i-1}, unif_k$
return $\texttt{ANNOTATE}(c, \beta_{in}^c)$

G.7 Leftmost green cut insertion

This operation inserts a green cut at the leftmost position of each clause (except for the last clause). A cut is inserted at a position in a clause only if the sequence of literals before that position is deterministic and exclusive with subsequent clauses.

$\texttt{INSERT\_CUT}(\tilde{pr}) = \tilde{pr}'$
Input: - an annotated procedure $\tilde{pr}$ (in the program P)
Output: - an annotated procedure $\tilde{pr}'$, where leftmost green cuts have been
              inserted in pr' for each clause of pr (except in the last clause)
              - $\langle pr, P \rangle \equiv_\theta \langle pr', P' \rangle$ for any $\theta \in Cc(\beta_{in}^{pr})$ (P' is the program P
              where pr is replaced by pr')

Let $\tilde{pr} = \langle B_{pr}, < \tilde{c}_1, ..., \tilde{c}_r > \rangle$ be an annotated procedure of the form:

$\tilde{c}_1 ::= ...$
$\quad \vdots$
$\tilde{c}_k ::= (\beta_{in}^{pr})h : - ... \tilde{l}_{i-1}, (B_{i-1})\tilde{l}_i, (B_i)\tilde{l}_{i+1}, ... \tilde{l}_{s_k}(B_{s_k}). \quad \langle B_{c_k}, acf_{c_k}, \beta_{c_k}^{cut}, \beta_k^{nocuts} \rangle$
$\quad \vdots$
$\tilde{c}_r ::= (\beta_{in}^{pr})h : - ... \quad \langle B_{c_r}, acf_{c_r}, \beta_{c_r}^{cut}, \beta_r^{nocuts} \rangle$

The operation $\texttt{INSERT\_CUT}(\tilde{pr})$ is implemented as follows.

for $k = 1$ **to** $r - 1$ **do**
  $i = 0$
  $insert\_cut = false$
  while $\neg insert\_cut \wedge i < s_k$ **do**
    $i = i + 1$
    $insert\_cut = (l_i = !) \vee \begin{pmatrix} \textbf{exclusive}(B_i, \{B_{c_{k+1}}, ..., B_r\}) \\ \wedge \textbf{ deterministic}(B_i) \end{pmatrix}$

  if $insert\_cut$
    $acf_{c_k} = \begin{cases} cut & \textbf{if } E^i_{sol} \Rightarrow \{[\![sol \geq 1]\!]\} \\ weakcut & \textbf{otherwise} \end{cases}$
    $\beta^{cut}_{c_k} = \beta^i_{ref}$
    $\beta^{nocuts}_{c_k} = \beta^i_{fails}$
  if $insert\_cut \wedge i = s_k \wedge l_{s_k} \neq !$
    $\tilde{c}'_k ::= (\beta^{pr}_{in})h : - ... \, \tilde{l}_{s_k}, (B_{s_k})!, (B_{s_k}). \ \langle B_{c_k}, acf_{c_k}, \beta^{cut}_{c_k}, \beta^{nocuts}_{c_k} \rangle$
  else if $insert\_cut \wedge 1 \leq i < s_k \wedge l_i \neq ! \wedge l_{i+1} \neq !$
    $\tilde{c}'_k ::= (\beta^{pr}_{in})h : - ... \, \tilde{l}_i, (B_i)!, (B_i), \tilde{l}_{i+1}, ... \ \langle B_{c_k}, acf_{c_k}, \beta^{cut}_{c_k}, \beta^{nocuts}_{c_k} \rangle$
  else
    $\tilde{c}'_k ::= \tilde{c}_k$
  return $\langle B_{pr}, < \tilde{c}'_1, ..., \tilde{c}'_{r-1}, \tilde{c}_r > \rangle$

G.8   Removing redundant literals

This operation removes redundant test literals (a test literal is deterministic and does not instantiate its arguments).

REMOVE_LIT$(\tilde{p}r) = \tilde{p}r'$
Input: - an annotated procedure $\tilde{p}r$ (in the program P)
Output: - an annotated procedure $\tilde{p}r'$, where the redundant literals in $\tilde{p}r$
                have been removed in pr'
              - $\langle pr, P \rangle \equiv_\theta \langle pr', P' \rangle$ for any $\theta \in Cc(\beta^{pr}_{in})$ (P' is the program P
                where pr is replaced by pr')

Let $\tilde{p}r$ be an annotated procedure of the form:

$\tilde{c}_1 ::= (\beta^{pr}_{in})h : - ... \ \langle B_{c_1}, acf_{c_1}, \beta^{cut}_{c_1}, \beta^{nocuts}_{c_1} \rangle$
$\vdots$
$\tilde{c}_k ::= (\beta^{pr}_{in})h : - ... \, \tilde{l}_{i-1}, (B_{i-1})\tilde{l}_i, (B_i)\tilde{l}_{i+1}, ... \, \tilde{l}_{s_k}(B_{s_k}). \ \langle B_{c_k}, acf_{c_k}, \beta^{cut}_{c_k}, \beta^{nocuts}_{c_k} \rangle$
$\vdots$
$\tilde{c}_r ::= ...$

The operation REMOVE_LIT$(\tilde{p}r)$ is implemented as follows.

$$\tilde{pr}' = \tilde{pr}$$

for $k = r$ **to** 1 **do**

    for $i = s_k$ **to** 1 **do**

        if remove$_k^i$

            $\tilde{c}'_k = (\beta_{in}^{pr})h : - ..., \tilde{l}_{i-1}, (B_{i-1})\tilde{l}_{i+1}, (B_{i+1})... \; \langle B_{c_k}, acf_{c_k}, \beta_{c_k}^{cut}, \beta_{c_k}^{nocuts} \rangle$

return $\tilde{pr}'$

where the condition **remove**$_k^i$ is true if the following conditions hold ($1 \le k \le r$, $1 \le i \le s_k$):

- l_i is not a cut
- **fully_deterministic**$(\tilde{l}_i)$

   $\vee$

   $\left(\begin{array}{l} \mathbf{deterministic}(\tilde{l}_i) \wedge \\ \exists z \in \{1, ..., k-1\} : acf_{c_z} = cut \wedge \beta_{l_i}^{sf} \le \beta_{c_z}^{cut} \wedge \beta_{l_i}^{sf} \sqcap \beta_{c_z}^{nocuts} = \bot \end{array} \right)$

- $(pvars(l_i) \backslash \mathbf{untouched}(\tilde{l}_i)) \cap (pvars(h) \cup pvars(l_{i+1}, ..., l_{s_k})) = \emptyset$
- **no_share**$((pvars(l_i) \backslash \mathbf{untouched}(\tilde{l}_i)), (pvars(c) \backslash \mathbf{untouched}(\tilde{l}_i)), B_i)$

G.9   Denormalisation

This operation instantiates the clause heads and subcalls as much as possible, and suppresses useless explicit unifications.

SYN_DENORM$(c) = c'$
Input: a Prolog clause c (in the program P)
Output: a Prolog clause c', where most explicit unifications of c have been removed and placed into clause's head and literals in c'
          - $\langle c, P \rangle \equiv_\theta \langle c', P' \rangle$ for any input substitution θ (P' is the program P where c is replaced by c')

The following rules take as input a Prolog clause c, and generate an equivalent Prolog clause c' where some explicit unification of c has been removed or placed into clause's head and literals in c'. Let o be a Prolog construct, X be a program variable, and t be a program term. Then $o\{X \mapsto t\}$ is the Prolog construct o where each occurrence of X has been replaced by t.

R13 $\left[\dfrac{c ::= h : -g_1, X = t, g_2.}{c' ::= h : -g_1, X = t, g_2\{X \mapsto t\}.} \right]$

R14 $\left[\dfrac{c ::= h \qquad\qquad : -X = t, g.}{c' ::= h\{X \mapsto t\} : -X = t, g\{X \mapsto t\}.} \right]$

R15 $\left[\dfrac{c ::= h : -g_1, X = t, g_2.}{c' ::= h : -g_1, g_2.} \right]$
   if $\Big\{$ X does not occur in g_1, t, g_2

The operation SYN_DENORM(c) is implemented as follows:

$c' = c$
while $\exists$ rule $\mathbf{R} \in \{\mathbf{R13}, \mathbf{R14}, \mathbf{R15}\}$ that can be applied to c' **do**
    $c' = \mathbf{R}(c')$
return c'

Appendix H

Experimental results of the optimiser

This appendix provides detailed tables on the experimental results described in Section 9.6. The optimiser has been tested on some classical programs, borrowed from [3, 45, 124] and from the Internet. The source programs, the formal specifications, the generated specialised codes, and the efficiency tests are available at *http://www.info.ucl.ac.be/~gobert*. The tests have been realised on a 1.5 GHz Pentium, 1 GB RAM, Linux Suse, with SWI-Prolog v 5.4.6 [132].

H.1 Checker and optimiser execution time

Table H.1 reports on the checker and optimiser execution time on 109 pairs of procedures/specifications. Table H.2 summarises the results. The legend of these tables is as follows.

Symbol	Description
Program	Name of the program
Input	Short description of the in part of the formal specification (v:var; g:ground; a:any; l:list; i:int)
T-Check (PPL)	Checker time (in sec) when PPL is enabled
T-Check (NoPPL)	Checker time (in sec) when PPL is disabled
T-Opt (SemNorm)	Optimiser time (in sec) spent for: semantic normalisation (Step D) + moving unifications forwards (Step E)
T-Opt (CutRm)	Optimiser time (in sec) spent for: cut insertion (Step F) + moving cut backwards (Step G) + removing redundant literals (Step H)
T-Opt (Denorm)	Optimiser time (in sec) spent for: denormalisation (Step I)
T-Total	**T-Check (PPL) + T-Opt**

Program	Input	T-Check		T-Opt			T-Total
		PPL	NoPPL	SemNorm	CutRm	Denorm	
ack	(i,i,v)	1.82	0.44	4.53	0.3	0.02	6.67
ack	(i,i,a)	2.96	0.72	7.88	0.55	0.04	11.43
append	(g,g,v)	0.53	0.12	0.44	0.06	0.02	1.05
append	(g,g,a)	0.44	0.08	0.33	0.04	0.01	0.82
append	(v,v,g)	0.8	0.15	0.87	0.1	0.01	1.78
bubblesort	(g,v)	3.17	0.46	3.09	0.58	0.07	6.91
bubblesort	(g,a)	2.81	0.46	2.97	0.55	0.07	6.4
bubble	(g,g,v,v)	2.2	0.25	2.38	0.5	0.06	5.14
close	(l)	0.45	0.14	0.43	0.02	0.01	0.91
close	(v)	0.08	0.02	0.06	0.01	0	0.15
close	(a)	0.3	0.08	0.22	0.07	0.01	0.6
compress	(g,v)	2.92	0.71	3.24	0.34	0.04	6.54
compress2	(v,g)	1.76	0.37	1.75	0.23	0.04	3.78
deriv	(g,v)	2.87	0.94	5.5	4.15	0.04	12.56
deriv	(g,a)	2.32	0.99	5.16	4.77	0.03	12.28
deriv	(a,g)	5.42	2.6	9.16	6.26	0.06	20.9
dutch	(g,v)	2.32	0.55	3.76	1.66	0.06	7.8
dutch	(g,a)	2.27	0.48	3.74	1.65	0.06	7.72
distribute	(g,v,v,v)	2.08	0.43	3.61	1.64	0.06	7.39
efface	(g,g,v)	0.85	0.26	0.76	0.1	0.02	1.73
efface	(g,g,a)	0.55	0.24	0.63	0.07	0.01	1.26
efface	(g,v,g)	0.59	0.23	0.96	0.08	0.01	1.64
flatten	(g,v)	1.75	0.42	1.32	0.21	0.03	3.31
flatten	(g,a)	2.71	0.69	2.09	0.34	0.04	5.18
flattendl	(g,v)	1.01	0.23	1.08	0.18	0.02	2.29
flattendl	(g,a)	1.41	0.38	1.55	0.3	0.02	3.28
flattree	(g,v)	1.62	0.33	1.21	0.11	0.03	2.97
flattree	(g,a)	2.77	0.57	2.2	0.2	0.05	5.22
flattree2	(v,g)	1.49	0.26	1.51	0.13	0.03	3.16
flattree2	(a,g)	1.28	0.32	1.31	0.13	0.02	2.74
hanoi	(g,g,g,g,v)	2.58	0.57	3.56	0.7	0.05	6.89
heapify	(g,a)	17.75	1.35	17.88	0.75	0.07	36.45
inorder	(g,v)	1.63	0.34	1.52	0.12	0.03	3.3
inorder	(g,a)	2.79	0.58	2.71	0.2	0.05	5.75
insertsort	(g,v)	2.21	0.39	2.28	0.49	0.04	5.02
insertsort	(g,a)	3.62	0.71	3.87	0.87	0.08	8.44
isotree	(v,g)	5.96	0.42	2.24	0.42	0.03	8.65
isotree	(a,g)	1.15	0.37	2.08	0.39	0.02	3.64
maxlist	(g,v)	1.61	0.31	1.15	0.13	0.04	2.93
maxlist	(g,a)	1.25	0.29	1.06	0.11	0.03	2.45
maximum	(i,i,v)	0.6	0.13	0.4	0.06	0.02	1.08
maximum	(i,i,a)	0.96	0.07	0.24	0.04	0.01	1.25
minimum	(i,i,v)	0.73	0.06	0.39	0.05	0.02	1.19
minimum	(i,i,a)	0.29	0.05	0.25	0.03	0.01	0.58
maxseq	(g,v)	3.23	0.6	2.72	0.63	0.06	6.64
maxseq	(g,a)	2.72	0.46	2.45	0.55	0.05	5.77
maxtree	(g,v)	2.42	0.45	1.74	0.14	0.05	4.35

Program	Input	T-Check		T-Opt			T-Total
		PPL	NoPPL	SemNorm	CutRm	Denorm	
maxtree	(g,a)	2.96	0.48	2.3	0.2	0.06	5.52
member	(a,g)	0.72	0.22	0.61	0.04	0.01	1.38
nonmember	(g,g)	0.35	0.05	0.32	0.02	0.01	0.7
mergesort	(g,v)	7.37	1.24	9.93	2.41	0.16	19.87
mergesort	(g,a)	12.08	2.1	16.51	4.45	0.27	33.31
merge	(g,g,v)	4.99	0.65	7.91	2.01	0.12	15.03
merge	(g,g,a)	3.76	0.57	5.58	1.74	0.09	11.17
mmult	(g,g,v)	5.7	0.86	6.48	2.75	0.08	15.01
nextcomb	(i,i,g,v)	10.87	1.33	23.35	2.2	0.2	36.62
numocc	(g,g,v)	1.25	0.31	1.54	0.38	0.02	3.19
numocc	(g,g,a)	1.98	0.52	2.77	0.72	0.03	5.5
permutsort	(g,v)	2.84	0.57	2.59	0.25	0.06	5.74
permutsort	(g,a)	2.19	0.51	2.18	0.22	0.04	4.63
postorder	(g,v)	1.89	0.38	2.26	0.12	0.04	4.31
postorder	(g,a)	3.25	0.65	4.01	0.21	0.05	7.52
prefix	(v,g)	0.87	0.22	0.66	0.07	0.03	1.63
prefix	(g,g)	0.51	0.07	0.41	0.03	0.01	0.96
preorder	(g,v)	1.69	0.34	1.57	0.12	0.03	3.41
preorder	(g,a)	2.86	0.58	2.88	0.2	0.05	5.99
qs	(g,v)	4.55	0.54	4.09	0.63	0.09	9.36
qs	(g,a)	5.66	0.79	5.4	0.71	0.11	11.88
part	(g,g,v,v)	2.5	0.24	2.53	0.52	0.07	5.62
remove_red	(g,v)	2.17	0.59	1.9	0.43	0.04	4.54
remove_red	(g,a)	1.65	0.46	1.84	0.36	0.02	3.87
revnaive	(g,v)	1.32	0.29	1.2	0.11	0.03	2.66
revnaive	(g,a)	2.27	0.48	2.11	0.19	0.04	4.61
revacc	(g,v)	0.6	0.12	0.52	0.1	0.01	1.23
revacc	(g,a)	0.48	0.11	0.41	0.04	0.01	0.94
revdl	(g,v)	0.54	0.1	0.5	0.05	0.01	1.1
revdl	(g,a)	0.42	0.07	0.38	0.04	0.01	0.85
sameleaves	(g,g)	1.87	0.37	1.65	0.45	0.03	4
select	(g,g,g)	1.42	0.32	1.12	0.11	0.02	2.67
select	(v,g,v)	1.14	0.16	1.43	0.15	0.02	2.74
select	(g,v,g)	0.66	0.14	0.91	0.09	0.01	1.67
selectsort	(g,v)	2.94	0.48	3.02	0.55	0.07	6.58
selectsort	(g,a)	1.97	0.44	2.16	0.47	0.06	4.66
substlist	(g,g,g,v)	1.45	0.44	1.5	0.41	0.03	3.39
substlist	(g,g,g,a)	0.86	0.28	1.16	0.37	0.02	2.41
substlist	(g,g,v,g)	1.15	0.17	1.76	0.34	0.02	3.27
substree	(g,g,g,v)	2.13	0.57	2.8	0.76	0.03	5.72
substree	(g,g,g,a)	1.31	0.41	2.09	0.78	0.04	4.22
substree	(g,g,v,g)	1.86	0.28	3.41	0.59	0.03	5.89
suffix	(v,g)	0.74	0.21	0.53	0.04	0.02	1.33
suffix	(g,g)	0.29	0.13	0.28	0.02	0.01	0.6
sumtree	(g,v)	1.89	0.31	2.54	0.1	0.02	4.55
sumtree	(g,i)	3.09	0.48	4.41	0.16	0.04	7.7
transpose	(g,v)	2.79	0.69	2.47	0.29	0.06	5.61

Program	Input	T-Check		T-Opt			T-Total
		PPL	NoPPL	SemNorm	CutRm	Denorm	
transpose	(g,a)	2.23	0.58	2.56	0.26	0.03	5.08
treememb	(v,g)	6.12	1.1	5.88	0.15	0.05	12.2
treememb	(a,g)	1.01	0.23	0.94	0.09	0.01	2.05
union	(g,g,v)	2.75	0.66	2.39	0.44	0.04	5.62
union	(g,g,a)	2.19	0.55	2.35	0.44	0.03	5.01
intersect	(g,g,v)	2.38	0.46	2.58	0.31	0.04	5.31
intersect	(g,g,a)	2.2	0.48	2.24	0.25	0.03	4.72
difference	(g,g,v)	2.4	0.46	2.46	0.46	0.04	5.36
difference	(g,g,a)	2.15	0.46	2.27	0.45	0.03	4.9
union2	(g,g,v)	4.31	0.44	5.87	1.57	0.13	11.88
union2	(g,g,a)	3.18	0.45	4.18	1.19	0.09	8.64
intersect2	(g,g,v)	4.21	0.35	4.73	1.17	0.11	10.22
intersect2	(g,g,a)	2.9	0.34	3.43	1.07	0.09	7.49
difference2	(g,g,v)	4.04	0.38	4.94	1.02	0.12	10.12
difference2	(g,g,a)	2.83	0.38	3.57	0.85	0.09	7.34

Table H.1: Checker and optimiser execution time.

♯ Procedures/Specifications		109	
T-Check (PPL)	Mean	-	2.46
	Max	heapify	17.75
	Min	close	0.08
T-Check (NoPPL)	Mean	-	0.46
	Max	deriv	2.6
	Min	close	0.02
T-Opt (SemNorm)	Mean	-	2.92
	Max	nextcomb	23.35
	Min	close	0.06
T-Opt (CutRm)	Mean	-	0.62
	Max	deriv	6.26
	Min	close	0.01
T-Opt (Denorm)	Mean	-	0.05
	Max	mergesort	0.27
	Min	close	0
T-Total	Mean	-	6.05
	Max	nextcomb	36.62
	Min	close	0.15

Table H.2: Summary of the checker and optimiser execution time.

H.2   Speedup of specialised code

Table H.3 and Table H.10 report on execution time speedup when indexing is disabled and when indexing is enabled, respectively. By default, SWI-Prolog enables indexing on the first argument position of each procedure. Speedup is defined as the ratio between the execution time spent for the source program and for the specialised program. A speedup greater than (resp. less than) one means that the specialised code is more (resp. less) efficient than the source code. We consider 57 procedures and 109 specifications (some procedures have several specifications, because they are multidirectional). We have performed 187 efficiency tests (there is at least one efficiency test for each specification of a procedure). For each efficiency test, the tables show the execution time and the speedup at each step of the optimisation strategy (see Section 9.4).

The speedup results are summarised in the following tables, by considering all the 187 efficiency tests (Table H.4 when indexing is disabled and Table H.11 when indexing is enabled), only the efficiency tests for the deterministic procedures (Table H.5 and Table H.12), only the efficiency tests for the procedures that surely succeed (Table H.6 and Table H.13), only the efficiency tests for the deterministic procedures that surely succeed (Table H.7 and Table H.14), only the efficiency tests for the procedures that contain negation (Table H.8 and Table H.15), and only the efficiency tests for the procedures that contain arithmetic comparison (Table H.9 and Table H.16). We use the following symbols in all the above-mentioned tables:

Symbol	Description
Input	Name of the program +
	Short description of the input (v:var; g:ground; a:any; i:int; l:list)+
	Success (ok) or Failure (ko) of the execution
No Index	Indexing is disabled
Default Index	Indexing is enabled (in SWI-Prolog, indexing is enabled on first argument position by default)
det	The procedure is deterministic (yes or no)
ss	The procedure surely succeeds (yes or no)
User	Original user version
Reorder	Reordered version
SynNorm	Syntactic normalised version
SemNorm	Semantic normalised version (Step D)
Cut	Version where leftmost green cuts are inserted (Step G)
RmCut	Version where redundant literals are removed (Step H)
Denorm	Denormalised version (Step I) (final specialised version)
T	Execution time (in ms)
Sdup	Speedup [= User T / Version T]

Input No Index	det	ss	User T	Reorder T	Reorder Sdup	SynNorm T	SynNorm Sdup	SemNorm T	SemNorm Sdup	Cut T	Cut Sdup	RmCut T	RmCut Sdup	Denorm T	Denorm Sdup
ack_iiv_3_4	yes	yes	150	150	1	240	0.63	289	0.52	260	0.58	259	0.58	130	1.15
ack_iia_3_4_ok	yes	no	149	150	0.99	240	0.62	280	0.53	259	0.58	259	0.58	130	1.15
ack_iia_3_4_ko	yes	no	150	150	1	240	0.63	280	0.54	250	0.6	250	0.6	131	1.15
append_ggv_1000	yes	yes	29	29	1	61	0.48	61	0.48	50	0.58	50	0.58	20	1.45
append_ggv_10000	yes	yes	219	219	1	489	0.45	489	0.45	490	0.45	490	0.45	180	1.22
append_ggv_20000	yes	yes	621	621	1	989	0.63	989	0.63	991	0.63	991	0.63	359	1.73
append_gga_1000_ok	yes	no	20	20	1	50	0.4	50	0.4	50	0.4	50	0.4	20	
append_gga_10000_ok	yes	no	270	270	1	559	0.48	559	0.48	550	0.49	550	0.49	220	1.23
append_gga_20000_ok	yes	no	690	690	1	1130	0.61	1130	0.61	1129	0.61	1129	0.61	440	1.57
append_gga_1000_ko	yes	no	10	10	1	30	0.33	30	0.33	20	0.5	20	0.5	10	1
append_gga_10000_ko	yes	no	91	91	1	250	0.36	250	0.36	250	0.36	250	0.36	89	1.02
append_gga_20000_ko	yes	no	21	21	1	51	0.41	51	0.41	51	0.41	51	0.41	11	1.91
append_vvg_1000	no	yes	530	530	1	561	0.94	600	0.88	600	0.88	600	0.88	530	1
bubblesort_gv_100	yes	yes	240	240	1	491	0.49	650	0.37	530	0.45	520	0.46	171	1.4
bubblesort_gv_200	yes	yes	1060	1060	1	2009	0.53	2710	0.39	2421	0.44	2359	0.45	789	1.34
bubblesort_ga_ok_100	yes	yes	240	240	1	500	0.48	650	0.37	469	0.51	461	0.52	150	1.6
bubblesort_ga_ok_150	yes	yes	570	570	1	1120	0.51	1519	0.38	1200	0.48	1190	0.48	340	1.68
bubblesort_ga_ko_100	yes	yes	239	239	1	481	0.5	650	0.37	470	0.51	470	0.51	150	1.59
close_1_10	yes	yes	1290	1359	0.95	1101	1.17	1101	1.17	950	1.36	200	6.45	160	8.06
close_v	yes	yes	231	231	1	190	1.22	190	1.22	190	1.22	180	1.28	161	1.43
close_a_ko	yes	no	120	120	1	120	1	120	1	120	1	100	1.2	60	2
compress_gv_10	no	no	20	20	1	40	0.5	50	0.4	41	0.49	39	0.51	19	1.05
compress_gv_15	no	no	289	289	1	591	0.49	700	0.41	669	0.43	669	0.43	269	1.07
compress2_vg_100	yes	no	80	80	1	150	0.53	151	0.53	141	0.57	141	0.57	70	1.14
compress2_vg_1000	yes	no	860	860	1	1540	0.56	1551	0.55	1450	0.59	1450	0.59	730	1.18
deriv_exprv	yes	yes	21	21	1	60	0.35	70	0.3	50	0.42	50	0.42	19	1.11
deriv_expra_ok	yes	no	80	79	1.01	210	0.38	221	0.36	150	0.53	150	0.53	70	1.14
deriv_expra_ko	yes	no	80	80	1	200	0.4	219	0.37	141	0.57	141	0.57	70	1.14

Input No Index	det	ss	User T	Reorder T	Reorder Sdup	SynNorm T	SynNorm Sdup	SemNorm T	SemNorm Sdup	Cut T	Cut Sdup	RmCut T	RmCut Sdup	Denorm T	Denorm Sdup
deriv_aexpr_ok	no	no	39	39	1	99	0.39	100	0.39	89	0.44	89	0.44	31	1.26
deriv_aexpr_ko	no	no	20	20	1	41	0.49	50	0.4	50	0.4	50	0.4	20	1
dutch_gv	yes	yes	20	19	1.05	50	0.4	70	0.29	60	0.33	60	0.33	19	1.05
dutch_gg_ok	yes	no	19	19	1	50	0.38	70	0.27	50	0.38	50	0.38	20	0.95
dutch_gg_ko	yes	no	60	50	1.2	159	0.38	230	0.26	190	0.32	190	0.32	50	1.2
distribute_gvvv	yes	yes	60	60	1	221	0.27	320	0.19	260	0.23	260	0.23	60	1
efface_ok_gv_100	yes	no	70	70	1	130	0.54	150	0.47	89	0.79	69	1.01	30	2.33
efface_ok_gv_1000	yes	no	670	661	1.01	1281	0.52	1471	0.46	870	0.77	610	1.1	221	3.03
efface_ko_ga_100	yes	no	40	40	1	110	0.36	130	0.31	91	0.44	69	0.58	20	2
efface_ko_ga_1000	yes	no	29	40	0.73	109	0.27	130	0.22	81	0.36	60	0.48	20	1.45
efface_ok_gv_100	yes	no	70	70	1	130	0.54	150	0.47	89	0.79	69	1.01	29	2.41
efface_ok_gv_1000	yes	no	670	661	1.01	1281	0.52	1471	0.46	870	0.77	610	1.1	21	31.9
efface_ok_gvg_100	no	no	1260	1260	1	1310	0.96	1380	0.91	130	9.69	130	9.69	70	18
efface_ko_gag_100	no	no	360	350	1	430	0.84	489	0.74	10	36	10	36	10	36
flatten_gv	yes	yes	20	11	1.82	30	0.67	30	0.67	21	0.95	21	0.95	10	2
flatten_ga_ok	yes	no	19	10	1.9	30	0.63	29	0.66	20	0.95	20	0.95	11	1.73
flatten_ga_ko	yes	no	20	19	1.05	30	0.67	30	0.67	20	1	20	1	19	1.05
flattendl_gv	yes	yes	60	60	1	80	0.75	90	0.67	80	0.75	80	0.75	60	1
flattendl_ga_ok	yes	no	60	60	1	80	0.75	90	0.67	81	0.74	81	0.74	50	1.2
flattendl_ga_ko	yes	no	60	50	1.2	81	0.74	91	0.66	80	0.75	80	0.75	51	1.18
flattree_gv	yes	yes	51	60	0.85	139	0.37	139	0.37	120	0.43	120	0.43	50	1.02
flattree_gg_ok	yes	no	50	60	0.83	140	0.36	140	0.36	120	0.42	120	0.42	50	1
flattree_gg_ko	yes	no	50	50	1	130	0.38	130	0.38	110	0.45	110	0.45	49	1.02
flattree2_vg	no	yes	20	20	1	50	0.4	60	0.33	49	0.41	49	0.41	19	1.05
flattree2_gg_ok	no	no	29	29	1	70	0.41	80	0.36	81	0.36	81	0.36	30	0.97
flattree2_gg_ko	no	no	20	20	1	41	0.49	50	0.4	50	0.4	50	0.4	20	1
hanoi_ggggv	yes	no	50	50	1	130	0.38	140	0.36	120	0.42	120	0.42	41	1.22

Input No Index	det	ss	User T	Reorder T	Reorder Sdup	SynNorm T	SynNorm Sdup	SemNorm T	SemNorm Sdup	Cut T	Cut Sdup	RmCut T	RmCut Sdup	Denorm T	Denorm Sdup
heapify_gv	no	no	60	60	1	120	0.5	149	0.4	139	0.43	131	0.46	60	1
heapify_ga_ok	no	no	60	60	1	120	0.5	140	0.43	130	0.46	129	0.47	50	1.2
heapify_ga_ko	no	no	60	60	1	110	0.55	140	0.43	130	0.46	130	0.46	50	1.2
inorder_gv	yes	yes	29	29	1	60	0.48	60	0.48	50	0.58	50	0.58	21	1.38
inorder_ga_ok	yes	no	29	29	1	60	0.48	60	0.48	50	0.58	50	0.58	20	1.45
inorder_ga_ko	yes	no	29	29	1	60	0.48	60	0.48	50	0.58	50	0.58	20	1.45
insertsort_gv	yes	yes	49	41	1.2	89	0.55	130	0.38	130	0.38	130	0.38	41	1.2
insertsort_ga_ok	yes	no	49	41	1.2	91	0.54	130	0.38	130	0.38	120	0.41	40	1.23
insertsort_ga_ko	yes	no	50	41	1.22	89	0.56	130	0.38	130	0.38	119	0.42	40	1.25
isotree_vg	no	yes	31	31	1	100	0.31	170	0.18	159	0.19	159	0.19	31	1
isotree_ag_ok	no	no	69	69	1	209	0.33	279	0.25	269	0.26	269	0.26	70	0.99
isotree_ag_ko	no	no	50	50	1	151	0.33	211	0.24	201	0.25	201	0.25	50	1
maxlist_gv	yes	yes	91	90	1.01	141	0.65	141	0.65	120	0.76	119	0.76	70	1.3
maxlist_ga_ok	yes	no	90	90	1	140	0.64	140	0.64	120	0.75	120	0.75	70	1.29
maxlist_ga_ko	yes	no	91	89	1.02	141	0.65	141	0.65	120	0.76	120	0.76	70	1.3
maximum_iiv	yes	yes	41	40	1.02	40	1.02	40	1.02	41	1	40	1.02	39	1.05
maximum_iiv2	yes	yes	40	40	1	40	1	40	1	40	1	40	1	40	1
maximum_iia_ok	yes	no	40	40	1	40	1	40	1	40	1	40	1	39	1.03
maximum_iia_ok2	yes	no	40	40	1	40	1	40	1	31	1.29	31	1.29	40	1
maximum_iia_ko	yes	no	40	30	1.33	40	1	40	1	40	1	40	1	40	1
minimum_iiv	yes	yes	40	40	1	40	1	40	1	40	1	40	1	40	1
minimum_iiv2	yes	yes	40	40	1	40	1	40	1	40	1	40	1	40	1
minimum_iia_ok	yes	no	40	40	1	40	1	40	1	39	1.03	39	1.03	39	1.03
minimum_iia_ok2	yes	no	39	30	1.3	41	0.95	41	0.95	41	0.95	41	0.95	39	1
minimum_iia_ko	yes	no	39	40	0.98	39	1	39	1	30	1.3	30	1.3	31	1.26
maxseq_gv	yes	no	31	31	1	50	0.62	50	0.62	39	0.79	40	0.78	20	1.55
maxseq_ga_ok	yes	no	31	31	1	40	0.78	50	0.62	31	1	39	0.79	20	1.55

Input No Index	det	ss	User T	Reorder		SynNorm		SemNorm		Cut		RmCut		Denorm	
				T	Sdup	T	Sdup	T	Sdup	T	Sdup	T	Sdup	T	Sdup
maxseq_ga_ko	yes	no	29	29	1	50	0.58	50	0.58	39	0.74	40	0.73	21	1.38
maxtree_gv	yes	yes	21	20	1.05	40	0.53	40	0.53	31	0.68	31	0.68	20	1.05
maxtree_ga_ok	yes	no	21	21	1	40	0.53	40	0.53	31	0.68	31	0.68	20	1.05
maxtree_ga_ko	yes	no	21	21	1	41	0.51	41	0.51	31	0.68	31	0.68	20	1.05
member_vg	no	no	61	61	1	91	0.67	100	0.61	100	0.61	100	0.61	61	1
member_gg_ok	no	no	20	20	1	50	0.4	61	0.33	61	0.33	61	0.33	20	1
member_gg_ko	no	no	20	20	1	51	0.39	60	0.33	60	0.33	60	0.33	20	1
nonmember_gg_ok	yes	no	51	49	1.04	80	0.64	80	0.64	80	0.64	80	0.64	50	1.02
nonmember_gg_ko	yes	no	29	29	1	40	0.73	40	0.73	40	0.73	40	0.73	29	1
mergesort_gv_100	yes	yes	10	10	1	31	0.32	39	0.26	31	0.32	31	0.32	10	1
mergesort_gv_200	yes	yes	31	20	1.55	60	0.52	81	0.38	70	0.44	70	0.44	20	1.55
mergesort_ga_ok_100	yes	no	10	20	0.5	39	0.26	50	0.2	40	0.25	40	0.25	10	1
mergesort_ga_ok_150	yes	no	20	21	0.95	60	0.33	81	0.25	60	0.33	60	0.33	20	1
mergesort_ga_ko_100	yes	no	19	19	1	41	0.46	50	0.38	41	0.46	40	0.48	10	1.9
mergesort_ga_ko_150	yes	no	21	21	1	60	0.35	80	0.26	70	0.3	60	0.35	10	2.1
merge_ggv_100	yes	yes	170	169	1.01	430	0.4	651	0.26	550	0.31	550	0.31	130	1.31
merge_ggv_1000	yes	yes	1630	1610	1.01	4230	0.39	6500	0.25	5451	0.3	5460	0.3	1271	1.28
merge_gga_ok_10	yes	no	29	30	0.97	90	0.32	120	0.24	81	0.36	81	0.36	20	1.45
merge_gga_ko	yes	no	29	29	1	79	0.37	120	0.24	80	0.36	80	0.36	20	1.45
mmult_ggv	yes	yes	71	71	1	160	0.44	240	0.3	220	0.32	220	0.32	70	1.01
nextcomb_iigv	yes	no	40	40	1	79	0.51	89	0.45	69	0.58	70	0.57	31	1.29
numocc_ggv	yes	yes	20	20	1	31	0.65	40	0.5	30	0.67	30	0.67	10	2
numocc_gga_ok	yes	no	20	20	1	30	0.67	30	0.67	30	0.67	30	0.67	10	2
numocc_gga_ko	yes	no	20	20	1	30	0.67	30	0.67	30	0.67	29	0.69	10	2
permutsort_gv	no	no	30	30	1	80	0.38	100	0.3	99	0.3	99	0.3	30	1
permutsort_ga_ok	no	no	49	49	1	130	0.38	151	0.32	150	0.33	150	0.33	49	1
permutsort_ga_ko	no	no	51	51	1	120	0.43	179	0.28	179	0.28	179	0.28	51	1

Input No Index	det	ss	User T	Reorder T	Reorder Sdup	SynNorm T	SynNorm Sdup	SemNorm T	SemNorm Sdup	Cut T	Cut Sdup	RmCut T	RmCut Sdup	Denorm T	Denorm Sdup
postorder_gv	yes	yes	39	39	1	90	0.43	90	0.43	80	0.49	80	0.49	31	1.26
postorder_ga_ok	yes	no	39	39	1	90	0.43	90	0.43	80	0.49	80	0.49	30	1.3
postorder_ga_ko	yes	no	39	39	1	91	0.43	91	0.43	80	0.49	80	0.49	30	1.3
prefix_vg	no	yes	31	31	1	59	0.53	81	0.38	81	0.38	81	0.38	31	1
prefix_gg_ok	yes	no	90	90	1	220	0.41	220	0.41	220	0.41	220	0.41	90	1
prefix_gg_ko	yes	no	51	51	1	120	0.43	120	0.43	120	0.43	120	0.43	50	1.02
preorder_gv	yes	yes	31	31	1	79	0.39	79	0.39	69	0.45	69	0.45	30	1.03
preorder_ga_ok	yes	no	30	30	1	79	0.38	79	0.38	69	0.43	69	0.43	30	1
preorder_ga_ko	yes	no	31	31	1	79	0.39	79	0.39	71	0.44	71	0.44	20	1.55
qs_gv_100	yes	yes	20	20	1	40	0.5	50	0.4	39	0.51	39	0.51	10	2
qs_gv_200	yes	yes	71	70	1.01	141	0.5	190	0.37	140	0.51	130	0.55	40	1.78
qs_ga_ok_100	yes	no	49	49	1	100	0.49	130	0.38	99	0.49	99	0.49	30	1.63
qs_ga_ok_150	yes	no	110	110	1	240	0.46	320	0.34	220	0.5	211	0.52	70	1.57
qs_ga_ko_100	yes	no	50	50	1	100	0.5	130	0.38	91	0.55	90	0.56	20	2.5
qs_ga_ko_150	yes	no	110	120	0.92	240	0.46	321	0.34	219	0.5	219	0.5	61	1.8
part_ggvv_100	yes	yes	51	50	1.02	100	0.51	130	0.39	110	0.46	100	0.51	40	1.27
part_ggvv_200	yes	yes	100	100	1	189	0.53	260	0.38	210	0.48	209	0.48	69	1.45
remove_red_gv	no	no	40	40	1	80	0.5	100	0.4	99	0.4	101	0.4	40	1
remove_red_ga_ok	no	no	30	30	1	70	0.43	80	0.38	80	0.38	80	0.38	31	0.97
remove_red_ga_ko	no	no	20	20	1	39	0.51	51	0.39	50	0.4	39	0.51	19	1.05
revnaive_gv	yes	yes	20	20	1	40	0.5	40	0.5	41	0.49	41	0.49	20	1
revnaive_ga_ok	yes	no	20	20	1	40	0.5	40	0.5	40	0.5	40	0.5	10	2
revnaive_ga_ko	yes	no	20	20	1	40	0.5	41	0.49	40	0.5	40	0.5	10	2
revacc_gv	yes	yes	31	31	1	89	0.35	89	0.35	90	0.34	90	0.34	30	1.03
revacc_ga_ok	yes	no	39	39	1	90	0.43	90	0.43	90	0.43	90	0.43	30	1.3
revacc_ga_ko	yes	no	39	39	1	90	0.43	90	0.43	90	0.43	90	0.43	31	1.26
revdl_gv	yes	yes	30	30	1	90	0.33	90	0.33	90	0.33	90	0.33	30	1

Input No Index	det	ss	User T	Reorder		SynNorm		SemNorm		Cut		RmCut		Denorm	
				T	Sdup	T	Sdup	T	Sdup	T	Sdup	T	Sdup	T	Sdup
revdl_ga_ok	yes	no	30	30	1	91	0.33	91	0.33	90	0.33	90	0.33	31	0.97
revdl_ga_ko	yes	no	30	30	1	90	0.33	90	0.33	90	0.33	90	0.33	31	0.97
sameleaves_gg_ok	yes	no	90	90	1	189	0.48	201	0.45	180	0.5	180	0.5	99	0.91
sameleaves_gg_ko	yes	no	41	41	1	70	0.59	79	0.52	70	0.59	70	0.59	40	1.02
select_ggg_ok	no	no	10	10	1	29	0.34	40	0.25	40	0.25	40	0.25	10	1
select_ggg_ko	no	no	20	20	1	49	0.41	71	0.28	71	0.28	71	0.28	20	1
select_vgv	no	no	40	40	1	59	0.68	90	0.44	90	0.44	90	0.44	40	1
select_gvg	no	yes	40	40	1	59	0.68	90	0.44	90	0.44	90	0.44	40	1
selectsort_gv	yes	yes	79	79	1	151	0.52	230	0.34	179	0.44	180	0.44	41	1.93
selectsort_ga_ok	yes	no	81	81	1	160	0.51	210	0.39	159	0.51	159	0.51	49	1.65
selectsort_ga_ko	yes	no	79	79	1	160	0.49	220	0.36	150	0.53	159	0.5	49	1.61
substlist_gggv	yes	yes	550	551	1	951	0.58	1039	0.53	280	1.96	230	2.39	110	5
substlist_ggga_ok	yes	no	150	150	1	270	0.56	299	0.5	281	0.53	231	0.65	110	1.36
substlist_ggga_ko	yes	no	160	160	1	280	0.57	311	0.51	59	2.71	49	3.27	51	3.14
substlist_ggvg_ok	no	no	100	100	1	181	0.55	250	0.4	210	0.48	210	0.48	80	1.25
substlist_ggvg_ko	no	no	269	269	1	520	0.52	730	0.37	71	3.79	71	3.79	51	5.27
substree_gggv	yes	yes	250	250	1	461	0.54	510	0.49	250	1	230	1.09	110	2.27
substree_ggga_ok	yes	no	150	150	1	290	0.52	319	0.47	250	0.6	220	0.68	120	1.25
substree_ggga_ko	yes	no	150	151	0.99	290	0.52	321	0.47	59	2.54	59	2.54	51	2.94
substree_ggvg_ok	no	no	230	230	1	500	0.46	760	0.3	701	0.33	701	0.33	201	1.14
substree_ggvg_ko	no	no	160	160	1	300	0.53	460	0.35	80	2	80	2	50	3.2
suffix_vg	no	yes	30	30	1	41	0.73	49	0.61	49	0.61	49	0.61	30	1
suffix_gg_ok	yes	no	20	20	1	30	0.67	30	0.67	20	1	20	1	10	2
suffix_gg_ko	yes	no	20	20	1	20	1	20	1	30	0.67	30	0.67	10	2
sumtree_gv	yes	yes	49	49	1	90	0.54	90	0.54	80	0.61	80	0.61	49	1
sumtree_gi_ok	yes	no	51	51	1	90	0.57	90	0.57	90	0.57	90	0.57	49	1.04
sumtree_gi_ko	yes	no	51	51	1	91	0.56	91	0.56	81	0.63	81	0.63	49	1.04

Input No Index	det	ss	User T	Reorder T	Reorder Sdup	SynNorm T	SynNorm Sdup	SemNorm T	SemNorm Sdup	Cut T	Cut Sdup	RmCut T	RmCut Sdup	Denorm T	Denorm Sdup
transpose_gv	yes	no	50	40	1.25	89	0.56	61	0.82	60	0.83	60	0.83	20	2.5
transpose_gg_ok	yes	no	80	80	1	201	0.4	210	0.38	200	0.4	200	0.4	69	1.16
transpose_gg_ko	yes	no	40	40	1	60	0.67	60	0.67	60	0.67	60	0.67	30	1.33
treememb_vg	no	yes	30	30	1	80	0.38	90	0.33	90	0.33	90	0.33	30	1
treememb_ag_ok	no	no	30	30	1	71	0.42	80	0.38	80	0.38	80	0.38	30	1
treememb_ag_ko	no	no	30	30	1	71	0.42	80	0.38	80	0.38	80	0.38	30	1
union_ggv	no	no	69	69	1	130	0.53	140	0.49	140	0.49	140	0.49	61	1.13
union_gga_ok	no	no	61	61	1	119	0.51	130	0.47	130	0.47	130	0.47	59	1.03
union_gga_ko	no	no	61	61	1	120	0.51	130	0.47	130	0.47	130	0.47	59	1.03
intersect_ggv	no	no	71	71	1	130	0.55	140	0.51	140	0.51	140	0.51	61	1.16
intersect_gga_ok	no	no	51	51	1	91	0.56	100	0.51	100	0.51	100	0.51	51	1
intersect_gga_ko	no	no	90	90	1	160	0.56	180	0.5	171	0.53	170	0.53	90	1
difference_ggv	no	no	69	69	1	130	0.53	140	0.49	140	0.49	140	0.49	69	1
difference_gga_ok	no	no	59	59	1	120	0.49	130	0.45	130	0.45	130	0.45	61	0.97
difference_gga_ko	no	no	59	59	1	109	0.54	120	0.49	110	0.54	120	0.49	60	0.98
union2_ggv	yes	yes	20	19	1.05	41	0.49	70	0.29	59	0.34	49	0.41	20	1
union2_gga_ok	yes	no	20	20	1	49	0.41	69	0.29	49	0.41	49	0.41	20	1
union2_gga_ko	yes	no	10	10	1	30	0.33	50	0.2	31	0.32	31	0.32	10	1
intersect2_ggv	yes	yes	19	20	0.95	40	0.48	59	0.32	40	0.48	41	0.46	10	1.9
intersect2_gga_ok	yes	no	19	20	0.95	40	0.48	61	0.31	49	0.39	40	0.48	20	0.95
intersect2_gga_ko	yes	no	10	10	1	30	0.33	40	0.25	31	0.32	30	0.33	10	1
difference2_ggv	yes	yes	20	19	1.05	40	0.5	61	0.33	49	0.41	49	0.41	10	2
difference2_gga_ok	yes	no	20	20	1	40	0.5	49	0.41	51	0.39	51	0.39	19	1.05
difference2_gga_ko	yes	no	71	71	1	140	0.51	191	0.37	150	0.47	150	0.47	61	1.16

Table H.3: Speedup of specialised programs generated by the optimiser when indexing is disabled.

Efficiency Tests (No Index ; all)		187/187	
Denorm w.r.t. **User**		**Input**	**Sdup**
	Mean	-	1.83
	Max	efface_ko_gag_100	36
	Min	sameleaves_gg_ok	0.91
Denorm w.r.t. **SynNorm**		**Input**	**Sdup**
	Mean	-	3.38
	Max	efface_ok_gv_1000	61
	Min	minimum_iiv2	1

Table H.4: Summary of the speedup for all procedures when indexing is disabled.

Efficiency Tests (No Index ; det)		140/187	
Denorm w.r.t. **User**		**Input**	**Sdup**
	Mean	-	1.68
	Max	efface_ok_gv_1000	31.9
	Min	sameleaves_gg_ok	0.91
Denorm w.r.t. **SynNorm**		**Input**	**Sdup**
	Mean	-	3.28
	Max	efface_ok_gv_1000	61
	Min	minimum_iiv2	1

Table H.5: Summary of the speedup for procedures that are deterministic when indexing is disabled.

Efficiency Tests (No Index ; ss)		54/187	
Denorm w.r.t. **User**		**Input**	**Sdup**
	Mean	-	1.5
	Max	close_l_10	8.06
	Min	union2_ggv	1
Denorm w.r.t. **SynNorm**		**Input**	**Sdup**
	Mean	-	2.79
	Max	substlist_gggv	8.65
	Min	minimum_iiv2	1

Table H.6: Summary of the speedup for procedures that surely succeed when indexing is disabled.

Efficiency Tests (No Index ; det+ss)		47/187	
Denorm w.r.t. **User**		**Input**	**Sdup**
	Mean	-	1.57
	Max	close_l_10	8.06
	Min	union2_ggv	1
Denorm w.r.t. **SynNorm**		**Input**	**Sdup**
	Mean	-	2.9
	Max	substlist_gggv	8.65
	Min	minimum_iiv2	1

Table H.7: Summary of the speedup for procedures that are deterministic and surely succeed when indexing is disabled.

Efficiency Tests (No Index ; ♯Not≥1)		55/187	
Denorm w.r.t. **User**		**Input**	**Sdup**
	Mean	-	3.09
	Max	efface_ko_gag_100	36
	Min	intersect2_gga_ok	0.95
Denorm w.r.t. **SynNorm**		**Input**	**Sdup**
	Mean	-	5.13
	Max	efface_ok_gv_1000	61
	Min	flattendl_gv	1.33

Table H.8: Summary of the speedup for procedures that contain negation when indexing is disabled.

Efficiency Tests (No Index ; ♯Arith≥1)		78/187	
Denorm w.r.t. **User**		**Input**	**Sdup**
	Mean	-	1.32
	Max	qs_ga_ko_100	2.5
	Min	intersect2_gga_ok	0.95
Denorm w.r.t. **SynNorm**		**Input**	**Sdup**
	Mean	-	2.57
	Max	mergesort_ga_ko_150	6
	Min	minimum_iiv2	1

Table H.9: Summary of the speedup for procedures that contain arithmetic comparison when indexing is disabled.

Input / Default Index	det	ss	User T	Reorder T	Reorder Sdup	SynNorm T	SynNorm Sdup	SemNorm T	SemNorm Sdup	Cut T	Cut Sdup	RmCut T	RmCut Sdup	Denorm T	Denorm Sdup
ack_iiv_3_4	yes	yes	149	149	1	241	0.62	280	0.53	250	0.6	250	0.6	129	1.16
ack_iia_3_4_ok	yes	no	149	150	0.99	240	0.62	280	0.53	259	0.58	250	0.6	129	1.16
ack_iia_3_4_ko	yes	no	149	150	0.99	241	0.62	281	0.53	260	0.57	250	0.6	130	1.15
append_ggv_1000	yes	yes	39	39	1	99	0.39	99	0.39	60	0.65	60	0.65	20	1.95
append_ggv_10000	yes	yes	159	159	1	490	0.32	490	0.32	500	0.32	500	0.32	139	1.14
append_ggv_20000	yes	yes	311	311	1	1020	0.3	1020	0.3	1020	0.3	1020	0.3	290	1.07
append_gga_1000_ok	yes	no	20	20	1	59	0.34	59	0.34	60	0.33	60	0.33	20	1
append_gga_10000_ok	yes	no	200	200	1	571	0.35	571	0.35	570	0.35	570	0.35	190	1.05
append_gga_20000_ok	yes	no	400	400	1	1159	0.35	1159	0.35	1161	0.34	1161	0.34	390	1.03
append_gga_1000_ko	yes	no	10	10	1	30	0.33	30	0.33	30	0.33	30	0.33	10	1
append_gga_10000_ko	yes	no	80	80	1	261	0.31	261	0.31	261	0.31	261	0.31	81	0.99
append_gga_20000_ko	yes	no	20	20	1	60	0.33	60	0.33	51	0.39	51	0.39	10	2
append_vvg_1000	no	yes	540	540	1	579	0.93	610	0.89	610	0.89	610	0.89	540	1
bubblesort_gv_100	yes	yes	240	240	1	480	0.5	650	0.37	520	0.46	511	0.47	170	1.41
bubblesort_gv_200	yes	yes	1051	1351	1	2000	0.53	2681	0.39	2410	0.44	2361	0.45	799	1.32
bubblesort_ga_ok_100	yes	yes	239	239	1	480	0.5	651	0.37	460	0.52	470	0.51	139	1.72
bubblesort_ga_ok_150	yes	yes	559	559	1	1120	0.5	1519	0.37	1199	0.47	1200	0.47	331	1.69
bubblesort_ga_ko_100	yes	yes	240	240	1	480	0.5	650	0.37	470	0.51	460	0.52	150	1.6
close_1_10	yes	yes	1289	359	0.95	1100	1.17	1090	1.18	940	1.37	201	6.41	159	8.11
close_v	yes	yes	231	231	1	190	1.22	190	1.22	190	1.22	180	1.28	161	1.43
close_a_ko	yes	no	120	121	0.99	120	1	120	1	120	1	100	1.2	50	2.4
compress_gv_10	no	no	19	19	1	39	0.49	40	0.48	41	0.46	41	0.46	20	0.95
compress_gv_15	no	no	290	290	1	591	0.49	700	0.41	670	0.43	670	0.43	270	1.07
compress2_vg_100	yes	no	80	80	1	150	0.53	159	0.5	141	0.57	141	0.57	70	1.14
compress2_vg_1000	yes	no	771	771	1	1540	0.5	1560	0.49	1450	0.53	1450	0.53	700	1.1
deriv_exprv	yes	yes	10	10	1	60	0.17	70	0.14	50	0.2	50	0.2	11	0.91
deriv_expra_ok	yes	no	40	40	1	209	0.19	221	0.18	149	0.27	149	0.27	60	0.67
deriv_expra_ko	yes	no	41	40	1.02	201	0.2	221	0.19	140	0.29	140	0.29	60	0.68

Input / Default Index	det	ss	User T	Reorder T	Reorder Sdup	SynNorm T	SynNorm Sdup	SemNorm T	SemNorm Sdup	Cut T	Cut Sdup	RmCut T	RmCut Sdup	Denorm T	Denorm Sdup
deriv_aexpr_ok	no	no	21	21	1	101	0.21	101	0.21	81	0.26	81	0.26	29	0.72
deriv_aexpr_ko	no	no	20	20	1	41	0.49	50	0.4	50	0.4	50	0.4	20	1
dutch_gv	yes	yes	20	19	1.05	50	0.4	70	0.29	60	0.33	60	0.33	10	2
dutch_gg_ok	yes	no	19	20	0.95	50	0.38	70	0.27	59	0.32	59	0.32	10	1.9
dutch_gg_ko	yes	no	50	50	1	159	0.31	230	0.22	180	0.28	180	0.28	41	1.22
distribute_gvvv	yes	yes	60	60	1	219	0.27	320	0.19	270	0.22	270	0.22	60	1
efface_ok_gv_100	yes	no	70	70	1	130	0.54	150	0.47	91	0.77	60	1.17	29	2.41
efface_ok_gv_1000	yes	no	670	671	1	1280	0.52	1480	0.45	880	0.76	610	1.1	219	3.06
efface_ko_ga_100	yes	no	40	40	1	111	0.36	130	0.31	89	0.45	60	0.67	21	1.9
efface_ko_ga_1000	yes	no	40	40	1	101	0.4	130	0.31	89	0.45	70	0.57	20	2
efface_ok_gv_100	yes	no	70	70	1	130	0.54	150	0.47	91	0.77	60	1.17	29	2.41
efface_ok_gv_1000	yes	no	670	671	1	1280	0.52	1480	0.45	880	0.76	610	1.1	20	33.5
efface_ok_gvg_100	no	no	1270	1270	1	1321	0.96	1400	0.91	139	9.14	139	9.14	70	18.14
efface_ko_gag_100	no	no	360	360	1	430	0.84	490	0.73	10	36	10	36	11	32.73
flatten_gv	yes	yes	11	19	0.58	30	0.37	30	0.37	30	0.37	30	0.37	10	1.1
flatten_ga_ok	yes	no	20	19	1.05	30	0.67	30	0.67	21	0.95	21	0.95	11	1.82
flatten_ga_ko	yes	no	20	21	0.95	29	0.69	30	0.67	30	0.67	30	0.67	11	1.82
flattendl_gv	yes	yes	60	60	1	90	0.67	100	0.6	80	0.75	80	0.75	60	1
flattendl_ga_ok	yes	no	60	60	1	90	0.67	100	0.6	89	0.67	89	0.67	60	1
flattendl_ga_ko	yes	no	60	50	1.2	90	0.67	99	0.61	80	0.75	80	0.75	50	1.2
flattree_gv	yes	yes	41	40	1.02	140	0.29	140	0.29	120	0.34	120	0.34	41	1
flattree_gg_ok	yes	no	41	41	1	140	0.29	140	0.29	120	0.34	120	0.34	40	1.02
flattree_gg_ko	yes	no	40	39	1.03	130	0.31	130	0.31	110	0.36	110	0.36	40	1
flattree2_vg	no	yes	19	19	1	50	0.38	59	0.32	50	0.38	50	0.38	20	0.95
flattree2_gg_ok	no	no	29	29	1	70	0.41	81	0.36	81	0.36	81	0.36	31	0.94
flattree2_gg_ko	no	no	20	20	1	41	0.49	50	0.4	51	0.39	51	0.39	20	1
hanoi_ggggv	yes	no	50	50	1	131	0.38	140	0.36	120	0.42	120	0.42	40	1.25

Input Default Index	det	ss	User T	Reorder T	Reorder Sdup	SynNorm T	SynNorm Sdup	SemNorm T	SemNorm Sdup	Cut T	Cut Sdup	RmCut T	RmCut Sdup	Denorm T	Denorm Sdup
heapify_gv	no	no	60	60		120	0.5	140	0.43	139	0.43	131	0.46	60	1
heapify_ga_ok	no	no	60	60	1	120	0.5	141	0.43	130	0.46	130	0.46	50	1.2
heapify_ga_ko	no	no	60	60	1	111	0.54	140	0.43	130	0.46	130	0.46	51	1.18
inorder_gv	yes	yes	20	20	1	60	0.33	60	0.33	51	0.39	51	0.39	20	1
inorder_ga_ok	yes	no	20	20	1	60	0.33	60	0.33	60	0.33	60	0.33	20	
inorder_ga_ko	yes	no	21	21	1	60	0.35	60	0.35	60	0.35	60	0.35	20	1.05
insertsort_gv	yes	yes	49	49		90	0.54	130	0.38	130	0.38	120	0.41	40	1.23
insertsort_ga_ok	yes	no	50	49	1.02	89	0.56	130	0.38	130	0.38	129	0.39	40	1.25
insertsort_ga_ko	yes	no	50	50	1	89	0.56	130	0.38	130	0.38	120	0.42	31	1.61
isotree_vg	no	yes	31	31	1	99	0.31	159	0.19	161	0.19	161	0.19	31	1
isotree_ag_ok	no	no	50	50	1	201	0.25	281	0.18	269	0.19	269	0.19	60	0.83
isotree_ag_ko	no	no	40	40	1	150	0.27	211	0.19	209	0.19	209	0.19	50	0.8
maxlist_gv	yes	yes	81	80	1.01	149	0.54	149	0.54	120	0.68	120	0.68	60	1.35
maxlist_ga_ok	yes	no	81	81	1	140	0.58	140	0.58	120	0.68	120	0.68	60	1.35
maxlist_ga_ko	yes	no	80	80	0.99	140	0.57	140	0.57	120	0.67	119	0.67	60	1.33
maximum_iiv	yes	yes	100	69	1.45	61	1.64	61	1.64	40	2.5	41	2.44	40	2.5
maximum_iiv2	yes	yes	40	40	1	40	1	40	1	40	1	39	1.03	40	1
maximum_iia_ok	no	no	40	40	1	29	1.38	29	1.38	40	1	40	1	40	1
maximum_iia_ok2	no	no	40	39	1.03	40	1	40	1	40	1	40	1	30	1.33
maximum_iia_ko	no	no	40	40	1	40	1	40	1	39	1.03	39	1.03	40	1
minimum_iiv	yes	yes	40	40	1	40	1	40	1	40	1	40	1	40	1
minimum_iiv2	yes	yes	40	40	1	40	1	40	1	40	1	40	1	39	1.03
minimum_iia_ok	yes	no	39	39	1	39	1	39	1	39	1	39	1	39	1
minimum_iia_ok2	yes	no	39	39	1	39	1	39	1	39	1	39	1	39	1
minimum_iia_ko	yes	no	41	39	1.05	39	1.05	39	1.05	40	1.02	40	1.02	31	1.32
maxseq_gv	yes	no	31	31	1	49	0.63	49	0.63	39	0.79	40	0.78	20	1.55
maxseq_ga_ok	yes	no	30	31	0.97	41	0.73	50	0.6	39	0.77	40	0.75	19	1.58

Input / Default Index	det	ss	User T	Reorder T	Reorder Sdup	SynNorm T	SynNorm Sdup	SemNorm T	SemNorm Sdup	Cut T	Cut Sdup	RmCut T	RmCut Sdup	Denorm T	Denorm Sdup
maxseq_ga_ko	yes	no	29	29	1	40	0.73	50	0.58	40	0.73	39	0.74	20	1.45
maxtree_gv	yes	yes	20	21	0.95	40	0.5	40	0.5	31	0.65	31	0.55	20	1
maxtree_ga_ok	yes	no	20	20	1	41	0.49	41	0.49	29	0.69	31	0.65	20	1
maxtree_ga_ko	yes	no	20	20	1	41	0.49	41	0.49	31	0.65	31	0.65	20	1
member_vg	no	no	120	120	1	121	0.99	109	1.1	109	1.1	109	1.1	120	1
member_gg_ok	no	no	21	21	1	50	0.42	60	0.35	60	0.35	60	0.35	21	1
member_gg_ko	no	no	20	20	1	51	0.39	60	0.33	60	0.33	60	0.33	20	1
nonmember_gg_ok	yes	no	51	51		80	0.64	80	0.64	80	0.64	80	0.64	50	1.02
nonmember_gg_ko	yes	no	30	29	1.03	40	0.75	40	0.75	40	0.75	40	0.75	29	1.03
mergesort_gv_100	yes	yes	9	10	0.9	31	0.29	40	0.23	31	0.29	31	0.29	10	0.9
mergesort_gv_200	yes	yes	21	20	1.05	60	0.35	80	0.26	69	0.3	70	0.3	20	1.05
mergesort_ga_ok_100	yes	no	11	11	1	39	0.28	51	0.22	40	0.28	39	0.28	10	1.1
mergesort_ga_ok_150	yes	no	21	21	1	60	0.35	80	0.26	61	0.34	60	0.35	20	1.05
mergesort_ga_ko_100	yes	no	10	10	1	40	0.25	50	0.2	41	0.24	40	0.25	10	1
mergesort_ga_ko_150	yes	no	20	20	1	60	0.33	81	0.25	70	0.29	60	0.33	19	1.05
merge_ggv_100	yes	yes	161	160	1.01	430	0.37	651	0.25	550	0.29	550	0.29	120	1.34
merge_ggv_1000	yes	yes	1599	1529	1.05	4230	0.38	6490	0.25	5451	0.29	5459	0.29	1210	1.32
merge_gga_ok_10	yes	no	29	29	1	80	0.36	119	0.24	81	0.36	81	0.36	20	1.45
merge_gga_ko	yes	no	29	20	1.45	80	0.36	119	0.24	81	0.36	81	0.36	20	1.45
mmult_ggv	yes	yes	71	79	0.9	161	0.44	240	0.3	229	0.31	219	0.32	70	1.01
nextcomb_iigv	yes	no	40	40	1	71	0.56	90	0.44	71	0.56	71	0.56	31	1.29
numocc_ggv	yes	yes	21	20	1.05	30	0.7	39	0.54	30	0.7	29	0.72	10	2.1
numocc_gga_ok	yes	no	20	20	1	31	0.65	39	0.51	30	0.67	30	0.67	10	2
numocc_gga_ko	yes	no	20	10	2	30	0.67	31	0.65	30	0.67	30	0.67	10	2
permutsort_gv	no	no	30	30	1	79	0.38	100	0.3	100	0.3	100	0.3	30	1
permutsort_ga_ok	no	no	50	50	1	130	0.38	151	0.33	150	0.33	150	0.33	50	1
permutsort_ga_ko	no	no	50	50	1	120	0.42	179	0.28	180	0.28	180	0.28	51	0.98

Input / Default Index	det	ss	User T	Reorder T	Reorder Sdup	SynNorm T	SynNorm Sdup	SemNorm T	SemNorm Sdup	Cut T	Cut Sdup	RmCut T	RmCut Sdup	Denorm T	Denorm Sdup
postorder_gv	yes	yes	30	30	1	91	0.33	91	0.33	80	0.38	80	0.38	30	1
postorder_ga_ok	yes	no	30	30	1	99	0.3	99	0.3	81	0.37	81	0.37	30	1
postorder_ga_ko	yes	no	30	30	1	91	0.33	91	0.33	80	0.38	80	0.38	30	1
prefix_vg	no	yes	39	39	1	59	0.66	81	0.48	81	0.48	81	0.48	39	1
prefix_gg_ok	yes	no	80	80	1	220	0.36	220	0.36	220	0.36	220	0.36	69	1.16
prefix_gg_ko	yes	no	51	51	1	120	0.43	120	0.43	120	0.43	120	0.43	49	1.04
preorder_gv	yes	yes	30	30	1	79	0.38	79	0.38	69	0.43	69	0.43	29	1.03
preorder_ga_ok	yes	no	30	30	1	80	0.38	80	0.38	69	0.43	69	0.43	20	1.5
preorder_ga_ko	yes	no	30	30	1	79	0.38	79	0.38	70	0.43	70	0.43	30	1
qs_gv_100	yes	yes	20	20	1	40	0.5	50	0.4	40	0.5	39	0.51	10	2
qs_gv_200	yes	yes	71	71	1	140	0.51	191	0.37	140	0.51	131	0.54	40	1.78
qs_ga_ok_100	yes	no	49	51	0.96	100	0.49	130	0.38	91	0.54	100	0.49	30	1.63
qs_ga_ok_150	yes	no	110	120	0.92	240	0.46	319	0.34	210	0.52	210	0.52	69	1.59
qs_ga_ko_100	yes	no	50	51	0.98	100	0.5	130	0.38	91	0.55	91	0.55	29	1.72
qs_ga_ko_150	yes	no	110	110	1	230	0.48	319	0.34	219	0.5	220	0.5	61	1.8
part_ggvv_100	yes	yes	49	50	0.98	100	0.49	130	0.38	109	0.45	101	0.49	39	1.26
part_ggvv_200	yes	yes	100	100	1	191	0.52	260	0.38	210	0.48	209	0.48	71	1.41
remove_red_gv	no	no	31	31	1	91	0.34	100	0.31	99	0.31	101	0.31	29	1.07
remove_red_ga_ok	no	no	29	29	1	70	0.41	89	0.33	80	0.36	80	0.36	31	0.94
remove_red_ga_ko	no	no	10	10	1	39	0.26	50	0.2	49	0.2	49	0.2	10	1
revnaive_gv	yes	yes	10	10	1	40	0.25	40	0.25	41	0.24	41	0.24	10	1
revnaive_ga_ok	yes	no	10	10	1	40	0.25	40	0.25	40	0.25	40	0.25	10	1
revnaive_ga_ko	yes	no	10	10	1	40	0.25	41	0.24	40	0.25	40	0.25	10	1
revacc_gv	yes	yes	30	30	1	89	0.34	89	0.34	81	0.37	81	0.37	20	1.5
revacc_ga_ok	yes	no	30	30	1	90	0.33	90	0.33	90	0.33	90	0.33	30	1
revacc_ga_ko	yes	no	30	30	1	90	0.33	90	0.33	90	0.33	90	0.33	29	1.03
revdl_gv	yes	yes	20	20	1	90	0.22	90	0.22	89	0.22	89	0.22	20	1

Input / Default Index	det	ss	User T	Reorder T	Reorder Sdup	SynNorm T	SynNorm Sdup	SemNorm T	SemNorm Sdup	Cut T	Cut Sdup	RmCut T	RmCut Sdup	Denorm T	Denorm Sdup
revdl_ga_ok	yes	no	30	30	1	91	0.33	91	0.33	90	0.33	90	0.33	30	1
revdl_ga_ko	yes	no	30	30	1	90	0.33	90	0.33	89	0.34	89	0.34	30	1
sameleaves_gg_ok	yes	no	71	71	1	190	0.37	201	0.35	179	0.4	179	0.4	89	0.8
sameleaves_gg_ko	yes	no	40	40	1	71	0.56	79	0.51	69	0.58	69	0.58	40	1
select_ggg_ok	no	no	10	10	1	30	0.33	39	0.26	39	0.26	39	0.26	10	1
select_ggg_ko	no	no	20	20	1	49	0.41	69	0.29	69	0.29	69	0.29	20	1
select_vgv	no	no	39	39	1	61	0.64	90	0.43	90	0.43	90	0.43	39	1
select_gvg	no	yes	40	40	1	61	0.66	80	0.5	80	0.5	80	0.5	40	1
selectsort_gv	yes	yes	71	71	1	160	0.44	230	0.31	179	0.4	179	0.4	50	1.42
selectsort_ga_ok	yes	no	71	71	1	160	0.44	219	0.32	160	0.44	150	0.47	50	1.42
selectsort_ga_ko	yes	no	71	71	1	160	0.44	220	0.32	160	0.44	160	0.44	50	1.42
substlist_gggv	yes	yes	559	550	1.02	950	0.59	1049	0.53	280	2	230	2.43	110	5.08
substlist_ggga_ok	yes	no	150	150	1	270	0.56	309	0.49	289	0.52	240	0.63	110	1.36
substlist_ggga_ko	yes	no	160	159	1.01	270	0.59	311	0.51	61	2.62	59	2.71	49	3.27
substlist_ggvg_ok	no	no	100	100	1	181	0.55	250	0.4	210	0.48	210	0.48	80	1.25
substlist_ggvg_ko	no	no	270	270	1	520	0.52	731	0.37	70	3.86	70	3.86	51	5.29
substree_gggv	yes	yes	250	260	0.96	459	0.54	500	0.5	240	1.04	219	1.14	101	2.48
substree_ggga_ok	yes	no	141	140	1.01	280	0.5	311	0.45	250	0.56	219	0.64	120	1.18
substree_ggga_ko	yes	no	140	150	0.93	281	0.5	319	0.44	59	2.37	59	2.37	50	2.8
substree_ggvg_ok	no	no	220	220	1	480	0.46	740	0.3	701	0.31	701	0.31	199	1.11
substree_ggvg_ko	no	no	160	160	1	311	0.51	460	0.35	80	2	80	2	51	3.14
suffix_vg	no	yes	30	30	1	40	0.75	51	0.59	51	0.59	51	0.59	30	1
suffix_gg_ok	yes	no	20	20	1	30	0.67	30	0.67	19	1.05	19	1.05	10	2
suffix_gg_ko	yes	no	19	19	1	30	0.63	30	0.63	30	0.63	30	0.63	19	1
sumtree_gv	yes	yes	40	40	1	90	0.44	90	0.44	81	0.49	81	0.49	40	1
sumtree_gi_ok	yes	no	40	40	1	90	0.44	90	0.44	80	0.5	80	0.5	40	1
sumtree_gi_ko	yes	no	41	41	1	90	0.46	90	0.46	81	0.51	81	0.51	41	1

Input / Default Index	det	ss	User T	Reorder T	Reorder Sdup	SynNorm T	SynNorm Sdup	SemNorm T	SemNorm Sdup	Cut T	Cut Sdup	RmCut T	RmCut Sdup	Denorm T	Denorm Sdup
transpose_gv	yes	no	40	40	1	90	0.44	60	0.67	59	0.68	59	0.68	11	3.64
transpose_gg_ok	yes	no	70	70	1	210	0.33	210	0.33	199	0.35	199	0.35	61	1.15
transpose_gg_ko	yes	no	40	40	1	59	0.68	59	0.68	59	0.68	59	0.68	40	1
treememb_vg	no	yes	30	30	1	80	0.38	89	0.34	89	0.34	89	0.34	30	1
treememb_ag_ok	no	no	29	29	1	71	0.41	80	0.36	80	0.36	80	0.36	29	1
treememb_ag_ko	no	no	30	30	1	70	0.43	80	0.38	80	0.38	80	0.38	30	1
union_ggv	no	no	71	71	1	130	0.55	140	0.51	140	0.51	140	0.51	61	1.16
union_gga_ok	no	no	59	59	1	120	0.49	130	0.45	130	0.45	131	0.45	60	0.98
union_gga_ko	no	no	59	59	1	120	0.49	130	0.45	130	0.45	130	0.45	61	0.97
intersect_ggv	no	no	69	69	1	130	0.53	140	0.49	140	0.49	141	0.49	61	1.13
intersect_gga_ok	no	no	51	51	1	90	0.57	110	0.46	101	0.5	100	0.51	51	1
intersect_gga_ko	no	no	90	90	1	160	0.56	180	0.5	179	0.5	179	0.5	90	1
difference_ggv	no	no	69	69	1	130	0.53	140	0.49	141	0.49	140	0.49	59	1.17
difference_gga_ok	no	no	59	59	1	110	0.54	130	0.45	130	0.45	130	0.45	61	0.97
difference_gga_ko	no	no	59	59	1	110	0.54	120	0.49	120	0.49	120	0.49	59	1
union2_ggv	yes	yes	20	20	1	49	0.41	71	0.28	61	0.33	50	0.4	10	2
union2_gga_ok	yes	no	20	19	1.05	49	0.41	69	0.29	49	0.41	49	0.41	20	1
union2_gga_ko	yes	no	10	11	0.91	30	0.33	49	0.2	39	0.26	39	0.26	10	1
intersect2_ggv	yes	yes	19	20	0.95	40	0.48	60	0.32	40	0.48	41	0.46	11	1.73
intersect2_gga_ok	yes	no	19	20	0.95	40	0.48	59	0.32	41	0.46	40	0.48	10	1.9
intersect2_gga_ko	yes	no	10	10	1	30	0.33	40	0.25	30	0.33	30	0.33	10	1
difference2_ggv	yes	yes	19	20	0.95	40	0.48	59	0.32	49	0.39	49	0.39	10	1.9
difference2_gga_ok	yes	no	10	19	0.53	40	0.25	61	0.16	40	0.25	40	0.25	10	1
difference2_gga_ko	yes	no	69	70	0.99	140	0.49	191	0.36	159	0.43	159	0.43	59	1.17

Table H.10 Speedup of specialised programs generated by the optimiser when indexing is enabled. By default, indexing is enabled on first argument position in SWI-Prolog.

Efficiency Tests (Default Index ; all)		187/187	
Denorm w.r.t. **User**		**Input**	**Sdup**
	Mean	-	1.8
	Max	efface_ok_gv_1000	33.5
	Min	deriv_expra_ok	0.67
Denorm w.r.t. **SynNorm**		**Input**	**Sdup**
	Mean	-	3.57
	Max	efface_ok_gv_1000	64
	Min	maximum_iia_ok	0.73

Table H.11: Summary of the speedup for all procedures when indexing is enabled.

Efficiency Tests (Default Index ; det)		140/187	
Denorm w.r.t. **User**		**Input**	**Sdup**
	Mean	-	1.67
	Max	efface_ok_gv_1000	33.5
	Min	deriv_expra_ok	0.67
Denorm w.r.t. **SynNorm**		**Input**	**Sdup**
	Mean	-	3.54
	Max	efface_ok_gv_1000	64
	Min	maximum_iia_ok	0.73

Table H.12: Summary of the speedup for procedures that are deterministic when indexing is enabled.

Efficiency Tests (Default Index ; ss)		54/187	
Denorm w.r.t. **User**		**Input**	**Sdup**
	Mean	-	1.52
	Max	close_l_10	8.11
	Min	mergesort_gv_100	0.9
Denorm w.r.t. **SynNorm**		**Input**	**Sdup**
	Mean	-	3.12
	Max	substlist_gggv	8.64
	Min	minimum_iiv	1

Table H.13: Summary of the speedup for procedures that surely succeed when indexing is enabled.

Efficiency Tests (Default Index ; det+ss)		47/187	
		Input	**Sdup**
Denorm w.r.t. **User**	Mean	-	1.6
	Max	close_1_10	8.11
	Min	mergesort_gv_100	0.9
		Input	**Sdup**
Denorm w.r.t. **SynNorm**	Mean	-	3.29
	Max	substlist_gggv	8.64
	Min	minimum_iiv	1

Table H.14: Summary of the speedup for procedures that are deterministic and surely succeed when indexing is enabled.

Efficiency Tests (Default Index ; ♯Not≥1)		55/187	
		Input	**Sdup**
Denorm w.r.t. **User**	Mean	-	3.11
	Max	efface_ok_gv_1000	33.5
	Min	remove_red_ga_ok	0.94
		Input	**Sdup**
Denorm w.r.t. **SynNorm**	Mean	-	5.3
	Max	efface_ok_gv_1000	64
	Min	nonmember_gg_ko	1.38

Table H.15: Summary of the speedup for procedures that contain negation when indexing is enabled.

Efficiency Tests (Default Index ; ♯Arith≥1)		78/187	
		Input	**Sdup**
Denorm w.r.t. **User**	Mean	-	1.32
	Max	maximum_iiv	2.5
	Min	mergesort_gv_100	0.9
		Input	**Sdup**
Denorm w.r.t. **SynNorm**	Mean	-	2.63
	Max	union2_ggv	4.9
	Min	maximum_iia_ok	0.73

Table H.16: Summary of the speedup for procedures that contain arithmetic comparison when indexing is enabled.

Table H.17 compares the speedup of the specialised code (**Denorm**) with respect to the original code (**User**) for the 187 efficiency tests, when indexing is enabled on the first argument position (**Default Index**), and when indexing is disabled (**No Index**). The following tables summarise the indexing comparison results, by considering all the 187 efficiency tests (Table H.18), only the efficiency tests for the deterministic procedures (Table H.19), only the efficiency tests for the procedures that surely succeed (Table H.20), only the efficiency tests for the deterministic procedures that surely succeed (Table H.21), only the efficiency tests for the procedures that contain negation (Table H.22), and only the efficiency tests for the procedures that contain arithmetic comparison (Table H.23).

Input	det	ss	Default Index			No Index		
			User	Denorm		User	Denorm	
			T	T	Sdup	T	T	Sdup
ack_iiv_3_4	yes	yes	149	129	1.16	150	130	1.15
ack_iia_3_4_ok	yes	no	149	129	1.16	149	130	1.15
ack_iia_3_4_ko	yes	no	149	130	1.15	150	131	1.15
append_ggv_1000	yes	yes	39	20	1.95	29	20	1.45
append_ggv_10000	yes	yes	159	139	1.14	219	180	1.22
append_ggv_20000	yes	yes	311	290	1.07	621	359	1.73
append_gga_1000_ok	yes	no	20	20	1	20	20	1
append_gga_10000_ok	yes	no	200	190	1.05	270	220	1.23
append_gga_20000_ok	yes	no	400	390	1.03	690	440	1.57
append_gga_1000_ko	yes	no	10	10	1	10	10	1
append_gga_10000_ko	yes	no	80	81	0.99	91	89	1.02
append_gga_20000_ko	yes	no	20	10	2	21	11	1.91
append_vvg_1000	no	yes	540	540	1	530	530	1
bubblesort_gv_100	yes	yes	240	170	1.41	240	171	1.4
bubblesort_gv_200	yes	yes	1051	799	1.32	1060	789	1.34
bubblesort_ga_ok_100	yes	yes	239	139	1.72	240	150	1.6
bubblesort_ga_ok_150	yes	yes	559	331	1.69	570	340	1.68
bubblesort_ga_ko_100	yes	yes	240	150	1.6	239	150	1.59
close_l_10	yes	yes	1289	159	8.11	1290	160	8.06
close_v	yes	yes	231	161	1.43	231	161	1.43
close_a_ko	yes	no	120	50	2.4	120	60	2
compress_gv_10	no	no	19	20	0.95	20	19	1.05
compress_gv_15	no	no	290	270	1.07	289	269	1.07
compress2_vg_100	yes	no	80	70	1.14	80	70	1.14
compress2_vg_1000	yes	no	771	700	1.1	860	730	1.18
deriv_exprv	yes	yes	10	11	0.91	21	19	1.11
deriv_expra_ok	yes	no	40	60	0.67	80	70	1.14
deriv_expra_ko	yes	no	41	60	0.68	80	70	1.14
deriv_aexpr_ok	no	no	21	29	0.72	39	31	1.26
deriv_aexpr_ko	no	no	20	20	1	20	20	1
dutch_gv	yes	yes	20	10	2	20	19	1.05
dutch_gg_ok	yes	no	19	10	1.9	19	20	0.95
dutch_gg_ko	yes	no	50	41	1.22	60	50	1.2
distribute_gvvv	yes	yes	60	60	1	60	60	1

Input	det	ss	Default Index			No Index		
			User	Denorm		User	Denorm	
			T	T	Sdup	T	T	Sdup
efface_ok_gv_100	yes	no	70	29	2.41	70	30	2.33
efface_ok_gv_1000	yes	no	670	219	3.06	670	221	3.03
efface_ko_ga_100	yes	no	40	21	1.9	40	20	2
efface_ko_ga_1000	yes	no	40	20	2	29	20	1.45
efface_ok_gv_100	yes	no	70	29	2.41	70	29	2.41
efface_ok_gv_1000	yes	no	670	20	33.5	670	21	31.9
efface_ok_gvg_100	no	no	1270	70	18.14	1260	70	18
efface_ko_gag_100	no	no	360	11	32.73	360	10	36
flatten_gv	yes	yes	11	10	1.1	20	10	2
flatten_ga_ok	yes	no	20	11	1.82	19	11	1.73
flatten_ga_ko	yes	no	20	11	1.82	20	19	1.05
flattendl_gv	yes	yes	60	60	1	60	60	1
flattendl_ga_ok	yes	no	60	60	1	60	50	1.2
flattendl_ga_ko	yes	no	60	50	1.2	60	51	1.18
flattree_gv	yes	yes	41	41	1	51	50	1.02
flattree_gg_ok	yes	no	41	40	1.02	50	50	1
flattree_gg_ko	yes	no	40	40	1	50	49	1.02
flattree2_vg	no	yes	19	20	0.95	20	19	1.05
flattree2_gg_ok	no	no	29	31	0.94	29	30	0.97
flattree2_gg_ko	no	no	20	20	1	20	20	1
hanoi_ggggv	yes	no	50	40	1.25	50	41	1.22
heapify_gv	no	no	60	60	1	60	60	1
heapify_ga_ok	no	no	60	50	1.2	60	50	1.2
heapify_ga_ko	no	no	60	51	1.18	60	50	1.2
inorder_gv	yes	yes	20	20	1	29	21	1.38
inorder_ga_ok	yes	no	20	20	1	29	20	1.45
inorder_ga_ko	yes	no	21	20	1.05	29	20	1.45
insertsort_gv	yes	yes	49	40	1.23	49	41	1.2
insertsort_ga_ok	yes	no	50	40	1.25	49	40	1.23
insertsort_ga_ko	yes	no	50	31	1.61	50	40	1.25
isotree_vg	no	yes	31	31	1	31	31	1
isotree_ag_ok	no	no	50	60	0.83	69	70	0.99
isotree_ag_ko	no	no	40	50	0.8	50	50	1
maxlist_gv	yes	yes	81	60	1.35	91	70	1.3
maxlist_ga_ok	yes	no	81	60	1.35	90	70	1.29
maxlist_ga_ko	yes	no	80	60	1.33	91	70	1.3
maximum_iiv	yes	yes	100	40	2.5	41	39	1.05
maximum_iiv2	yes	yes	40	40	1	40	40	1
maximum_iia_ok	yes	no	40	40	1	40	39	1.03
maximum_iia_ok2	yes	no	40	30	1.33	40	40	1
maximum_iia_ko	yes	no	40	40	1	40	40	1
minimum_iiv	yes	yes	40	40	1	40	40	1
minimum_iiv2	yes	yes	40	39	1.03	40	40	1
minimum_iia_ok	yes	no	39	39	1	40	39	1.03
minimum_iia_ok2	yes	no	39	39	1	39	39	1
minimum_iia_ko	yes	no	41	31	1.32	39	31	1.26

Input	det	ss	Default Index			No Index		
			User	Denorm		User	Denorm	
			T	T	Sdup	T	T	Sdup
maxseq_gv	yes	no	31	20	1.55	31	20	1.55
maxseq_ga_ok	yes	no	30	19	1.58	31	20	1.55
maxseq_ga_ko	yes	no	29	20	1.45	29	21	1.38
maxtree_gv	yes	yes	20	20	1	21	20	1.05
maxtree_ga_ok	yes	no	20	20	1	21	20	1.05
maxtree_ga_ko	yes	no	20	20	1	21	20	1.05
member_vg	no	no	120	120	1	61	61	1
member_gg_ok	no	no	21	21	1	20	20	1
member_gg_ko	no	no	20	20	1	20	20	1
nonmember_gg_ok	yes	no	51	50	1.02	51	50	1.02
nonmember_gg_ko	yes	no	30	29	1.03	29	29	1
mergesort_gv_100	yes	yes	9	10	0.9	10	10	1
mergesort_gv_200	yes	yes	21	20	1.05	31	20	1.55
mergesort_ga_ok_100	yes	no	11	10	1.1	10	10	1
mergesort_ga_ok_150	yes	no	21	20	1.05	20	20	1
mergesort_ga_ko_100	yes	no	10	10	1	19	10	1.9
mergesort_ga_ko_150	yes	no	20	19	1.05	21	10	2.1
merge_ggv_100	yes	yes	161	120	1.34	170	130	1.31
merge_ggv_1000	yes	yes	1599	1210	1.32	1630	1271	1.28
merge_gga_ok_10	yes	no	29	20	1.45	29	20	1.45
merge_gga_ko	yes	no	29	20	1.45	29	20	1.45
mmult_ggv	yes	yes	71	70	1.01	71	70	1.01
nextcomb_iigv	yes	no	40	31	1.29	40	31	1.29
numocc_ggv	yes	yes	21	10	2.1	20	10	2
numocc_gga_ok	yes	no	20	10	2	20	10	2
numocc_gga_ko	yes	no	20	10	2	20	10	2
permutsort_gv	no	no	30	30	1	30	30	1
permutsort_ga_ok	no	no	50	50	1	49	49	1
permutsort_ga_ko	no	no	50	51	0.98	51	51	1
postorder_gv	yes	yes	30	30	1	39	31	1.26
postorder_ga_ok	yes	no	30	30	1	39	30	1.3
postorder_ga_ko	yes	no	30	30	1	39	30	1.3
prefix_vg	no	yes	39	39	1	31	31	1
prefix_gg_ok	yes	no	80	69	1.16	90	90	1
prefix_gg_ko	yes	no	51	49	1.04	51	50	1.02
preorder_gv	yes	yes	30	29	1.03	31	30	1.03
preorder_ga_ok	yes	no	30	20	1.5	30	30	1
preorder_ga_ko	yes	no	30	30	1	31	20	1.55
qs_gv_100	yes	yes	20	10	2	20	10	2
qs_gv_200	yes	yes	71	40	1.78	71	40	1.78
qs_ga_ok_100	yes	no	49	30	1.63	49	30	1.63
qs_ga_ok_150	yes	no	110	69	1.59	110	70	1.57
qs_ga_ko_100	yes	no	50	29	1.72	50	20	2.5
qs_ga_ko_150	yes	no	110	61	1.8	110	61	1.8
part_ggvv_100	yes	yes	49	39	1.26	51	40	1.27
part_ggvv_200	yes	yes	100	71	1.41	100	69	1.45

Input	det	ss	Default Index			No Index		
			User	Denorm		User	Denorm	
			T	T	Sdup	T	T	Sdup
remove_red_gv	no	no	31	29	1.07	40	40	1
remove_red_ga_ok	no	no	29	31	0.94	30	31	0.97
remove_red_ga_ko	no	no	10	10	1	20	19	1.05
revnaive_gv	yes	yes	10	10	1	20	20	1
revnaive_ga_ok	yes	no	10	10	1	20	10	2
revnaive_ga_ko	yes	no	10	10	1	20	10	2
revacc_gv	yes	yes	30	20	1.5	31	30	1.03
revacc_ga_ok	yes	no	30	30	1	39	30	1.3
revacc_ga_ko	yes	no	30	29	1.03	39	31	1.26
revdl_gv	yes	yes	20	20	1	30	30	1
revdl_ga_ok	yes	no	30	30	1	30	31	0.97
revdl_ga_ko	yes	no	30	30	1	30	31	0.97
sameleaves_gg_ok	yes	no	71	89	0.8	90	99	0.91
sameleaves_gg_ko	yes	no	40	40	1	41	40	1.02
select_ggg_ok	no	no	10	10	1	10	10	1
select_ggg_ko	no	no	20	20	1	20	20	1
select_vgv	no	no	39	39	1	40	40	1
select_gvg	no	yes	40	40	1	40	40	1
selectsort_gv	yes	yes	71	50	1.42	79	41	1.93
selectsort_ga_ok	yes	no	71	50	1.42	81	49	1.65
selectsort_ga_ko	yes	no	71	50	1.42	79	49	1.61
substlist_gggv	yes	yes	559	110	5.08	550	110	5
substlist_ggga_ok	yes	no	150	110	1.36	150	110	1.36
substlist_ggga_ko	yes	no	160	49	3.27	160	51	3.14
substlist_ggvg_ok	no	no	100	80	1.25	100	80	1.25
substlist_ggvg_ko	no	no	270	51	5.29	269	51	5.27
substree_gggv	yes	yes	250	101	2.48	250	110	2.27
substree_ggga_ok	yes	no	141	120	1.18	150	120	1.25
substree_ggga_ko	yes	no	140	50	2.8	150	51	2.94
substree_ggvg_ok	no	no	220	199	1.11	230	201	1.14
substree_ggvg_ko	no	no	160	51	3.14	160	50	3.2
suffix_vg	no	yes	30	30	1	30	30	1
suffix_gg_ok	yes	no	20	10	2	20	10	2
suffix_gg_ko	yes	no	19	19	1	20	10	2
sumtree_gv	yes	yes	40	40	1	49	49	1
sumtree_gi_ok	yes	no	40	40	1	51	49	1.04
sumtree_gi_ko	yes	no	41	41	1	51	49	1.04
transpose_gv	yes	no	40	11	3.64	50	20	2.5
transpose_gg_ok	yes	no	70	61	1.15	80	69	1.16
transpose_gg_ko	yes	no	40	40	1	40	30	1.33
treememb_vg	no	yes	30	30	1	30	30	1
treememb_ag_ok	no	no	29	29	1	30	30	1
treememb_ag_ko	no	no	30	30	1	30	30	1
union_ggv	no	no	71	61	1.16	69	61	1.13
union_gga_ok	no	no	59	60	0.98	61	59	1.03
union_gga_ko	no	no	59	61	0.97	61	59	1.03

Input	det	ss	Default Index			No Index		
			User	**Denorm**		**User**	**Denorm**	
			T	**T**	**Sdup**	**T**	**T**	**Sdup**
intersect_ggv	no	no	69	61	1.13	71	61	1.16
intersect_gga_ok	no	no	51	51	1	51	51	1
intersect_gga_ko	no	no	90	90	1	90	90	1
difference_ggv	no	no	69	59	1.17	69	69	1
difference_gga_ok	no	no	59	61	0.97	59	61	0.97
difference_gga_ko	no	no	59	59	1	59	60	0.98
union2_ggv	yes	yes	20	10	2	20	20	1
union2_gga_ok	yes	no	20	20	1	20	20	1
union2_gga_ko	yes	no	10	10	1	10	10	1
intersect2_ggv	yes	yes	19	11	1.73	19	10	1.9
intersect2_gga_ok	yes	no	19	10	1.9	19	20	0.95
intersect2_gga_ko	yes	no	10	10	1	10	10	1
difference2_ggv	yes	yes	19	10	1.9	20	10	2
difference2_gga_ok	yes	no	10	10	1	20	19	1.05
difference2_gga_ko	yes	no	69	59	1.17	71	61	1.16

Table H.17: Speedup comparison of specialised programs generated by the optimiser when indexing is enabled (**Default Index**) or disabled (**No Index**). Time execution (**T**) is expressed in milliseconds. Speedup (**Sdup**) is the ratio between the execution time spent for the source program (**User**) and the specialised program (**Denorm**).

Efficiency Tests (all)		187/187	
		Input	**Sdup**
Denorm w.r.t. **User (Default Index)**	Mean	-	1.8
	Max	efface_ok_gv_1000	33.5
	Min	deriv_expra_ok	0.67
		Input	**Sdup**
Denorm w.r.t. **User (No Index)**	Mean	-	1.83
	Max	efface_ko_gag_100	36
	Min	sameleaves_gg_ok	0.91

Table H.18: Summary of the speedup for all procedures (comparison when indexing is enabled and when indexing is disabled).

Efficiency Tests (det)		140/187	
		Input	**Sdup**
Denorm w.r.t. User (Default Index)	Mean	-	1.67
	Max	efface_ok_gv_1000	33.5
	Min	deriv_expra_ok	0.67
		Input	**Sdup**
Denorm w.r.t. User (No Index)	Mean	-	1.68
	Max	efface_ok_gv_1000	31.9
	Min	sameleaves_gg_ok	0.91

Table H.19: Summary of the speedup for procedures that are deterministic (comparison when indexing is enabled and when indexing is disabled).

Efficiency Tests (ss)		54/187	
		Input	**Sdup**
Denorm w.r.t. User (Default Index)	Mean	-	1.52
	Max	close_l_10	8.11
	Min	mergesort_gv_100	0.9
		Input	**Sdup**
Denorm w.r.t. User (No Index)	Mean	-	1.5
	Max	close_l_10	8.06
	Min	union2_ggv	1

Table H.20: Summary of the speedup for procedures that surely succeed (comparison when indexing is enabled and when indexing is disabled).

Efficiency Tests (det+ss)		47/187	
		Input	**Sdup**
Denorm w.r.t. User (Default Index)	Mean	-	1.6
	Max	close_l_10	8.11
	Min	mergesort_gv_100	0.9
		Input	**Sdup**
Denorm w.r.t. User (No Index)	Mean	-	1.57
	Max	close_l_10	8.06
	Min	union2_ggv	1

Table H.21: Summary of the speedup for procedures that are deterministic and surely succeed (comparison when indexing is enabled and when indexing is disabled).

Efficiency Tests ($\sharp$Not$\geq$1)		55/187	
		Input	**Sdup**
Denorm w.r.t. **User (Default Index)**	Mean	-	3.11
	Max	efface_ok_gv_1000	33.5
	Min	remove_red_ga_ok	0.94
		Input	**Sdup**
Denorm w.r.t. **User (No Index)**	Mean	-	3.09
	Max	efface_ko_gag_100	36
	Min	intersect2_gga_ok	0.95

Table H.22: Summary of the speedup for procedures that contain negation (comparison when indexing is enabled and when indexing is disabled).

Efficiency Tests ($\sharp$Arith$\geq$1)		78/187	
		Input	**Sdup**
Denorm w.r.t. **User (Default Index)**	Mean	-	1.32
	Max	maximum_iiv	2.5
	Min	mergesort_gv_100	0.9
		Input	**Sdup**
Denorm w.r.t. **User (No Index)**	Mean	-	1.32
	Max	qs_ga_ko_100	2.5
	Min	intersect2_gga_ok	0.95

Table H.23: Summary of the speedup for procedures that contain arithmetic comparison (comparison when indexing is enabled and when indexing is disabled).

H.3 Local stack utilisation

Table H.24 compares the local stack utilisation of the source and specialised code of 57 procedures. The size to which the local stack is allowed to grow is 2048000 B. The efficiency tests have been performed when indexing was enabled on the first argument position (**Default Indexing**) and when indexing was disabled (**No Indexing**).

When indexing is enabled. The maximal amount of local stack used during the execution of the generated code is either reduced (for 33 procedures), or identical (for 11 procedures), or slightly increased (for 13 procedures) w.r.t. the maximal amount of local stack used during the execution of the source code. Furthermore, 17 specialised procedures use a constant amount of local stack (this is the case for only 9 original procedures).

When indexing is disabled. The maximal amount of local stack used during the execution of the generated code is either reduced (for 46 procedures), or identical (for 9 procedures), or slightly increased (for 2 procedures) w.r.t. the maximal amount of local stack used during the execution of the source code. Furthermore, 17 specialised procedures use a constant amount of local stack (this is the case for only 4 original procedures).

The following symbols are used in Table H.17:

Symbol	Description
Program	Name of the program +
	Short description of the input (v:var; g:ground; a:any; i:int; l:list)
Input	Short description on the size of the input (e.g., list-length, tree-depth)
No Index	Indexing is disabled
Default Index	Indexing is enabled (in SWI-Prolog, indexing is enabled on first argument position by default)
det	The procedure is deterministic (*yes* or *no*)
ss	The procedure surely succeeds (*yes* or *no*)
User	Amount of local stack used by the original user version (in Bytes)
Denorm	Amount of local stack used by the specialised version (in Bytes)
ERROR	Local stack overflow during the execution

Program	Input	det	ss	Default Indexing Used Local Stack		No Indexing Used Local Stack	
				User (B)	Denorm (B)	User (B)	Denorm (B)
ack(i,i,v)	2-3	yes	yes	2992	572	2992	572
ack(i,i,v)	3-3	yes	yes	156448	3484	156448	3484
ack(i,i,v)	3-6	yes	yes	ERROR	28572	ERROR	28572
append(g,g,v)	10000	yes	yes	108	152	840108	180
append(g,g,v)	20000	yes	yes	108	152	1680108	180
append(g,g,v)	100000	yes	yes	108	152	ERROR	180
bubblesort(g,v)	10	yes	yes	4668	1036	4948	1036
bubblesort(g,v)	100	yes	yes	441708	8956	444508	8956
bubblesort(g,v)	1000	yes	yes	ERROR	88156	ERROR	88156
bubble(g,g,v,v)	100	yes	yes	8908	272	8908	272
bubble(g,g,v,v)	1000	yes	yes	88108	272	88108	272
bubble(g,g,v,v)	10000	yes	yes	880108	272	880108	272
bubble(g,g,v,v)	100000	yes	yes	ERROR	272	ERROR	272
close(a)	10000	yes	no	172	172	172	172
close(a)	100000	yes	no	172	172	172	172
compress(g,v)	10	no	no	1716	1336	1800	1336
compress(g,v)	100	no	no	16236	10500	17020	10500
compress(g,v)	1000	no	no	161556	102856	169200	102856
compress2(v,g)	100	yes	no	30348	6180	61260	6180
compress2(v,g)	1000	yes	no	301548	60180	609660	60180
compress2(v,g)	5000	yes	no	1506748	300180	ERROR	300180
compress2(v,g)	10000	yes	no	ERROR	600180	ERROR	600180
deriv(g,v)	10	yes	yes	668	708	148532	1016
deriv(g,v)	13	yes	yes	836	876	1187892	1268
deriv(g,v)	15	yes	yes	948	988	ERROR	1436
dutch(g,v)	1000	yes	yes	58860	58820	114964	58848
dutch(g,v)	10000	yes	yes	586860	586820	1146964	586848
dutch(g,v)	20000	yes	yes	1173556	1173516	ERROR	1173544
distribute(g,v,v,v)	1000	yes	yes	58804	58764	58880	58792
distribute(g,v,v,v)	10000	yes	yes	586804	586764	586880	586792
distribute(g,v,v,v)	20000	yes	yes	1173500	1173460	1173576	1173488
distribute(g,v,v,v)	25000	yes	yes	1466804	1466764	1466880	1466792
distribute(g,v,v,v)	50000	yes	yes	ERROR	ERROR	ERROR	ERROR
efface(g,g,v)	1000	yes	no	42024	184	42024	184
efface(g,g,v)	10000	yes	no	420024	184	420024	184
efface(g,g,v)	25000	yes	no	ERROR	184	ERROR	184
efface(g,g,a)	1000	yes	no	42024	184	42024	184
efface(g,g,a)	10000	yes	no	420024	184	420024	184
efface(g,g,a)	25000	yes	no	ERROR	184	ERROR	184
efface(g,v,g)	200	no	no	16908	8424	16908	8424
efface(g,v,g)	500	no	no	42108	21024	42108	21024
efface(g,v,g)	25000	no	no	ERROR	840024	ERROR	840024
flatten(g,v)	100	yes	yes	72176	6176	191776	6204
flatten(g,v)	1000	yes	yes	720176	56576	1916176	56604
flatten(g,v)	1200	yes	yes	864176	67776	ERROR	67804
flatten(g,v)	10000	yes	yes	ERROR	560576	ERROR	560604

Program	Input	det	ss	Default Indexing Used Local Stack		No Indexing Used Local Stack	
				User (B)	Denorm (B)	User (B)	Denorm (B)
flattendl(g,v)	10	yes	yes	7588	964	10616	964
flattendl(g,v)	100	yes	yes	73828	6004	104216	6004
flattendl(g,v)	1000	yes	yes	736228	56404	1040216	56404
flattendl(g,v)	2000	yes	yes	1472228	112404	ERROR	112404
flattendl(g,v)	10000	yes	yes	ERROR	560404	ERROR	560404
flattree(g,v)	5	yes	yes	428	468	8384	496
flattree(g,v)	10	yes	yes	748	788	479360	816
flattree(g,v)	11	yes	yes	812	852	1044608	880
flattree(g,v)	15	yes	yes	1068	1108	ERROR	1136
flattree2(v,g)	10	no	yes	5276	4596	5276	4596
flattree2(v,g)	100	no	yes	429176	422376	429176	422376
flattree2(v,g)	1000	no	yes	ERROR	ERROR	ERROR	ERROR
hanoi(g,g,g,g,v)	5	yes	no	1488	444	5604	444
hanoi(g,g,g,g,v)	10	yes	no	47120	764	391268	764
hanoi(g,g,g,g,v)	100	yes	no	ERROR	ERROR	ERROR	ERROR
heapify(g,a)	10	no	no	125068	764	184432	764
heapify(g,a)	11	no	no	249996	824	368752	824
heapify(g,a)	12	no	no	499852	884	737392	884
heapify(g,a)	13	no	no	999564	944	1474672	944
inorder(g,v)	5	yes	yes	408	448	6952	476
inorder(g,v)	10	yes	yes	708	748	434280	776
inorder(g,v)	11	yes	yes	768	808	954472	836
inorder(g,v)	12	yes	yes	828	868	ERROR	896
insertsort(g,v)	100	yes	yes	13248	5348	16100	5376
insertsort(g,v)	1000	yes	yes	132048	52148	160100	52176
insertsort(g,v)	10000	yes	yes	1320048	520148	1600100	520176
insertsort(g,v)	15000	yes	yes	1980048	780148	ERROR	780176
insertsort(g,v)	20000	yes	yes	ERROR	1040148	ERROR	1040176
isotree(v,g)	10	no	yes	90132	90132	90132	90132
isotree(v,g)	11	no	yes	180244	180244	180244	180244
isotree(v,g)	13	no	yes	720916	720916	720916	720916
maxlist(g,v)	1000	yes	yes	236	236	84096	236
maxlist(g,v)	2000	yes	yes	236	236	168096	236
maxlist(g,v)	20000	yes	yes	236	236	1680096	236
maxlist(g,v)	50000	yes	yes	236	236	ERROR	236
maxseq(g,v)	100	yes	no	16880	276	16960	276
maxseq(g,v)	1000	yes	no	168080	276	168160	276
maxseq(g,v)	10000	yes	no	1680080	276	1680160	276
maxseq(g,v)	20000	yes	no	ERROR	276	ERROR	276
maxtree(g,v)	11	yes	yes	278500	884	335816	884
maxtree(g,v)	12	yes	yes	557028	948	671688	948
maxtree(g,v)	13	yes	yes	1114084	1012	1343432	1012
maxtree(g,v)	14	yes	yes	ERROR	1076	ERROR	1076
member(a,g)	1000	no	no	72108	72108	72108	72108
member(a,g)	10000	no	no	720108	720108	720108	720108
member(a,g)	100000	no	no	ERROR	ERROR	ERROR	ERROR

Program	Input	det	ss	Default Indexing Used Local Stack		No Indexing Used Local Stack	
				User (B)	Denorm (B)	User (B)	Denorm (B)
nonmember(g,g)	1000	yes	no	76108	176	76108	176
nonmember(g,g)	10000	yes	no	760108	176	760108	176
nonmember(g,g)	100000	yes	no	ERROR	176	ERROR	176
mergesort(g,v)	100	yes	yes	45992	4668	107160	4696
mergesort(g,v)	1000	yes	yes	601848	46068	1510792	46096
mergesort(g,v)	2000	yes	yes	1295656	92068	ERROR	92096
mergesort(g,v)	10000	yes	yes	ERROR	460068	ERROR	460096
mergesort(g,v)	50000	yes	yes	ERROR	ERROR	ERROR	ERROR
merge(g,g,v)	1000	yes	yes	92108	92068	92188	92096
merge(g,g,v)	10000	yes	yes	920108	920068	920188	920096
merge(g,g,v)	20000	yes	yes	1840108	1840068	1840188	1840096
merge(g,g,v)	30000	yes	yes	ERROR	ERROR	ERROR	ERROR
mmult(g,g,v)	10*10	yes	yes	107468	1312	107748	1312
mmult(g,g,v)	50*50	yes	yes	ERROR	5312	ERROR	5312
mmult(g,g,v)	100*100	yes	yes	ERROR	10312	ERROR	10312
nextcomb(i,i,g,v)	100	yes	no	9900	244	17928	244
nextcomb(i,i,g,v)	1000	yes	no	96300	244	176328	244
nextcomb(i,i,g,v)	10000	yes	no	960300	244	1760328	244
nextcomb(i,i,g,v)	20000	yes	no	1920300	244	ERROR	244
nextcomb(i,i,g,v)	100000	yes	no	ERROR	244	ERROR	244
numocc(g,g,v)	1000	yes	yes	80108	80180	80108	80180
numocc(g,g,v)	10000	yes	yes	800108	800180	800108	800180
numocc(g,g,v)	20000	yes	yes	1600108	1600180	1600108	1600180
numocc(g,g,v)	30000	yes	yes	ERROR	ERROR	ERROR	ERROR
permutsort(g,v)	5	no	no	1248	1248	1388	1388
permutsort(g,v)	10	no	no	1248	1248	1388	1388
postorder(g,v)	10	yes	yes	748	792	782520	820
postorder(g,v)	11	yes	yes	812	856	1736888	884
postorder(g,v)	12	yes	yes	876	920	ERROR	948
prefix(g,g)	500	yes	no	108	148	40108	176
prefix(g,g)	5000	yes	no	108	148	400108	176
prefix(g,g)	30000	yes	no	108	148	ERROR	176
preorder(g,v)	10	yes	yes	708	748	520212	776
preorder(g,v)	11	yes	yes	768	808	1126420	836
preorder(g,v)	12	yes	yes	828	868	ERROR	896
qs(g,v)	10	yes	yes	5468	824	9528	824
qs(g,v)	100	yes	yes	449708	6584	868308	6584
qs(g,v)	200	yes	yes	1779308	12984	ERROR	12984
qs(g,v)	500	yes	yes	ERROR	32184	ERROR	32184
part(g,g,v,v)	100	yes	yes	4496	4584	4496	4584
part(g,g,v,v)	1000	yes	yes	44096	44184	44096	44184
part(g,g,v,v)	10000	yes	yes	440096	440184	440096	440184
part(g,g,v,v)	100000	yes	yes	ERROR	ERROR	ERROR	ERROR
remove_red(g,v)	10	no	no	2728	2728	2968	2728
remove_red(g,v)	100	no	no	349768	349768	350008	349768
revnaive(g,v)	10	yes	yes	628	668	4688	696

Program	Input	det	ss	Default Indexing Used Local Stack		No Indexing Used Local Stack	
				User (B)	Denorm (B)	User (B)	Denorm (B)
revnaive(g,v)	100	yes	yes	5308	5348	423908	5376
revnaive(g,v)	1000	yes	yes	52108	52148	ERROR	52176
revacc(g,v)	1000	yes	yes	148	152	80108	180
revacc(g,v)	10000	yes	yes	148	152	800108	180
revacc(g,v)	20000	yes	yes	148	152	1600108	180
revacc(g,v)	100000	yes	yes	148	152	ERROR	180
revdl(g,v)	1000	yes	yes	148	152	80108	180
revdl(g,v)	10000	yes	yes	148	152	800108	180
revdl(g,v)	20000	yes	yes	148	152	1600108	180
revdl(g,v)	100000	yes	yes	148	152	ERROR	180
sameleaves(g,g)	5	yes	no	80	80	80	80
sameleaves(g,g)	10	yes	no	80	80	80	80
sameleaves(g,g)	11	yes	no	80	80	80	80
select(g,g,g)	1000	no	no	84108	84108	84108	84108
select(g,g,g)	10000	no	no	840108	840108	840108	840108
select(g,g,g)	100000	no	no	ERROR	ERROR	ERROR	ERROR
selectsort(g,v)	10	yes	yes	4628	1032	4908	1032
selectsort(g,v)	100	yes	yes	441308	8952	444108	8952
selectsort(g,v)	1000	yes	yes	ERROR	88152	ERROR	88152
substlist(g,g,g,v)	100	yes	yes	8508	8584	8508	8584
substlist(g,g,g,v)	1000	yes	yes	84108	84184	84108	84184
substlist(g,g,g,v)	10000	yes	yes	840108	840184	840108	840184
substlist(g,g,g,v)	100000	yes	yes	ERROR	ERROR	ERROR	ERROR
substree(g,g,g,v)	11	yes	yes	80	80	80	80
substree(g,g,g,v)	12	yes	yes	80	80	80	80
substree(g,g,g,v)	13	yes	yes	80	80	80	80
substree(g,g,g,v)	14	yes	yes	80	80	80	80
suffix(g,g)	500	yes	no	36108	176	36108	176
suffix(g,g)	5000	yes	no	360108	176	360108	176
suffix(g,g)	30000	yes	no	ERROR	176	ERROR	176
sumtree(g,v)	12	yes	yes	828	868	360468	896
sumtree(g,v)	13	yes	yes	888	928	720916	956
sumtree(g,v)	14	yes	yes	948	988	1441812	1016
sumtree(g,v)	15	yes	yes	1008	1048	ERROR	1076
transpose(g,v)	50*50	yes	no	4308	260	234376	316
transpose(g,v)	100*100	yes	no	8508	260	928576	316
transpose(g,v)	200*200	yes	no	16908	260	ERROR	316
treememb(a,g)	5	no	no	396	396	396	396
treememb(a,g)	10	no	no	756	756	756	756
union(g,g,v)	100	no	no	285108	92432	286508	92432
union(g,g,v)	200	no	no	1130108	364632	1132908	364632
union(g,g,v)	300	no	no	ERROR	816832	ERROR	816832
intersect(g,g,v)	100	no	no	285108	92628	286508	92628
intersect(g,g,v)	200	no	no	1130108	365028	1132908	365028
intersect(g,g,v)	300	no	no	ERROR	817428	ERROR	817428
difference(g,g,v)	100	no	no	285108	92432	286508	92432

Program	Input	det ss		Default Indexing Used Local Stack		No Indexing Used Local Stack	
				User (B)	Denorm (B)	User (B)	Denorm (B)
difference(g,g,v)	200	no no		1130108	364632	1132908	364632
difference(g,g,v)	300	no no		ERROR	816832	ERROR	816832
union2(g,g,v)	1000	yes yes		46180	44152	46180	44152
union2(g,g,v)	10000	yes yes		460180	440152	460180	440152
union2(g,g,v)	30000	yes yes		1380180	1320152	1380180	1320152
union2(g,g,v)	50000	yes yes		ERROR	ERROR	ERROR	ERROR
intersect2(g,g,v)	1000	yes yes		46180	44152	46180	44152
intersect2(g,g,v)	10000	yes yes		460180	440152	460180	440152
intersect2(g,g,v)	30000	yes yes		1380180	1320152	1380180	1320152
intersect2(g,g,v)	50000	yes yes		ERROR	ERROR	ERROR	ERROR
difference2(g,g,v)	1000	yes yes		44180	40152	44180	40152
difference2(g,g,v)	10000	yes yes		440180	400152	440180	400152
difference2(g,g,v)	30000	yes yes		1320180	1200152	1320180	1200152
difference2(g,g,v)	50000	yes yes		ERROR	2000152	ERROR	2000152

Table H.24: Used local stack of the original and the specialised codes when indexing is enabled (**Default Indexing**) and when indexing is disabled (**No Indexing**).

Appendix I

System utilisation with modules

This appendix illustrates how to use the system: the *checker* presented in Part I and the *optimiser* presented in Part II.[1]

Module systems are an essential feature of programming languages as they facilitate the reuse of existing code and the development of general purpose libraries and of larger programs. Our analyser is able to verify and optimise programs decomposed in modules. The system analyses a module without having to reanalyse its imported modules (except if they have been modified since their last verification). The analysis remains entirely compositional.

I.1 Using the checker

Figure I.1 depicts the inputs and outputs of the checker.

Input modules

A module contains a name, the list of the imported modules, the code of some Prolog procedures, and several annotations: the type and norm declarations (see Section 5.2 and Section 5.3), and the formal specifications of the procedures (see Section 3.1.1 and its extensions). The annotations are either `public` or `private`. When a module mod_1 imports another module mod_2, then all the public specifications, types and norms declarations of mod_2 are imported to the module mod_1. By default, if it is not specified, an annotation in a module is public.

An input module whose name is mod can exist in two versions: a *source module* (contained in a file $mod.pl$) and/or a *normalised source module* (contained in a file $mod.mo$). Note that the file containing a module has the same name as the module name. A source module is the file provided by the user. The normalised

---

[1]The tool is available at the website `http://www.info.ucl.ac.be/~gobert`, where you can find all the sources, documentation, and benchmark.

319

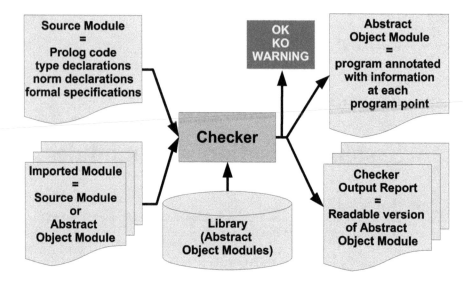

Figure I.1: Checker inputs and outputs.

source module is a binary file corresponding to a source module, where several normalisation have been realized (types and norms declarations, formal specifications, procedures), and can be processed more directly and quickly by the checker when it is imported by another source module.

In a source module, the annotations are written between the symbols /** (followed by a *keyword*) and **/. The module name is written after the keyword MODULE, the imported modules are listed after the keyword IMPORT, the types and the norms declarations are written after the keyword TYPE and NORM respectively, and the formal specifications attached to the procedures are described after the keyword SPECIFICATION.

For instance, the source module flattree.pl, depicted in Figure I.2, contains the program flattree (Procedure 5.2, page 108) and is annotated with Type definition 5.3, Norm Definition 5.2, and Specification 6.9. The procedure flattree calls the procedure append (Procedure 2.4, page 12), whose code and specifications are defined in the module list.pl. A part of the source module list.pl, containing some usual procedures using lists, is depicted in Figure I.3. The module flattree.pl imports the module list.pl. By default, all formal specifications are public: thus, in this case, the specifications of append can be used during the verification analysis of flattree.

```
/** MODULE flattree **/

/** IMPORT list **/

/** TYPE
     tree(T) ::= void | t(T,tree(T),tree(T))
**/

/** NORM
     (elems) void       = 0
     (elems) t(_,LT,RT) = 1 + (elems)LT + (elems)RT
**/

/** SPECIFICATION
   flattree/2
     in(T:tree(ground), L:var)
     out(_, list(ground))
     srel( (elems)T_in = (list)L_out )
     sol(sol = 1)
     sexpr(< (gen)T >)
**/

flattree(void, []).
flattree(t(X,LT,RT), [X|Xs]) :-
   flattree(LT, LLT),
   flattree(RT, LRT),
   append(LLT, LRT, Xs).
```

Figure I.2: File `flattree.pl`

Libraries modules

The system provides several library modules that specify the Prolog built-ins. For instance, Figure I.4 shows a part of the library module describing the behaviours of test predicates, and Figure I.5 shows part of the library module specifying arithmetics built-ins. The specifications are assumed (i.e., not checked) and public. The complete contents of the library modules can be viewed at the website of the analyser [55].

```
/** MODULE list **/

/** SPECIFICATION
  list/1
    in(T:ground)
    ref(list)
    sol(sol = 1)
    sexpr(< (list)X >)

  list/1
    in(T:list(any))
    untouched(T)
    sol(sol = 1)
    sexpr(< (list)X >)
**/
list([]).
list([_|T]) :- list(T).

/** SPECIFICATION
  append/3
    in(L1:list(ground),L2:list(ground),L3:var)
    out(_,_,list(ground))
    srel( (list)L1_in+(list)L2_in = (list)L3_out )
    sol(sol = 1)
    sexpr(< (list)L1 >)

  append/3
    in(L1:var,L2:var,L3:list(ground); noshare(<L1,L2>))
    out(list(ground),list(ground),_)
    srel( (list)L1_out+(list)L2_out = (list)L3_in )
    sol(sol = L3_in+1)
    sexpr(< (list)L3 >)

  /* other specifications for append */
**/
append([], L2, L2).
append([X|L1], L2, [X|L3]) :- append(L1, L2, L3).

/* other procedures and specifications */
```

Figure I.3: File list.pl

```
/** MODULE test_predicates **/

/** SPECIFICATION
  public assume unlogic var/1
    in(X:any)
    ref(var)
    untouched(X)
    sol(sol = 1)

  public assume unlogic nonvar/1
    in(X:any)
    ref(novar)
    untouched(X)
    sol(sol = 1)

  public assume unlogic integer/1
    in(X:any)
    ref(int)
    untouched(X)
    sol(sol = 1)

  /* other specifications for test predicates */
**/
```

Figure I.4: File test_predicates.pl

```
/** MODULE arithmetics **/

/** SPECIFICATION
  public assume =:=/2
    in(X:int, Y:int)
    srel((int)X_ref = (int)Y_ref)
    sol(sol = 1)

  public assume >/2
    in(X:int, Y:int)
    srel((int)X_ref > (int)Y_ref)
    sol(sol = 1)

  public assume is/2
    in(X:var, Y:int)
    out(int, _)
    srel((int)X_out = (int)Y_int)
    sol(sol = 1)

  public assume is/2
    in(X:var, Y:+(A:int,B:int))
    out(int, _)
    srel((int)X_out = (int)A_in+(int)B_in)
    sol(sol = 1)

  /* other specifications for arithmetics */
**/
```

Figure I.5: File arithmetics.pl

Outputs modules

The checker generates OK/KO/WARNING messages on the output prompt, depending on the success or failure of the verification analysis. For each pair procedure/specification, the checker may generate an *abstract object module* as well as well as a *checker output report*. An abstract object module contains the same information as an *normalised source module*, plus the abstract information that has been collected and verified during the abstract execution. The output report is a user-readable version of the abstract object module, where the syntax of formal specifications is used to describe the abstract sequences at each program point. The abstract information contained in an abstract object module can serve to perform further optimisation, by using the *optimiser*.

Command lines

Given the source modules `flattree.pl` (depicted in Figure I.2) and `list.pl` (depicted in Figure I.3), the program `flattree` can be checked by using the following command:

```
analyser -mode checker flattree.pl
```

Figure I.6 shows the output prompt of the analyser: the checker succeeds to verify the procedure `flattree` with respect to Specification 6.9. A checker output report `flattree.3.1.out` is generated. It contains the result of the analysis, i.e., the abstract sequences collected at each program point (expressed with the language of formal specifications). This allows deeper diagnostic of errors (if any).

Suppose now that some programmer has incorrectly replaced the first recursive call `flattree(LT, LLT)` by `flattree(LLT, LT)`. In such a case, the checker generates a warning message explaining the possible error, as it depicted in Figure I.7.

Table I.1 reports on the various options of the checker. For instance, the option `check-term` tells the checker to not verify the termination of the procedures. This can be achieved with the following command:

```
analyser -mode checker -check-term no flattree.pl
```

```
gobert@alonzi:~> analyser -mode checker flattree.pl

*****************************************************************
* Automated verification and optimisation of Prolog programs *
*****************************************************************

-----------------------------------------------------------------
| PrologAnalyser version 0.3, Copyright (C) 2004-2007 F.Gobert. |
| This comes with ABSOLUTELY NO WARRANTY. This is free software |
| and you are welcome to redistribute it under some conditions. |
| See the file COPYING in the distribution for details.         |
-----------------------------------------------------------------

Loading and normalizing modules.
  - list.mo.................................(load)[0,687 seconds]
  - flattree.pl..................(load,normalize)[0,167 seconds]

The analysis process begins.
Checking module flattree
  - flattree.2.1(g,v)............(rec,ss,det) OK: [1,188 seconds]
The analysis process is finished.

  ==> Global analysis succeeds                     [OK:1 / KO:0]

Loaded files....................................................[2]
Global loading time.................................[0,768 seconds]
Global normalizing time.............................[0,086 seconds]
Global analysis time................................[1,188 seconds]
Global time.........................................[2,042 seconds]
Number of warnings..............................................[0]
Number of analysed predicates...................................[1]
Number of analysed specifications...............................[1]
Number of program clauses.......................................[2]
Number of clauses per procedure (mean)........................[2.0]
Number of literals..............................................[7]
Number of analyzed literals.....................................[7]
Number of analyzed cuts.........................................[0]
Maximal time..............['flattree.2.1(g,v)' => 1,188 seconds]
Mean time per specification......................[1,188 seconds]

GoodBye and see you later!
```

Figure I.6: Successful checker execution of Procedure 5.2 flattree according to Specification 6.9. The symbols rec, ss and det mean that the procedure (in the context of a formal specification) is recursive, surely succeeds, and is deterministic, respectively. Some statistics about the program and the analyser execution time are provided.

```
gobert@alonzi:~> analyser -mode checker flattree.pl

 ******************************************************************
 * Automated verification and optimisation of Prolog programs *
 ******************************************************************


 ----------------------------------------------------------------
 | PrologAnalyser version 0.3, Copyright (C) 2004-2007 F.Gobert. |
 | This comes with ABSOLUTELY NO WARRANTY. This is free software |
 | and you are welcome to redistribute it under some conditions. |
 | See the file COPYING in the distribution for details.         |
 ----------------------------------------------------------------


Loading and normalizing modules.
  - list.mo..............................(load)[0,505 seconds]
  - flattree.pl..................(load,normalize)[0,150 seconds]

The analysis process begins.
Checking module flattree
  - flattree.2.1(g,v)
    ******** WARNING *******
    * The analyser cannot lookup an applicable specification for
    * literal flattree(v,g) executed at position 1 in clause 2
    ***********************
  - flattree.2.1(g,v)...............(ss,det) KO: [0,597 seconds]
The analysis process is finished.

  ==> Global analysis fails                       [OK:0 / KO:1]


Loaded files...................................................[2]
Global loading time..............................[0,576 seconds]
Global normalizing time..........................[0,079 seconds]
Global analysis time.............................[0,597 seconds]
Global time......................................[1,252 seconds]
Number of warnings.............................................[1]
Number of analysed predicates..................................[1]
Number of analysed specifications..............................[1]
Number of program clauses......................................[2]
Number of clauses per procedure (mean).......................[2.0]
Number of literals.............................................[7]
Number of analyzed literals....................................[7]
Number of analyzed cuts........................................[0]
Maximal time..............['flattree.2.1(g,v)' => 0,597 seconds]
Mean time per specification......................[0,597 seconds]

GoodBye and see you later!
```

Figure I.7: Unsuccessful checker execution of the procedure `flattree` (modified version of Procedure 5.2 where the first recursive call has been replaced by `flattree(LLT, LT)`), according to Specification 6.9.

I.2 Using the optimiser

Consider the predicate efface(X,T,TEff) that holds iff X is an element of
the list T and if TEff is the list T without the first occurrence of X. The module
containing that procedure is depicted in Figure I.8, which is annotated with four
formal specifications.

```
/** MODULE efface **/

/** SPECIFICATION
  efface/3
    in(X:ground, T:list(ground), TEff:var)
    out(_, _, list(ground))
    sol(sol =< 1)
    sexpr(< (list)T >)

  efface/3
    in(X:ground, T:list(ground), TEff:any)
    out(_, _, list(ground))
    sol(sol =< 1)
    sexpr(< (list)T >)

  efface/3
    in(X:ground, T:any, TEff:list(ground))
    out(_, list(ground), _)
    sol(sol =< (list)TEff_in+1)
    sexpr(< (list)TEff >)

  efface/3
    in(X:var,T:list(ground),TEff:any;
       noshare(<X,TEff>))
    out(ground, _, list(ground))
    sol(sol =< (list)T_in)
    sexpr(< (list)T >)
**/
efface(X,[H|T],[H|TEff]) :- efface(X,T,TEff), not(X=H).
efface(X,[X|T],T).
```

Figure I.8: File efface.pl

The specialised versions of that procedure (one for each of its formal specifications) are generated by using the following command.

```
analyser -mode optimiser efface.pl
```

The specialised versions of efface are generated by the optimiser in the file
o_efface.pl, which is depicted in Figure I.9.   The output report
efface.3.1.out, generated by the checker during the verification of the first
specification of efface, is given on Page 332 and on Page 338.

The Prolog code versions related to each optimisation step of the optimiser strategy presented in Section 9.4 are generated by using the following command (Figure I.10 shows part of the generated file o_efface.pl):

```
analyser -mode optimiser -osteps efface.pl
```

Table I.2 reports on the optimiser options, which enable or disable source-to-source transformations.

Option	Value	Description
polyhedra	ppl*,none	Enable or not the polyhedra library
check-ocf	yes*,no	Check or not occur-check freeness
check-term	yes*,no	Check or not termination
check-green-cut	yes*,no	Check or not that cuts are green
check-sound-not	yes*,no	Check or not that negations are sound
warning	yes*,no	Generate or not warning messages
generate	out*,am,none	Generate or not output reports (out) and abstract object modules (am)

Table I.1: Checker options. Default options are annotated by an asterisk. They can be set up in the file properties/analyser.prop of the distribution.

Option	Value
clause-reordering	yes*,no
semantic-normalisation	yes*,no
advance-unification	yes*,no
cut-insertion	yes*,no
move-back-cut	yes*,no
remove-literals	yes*,no
denormalisation	yes*,no

Table I.2: Optimiser options. Code transformations can be enabled (*yes*) or disabled (*no*). Default options are annotated by an asterisk. They can be set up in the file properties/analyser.prop of the distribution.

```
%------------------------------------------------------------%
%  This file was automatically generated by the optimiser  %
%------------------------------------------------------------%

/** MODULE o_efface **/

/** SPECIFICATION
  o_efface_3_1/3
    in(X:ground, T:list(ground), TEff:var)
    out(_, _, list(ground))
    sol( 1 >= sol )
    sexpr(< (list)T >)
**/
o_efface_3_1(X3,[X3|X2],X1) :- !.
o_efface_3_1(X4,[X3|X2],[X3|X1]) :- o_efface_3_1(X4,X2,X1).

/** SPECIFICATION
  o_efface_3_2/3
    in(X:ground, T:list(ground), TEff:any)
    out(_, _, list(ground))
    sol( 1 >= sol )
    sexpr(< (list)T >)
**/
o_efface_3_2(X3,[X3|X2],X1) :- !, X1=X2.
o_efface_3_2(X4,[X3|X2],[X3|X1]) :- o_efface_3_2(X4,X2,X1).

/** SPECIFICATION
  o_efface_3_3/3
    in(X:ground, T:any, TEff:list(ground))
    out(_, list(ground), _)
    sol( TEff_in + 1 >= sol )
    sexpr(< (list)TEff >)
**/
o_efface_3_3(X2,[X2|X1],X1).
o_efface_3_3(X4,[X3|X2],[X3|X1]) :- not(X4=X3),
                                    o_efface_3_3(X4,X2,X1).

/** SPECIFICATION
  o_efface_3_4/3
    in(X:var,T:list(ground),TEff:any; noshare(<X,TEff>))
    out(ground, _, list(ground))
    sol(sol =< (list)T_in)
    sexpr(< (list)T >)
**/
o_efface_3_4(X,[H|T],[H|TEff]) :- o_efface_3_4(X,T,TEff),
                                  not(X=H).
o_efface_3_4(X,[X|T],T).
```

Figure I.9: File o_efface.pl

```
%----------------------------------------------------------------%
%      This file was automatically generated by the optimiser     %
%----------------------------------------------------------------%

/** MODULE o_efface **/

/** SPECIFICATION
  o_efface_3_1/3
    in(X:ground, T:list(ground), TEff:var)
    out(_, _, list(ground))
    sol( 1 >= sol )
    sexpr(< (list)T >)
**/
% Version after syntactic normalisation
  synnorm_efface_3_1(X1,X2,X3) :-
      X2=[X4|X5], X3=[X4|X6],
      synnorm_efface_3_1(X1,X5,X6), not(X1=X4).
  synnorm_efface_3_1(X1,X2,X3) :- X2=[X1|X3].

% Version after clause reordering
  reorder_efface_3_1(X1,X2,X3) :- X2=[X1|X3].
  reorder_efface_3_1(X1,X2,X3) :-
      X2=[X4|X5], X3=[X4|X6],
      reorder_efface_3_1(X1,X5,X6), not(X1=X4).

% Version after semantic normalisation
  semnorm_efface_3_1(X1,X2,X3) :- X2=[X4|X5], X4=X1, X5=X3.
  semnorm_efface_3_1(X1,X2,X3) :-
      X2=[X4|X5], X3=[X4|X6],
      semnorm_efface_3_1(X1,X5,X6), not(X1=X4).

% Version after moving unification and negation forwards
  moveunif_efface_3_1(X1,X2,X3) :- X2=[X4|X5], X4=X1, X5=X3.
  moveunif_efface_3_1(X1,X2,X3) :-
      X2=[X4|X5], X3=[X4|X6], not(X1=X4),
      moveunif_efface_3_1(X1,X5,X6).

% Version after cut insertion
  cut_efface_3_1(X1,X2,X3) :- X2=[X4|X5], X4=X1, !, X5=X3.
  cut_efface_3_1(X1,X2,X3) :-
      X2=[X4|X5], X3=[X4|X6], not(X1=X4),
      cut_efface_3_1(X1,X5,X6).

% Version after moving cut backwards
  movecut_efface_3_1(X1,X2,X3) :- X2=[X4|X5], X4=X1, X5=X3, !.
  movecut_efface_3_1(X1,X2,X3) :-
      X2=[X4|X5], X3=[X4|X6], not(X1=X4),
      movecut_efface_3_1(X1,X5,X6).

% Version after removing redundant literals
  remove_efface_3_1(X1,X2,X3) :- X2=[X4|X5], X4=X1, !, X5=X3.
  remove_efface_3_1(X1,X2,X3) :-
      X2=[X4|X5], X3=[X4|X6], remove_efface_3_1(X1,X5,X6).

% Version after denormalisation
  o_efface_3_1(X2,[X2|X1],X1) :- !.
  o_efface_3_1(X4,[X3|X2],[X3|X1]) :-
      o_efface_3_1(X4,X2,X1).
```

Figure I.10: File `o_efface.pl` with explicit optimisation steps. Only the specialised code corresponding to the first specification of `efface` is shown.

Output report `efface.3.1.out` (1/6)

```
*************************************
*      ANNOTATION OF PROCEDURE      *
*************************************


  'efface'(X1,X2,X3) :- X2=[X4|X5], X3=[X4|X6],
                        'efface'(X1,X5,X6), not(X1=X4).
  'efface'(X1,X2,X3) :- X2=[X1|X3].


*************************************
*      FORMAL SPECIFICATION         *
*************************************


  logic no-side-effect
  'efface'
    in(X1:ground, X2:list(ground), X3:var)
    out(_, _, list(ground))
    sol( 1 >= sol )
    sexpr(< (list)X2 >)


*************************************
*         CHECKER ANALYSIS          *
*************************************


>>>>>>>>>>>>>>>>>>>>>>>>>>>>>>>>>>>>>>>>>>>>>>>>>>>>>>>>>
==>  Clause (1) to analyze:
     c = 'efface'(X1,X2,X3) :- X2=[X4|X5], X3=[X4|X6],
                               'efface'(X1,X5,X6), not(X1=X4).


---------------------------------------
EXTC(c,betaIn) = B_0
---------------------------------------


   B_0:
     in(X1:ground, X2:list(ground), X3:var)
     ref(X1:ground, X2:list(ground), X3:var)
     out(X1:ground, X2:list(ground), X3:var,
        X4:var, X5:var, X6:var ;
        noshare(<X3,X4>,<X3,X5>,<X3,X6>,<X4,X5>,
                <X4,X6>,<X5,X6>))
     untouched(X1,X2,X3)
     sol( sol = 1 )


---------------------------------------
Literal to abstractly execute: l1 = X2=[X4|X5]
---------------------------------------


      ---------------------------------------
      RESTRG(l1,B_0) = beta^1_inter
      ---------------------------------------
           beta^1_inter(X1:list(ground), X2:var, X3:var ;
                        noshare(<X2,X3>) )
```

Output report `efface.3.1.out` (2/6)

```
---------------------------------------
UNIF_FUNC(beta^1_inter[X4|X5]) = B^1_aux
---------------------------------------

    B^1_aux:
        in(X1:list(ground), X2:var, X3:var ;
            noshare(<X2,X3>) )
        ref(X1:[R4:ground|R5:list(ground)],
            X2:var, X3:var ; noshare(<X2,X3>))
        out(X1:[R4:ground|R5:list(ground)],
            R4:ground, R5:list(ground))
        untouched(X1,R4,R5)
        srel( )
        sol( sol = 1 )


---------------------------------------
EXTG(l1,B_0,B^1_aux) = B_1
---------------------------------------

    B_1:
        in(X1:ground, X2:list(ground), X3:var)
        ref(X1:ground, X2:[R4:ground|R5:list(ground)],
            X3:var)
        out(X1:ground, X2:[R4:ground|R5:list(ground)],
            X3:var, R4:ground, R5:list(ground), X6:var ;
            noshare(<X3,X6>))
        untouched(X1,X2,X3,R4,R5)
        srel( (list)X2_ref = (list)R5_ref + 1)
        sol( sol = 1 )

---------------------------------------
Literal to abstractly execute: l2 = X3=[X4|X6]
---------------------------------------


---------------------------------------
RESTRG(l2,B_1) = beta^2_inter
---------------------------------------

    beta^2_inter(X1:var, X2:ground, X3:var ;
                noshare(<X1,X3>))


---------------------------------------
UNIF_FUNC(beta^2_inter[X4|X6]) = B^2_aux
---------------------------------------

    B^2_aux:
        in(X1:var, X2:ground, X3:var ;
            noshare(<X1,X3>) )
        ref(X1:var, X2:ground, X3:var ;
            noshare(<X1,X3>))
        out(X1:ngv [X2:ground|X3:var], X2:ground, X3:var)
        untouched(X2,X3)
        srel( )
        sol( sol = 1 )
```

Output report `efface.3.1.out` (3/6)

```
----------------------------------------
    EXTG(l2,B_1,B^2_aux) = B_2
----------------------------------------

      B_2:
          in(X1:ground, X2:list(ground), X3:var)
          ref(X1:ground, X2:[R4:ground|R5:list(ground)],
              X3:var)
          out(X1:ground, X2:[R4:ground|R5:list(ground)],
              X3:ngv [R4:ground|X6:var], R4:ground,
              R5:list(ground), X6:var)
          untouched(X1,X2,R4,R5)
          srel( (list)X6_out + 1 = (list)X3_out,
                (list)X2_ref = (list)R5_ref + 1 )
          sol( sol = 1 )


----------------------------------------
Literal to abstractly execute: l3 = 'efface'(X1,X5,X6)
----------------------------------------


    ----------------------------------------
    RESTRG(l3,B_2) = beta^3_inter
    ----------------------------------------

        beta^3_inter(X1:ground, X2:list(ground), X3:var)


    ----------------------------------------
    LOOKUP(beta^3_inter,'efface'(X1,X5,X6),sbeh) = B^3_aux
    ----------------------------------------

        B^3_aux:
            in(X1:ground, X2:list(ground), X3:var)
            ref(X1:ground, X2:list(ground), X3:var)
            out(X1:ground, X2:list(ground), X3:list(ground))
            untouched(X1,X2)
            srel( )
            sol( 1 >= sol )


    ----------------------------------------
    Call to l3 is logic
    ----------------------------------------


    ----------------------------------------
    Call to l3 has no side-effect
    ----------------------------------------


    ----------------------------------------
    CHECK_TERM(l3,B3,seMutRec,se) = true
    ----------------------------------------
```

Output report `efface.3.1.out` (4/6)

```
----------------------------------------
    EXTG(13,B_2,B^3_aux) = B_3
----------------------------------------

    B_3:
        in(X1:ground, X2:list(ground), X3:var)
        ref(X1:ground, X2:[R4:ground|R5:list(ground)],
            X3:var)
        out(X1:ground, X2:[R4:ground|R5:list(ground)],
            X3:[R4:ground|X6:list(ground)],
            R4:ground, R5:list(ground), X6:list(ground))
        untouched(X1,X2,R4,R5)
        srel( (list)X2_ref = (list)R5_ref + 1 )
        sol( 1 >= sol )


----------------------------------------
Literal to abstractly execute: 14 = not(X1=X4)
----------------------------------------


    ----------------------------------------
    RESTRG(14,B_3) = beta^4_inter
    ----------------------------------------

        beta^4_inter(X1:ground, X2:ground)


    ----------------------------------------
    NOT_AI(not(X1=X4),beta^4_inter) = B^4_aux
    ----------------------------------------

        B^4_aux:
            in(X1:ground, X2:ground)
            fail(X1:ground, X1:ground)
            ref(X1:ground, X2:ground)
            out(X1:ground, X2:ground)
            untouched(X1,X2)
            srel(   )
            sol( sol = 1 )


    ----------------------------------------
    EXTG(14,B_3,B^4_aux) = B_4
    ----------------------------------------

        B_4:
            in(X1:ground, X2:list(ground), X3:var)
            fail(X1:ground, X2:[X1:ground|R4:list(ground)],
                X3:var)
            ref(X1:ground, X2:[R4:ground|R5:list(ground)],
                X3:var)
            out(X1:ground, X2:[R4:ground|R5:list(ground)],
                X3:[R4:ground|X6:list(ground)], R4:ground,
                R5:list(ground), X6:list(ground))
            untouched(X1,X2,R4,R5)
            srel( (list)X6_out + 1 = (list)X3_out,
                (list)X2_ref = (list)R5_ref + 1 )
            sol( 1 >= sol )
```

Output report `efface.3.1.out` (5/6)

```
---------------------------------------
RESTRC(c,B_k) = B_out
---------------------------------------

    B_out:
        in(X1:ground, X2:list(ground), X3:var)
        fail(X1:ground, X2:[X1:ground|R4:list(ground)], X3:var)
        ref(X1:ground, X2:[R4:ground|R5:list(ground)], X3:var)
        out(X1:ground, X2:[R4:ground|R5:list(ground)],
             X3:[R4:ground|O6:list(ground)])
        untouched(X1,X2,R4,R5)
        srel( (list)O6_out + 1 = (list)X3_out,
             (list)X2_ref = (list)R5_ref + 1)
        sol( 1 >= sol )
>>>>>>>>>>>>>>>>>>>>>>>>>>>>>>>>>>>>>>>>>>>>>>>>>>>>>>>>>>>>


>>>>>>>>>>>>>>>>>>>>>>>>>>>>>>>>>>>>>>>>>>>>>>>>>>>>>>>>>>>>
==>  Clause (2) to analyze:
     c = 'efface'(X1,X2,X3) :- X2=[X1|X3].


---------------------------------------
EXTC(c,betaIn) = B_0
---------------------------------------

    B_0:
        in(X1:ground, X2:list(ground), X3:var)
        ref(X1:ground, X2:list(ground), X3:var)
        out(X1:ground, X2:list(ground), X3:var)
        untouched(X1,X2,X3)
        sol( sol = 1 )


---------------------------------------
Literal to abstractly execute: l1 = X2=[X1|X3]
---------------------------------------

    ---------------------------------------
    RESTRG(l1,B_0) = beta^1_inter
    ---------------------------------------

        beta^1_inter(X1:list(ground), X2:ground, X3:var)


    ---------------------------------------
    UNIF_FUNC(beta^1_inter[X1|X3]) = B^1_aux
    ---------------------------------------

        B^1_aux:
            in(X1:list(ground), X2:ground, X3:var)
            ref(X1:[X2:ground|R4:list(ground)],
                 X2:ground, X3:var)
            out(X1:[X2:ground|R4:list(ground)],
                 X2:ground, R4:list(ground))
            untouched(X2,X1,R4)
            srel( )
            sol( sol = 1 )
```

Output report `efface.3.1.out` (6/6)

```
--------------------------------------
EXTG(l1,B_0,B^1_aux) = B_1
--------------------------------------

    B_1:
        in(X1:ground, X2:list(ground), X3:var)
        ref(X1:ground, X2:[X1:ground|R4:list(ground)],
            X3:var)
        out(X1:ground, X2:[X1:ground|R4:list(ground)],
            R4:list(ground))
        untouched(X1,X2,R4)
        srel( (list)X2_ref = (list)R4_ref + 1 )
        sol( sol = 1 )
--------------------------------------
RESTRC(c,B_k) = B_out
--------------------------------------

    B_out:
        in(X1:ground, X2:list(ground), X3:var)
        ref(X1:ground, X2:[X1:ground|R4:list(ground)],
            X3:var)
        out(X1:ground, X2:[X1:ground|R4:list(ground)],
            R4:list(ground))
        untouched(X1,X2,R4)
        srel( (list)X2_ref = (list)R4_ref + 1 )
        sol( sol = 1 )
>>>>>>>>>>>>>>>>>>>>>>>>>>>>>>>>>>>>>>>>>>>>>>>>>>>>>>>>>>>>
*_*_*_*_*_*_*_*_*_*_*_*_*_*_*_*_*_*_*_*
ABSTRACT CONCATENATION OF THE CLAUSES
*_*_*_*_*_*_*_*_*_*_*_*_*_*_*_*_*_*_*_*
B1:    in(X1:ground, X2:list(ground), X3:var)
       fail(X1:ground, X2:[], X3:var)
       fail(X1:ground, X2:[X1:ground|R4:list(ground)], X3:var)
       ref(X1:ground, X2:[R4:ground|R5:list(ground)], X3:var)
       out(X1:ground, X2:[R4:ground|R5:list(ground)],
           X3:[R4:ground|O6:list(ground)])
       untouched(X1,X2,R4,R5)
       srel( (list)O6_out + 1 = (list)X3_out,
             (list)X2_ref = (list)R5_ref + 1 )
       sol( 1 >= sol )

B2:    in(X1:ground, X2:list(ground), X3:var)
       ref(X1:ground, X2:[X1:ground|R4:list(ground)],
           X3:var)
       out(X1:ground, X2:[X1:ground|R4:list(ground)],
           R4:list(ground))
       untouched(X1,X2,R4)
       srel( (list)X2_ref = (list)R4_ref + 1 )
       sol( sol = 1 )

We have:
 - B1 and B2 are exclusive
 - B1 implies specification
 - B2 implies specification
*_*_*_*_*_*_*_*_*_*_*_*_*_*_*_*_*_*_*_*
==> We can infer the verification.
*_*_*_*_*_*_*_*_*_*_*_*_*_*_*_*_*_*_*_*
```

Output report (internal representation) `efface.3.1.out` (1/12)

```
***************************************
*      ANNOTATION OF PROCEDURE      *
***************************************


  'efface'(X1,X2,X3)  :- X2=[X4|X5],  X3=[X4|X6],
                         'efface'(X1,X5,X6), not(X1=X4).
  'efface'(X1,X2,X3)  :- X2=[X1|X3].


***************************************
*      FORMAL SPECIFICATION         *
***************************************


  logic no-side-effect
  %==============='efface'/3================
  beta_in: sv = {X1->1,X2->2,X3->3}
           frm = {}
           mo = {1->ground,2->ground,3->var}
           ty = {1->ground,2->list(ground),3->any}
           ps = {<3,3>}
           lin = {1,2,3}
  beta_ref: sv = {X1->2,X2->3,X3->1}
           frm = {}
           mo = {1->var,2->ground,3->ground}
           ty = {1->any,2->ground,3->list(ground)}
           ps = {<1,1>}
           lin = {1,2,3}
  beta_out: sv = {X1->2,X2->3,X3->4}
           frm = {}
           mo = {2->ground,3->ground,4->ground}
           ty = {2->ground,3->list(ground),4->list(ground)}
           ps = {}
           lin = {2,3,4}
  E_refoutsol = {   }
  sexpr = <(list)X2>
  %=========================================


***************************************
*      CHECKER ANALYSIS             *
***************************************

>>>>>>>>>>>>>>>>>>>>>>>>>>>>>>>>>>>>>>>>>>>>>>>>>>>>>>>>>>>>>>>>
==>  Clause (1) to analyze:
     c = 'efface'(X1,X2,X3)  :- X2=[X4|X5],  X3=[X4|X6],
                               'efface'(X1,X5,X6), not(X1=X4).


-----------------------------------------
EXTC(c,betaIn) = B_0
-----------------------------------------


  %===============B_0================
  beta_in: sv = {X1->1,X2->2,X3->3}
           frm = {}
           mo = {1->ground,2->ground,3->var}
           ty = {1->ground,2->list(ground),3->any}
           ps = {<3,3>}
           lin = {1,2,3}
```

Output report (internal representation) `efface.3.1.out` (2/12)

```
 beta_ref:  sv = {X1->1,X2->2,X3->3}
            frm = {}
            mo = {1->ground,2->ground,3->var}
            ty = {1->ground,2->list(ground),3->any}
            ps = {<3,3>}
            lin = {1,2,3}
 beta_out:  sv = {X1->1,X2->2,X3->3,X4->4,X5->5,X6->6}
            frm = {}
            mo = {1->ground,2->ground,3->var,4->var,5->var,
                  6->var}
            ty = {1->ground,2->list(ground),3->any,4->any,
                  5->any,6->any}
            ps = {<3,3>,<4,4>,<5,5>,<6,6>}
            lin = {1,2,3,4,5,6}
 E_refoutsol = { sol = 1 }
 %====================================


----------------------------------------
Literal to abstractly execute: l1 = X2=[X4|X5]
----------------------------------------


    ----------------------------------------
    RESTRG(l1,B_0) = beta^1_inter
    ----------------------------------------

        beta^1_inter:  sv = {X1->1,X2->2,X3->3}
                       frm = {}
                       mo = {1->ground,2->var,3->var}
                       ty = {1->list(ground),2->any,3->any}
                       ps = {<2,2>,<3,3>}
                       lin = {1,2,3}
    ----------------------------------------
    UNIF_FUNC(beta^1_inter[X4|X5]) = B^1_aux
    ----------------------------------------

        %===============B^1_aux===============
        beta_in:  sv = {X1->1,X2->2,X3->3}
                  frm = {}
                  mo = {1->ground,2->var,3->var}
                  ty = {1->list(ground),2->any,3->any}
                  ps = {<2,2>,<3,3>}
                  lin = {1,2,3}
        beta_ref:  sv = {X1->3,X2->1,X3->2}
                   frm = {3->[4|5]}
                   mo = {1->var,2->var,3->ground,4->ground,
                         5->ground}
                   ty = {1->any,2->any,
                         3->('[]/2'(ground,list(ground))),
                         4->ground,5->list(ground)}
                   ps = {<1,1>,<2,2>}
                   lin = {1,2,4,5}
        beta_out:  sv = {X1->3,X2->4,X3->5}
                   frm = {3->[4|5]}
                   mo = {3->ground,4->ground,5->ground}
                   ty = {3->('[]/2'(ground,list(ground))),
                         4->ground,5->list(ground)}
                   ps = {}
                   lin = {4,5}
        E_refoutsol = { sol = 1 }
        %====================================
```

Output report (internal representation) efface.3.1.out (3/12)

```
----------------------------------------
EXTG(11,B_0,B^1_aux) = B_1
----------------------------------------

    %=================B_1================
    beta_in: sv = {X1->1,X2->2,X3->3}
             frm = {}
             mo = {1->ground,2->ground,3->var}
             ty = {1->ground,2->list(ground),3->any}
             ps = {<3,3>}
             lin = {1,2,3}
    beta_ref: sv = {X1->1,X2->2,X3->3}
              frm = {2->[4|5]}
              mo = {1->ground,2->ground,3->var,4->ground,
                    5->ground}
              ty = {1->ground,
                    2->('[]/2'(ground,list(ground))),
                    3->any,4->ground,5->list(ground)}
              ps = {<3,3>}
              lin = {1,3,4,5}
    beta_out: sv = {X1->1,X2->2,X3->3,X4->4,X5->5,X6->6}
              frm = {2->[4|5]}
              mo = {1->ground,2->ground,3->var,4->ground,
                    5->ground,6->var}
              ty = {1->ground,
                    2->('[]/2'(ground,list(ground))),
                    3->any,4->ground,5->list(ground),
                    6->any}
              ps = {<3,3>,<6,6>}
              lin = {1,3,4,5,6}
    E_refoutsol = { (list)sz(2) = (list)sz(5)+1, sol = 1 }
    %==================================
----------------------------------------
Literal to abstractly execute: 12 = X3=[X4|X6]
----------------------------------------


    ------------------------------------
    RESTRG(12,B_1) = beta^2_inter
    ------------------------------------

    beta^2_inter: sv = {X1->1,X2->2,X3->3}
                  frm = {}
                  mo = {1->var,2->ground,3->var}
                  ty = {1->any,2->ground,3->any}
                  ps = {<1,1>,<3,3>}
                  lin = {1,2,3}


    ----------------------------------------
    UNIF_FUNC(beta^2_inter[X4|X6]) = B^2_aux
    ----------------------------------------

    %=================B^2_aux===============
    beta_in: sv = {X1->1,X2->2,X3->3}
             frm = {}
             mo = {1->var,2->ground,3->var}
             ty = {1->any,2->ground,3->any}
             ps = {<1,1>,<3,3>}
             lin = {1,2,3}
```

Output report (internal representation) `efface.3.1.out` (4/12)

```
         beta_ref: sv = {X1->1,X2->2,X3->3}
                   frm = {}
                   mo = {1->var,2->ground,3->var}
                   ty = {1->any,2->ground,3->any}
                   ps = {<1,1>,<3,3>}
                   lin = {1,2,3}
         beta_out: sv = {X1->4,X2->2,X3->3}
                   frm = {4->[2|3]}
                   mo = {2->ground,3->var,4->ngv}
                   ty = {2->ground,3->any,4->any}
                   ps = {<3,3>}
                   lin = {2,3}
         E_refoutsol = { sol = 1 }
            %=======================================


         ---------------------------------------
         EXTG(l2,B_1,B^2_aux) = B_2
         ---------------------------------------
            %===============B_2===============
         beta_in: sv = {X1->1,X2->2,X3->3}
                  frm = {}
                  mo = {1->ground,2->ground,3->var}
                  ty = {1->ground,2->list(ground),3->any}
                  ps = {<3,3>}
                  lin = {1,2,3}
         beta_ref: sv = {X1->2,X2->3,X3->1}
                   frm = {3->[4|5]}
                   mo = {1->var,2->ground,3->ground,
                         4->ground,5->ground}
                   ty = {1->any,2->ground,
                         3->('[]/2'(ground,list(ground))),
                         4->ground,5->list(ground)}
                   ps = {<1,1>}
                   lin = {1,2,4,5}
         beta_out: sv = {X1->2,X2->3,X3->7,X4->4,X5->5,
                         X6->6}
                   frm = {3->[4|5],7->[4|6]}
                   mo = {2->ground,3->ground,4->ground,
                         5->ground,6->var,7->ngv}
                   ty = {2->ground,
                         3->('[]/2'(ground,list(ground))),
                         4->ground,5->list(ground),6->any,
                         7->any}
                   ps = {<6,6>}
                   lin = {2,4,5,6}
         E_refoutsol = { (list)sz(6)+1=(list)sz(7),
                         (list)sz(3)=(list)sz(5)+1, sol=1 }
            %=================================


---------------------------------------
Literal to abstractly execute: l3 = 'efface'(X1,X5,X6)
---------------------------------------
```

Output report (internal representation) `efface.3.1.out` (5/12)

```
-------------------------------------
RESTRG(l3,B_2) = beta^3_inter
-------------------------------------

  beta^3_inter: sv = {X1->1,X2->2,X3->3}
                frm = {}
                mo = {1->ground,2->ground,3->var}
                ty = {1->ground,2->list(ground),3->any}
                ps = {<3,3>}
                lin = {1,2,3}


-------------------------------------
LOOKUP(beta^3_inter,'efface'(X1,X5,X6),sbeh) = B^3_aux
-------------------------------------

    %================B^3_aux================
    beta_in: sv = {X1->1,X2->2,X3->3}
             frm = {}
             mo = {1->ground,2->ground,3->var}
             ty = {1->ground,2->list(ground),3->any}
             ps = {<3,3>}
             lin = {1,2,3}
    beta_ref: sv = {X1->2,X2->3,X3->1}
              frm = {}
              mo = {1->var,2->ground,3->ground}
              ty = {1->any,2->ground,3->list(ground)}
              ps = {<1,1>}
              lin = {1,2,3}
    beta_out: sv = {X1->2,X2->3,X3->4}
              frm = {}
              mo = {2->ground,3->ground,4->ground}
              ty = {2->ground,3->list(ground),
                    4->list(ground)}
              ps = {}
              lin = {2,3,4}
    E_refoutsol = { 1 >= sol }
    %=====================================
-------------------------------------
Call to l3 is logic
-------------------------------------
Call to l3 has no side-effect
-------------------------------------
CHECK_TERM(l3,B3,seMutRec,se) = true
-------------------------------------


-------------------------------------
EXTG(l3,B_2,B^3_aux) = B_3
-------------------------------------

    %================B_3================
    beta_in: sv = {X1->1,X2->2,X3->3}
             frm = {}
             mo = {1->ground,2->ground,3->var}
             ty = {1->ground,2->list(ground),3->any}
             ps = {<3,3>}
             lin = {1,2,3}
```

Output report (internal representation) `efface.3.1.out` (6/12)

```
        beta_ref: sv = {X1->2,X2->3,X3->1}
                  frm = {3->[4|5]}
                  mo = {1->var,2->ground,3->ground,
                        4->ground,5->ground}
                  ty = {1->any,2->ground,
                        3->('[]/2'(ground,list(ground))),
                        4->ground,5->list(ground)}
                  ps = {<1,1>}
                  lin = {1,2,4,5}
        beta_out: sv = {X1->2,X2->3,X3->7,X4->4,X5->5,X6->6}
                  frm = {3->[4|5],7->[4|6]}
                  mo = {2->ground,3->ground,4->ground,
                        5->ground,6->ground,7->ground}
                  ty = {2->ground,
                        3->('[]/2'(ground,list(ground))),
                        4->ground,5->list(ground),
                        6->list(ground),
                        7->('[]/2'(ground,list(ground)))}
                  ps = {}
                  lin = {2,4,5,6}
        E_refoutsol = { (list)sz(3)=(list)sz(5)+1, 1 >= sol }
        %===================================

-------------------------------------
Literal to abstractly execute: 14 = not(X1=X4)
-------------------------------------


        -------------------------------------
        RESTRG(14,B_3) = beta^4_inter
        -------------------------------------

            beta^4_inter: sv = {X1->1,X2->2}
                          frm = {}
                          mo = {1->ground,2->ground}
                          ty = {1->ground,2->ground}
                          ps = {}
                          lin = {1,2}


        -------------------------------------
        NOT_AI(not(X1=X4),beta^4_inter) = B^4_aux
        -------------------------------------

            %===============B^4_aux===============
        beta_in: sv = {X1->1,X2->2}
                 frm = {}
                 mo = {1->ground,2->ground}
                 ty = {1->ground,2->ground}
                 ps = {}
                 lin = {1,2}
        beta_fail: sv = {X1->1,X2->1}
                   frm = {}
                   mo = {1->ground}
                   ty = {1->ground}
                   ps = {}
                   lin = {1}
```

Output report (internal representation) `efface.3.1.out` (7/12)

```
        beta_ref: sv = {X1->1,X2->2}
                  frm = {}
                  mo = {1->ground,2->ground}
                  ty = {1->ground,2->ground}
                  ps = {}
                  lin = {1,2}
        beta_out: sv = {X1->1,X2->2}
                  frm = {}
                  mo = {1->ground,2->ground}
                  ty = {1->ground,2->ground}
                  ps = {}
                  lin = {1,2}
        E_refoutsol = { sol = 1 }
        %=======================================


-------------------------------------------
EXTG(14,B_3,B^4_aux) = B_4
-------------------------------------------

        %===============B_4================
        beta_in: sv = {X1->1,X2->2,X3->3}
                 frm = {}
                 mo = {1->ground,2->ground,3->var}
                 ty = {1->ground,2->list(ground),3->any}
                 ps = {<3,3>}
                 lin = {1,2,3}
       beta_fail: sv = {X1->1,X2->2,X3->3}
                  frm = {2->[1|4]}
                  mo = {1->ground,2->ground,3->var,
                        4->ground}
                  ty = {1->ground,
                        2->('[]/2'(ground,list(ground))),
                        3->any,4->list(ground)}
                  ps = {<3,3>}
                  lin = {1,2,3,4}
        beta_ref: sv = {X1->2,X2->3,X3->1}
                  frm = {3->[4|5]}
                  mo = {1->var,2->ground,3->ground,
                        4->ground,5->ground}
                  ty = {1->any,2->ground,
                        3->('[]/2'(ground,list(ground))),
                        4->ground,5->list(ground)}
                  ps = {<1,1>}
                  lin = {1,2,4,5}
        beta_out: sv = {X1->2,X2->3,X3->7,X4->4,X5->5,X6->6}
                  frm = {3->[4|5],7->[4|6]}
                  mo = {2->ground,3->ground,4->ground,
                        5->ground,6->ground,7->ground}
                  ty = {2->ground,
                        3->('[]/2'(ground,list(ground))),
                        4->ground,5->list(ground),
                        6->list(ground),
                        7->('[]/2'(ground,list(ground)))}
                  ps = {}
                  lin = {2,4,5,6}
        E_refoutsol = { (list)sz(3)=(list)sz(5)+1,
                        (list)sz(6)+1=(list)sz(7), 1>=sol }
        %=======================================
```

Output report (internal representation) `efface.3.1.out` (8/12)

```
--------------------------------------
RESTRC(c,B_k) = B_out
--------------------------------------


    %================B_out================
    beta_in: sv = {X1->1,X2->2,X3->3}
             frm = {}
             mo = {1->ground,2->ground,3->var}
             ty = {1->ground,2->list(ground),3->any}
             ps = {<3,3>}
             lin = {1,2,3}
    beta_fail: sv = {X1->1,X2->2,X3->3}
               frm = {2->[1|4]}
               mo = {1->ground,2->ground,3->var,4->ground}
               ty = {1->ground,
                     2->('[]/2'(ground,list(ground))),
                     3->any,4->list(ground)}
               ps = {<3,3>}
               lin = {1,2,3,4}
    beta_ref: sv = {X1->2,X2->3,X3->1}
              frm = {3->[4|5]}
              mo = {1->var,2->ground,3->ground,4->ground,
                    5->ground}
              ty = {1->any,2->ground,
                    3->('[]/2'(ground,list(ground))),
                    4->ground,5->list(ground)}
              ps = {<1,1>}
              lin = {1,2,4,5}
    beta_out: sv = {X1->2,X2->3,X3->7}
              frm = {3->[4|5],7->[4|6]}
              mo = {2->ground,3->ground,4->ground,5->ground,
                    6->ground,7->ground}
              ty = {2->ground,3->('[]/2'(ground,list(ground))),
                    4->ground,5->list(ground),6->list(ground),
                    7 >('[]/2'(ground,list(ground)))}
              ps = {}
              lin = {2,4,5,6}
    E_refoutsol = { (list)sz(6)+1=(list)sz(7),
                    (list)sz(3)=(list)sz(5)+1, 1>=sol }
    %====================================
>>>>>>>>>>>>>>>>>>>>>>>>>>>>>>>>>>>>>>>>>>>>>>>>>>>>>>>>>>>>

>>>>>>>>>>>>>>>>>>>>>>>>>>>>>>>>>>>>>>>>>>>>>>>>>>>>>>>>>>>>
==> Clause (2) to analyze:
    c = 'efface'(X1,X2,X3) :- X2=[X1|X3].


--------------------------------------
EXTC(c,betaIn) = B_0
--------------------------------------
```

Output report (internal representation) efface.3.1.out (9/12)

```
%================B_0=================
beta_in: sv = {X1->1,X2->2,X3->3}
         frm = {}
         mo = {1->ground,2->ground,3->var}
         ty = {1->ground,2->list(ground),3->any}
         ps = {<3,3>}
         lin = {1,2,3}
beta_ref: sv = {X1->1,X2->2,X3->3}
         frm = {}
         mo = {1->ground,2->ground,3->var}
         ty = {1->ground,2->list(ground),3->any}
         ps = {<3,3>}
         lin = {1,2,3}
beta_out: sv = {X1->1,X2->2,X3->3}
         frm = {}
         mo = {1->ground,2->ground,3->var}
         ty = {1->ground,2->list(ground),3->any}
         ps = {<3,3>}
         lin = {1,2,3}
E_refoutsol = { sol = 1 }
%===================================


---------------------------------------
Literal to abstractly execute: l1 = X2=[X1|X3]
---------------------------------------


---------------------------------------
RESTRG(l1,B_0) = beta^1_inter
---------------------------------------
  beta^1_inter: sv = {X1->2,X2->1,X3->3}
               frm = {}
               mo = {1->ground,2->ground,3->var}
               ty = {1->ground,2->list(ground),3->any}
               ps = {<3,3>}
               lin = {1,2,3}


---------------------------------------
UNIF_FUNC(beta^1_inter[X1|X3]) = B^1_aux
---------------------------------------
    %===============B^1_aux===============
beta_in: sv = {X1->2,X2->1,X3->3}
         frm = {}
         mo = {1->ground,2->ground,3->var}
         ty = {1->ground,2->list(ground),3->any}
         ps = {<3,3>}
         lin = {1,2,3}
beta_ref: sv = {X1->3,X2->2,X3->1}
         frm = {3->[2|4]}
         mo = {1->var,2->ground,3->ground,4->ground}
         ty = {1->any,2->ground,
               3->('[]/2'(ground,list(ground))),
               4->list(ground)}
         ps = {<1,1>}
         lin = {1,2,4}
```

Output report (internal representation) efface.3.1.out (10/12)

```
            beta_out: sv = {X1->3,X2->2,X3->4}
                      frm = {3->[2|4]}
                      mo = {2->ground,3->ground,4->ground}
                      ty = {2->ground,
                            3->('[]/2'(ground,list(ground))),
                            4->list(ground)}
                      ps = {}
                      lin = {2,4}
            E_refoutsol = { sol = 1 }
            %=========================================


            ---------------------------------------
            EXTG(l1,B_0,B^1_aux) = B_1
            ---------------------------------------
               %===============B_1===============
            beta_in: sv = {X1->1,X2->2,X3->3}
                     frm = {}
                     mo = {1->ground,2->ground,3->var}
                     ty = {1->ground,2->list(ground),3->any}
                     ps = {<3,3>}
                     lin = {1,2,3}
            beta_ref: sv = {X1->2,X2->3,X3->1}
                      frm = {3->[2|4]}
                      mo = {1->var,2->ground,3->ground,
                            4->ground}
                      ty = {1->any,2->ground,
                            3->('[]/2'(ground,list(ground))),
                            4->list(ground)}
                      ps = {<1,1>}
                      lin = {1,2,4}
            beta_out: sv = {X1->2,X2->3,X3->4}
                      frm = {3->[2|4]}
                      mo = {2->ground,3->ground,4->ground}
                      ty = {2->ground,
                            3->('[]/2'(ground,list(ground))),
                            4->list(ground)}
                      ps = {}
                      lin = {2,4}
            E_refoutsol = { (list)sz(3)=(list)sz(4)+1, sol=1 }
               %================================

    ---------------------------------------
    RESTRC(c,B_k) = B_out
    ---------------------------------------
       %===============B_out===============
    beta_in: sv = {X1->1,X2->2,X3->3}
             frm = {}
             mo = {1->ground,2->ground,3->var}
             ty = {1->ground,2->list(ground),3->any}
             ps = {<3,3>}
             lin = {1,2,3}
```

Output report (internal representation) efface.3.1.out (11/12)

```
    beta_ref: sv = {X1->2,X2->3,X3->1}
              frm = {3->[2|4]}
              mo = {1->var,2->ground,3->ground,4->ground}
              ty = {1->any,2->ground,
                       3->('[]/2'(ground,list(ground))),
                       4->list(ground)}
              ps = {<1,1>}
              lin = {1,2,4}
    beta_out: sv = {X1->2,X2->3,X3->4}
              frm = {3->[2|4]}
              mo = {2->ground,3->ground,4->ground}
              ty = {2->ground,
                       3->('[]/2'(ground,list(ground))),
                       4->list(ground)}
              ps = {}
              lin = {2,4}
    E_refoutsol = { (list)sz(3)=(list)sz(4)+1, sol = 1 }
    %====================================
>>>>>>>>>>>>>>>>>>>>>>>>>>>>>>>>>>>>>>>>>>>>>>>>>>>>>>>>>>>>>>>
*-*-*-*-*-*-*-*-*-*-*-*-*-*-*-*-*-*-*
ABSTRACT CONCATENATION OF THE CLAUSES
*-*-*-*-*-*-*-*-*-*-*-*-*-*-*-*-*-*-*
    %=============== [(B1)] ===============
    beta_in: sv = {X1->1,X2->2,X3->3}
              frm = {}
              mo = {1->ground,2->ground,3->var}
              ty = {1->ground,2->list(ground),3->any}
              ps = {<3,3>}
              lin = {1,2,3}
    beta_fail: sv = {X1->1,X2->2,X3->3}
              frm = {2->[]}
              mo = {1->ground,2->ground,3->var}
              ty = {1->ground,2->('[]/0'),3->any}
              ps = {<3,3>}
              lin = {1,2,3}
    beta_fail: sv = {X1->1,X2->2,X3->3}
              frm = {2->[1|4]}
              mo = {1->ground,2->ground,3->var,4->ground}
              ty = {1->ground,
                       2->('[]/2'(ground,list(ground))),
                       3->any,4->list(ground)}
              ps = {<3,3>}
              lin = {1,2,3,4}
    beta_ref: sv = {X1->2,X2->3,X3->1}
              frm = {3->[4|5]}
              mo = {1->var,2->ground,3->ground,4->ground,
                       5->ground}
              ty = {1->any,2->ground,
                       3->('[]/2'(ground,list(ground))),
                       4->ground,5->list(ground)}
              ps = {<1,1>}
              lin = {1,2,4,5}
```

Output report (internal representation) `efface.3.1.out` (12/12)

```
 beta_out: sv = {X1->2,X2->3,X3->7}
           frm = {3->[4|5],7->[4|6]}
           mo = {2->ground,3->ground,4->ground,5->ground,
                 6->ground,7->ground}
           ty = {2->ground,3->('[]/2'(ground,list(ground))),
                 4->ground,5->list(ground),6->list(ground),
                 7->('[]/2'(ground,list(ground)))}
           ps = {}
           lin = {2,4,5,6}
 E_refoutsol = { (list)sz(6)+1=(list)sz(7),
                 (list)sz(3)=(list)sz(5)+1, 1>=sol }
 %=================================================


 %=============== [(B2)] =====================
 beta_in: sv = {X1->1,X2->2,X3->3}
          frm = {}
          mo = {1->ground,2->ground,3->var}
          ty = {1->ground,2->list(ground),3->any}
          ps = {<3,3>}
          lin = {1,2,3}
 beta_ref: sv = {X1->2,X2->3,X3->1}
           frm = {3->[2|4]}
           mo = {1->var,2->ground,3->ground,4->ground}
           ty = {1->any,2->ground,
                 3->('[]/2'(ground,list(ground))),
                 4->list(ground)}
           ps = {<1,1>}
           lin = {1,2,4}
 beta_out: sv = {X1->2,X2->3,X3->4}
           frm = {3->[2|4]}
           mo = {2->ground,3->ground,4->ground}
           ty = {2->ground,
                 3->('[]/2'(ground,list(ground))),
                 4->list(ground)}
           ps = {}
           lin = {2,4}
 E_refoutsol = { (list)sz(3) = (list)sz(4) + 1, sol = 1 }
 %=================================================

We have:
 - B1 and B2 are exclusive
 - B1 implies specification
 - B2 implies specification
*-*-*-*-*-*-*-*-*-*-*-*-*-*-*-*-*-*-*
==> We can infer the verification.
*-*-*-*-*-*-*-*-*-*-*-*-*-*-*-*-*-*-*
```

www.ingramcontent.com/pod-product-compliance
Lightning Source LLC
LaVergne TN
LVHW022300060326
832902LV00020B/3190